A CONCISE HISTORY
OF WESTERN CIVILIZATION

From Prehistoric to Early Modern Times

THIRD EDITION

by Gary Forsythe

DORRANCE
PUBLISHING CO
EST. 1920
PITTSBURGH, PENNSYLVANIA 15238

Dorrance Publishing Co
585 Alpha Drive
Pittsburgh, PA 15238
Visit our website at www.dorrancebookstore.com

ISBN: 978-1-6480-4063-4
eISBN: 978-1-6480-4923-1

CONTENTS

ACKNOWLEDGEMENTS

The author wishes to acknowledge the following friends and assistants for their help in proofreading and editing the text of this book and its companion volume (*Primary Sources for Western Civilization, Volume I, From Early Mesopotamia to the Reformation*): Joseph Anselmi, Justin Kirkland, Will Lizerazzo, Alex Milmine, Jason Roberts, Christopher San Miguel, Sandy Weller, and Travis West. As always, he further wishes to dedicate the work to his beloved deceased wife, Dorothy Alice Forsythe, whose love, support, and assistance in every capacity for thirty years (1972-2003) continue to be the single greatest inspiration of his entire life.

FOREWORD

The following set of 34 readings contains the content of the lectures that I have been presenting for many years in teaching an introductory college course for the first semester of a two semester sequence on the history of Western civilization. I have therefore entitled these 34 units not chapters, but lectures. The course, as I have been teaching it, begins with the earliest two civilizations of Mesopotamia and Egypt and ends shortly after 1600 in the Early Modern Period with the wars of religious intolerance resulting from the Protestant Reformation. Since teaching this course on a Monday, Wednesday, Friday schedule usually allows for 41 class meetings, and since three are taken up with in-class hourly exams, this results in four class meetings being available for treating additional topics. Consequently, besides doubling up lectures for a single class meeting, instructors who adopt this book as their basic textbook for teaching a similar course should have plenty of flexibility in adjusting these lectures to their own way of handling these subjects and adding their own. Moreover, since I have also prepared a companion volume of 46 primary source readings (*Primary Sources for Western Civilization, Volume I, From Early Mesopotamia to the Reformation*), allusions to these 46 readings are occasionally made throughout the lectures.

Anyone who teaches a course on such a broad topic as this one knows that the greatest difficulty facing the instructor is deciding what to include and what to exclude. My basic approach in teaching my own course is what I call the legacy approach. I try to present to students what seems to me to be the most historically important facets of human history during these roughly 5000 years that have exercised a significant influence in shaping the Western cultural tradition up to our day. This has resulted in making this volume different in three respects from most other textbooks covering the earlier history of Western civilization. One is that less space has been given to the 900 years of Medieval history (450-1350), and more attention paid to the earlier 4000 years of ancient history. Secondly, covering the civilizations of the ancient Near East has been done with a view to understanding the historical origins of ancient Judaism and the writings of *The Hebrew Bible* or *The Old Testament*. Despite the very important role that judaism and its writings have played in the Western tradition, many textbooks on Western civilization give these topics minimal attention. Without a doubt, Judaism and its sacred literature hare the single most important legacy from the civilizations of the ancient Near East. Thirdly, these lectures give more attention to the political history and political thought and practice of the ancient Greeks and Romans, to whom virtually all nations of the world today owe their political configurations. In addition, within those lectures the historical origins and spread of Christianity in the Roman Empire have received prominent attention. As the result of these emphases, the first half of these lectures treats roughly 4000 years of the ancient Near Eastern and Greco-Roman periods, and the second half covers roughly 1200 years of the Middle Ages and part of the Early Modern Period.

In keeping with one of the key words in the title of this book (i.e., Concise), all the lectures are relatively short and are roughly the same length, no more than what I can usually get through in a normal class meeting of 50 minutes. College students should therefore be expected to do their reading assignments for such a course without difficulty. Along these same lines, no notes or sections on "Further Reading" have been included, because virtually all college students taking such a course have no interest in these matters and will simply ignore them, and instructors who teach a course of this nature generally need no such additional guidance. Furthermore, given the easy availability of maps and illustrations on the internet with most instructors having their own websites designed specifically for their courses, it has seemed totally unnecessary to provide maps or illustrations to accompany the text. Accordingly, the result of these various factors is a relatively short and straightforward textbook of basic historical information.

LECTURE 1
Human Prehistory

- **History** = critical analysis, rigorous reconstruction of the past.
- Primary source material vs. secondary literature.
- Culture vs. biology = learned vs. inherited behavior.
- Culture vs. civilization.
- How do we define civilization?
- **Paleolithic (old stone) Age:** stone tools, hunting and gathering.
- **Neolithic (new stone) Age:** stone tools, agriculture = growing one's own food (wheat, barley, fruits, and vegetables), domestication of animals (cattle, pigs, sheep, goats).
- **agricultural revolution / transformation:** permanent residence in villages, food surplus, population growth, exchange of surplus commodities (trade), division and specialization of labor, development of crafts (pottery and metallurgy).
- **Prehistory vs. history** = lack vs. presence of written information for modern analysis.
- Archaeology useful for reconstructing material culture.
- **Ice Man:** body of prehistoric man discovered in the Alps,

dating to about 3200 B.C., body well preserved by freezing, prehistoric equipment found with him (boots, coat, cape, bow, arrows, quiver, knife, pieces of flint, copper axe, charcoal packet for making fire, etc.).

This course will survey about five thousand years of human history that have formed the tradition of Western civilization. In the first quarter we shall treat the major civilizations of the ancient Near East and will use this knowledge to develop an informed understanding of the formation of Judaism and the writings of The *Old Testament*, one of the most important collections of writings ever composed. Then in the second quarter of the course we will turn our attention to the ancient Greeks and Romans and will focus upon their political history and their development of the political ideas that have become fundamental to modern political thought and practice in Western society. The third quarter of the course will be devoted to the Middle Ages and will examine the important role of Christianity. The last quarter of the course will chart the intellectual advancement in Western Europe during the Early Modern Period that led to religious pluralism, the scientific revolution, and the beginnings of an integrated world economy. The course should provide you with a full appreciation of human behavior as exhibited in the historical process and should also enrich your understanding of the ideas and values of the Western tradition.

Although this is a course devoted to history, we will use this first lecture to survey a far longer period of human existence that we call prehistory, because it forms the first chapter, as it were, of human existence and laid the groundwork for the emergence of the earliest civilizations at the very beginning of human history. So, to begin with, what are history and prehistory? History is an intellectual discipline that uses human logic to assemble information about a past human society and to reconstruct as fully and as accurately as possible what the people of that society achieved, how they lived, what their values were, and how they worshipped. The principal source of information used by historians to carry out this logical reconstruction of past human behavior is what people have left behind in the form of writing, because written material gives us the most detailed account of people's thoughts and actions. Although the modern discipline of prehistory also attempts to reconstruct human actions and behavior of earlier times, it does so in reference to human societies that did not develop a writing system and have therefore not left behind any written evidence.

This important distinction between history and prehistory as scholarly disciplines leads us to two other contrasting pairs of concepts: biology and culture, and culture and civilization. All animal behavior (including human behavior) can be attributed to two sources: biology or culture. Most animals, especially the ones lower down in the evolutionary hierarchy, have much of their behavior determined by their biology, because their genes are responsible for how they are designed and operate within their environment. That part of their behavior which is not determined by their biology results from learning. As a general rule, the more advanced the animal, the greater is the role played by learning in the animal's behavior. In the case of mammals, for example, their biological make-up largely determines the environmental niche into which they fit and are well adapted, but their ultimate success to survive is also determined to a very large extent by their acquisition of complex learned behaviors.

Since the beginning of the Upper Paleolithic Age about 40,000 years ago we human beings have been the same biological creature with the same behavioral attributes. Unlike most other animals who possess a particular physical trait or set of attributes that suits them to an environment or gives them an adaptive advantage over other animals (birds' ability to fly, the swiftness of deer, the hunting and eating prowess of sharks, etc.), the three principal adaptive advantages that we humans have are our brain, our ability to formulate complex language, and our hands with which we can shape and fashion material objects in nature into all sorts of tools and useful things. Our brain, especially, gives us an extraordinary capacity to learn and to adapt to a seemingly infinite variety of conditions. In this sense our overall behavior is the least determined by biology and most dependent upon learning. In fact, unlike many other animals who can function fairly well within a very short time of their birth, we humans are so dependent upon learned behavior that when we are born, we are virtually helpless and require years and years of patient care by older humans before we can acquire enough learned behavior to make us relatively self sufficient. In fact, our learned behavior is so extremely complex that we have a special term for it: culture. It is the sum total of our learned behavior both as individuals and as well defined groups of humans. Thus, in observing the collective behavior of a society or well defined social group, we can use the term culture to refer to their overall patterns of behavior, interaction among themselves and with outsiders, etc.

Civilization, on the other hand, is a very special form of human culture, so that all civilizations are cultures, but not all cultures are civilizations. As we shall see in the next two lectures, the earliest civilizations of Mesopotamia and Egypt were the natural outgrowth of prehistoric human cultures. Once people within these two river valleys adopted agriculture and began to experience population growth, the complexity of human interaction increased so drastically that these human societies developed a very special form of culture that had previously never existed. They organized themselves into well defined state-like communities requiring so many actions and transactions that they had to develop a writing system in order to keep track of things. Consequently, there is a direct connection between civilization, writing, and history, because historians rely upon written records, and written records are produced only by civilizations. Anthropologists, on the other hand, unlike historians, frequently study human cultures, both present and past, that have not advanced to the point of civilization with writing as one of their salient characteristics.

There is one more pair of contrasting concepts that we need to examine in order to have a solid foundation upon which we can build. This is the distinction between primary and secondary sources. In order to produce their reconstructions of past civilizations, historians must assemble and carefully analyze primary source material. These are written records and other artifacts produced by the very society being studied. So, for example, the companion volume of this book, *Primary Sources For Western Civilization* (hereafter cited as PSWC), is a collection of primary sources, because all the writings contained in that volume are English translations of texts written by members of those various societies. Secondary sources, on the other hand, are the products of modern historians who have devoted considerable study to primary source material and have used their knowledge and expertise to describe in writing what they have succeeded in reconstructing from the primary source material.

This volume of lectures is therefore a secondary source, because it is the product of my own study of past societies through the surviving primary source material. It is also important to realize that as a general rule, the farther back into time we go, the less abundant is the primary source material that we have to study. Consequently, more recent societies can have their histories reconstructed in much more detail than earlier ones. Moreover, as we will see when we survey the earliest civilizations, our surviving primary source material varies considerably from place to place, depending upon how the evidence has either been destroyed or succeeded in being preserved over the centuries.

Although historians primarily rely upon written evidence, one very important supplemental form of evidence, especially for earlier times, is archaeology. This scholarly field has been in existence for about two hundred years; and it has become increasingly more sophisticated as all sorts of high-tech methods of scientific analysis have been developed to assist in the analysis of archaeological data. We need to remember, however, that like the chancy preservation of written records from the distant past, archaeological data are likewise subject to the vagaries of fortuitous discovery and survival. Archaeology seeks to find and analyze the material remains of a past society, but what has survived to the present to be discovered and analyzed may vary widely from place to place, depending upon the conditions of the local climate or soil, and what kinds of material the people used for making things. For example, we know much about the ancient Egyptians, because the dry conditions of the desert have preserved countless objects over the centuries, and the Egyptians had available to them and used durable building stone for making temples and other important structures, whereas the wet conditions of Mesopotamia have been very destructive of ancient artifacts, and the mud brick employed by the Mesopotamians for building has largely crumbled away over time. Consequently, although archaeology is extremely useful in providing us with additional information about past societies, we need to remember that it too is subject to the same laws of chance as our written records.

Let us now finally turn to examine briefly human prehistory. Here again, we are immediately confronted with yet another important pair of contrasting concepts: the Paleolithic and Neolithic Ages. They derive from Greek words that mean respectively "old stone" and "new stone," and they are used by modern scholars to distinguish between two very different prehistoric human lifestyles: hunting and gathering vs. agriculture. It is very sobering to realize that human civilization has been around for less than six thousand years, but human prehistory goes back into the past before then for hundreds of thousands of years. Thus, our civilized way of life is a very recent phenomenon that is dwarfed by our incredibly long prehistoric past.

During the very long Paleolithic Age our human ancestors eked out a precarious existence by hunting animals and gathering edible plants. Their overall numbers in Africa, Europe, and Asia were extremely small, and they clustered together in small groups. They were often moving about to follow the migratory patterns of animals that they hunted, or in response to the seasonal rhythms of vegetation upon which they also depended. Theirs was a very hard existence. Very few of them would have reached the age of thirty. There was probably a fairly clear division of lifestyles based upon gender, with the older males roaming farther afield in devoting much of their time and energy to hunting, and the females staying close to their camp-site or settlement and gathering plants because of their need to nurse the infants. Our Paleolithic ancestors possessed only the most primitive technology to assist them in dealing with the rigors of nature. They knew how to make fire and used it for heat against the cold, to drive off wild animals, and to cook their food. They shaped wood, horn, bone, and stone into various tools for cutting and stabbing. They used animal skins, furs, and grasses to make clothing and bags for carrying their few surplus commodities, such as berries or dried fish. The first really big step forward in human prehistory was taken about twelve thousand years ago at the close of the most recent Ice Age. As the glaciers melted and retreated to northern latitudes, the climate of the Mediterranean and western Asia became milder and produced such an abundance of animal and plant life that many small groups of humans throughout the Fertile Crescent (stretching from the head of the Persian Gulf to the eastern end of the Mediterranean Sea) were able to settle down in one place for long periods of time as they exploited nature's abundance that surrounded them. This sedentary existence encouraged people to begin experimenting with their way of life by figuring out how to plant and grow things and to catch certain kinds of wild animals to keep and raise them. Eventually these experiments brought about what we call today the agricultural revolution. For the very first time in human existence people could stay in one place while they planted and harvested things and tended to their herds of animals. Throughout the Fertile Crescent the two main grain staples were wheat and barley, supplemented with a large variety of fruits and vegetables. The main herd animals were cows, sheep, pigs, and goats. People soon figured out that they could store their surplus milk in the form of cheese, and that they could spin the wool of sheep into thread and weave it into cloth to make clothing to replace animal skins and furs.

Once people abandoned their former lifestyle of hunting and gathering and adopted agriculture, they made the transition from the Paleolithic to the Neolithic Age. They were still living in a stone age, because their hardest tools were still fashioned out of stone, but they had now adopted an entirely new way of life, which quickly began to have major consequences for human development. Since people were now able to grow more food than they could eat, these early farming settlements began to experience the first major population growth. Moreover, as people began to live in small villages, they had more free time on their hands, because they were not constantly on the move. Larger human groupings combined with a sedentary existence produced two other important aspects of human life: the division and specialization of labor. As there were more people with more time on their hands, some of them were able to spend part of their time in doing things other than farming or tending herds of animals. As people continued to experiment, they came up with new discoveries. For example, they eventually figured out that clay was an incredibly useful material. It could be formed by hand into any desired shape and then hardened by being baked in a fire. People now began to use clay pots for storing, cooking, and eating. In fact, for the next thousands of years, until the modern technique of making plastics came along, clay was one of the most widely used materials. Another Neolithic invention was the wheel, which enabled people to harness the pulling power of oxen. The horse did not come along as a domesticated beast of burden in Mesopotamia until about 2000 B.C., long after the development of the earliest civilizations.

The Neolithic Age lasted for a few thousands of years in the Fertile Crescent, an area of western Asia from the head of the Persian Gulf to the eastern coast of the Mediterranean, where the agricultural revolution seems to have first occurred, and where the earliest civilization of southern Mesopotamia arose. During this Neolithic Age most of the human inhabitants of this region were living a settled way of life in villages and were practicing agriculture and stock breeding. It was yet another major invention that spelled the ending of the Neolithic in this part of the world: namely, metallurgy. Some enterprising persons eventually figured out that metals could be melted out of rock ores. The first such discovery involved copper, because it melts at a relatively low temperature and is easy to work. So, in the modern scholarly terminology the Neolithic Age gave way to the Copper Age, or the Chalcolithic Age. But since copper is such a soft metal, people continued to use flint, obsidian, and other hard stone for making their most important cutting instruments. Once people figured out how to extract copper from rocks, they conducted more experiments and soon found that they could obtain lead, silver, and gold from other ores.

We have now succeeded in sketching human prehistory in the area of the Fertile Crescent down to the dawn of the first civilizations of Mesopotamia and Egypt, which we shall survey in the next two lectures. We will therefore end this lecture by looking more closely at one striking illustration of human prehistory, the case of the Ice Man, which gives us a very detailed example of how our prehistoric ancestors exercised great ingenuity in adapting themselves to their immediate environment.

In September of 1991 a German couple, while hiking through the Alps bordering western Austria and northern Italy southwest of Innsbruck, inadvertently came upon what might be considered the single most remarkable archaeological find of European prehistory: the frozen body of a man who had died some 5000 years ago. Summer melting of the Similaun Glacier had exposed the man's head and shoulders. At first he was thought to be another hiker who had met with a fatal accident, but the artifacts accompanying the corpse soon dispelled this presupposition. Before scientists arrived on the scene to extricate the dead man, some damage was inflicted upon the body's left hip by a jackhammer, and certain objects were removed by curiosity seekers. Nevertheless, a nearly intact corpse of a prehistoric man with all his gear was recovered and has become the focus of intense scientific analysis.

Carbon 14 dating indicates that this man lived around 3200 B.C., which makes him approximately as old as the earliest civilizations of Mesopotamia and Egypt. Moreover, unlike the mummies from ancient Egypt who had their internal organs removed when embalmed, the body of the Ice Man is almost fully preserved, and scientists have begun to study his internal anatomy in detail. He stood about five feet five inches tall and weighed about 134 pounds. His age at the time of his death was about 45 years, and skeletal analysis shows that he was beginning to suffer from degenerative arthritis. He had brownish black hair, wore a beard, and would easily blend into the local Alpine population today if put in contemporary dress. The hair on his head is only three and a half inches long, demonstrating that the people of his culture regularly cut their hair. His body also bears 61 tattoos in 19 groups of lines, including a cross behind the left knee, stripes on the right ankle, and three sets of short vertical parallel lines to the left of his spine on his lower back. Further examination has revealed these markings to be cauterized cuts, possibly intended to counter the pain of arthritis and acting as a kind of acupuncture.

But perhaps the most informative aspects of this discovery pertain to his clothing and other artifacts. Unlike the grave goods uncovered from prehistoric burials, which were placed with the dead according to the prevailing funerary customs and religious beliefs, the Ice Man was not formally buried but died with all his regular gear about him, and its remarkable state of preservation offers unique insights into the living conditions and technology of his culture. He wore leather boots bound around his legs with thongs and stuffed with straw for insulation against the cold. He was clad in a fur-lined coat composed of deer, chamois, and ibex skin stitched together, and over this he wore a cape of woven grass similar to those worn by local Tyrolean shepherds as late as the early twentieth century. A disk-shaped stone may have been worn around his neck as an amulet. He had with him a bow, fourteen arrow shafts, and what is now the world's oldest known quiver, made of deerskin. The arrows are fitted with feathers at an angle so as to impart spin for greater stability and accuracy. His bow measures six feet in length and is made of yew, the best wood available in Europe for bow making, the same as that used to make the famous English long bow of the High Middle Ages. His bow, however, had not yet been notched and fitted with a string, suggesting that the Ice Man had only recently obtained the wood from a tree. He also had a bone needle, a small flint knife fitted with a handle of ash wood, a copper axe, and a small tool of deer antler that was probably used for sharpening flint blades and arrowheads. The flint knife was carried in a delicately woven grass sheath. Pieces of charcoal contained in a grass packet were used for making a fire. Two mushrooms (Piptoporus betulinus) bound on a cord are conjectured to have constituted the Ice Man's medicine for fighting off stomach-ache and pain resulting from arthritis. The discovery of parasitic worms in the lower part of the large intestine suggests that the Ice Man suffered from the former ailment. His equipment was carried in a backpack made of wood and bark.

The body and all the artifacts were located in a natural depression, which accounts for the fact that they were not destroyed by glacial action but were covered in ice and snow until the present day. But his outer layer of skin on his body eventually deteriorated and fell away, thereby giving his body a rather dark appearance. The site is at an altitude of 10,530 feet, about 3000 feet above the tree line of that time. It has therefore been conjectured that the Ice Man was engaged in traveling across the mountains when the onset of a sudden snow storm forced him to seek refuge in the hollow where he froze to death, and his corpse and equipment were preserved. He could have belonged to one of several local Copper Age cultures that flourished then on both sides of the Alps, and the discovery offers striking testimony to the existence of human traffic across these mountains in prehistoric times. The shape and style of his copper axe closely resemble those of the so-called Remedello Culture of northern Italy, known from a series of 124 graves and dating to the third millennium. The Ice Man also had with him a collection of unshaped pieces of flint of high quality, which might have come from flint deposits in northern Italy.

LECTURE 2
Early Mesopotamia

- **3500-2300 B.C.:** Sumerian civilization.
- **2300-2150 B.C.:** Dynasty of Sargon, a Semite who unified the Sumerian city-states and expanded its influence by military conquest throughout the Fertile Crescent.
- **1900-1600 B.C.:** Old Babylonian Kingdom.
- **1792-1750 B.C.:** Reign of Hammurabi, King of Babylonia.
- Importance of rivers in fostering growth of civilization.
- **Mesopotamia** = "land between rivers," i.e. Tigris and Euphrates.
- **Fertile Crescent:** area from Egypt along Mediterranean coast and through Mesopotamia to the Persian Gulf, suitable for large-scale agriculture, region of the earliest civilizations.
- **city-state:** important early political organizational unit, consisting of a city or town center along with the surrounding countryside of farmland to form an independent, self governing, fully functioning political unit.
- **Cuneiform writing:** earliest known writing system, wedge-shaped symbols impressed on clay tablets with a reed stylus, requiring hundreds of different signs.
- **Epic of Gilgamesh:** Gilgamesh the legendary king of Uruk, performed heroic deeds with friend Enkidu, Enkidu's death, Gilgamesh's unsuccessful quest for personal immortality, his

meeting with Utnapishtim and the story of the great flood.

- **Polytheistic religion:** religion involving the worship of many different divinities.
- **anthropomorphic gods:** gods having the physical appearance and behavioral attributes of human beings.

In this lecture we will survey the general features of 1900 years of early Mesopotamian history, 3500-1600 B.C., covering the Sumerian civilization (3500-2300 B.C.), the Sargonid dynasty or Empire (2300-2150 B.C.), and the Old Babylonian Kingdom (1900-1600 B.C.). Please be aware that all these dates are approximate. Thus, if you encounter these periods in doing additional reading, you are likely to notice that slightly different dates are given.

As we saw in the previous lecture, during the Neolithic and Copper Ages people living throughout the Fertile Crescent adopted agriculture and began living in fixed villages. Their principal grain staples were wheat and barley, and their primary herd animals were cattle, sheep, pigs, and goats. The Fertile Crescent is a term developed by modern historians who have studied this early period of our human past. It is an area that begins at the head of the Persian Gulf, comes up through Iraq, into Syria, and down along the eastern coast of the Mediterranean. During the first several millennia following the end of the last Ice Age this region received more rainfall than it does today, and its soil was much more fertile than it now is from having been cultivated for thousands of years by human farming. It was therefore at first an area ideal for human habitation and is where human beings first developed agriculture and the earliest civilized way of life.

In fact, the two earliest civilizations arose along major river valleys: the Tigris and Euphrates of Mesopotamia and the Nile in Egypt. This was no coincidence. A rich and varied plant life arose along the rivers, which in turn produced an abundant animal life, and that in turn attracted human beings. Once people began to support themselves by agriculture and experienced population growth, villages arose along these rivers; and in order to take full advantage of the agricultural potential offered by an abundant water supply, the people needed to form a larger and more cohesive society, because they had to pool their labor and cooperate in a very organized way to dig irrigation ditches and catch basins. Thus, the peculiar nature of the environment and the human response to it were key elements in the rise of the two earliest civilized societies.

Mesopotamia is an ancient Greek term meaning "the land between the rivers," referring to the Tigris and Euphrates; and it was along the slower flowing Euphrates that the factors just described came together and crystalized around 3500 B.C. to form the earliest human civilization that we call Sumerian. This civilization endured for about 1200 years, 3500-2300 B.C. and was characterized by its population speaking a common Sumerian language, sharing a common Sumerian culture, but living in about a dozen separate, self-governing communities, such as Eridu, Kish, Lagash, Nippur, Sippar, Umma, Ur, and Uruk. Modern scholars use the term city-state to describe this type of community, and we will encounter it again when we study the ancient Greeks. Each of these communities had a single main city center and a sizable surrounding territory to form the total extent of the entire state. Since 80-90 percent of the entire population were farmers, most people lived outside the city center in the surrounding rural area. In fact, throughout this entire course we will be surveying pre-industrial societies that conform to this basic pattern. Each city-state was ruled by its own king; and since these city-states bordered upon one another, they were often engaged in warfare, as one state attempted to take over a bit more land from its neighbor.

As these large associations of people came into being, the earliest writing system gradually developed out of the need for people to keep track of commercial transactions. At first, in order to remember how many herd animals or measures of grain were bought and sold between two parties, the people used small clay objects to serve as counters. The next step in the evolutionary process of a writing system was to enclose the small clay counters inside a clay jacket or envelope and to place a picture-like marking (pictograph) on the outside to represent the number and nature of the transaction. As time passed, and as more symbols began to be used for a wider variety of products, there developed the general idea that the full range of complex language could be represented symbolically if enough signs were employed. Thus arose what is called the cuneiform writing system, which takes its name from two Latin words meaning "wedge shaped," because many of the symbols used in this system had markings that were thicker on one end than the other. This fact arose from the actual Mesopotamian writing materials: clay tablets and a pointed reed stylus to make the impressions on the soft clay. Once a clay tablet was filled with writing, it was placed in a fire and baked hard. This had the advantage of making the writing permanent, so that a bill of sale could not have its terms changed, but it has also meant that we now possess thousands and thousands of well preserved cuneiform clay tablets.

When the Sumerians finally developed the cuneiform writing system, it involved hundreds of signs that had to be mastered in order for a person to have the ability to read and write in this medium. Since, unlike our own simple alphabet of 26 letters, this required years and years of very hard work, only a very small fraction of the entire Sumerian population acquired the ability to read and write; and those who did were a special chosen few who attended a writing school in their city-state; and once they became masters of this rare skill, they became part of an elite class of scribes, upon whom everyone else in their society depended for writing out bills of sale, legal contracts, and other records. Since cuneiform was used in Mesopotamia for the next 3000 years, the literacy rate was extremely low; and those few who possessed the knowledge were an important part of the ruling establishment, because they controlled the recording and use of information. Thus, as we have seen, the first writing system came into being as the result of people's need to have a reliable method of record keeping. Unfortunately, virtually all the clay tablets for the first several centuries of Sumerian civilization are nothing but records of simple transactions, informing us of who bought what from whom and at what price. It is as if we were left to reconstruct our own contemporary history based upon thousands of purchase receipts from Wal-Mart. It is not until the close of the long period of Sumerian civilization that we begin to have clay tablets that record other, more interesting aspects of human life, such as religious hymns and the major deeds accomplished by kings and their communities.

Since very few people in ancient Mesopotamia knew how to read and write, but since everyone at one time or another had to signify his or her agreement to a transaction recorded on a clay tablet, the Mesopotamians developed an interesting equivalent of our "signing your name." This was accomplished by a cylinder seal, a small cylindrically shaped piece of stone on the outer rounded surface of which was carved a distinctive scene. When a person needed to "sign his name," he simply rolled the cylinder onto the surface of the soft clay, and it left an impression of the person's cylinder seal and thus served as his signature on the clay document. In order to have their cylinder seal always at hand and ready to use, like our modern-day driver's license kept in our wallet or purse, a hole was bored all the way through the cylinder along its axis, and a cord was passed through it, so that the person could wear the cylinder seal around the neck or on the wrist.

Sumerian society consisted of three classes. At the top was a very small class of nobles, who owned large amounts of land in comparison to other people; and as possessors of greater resources, they were better off than others. The vast majority of the population belonged to the peasant class, which was further subdivided into two parts: the free peasants and the tenants. Free peasants were relatively poor people who owned their own bit of land and supported themselves by farming. The tenants worked portions of land assigned to them by large landowners under contract and were obliged to pay the landowners a fixed amount of their crops as rent. Another part of the peasant class consisted of the various artisans, such as potters, carpenters, leather workers, and metal smiths, most of whom would have lived in the city center. At the very bottom of Sumerian society were the slaves. In fact, in all the societies that we will study in this course, there were slaves, because they were a necessity for human existence in pre-industrial times when there were virtually no labor-saving machines, but everything had to be performed either by human or animal labor. There were two principal ways in which a person became a slave in Mesopotamia: either as a captive taken in war, or through indebtedness. Captivity in warfare is understood easily enough, but indebtedness may not be. If a person took out a loan from another and then was unable to pay up when the time for payment arrived, the creditor could come before a judge and have the debtor or one of his dependents assigned to him as a slave in payment for the loan.

One very important institution in Sumerian society was organized religion. Although they lived in separate independent city-states, the Sumerians shared a common religion, in which they believed that the world and all aspects of nature were controlled by a whole host of gods and goddesses, each of whom had their own role to play. For example, Anu and his wife Antum presided over the vault of highest heaven; Enlil was the god of storms and weather; Inanna was the goddess of female beauty and sexuality; Enki was the lord of wisdom and of the fresh water beneath the earth; and Ereshkigal was the dreaded goddess of the dead in the underworld. Like many other ancient peoples whom we shall encounter, the Sumerians were polytheistic, and they conceived of their gods in very human-like terms, having both the shape and psychology of humans and therefore being entirely anthropomorphic. One of the important aspects of the city-state's city center was that it was where all the major temples to the various gods were located, and around which major public festivals were celebrated. These temples owned large tracts of land worked by tenant peasants, and it used the produce from the land to support the various employees of the temple: priests and priestesses for conducting religious ceremonies, musicians for playing religious hymns, craftsmen for making and repairing things, scribes for keeping all the necessary records, etc. Consequently, public religion in Mesopotamia was big business, and the temples constituted major enterprises in their cities. The Sumerians developed a very distinctive form of religious architecture known as the ziggurat. Since the land of southern Mesopotamia did not possess good building stone or timber, its primary building material was mud brick; and since much of it has crumbled over the centuries, we do not have the fine remains of Mesopotamian buildings as we do from ancient Egypt, where durable stone was ready at hand and used for construction. The ziggurat was a large multi-layered platform constructed of mud brick. It ascended in several layers, each being a square or rectangle placed on top of each other and diminishing in size like a wedding cake. A ramp built along one side formed a walk-way to the very top, where there stood the temple dedicated to a particular divinity, and in which was housed a statue of that god made out of precious materials, and to whom the priests and other worshippers made offerings of food every day. The Sumerians worshipped their gods both collectively and privately in order to make sure that there was no drought, their crops grew, people and their animals were healthy and reproduced, etc.

We have now surveyed the basic patterns of Sumerian civilization in terms of its political, social, economic, and religious organization and practices; and they remained basically the same throughout the subsequent periods of Mesopotamian history, which we will now proceed to survey. As we have seen, the Sumerians were united by a common language and culture, but they were not politically unified into a single nation, but were organized into several separate self-governing city-states. This situation changed around 2300 B.C. and brought Sumerian civilization to an end. At that time there arose a powerful figure named Sargon, who conquered all the Sumerian city-states and for the first time united them under his rule. This ushered in what is known as the Sargonid dynasty or Empire that lasted for about 150 years (2300-2150 B.C.), in which Sargon's kingdom was ruled successively by his descendants. Sargon therefore was the first great conqueror of this region; and as a result, many stories were told about him in later times, one of which you have as Text #1 in PSWC, and which closely resembles the story later attached to Moses in *The Bible*: namely, that Sargon was born of a priestess, who placed him in a basket and set him adrift on the river to be drowned, but instead, Sargon's destiny was so powerful that even as a vulnerable infant he survived, was taken in and raised by Aki, the drawer of water, and grew up to realize his destiny as a mighty conqueror.

Sargon was not a Sumerian, but a Semite; that is, he spoke a Semitic language. The Sumerian language is a linguistic isolate. It cannot be related to any other known language. Just to the west of Mesopotamia lay the eastern edges of the Arabian Desert, which was apparently the homeland of the Semitic people. As we will see in Lecture 20, the Arabs of Islam, another Semitic people, were native to the western edge of this same desert. Over the course of centuries small groups of Semites, who lived as animal-herding nomads along the livable fringes of the desert, moved into the Fertile Crescent and settled down to become farmers. This demographic movement ultimately resulted in the Fertile Crescent being inhabited entirely by Semitic-speaking peoples: Babylonians, Assyrians, Arimaeans, Phoenicians, and Hebrews. Sargon and his warriors formed an early and not so peaceful aspect of this larger Semitic infiltration into the Fertile Crescent. Sargon and his descendants carried out military campaigns beyond the Sumerian homeland into central and northern Mesopotamia, whose inhabitants had already begun to organize themselves into city-states, like those of the Sumerians, who, as the result of trading interaction, had acquainted them with the notion of civilization. Thus, the Sargonid dynasty represents the earliest unification of the various civilized peoples of Mesopotamia.

The unification, however, was relatively short lived. Recent excavations at a site in Syria have revealed the possible cause for the collapse of the Sargonid dynasty: major climatic change. Sometime around 2200 B.C. there was a gigantic volcanic eruption somewhere in the northern hemisphere, as shown by a layer of volcanic ash at the site of Tell Leilan. This apparently produced a major cooling-down of the climate and created drought conditions for a very long period of time. Since the people of the Fertile Crescent depended entirely upon agriculture, the prolonged drought must have been quite devastating to them and must have caused civilization throughout this region to collapse. It also seemed to have caused massive immigration into the Fertile Crescent from the edges of the Arabian Desert, which would have become unlivable during these drier times. As a result, when civilization arose once again in this region with the return of the earlier climatic conditions, the curtain is raised on a historical stage that looks quite different from earlier times. By 1900 B.C. central Mesopotamia had become dominated by a newly arrived Semitic people known as the Amorites, whose principal city was Babylon, conveniently situated at the hour-glass waist of Mesopotamia, where the Tigris and Euphrates nearly meet, so that the Babylonians had easy access to both rivers. This then marked the beginning of the Old Babylonian Kingdom that flourished for 300 years, 1900-1600 B.C. By this time Sumerian had become a dead language, and the people throughout this region now spoke a Semitic language that modern scholars call Akkadian. The Babylonian kings exercised their rule over a large area, including the old Sumerian city-states to the south. The most famous king of the Old Babylonian Kingdom was

Hammurabi, whose 42-year reign occurred around the midpoint of this whole period, 1792-1750 B.C. During his reign Babylon ruled over the largest area of that period. Hammurabi, however, is most famous for his law code, a series of 282 provisions inscribed in cuneiform on a tall pillar of stone that is now housed in the Louvre Museum in Paris, and portions of which are set out as Text #4 in PSWC. Although we possess portions of much earlier Mesopotamian law codes, they were written on clay tablets and are not complete because of damage to the tablets. Hammurabi's law code is the earliest surviving complete text and is most interesting, because it offers us important glimpses into Mesopotamian society, its values, attitudes, and various social institutions such as marriage, divorce, adultery, adoption, damage to property, and compensation for bodily harm. It also constitutes important comparative material for the Mosaic law in *The Old Testament*.

The Old Babylonian Kingdom came to a sudden end around 1600 B.C. as the result of foreign enemy attack. Two different peoples, the Hittites and the Kassites, formed an alliance and attacked Babylon, capturing and sacking it. As we will see in Lecture 4, the Hittites lived a considerable distance away in Anatolia and were just beginning to arise as the dominant people in that region. Their primary goal in attacking Babylon was quick and easy plunder. Thus, after capturing and sacking the city, the Hittites returned home. The Kassites, however, who lived nearby, toppled the Old Babylonian dynasty, replaced it with their own line of rulers, and formed the ruling elite in Babylonian society for the next several centuries.

We now come to the last element of this lecture, the Epic of Gilgamesh, portions of which you have as Text #3 in PSWC. I will summarize its plot, because it was one of the earliest major literary achievements of Mesopotamia and offers us an interesting view into the society that created it. First of all, what is an epic? It is a long narrative poem. It is therefore written in verse and tells a story, involving great heroes of the past engaged in struggles, journeys, and confronting the great mysteries of human existence, such as life and death. As the title suggests, the main character and hero of the epic is Gilgamesh, who was king of Uruk. We do not know whether he ever actually existed. If he did, he would have lived at some time during the later centuries of the

PSWC #3

Sumerian civilization, perhaps around 2700 or 2600 B.C. But in any case, whether he ever existed or was simply the creation of Mesopotamian story tellers, he figured as such an important hero to the Mesopotamians that they told all sorts of stories about him. Finally, during the time of the Old Babylonian Kingdom that we have just surveyed, many of these tales were put together to form a continuous narrative in the form of the Epic of Gilgamesh.

Here is the basic story line. When Gilgamesh, the king of Uruk, oppresses his people, they pray to the gods for assistance. The gods answer their prayers by having one of the goddesses fashion a man-like being out of clay. His name is Enkidu, who, as the poem describes him, was a huge, muscular, and hairy human being. Enkidu comes to Uruk, where he and Gilgamesh engage in a titanic wrestling match. Although Gilgamesh finally succeeds in getting the edge on Enkidu, the former suggests that they become friends and combine their enormous strength and power to perform great deeds. They first travel a long distance to the Cedar Forest, which is guarded by a gigantic creature named Huwawa or Humbaba. This Fairyland is to be located in what is now Lebanon along the eastern Mediterranean coast, where large cedar forests grew, and from which the Mesopotamians imported cedar as roof beams and timbers for similar construction. After killing Huwawa or Humbaba, they return to Mesopotamia. At this point the Semitic goddess Ishtar (Sumerian Inanna) falls in love with Gilgamesh and offers herself to him, but he rejects her, because he knows from past stories that Ishtar has taken mortal lovers, only to destroy them when she no longer wants them. Here we encounter another characteristic feature of epic poetry, the interaction between the human and the divine. Ishtar is so enraged by Gilgamesh's rejection that she comes to her father Anu, the god of heaven, and demands that he avenge her insult. Anu does so by sending upon the land the Bull of Heaven, a monstrous creature that tears up the land and causes all sorts of death and destruction. Gilgamesh and Enkidu overpower and kill the monster, but Enkidu further insults Ishtar by throwing a piece of the slain bull into her face. The gods now decree that one of the pair must die, and they decide upon Enkidu, who then falls ill and lingers on his sick bed. At one point he awakens from a dream and tells it to Gilgamesh. He dreamed that he had gone down into the underworld.

There he saw previous kings and priests sitting in the same silence and darkness as the other shades of ordinary people, covered over in feathers like birds. There they all sit in gloom. Dust is their food, and clay is their meat. It is a very dreary picture of the Mesopotamian view of life after death.

When Enkidu dies, Gilgamesh is not only shattered with grief for his friend, but he also becomes alarmed at his own impending death. He now decides to embark upon the ultimate quest, the quest for immortality. After much travel Gilgamesh passes through an area of perpetual darkness and emerges into a paradise called The Garden of the Gods, where he encounters a woman or divine being named Siduri. He asks her if she knows how he can obtain immortality. She replies that immortality is not for humans. The gods have reserved it for themselves. She advises Gilgamesh to give up his quest and to content himself with the simple pleasures of human life: bathing, clean clothes, playing with one's children, eating and drinking, enjoying time with one's friends. Despite her sage advice, Gilgamesh learns from Siduri how he might reach Utnapishtim, the Mesopotamian Noah, who survived the great flood of the distant past, and to whom the gods granted immortality. Gilgamesh goes down to the sea and goes aboard the ship of Urshanabi, the boatman, who conveys him to the faraway island of Dilmun, where live Utnapishtim and his wife in quiet bliss. When Gilgamesh asks him to tell him how he has become immortal, Utnapishtim proceeds to tell the story of the great flood.

When the earth abounded with humans, the land bellowed like a bull and disturbed the peace of the gods in heaven, so that Enlil decided to wipe out mankind so as to have peace and quiet. Enki, one of the other gods, however, informed Utnapishtim of the coming flood and instructed him to build a big ship and to load it with animals and all the craftsmen in order to save nature and civilization. It then stormed so violently for seven days that the gods fled to highest heaven to escape the fury, and they huddled together as if they were frightened dogs. Utnapishtim's ship eventually landed on a mountain top. He emerged, erected an altar, and performed a sacrifice of thanksgiving to the gods. When they smelled the sweet sacrifice, they descended to earth like flies, but when Enlil realized that there were some survivors of the flood, he flew into a rage until Enki and Ishtar persuaded him to let these people live. He then blessed Utnapishtim and his wife with the gift of immortality and had them taken away to live forever on the island of Dilmun.

In order to see if Gilgamesh is made of the right stuff to receive the gift of immortality, Utnapishtim challenges him to a contest to see if he can stay awake longer than himself. Gilgamesh loses and falls asleep, sleep being akin to the death that Gilgamesh is wanting to avoid. But as a consolation prize, Utnapishtim tells Gilgamesh of a plant that will not give him immortality, but will at least rejuvenate him. It grows on the bottom of the ocean and is called "man becomes young in old age." Gilgamesh then leaves Dilmun on Urshanabi's ship; and at one point he descends to the bottom of the ocean, finds the plant, cuts it from its root, and ascends to the surface with it, but rather than eating it right away, he keeps it until they make landfall. Then as Gilgamesh is traveling by land back to Uruk, he passes a cool pool of water and decides to take a bath. He lays the plant on the ground and proceeds to bathe himself, but while doing so, a snake smells the sweet fragrance of the plant and eats it. As soon as he does, he sheds his skin. This explains for the Mesopotamians why the snake, not human beings, can be rejuvenated. Gilgamesh now returns to Uruk a very sad man, because he has no hope of obtaining immortality, but he at least consoles himself with the knowledge that he has accomplished great things to be remembered.

PS WC #3
continued.

LECTURE 3
Ancient Egypt

- **3100-2200 B.C.:** the Old Kingdom, during which the Egyptians developed the basic forms of their culture and erected the great pyramids.
- **2200-2050 B.C.:** the First Intermediate Period, characterized by political disunity.
- **2050-1650 B.C.:** the Middle Kingdom.
- **1650-1550 B.C.:** the Second Intermediate Period, characterized by political disunity and rule by the foreign invaders called the Hyksos.
- **1550-1100 B.C.:** the New Kingdom, characterized by internal prosperity and the establishment of an empire in the Levant.
- 1352-1336 B.C.: reign of Akhenaten, the monotheistic pharaoh.
- Importance of the Nile River in fostering the development and prosperity of Egyptian civilization.
- **hieroglyphics** = sacred carvings: Egyptian form of writing, employing hundreds of symbols.
- **pharaoh:** title given to the ruler of Egypt.
- **monotheism:** belief in the existence of a single divinity.
- **Isis and Osiris:** most important sister-brother and wife-husband pair of divinities in Egyptian religion, in myth Isis revived Osiris after he was murdered by his evil brother Seth,

and he then became ruler over the dead.

Horus: son of Isis and Osiris, identified with the ruling pharaoh, while the preceding dead pharaoh was identified with Osiris who ruled over the dead.

This lecture will survey about two thousand years of ancient Egyptian history, 3100-1100 B.C., which falls into five distinct periods, consisting of three periods of political unity and prosperity and two intervening (or intermediate) periods characterized by political disunity: the Old Kingdom (3100-2200 B.C.), the First Intermediate Period (2200-2050 B.C.), the Middle Kingdom (2050-1650 B.C.), the Second Intermediate Period (1650-1550 B.C.), and the New Kingdom or period of the Empire (1550-1100 B.C.). Please be aware that all these dates are approximate. So, if you encounter these periods in doing additional reading in other modern works, you are likely to notice that slightly different dates are given.

Just as we saw in the case of Mesopotamia, a great river, the Nile, played a crucial role in the rise of civilization in ancient Egypt. Abundant plant and animal life along the river attracted human beings, who eventually adopted agriculture and began living in villages. Then around 3100 B.C. the whole land was united under the rule of the first pharaoh to mark the beginning of Egyptian civilization with the Old Kingdom.

Before proceeding further, we need to explain some of the important geographical features of the Nile Valley. The river is one of the longest in the world, and it flows through a desert, which, for most of the time, protected the ancient Egyptians from invaders from both the east and west. In addition, the very dry climate of the desert has been responsible for preserving countless Egyptian artifacts over the centuries, so that we know much more about Egyptian daily life than we do about that of early Mesopotamia. The land of Egypt actually consisted of two distinct parts: Lower Egypt, the area of the Nile delta; and Upper Egypt, the narrow band of fertile land (just a few miles wide) on either side of the Nile stretching south from the delta for several hundreds of miles. Once Egyptian civilization arose, these two areas each had twenty or so major towns that served as administrative centers during the three periods of the land's unity and as local centers of city-state-like entities during the two Intermediate Periods of disunity. In later Greek times these forty or so communities were termed nomes and had always served as the basic building blocks of the Egyptian kingdom. Even after the land was united under the pharaohs, the Egyptians always thought of their land as consisting of the two parts of Upper and Lower Egypt, and the pharaoh was always termed the ruler of Upper and Lower Egypt. His royal crown consisted of two parts: a low red brim representing Lower Egypt, and a white taller conical part that represented Upper Egypt. Unlike southern Mesopotamia, Egypt possessed fine building stone and some metal ores (principally copper) in easy reach of the Nile Valley. As a result, the Egyptians constructed numerous temples and other monuments that have survived in good condition up to the modern day. Moreover, the flooding pattern of the Nile was far more beneficent than that of the Tigris and Euphrates. As the snows in the mountains of central Africa melted, and as the monsoon rains from the Indian Ocean fell upon eastern Africa during the summer, the Nile received a large volume of water, rose out of its banks, and flooded the land of Upper Egypt for a period of several months. When the waters finally receded, there was left behind on the land a rich and fertile silt that acted as a natural fertilizer. The Egyptians then planted their crops and harvested them before the next annual inundation of the land. Consequently, unless the Nile did not flood sufficiently or did so in excess, the land was extremely bountiful in producing crops.

During the long period of the Old Kingdom the Egyptians worked out all the basic forms of their civilization. As we saw in the previous lecture with the Mesopotamians, the complexity of human organization and need for record keeping led to the development of the first writing system. The same thing occurred in ancient Egypt, but they developed their own distinctive system and writing materials. Their writing system is termed hieroglyphics, taking its name from two Greek words meaning "sacred carvings," because when the Greeks centuries later visited Egypt to see the great monuments, they saw them adorned with the Egyptian writing. Like cuneiform, hieroglyphics was a system that employed hundreds of signs to represent entire words. As a result, just as in Mesopotamia, the literacy rate in ancient Egypt was incredibly low, and reading and writing were skills possessed only by very few people, who had to be trained for years and years. Once they had mastered the system, they became part of the ruling establishment, because they were employed by the Pharaoh's administration or the temples to do all their necessary record keeping. Egyptian scribes eventually developed a simplified form of writing in which they used a few dozen signs to represent consonant sounds, but no vowels, for spelling words. But despite the creation of this much simpler script, the literacy rate in ancient Egypt remained very low. Rather than writing on clay tablets like the Mesopotamians, the Egyptians developed a kind of paper from the papyrus plant that grew in the shallow waters of the Nile. Its stalk was prism-shaped, and the Egyptians cut it into long thin strips. They used the tougher outer pieces to weave into rope or to fashion into sandals and other objects, but the softer inner strips were laid side by side with another layer placed on top of them in the opposite direction. The material was pressed together and then left to dry out in the sun, and the natural moisture in the papyrus strips acted as a binding glue to hold the pieces together. In fact, our word paper derives from papyrus. It was light brown or yellowish brown in color. The Egyptians produced ink from vegetable dyes, usually black or red, and applied it to the papyrus with a brush-like writing instrument. For long documents the Egyptians made papyrus several feet long, and they wrote on the material in columns placed side by side along the length of the papyrus; and when the document was finished, they rolled up the papyrus into the form of a scroll.

Another major difference between Egypt and early Mesopotamia was their political organization and ideology. Whereas the Sumerian civilization consisted of separate self-governing city-states, Egypt from the beginning of the Old Kingdom was united under the rule of a single pharaoh. Its capital was located at Memphis near the junction of Upper and Lower Egypt at the apex of the delta. In addition, although the ordinary Mesopotamian regarded his king as an exalted figure, he was not believed to be divine, as was the pharaoh. Egyptians thought that pharaoh was in fact the incarnation of one of their gods, Horus; and they had a myth to explain the cycle of the royal succession. According to this myth, the god Osiris was once deceived and

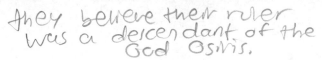
they believe their ruler was a descendant of the God Osiris.

murdered by his evil brother Seth, who dismembered his body and scattered its parts all over the land of Egypt. Osiris' divine wife, Isis, traveled through the land and found each of his body parts, after which she put Osiris back together and used her magical spells to bring him back to life. At that point Osiris became the ruler of the dead, and his son, Horus, became ruler over the living (that is, the Egyptians). Then whenever a pharaoh died, he was thought to become or merge with Osiris in the underworld, while his son became the new incarnation of Horus to rule over the living. The hieroglyphic character for the goddess Isis was shaped like a throne, because when Horus sat on his royal throne, he was regarded as sitting in the lap of his divine mother.

As a god-king, the pharaoh was believed to own the entire land of Egypt, so that people paid a portion of their crops to him every year as a kind of rent for using his land. In good years the land produced more than enough to feed everyone, and the pharaoh was able to build up reserves in granaries, so that there would be food available in bad years.

Both the Mesopotamians and Egyptians were polytheists and conceived of their divinities in human form, but the Egyptians represented their gods in art with the heads of animals in order to symbolize some important trait of the divinity. For example, Sakhmet, the goddess of war, had the head of a lion; Horus had the head of a falcon; and Thoth, the god of wisdom, writing, and of other human skills, had either the head of a baboon or of an ibis.

The Old Kingdom is most famous for the great pyramids. The three largest and most famous were built during the middle part of the Old Kingdom, c.2600-2500 B.C., and they were the culmination of a very long process of architectural evolution and experimentation. The people who were responsible for their building comprised two distinct groups: a very small number of highly skilled engineers and technicians who possessed the necessary knowledge for how these complex structures could be built, and an enormous unskilled peasant labor force. Contrary to modern popular belief, the pyramids were not built by slaves, nor by the Hebrews of *The Old Testament*, but by ordinary free Egyptian peasants, who had little to do during the months of inundation each year. They were therefore available to donate their labor to the service of their god-king to build him a truly grand tomb that would last for eternity. The pyramids were built with the simplest tools, but they exhibit a precision of construction that still astonishes all modern experts who study them. The mere organization alone that was needed to coordinate the labor and building materials would have been extraordinary. While the small number of experts were on site the year around to oversee everything, whole families of men, women, and children were brought in from different districts in relays to keep the stone cutting, hauling, and positioning of the multi-ton blocks moving right along with no or little interruptions. Even so, it would have taken perhaps as long as ten or twenty years to build one of the larger pyramids. When completed, their outer faces were rendered perfectly smooth by being fitted with sections of polished limestone, so that the whole monument was gleaming white. In later times, when the Arabs conquered Egypt and made it part of their Islamic Empire, the outer limestone casing of the pyramids was stripped away and recycled as building material.

The largest of the pyramids was constructed for King Khufu (or Cheops, as the Greeks called him). The base of the pyramid covers thirteen and a half acres. Its base measures 756 feet square. Its height is 480 feet. In fact, this pyramid was the tallest man-made structure on the entire planet for 4500 years until the erection of the Eiffel Tower in Paris (1887-1889). Khufu's pyramid is composed of about two million massive blocks of limestone, whose average weight is about two and a half tons.

According to the ancient Egyptian myth of Creation, the god Ptah brought everything into existence by merely pronouncing their names as he sat upon a mound that had emerged from the primordial waters. The shape of the pyramid may have been a stylized representation of this primordial mound of Creation; and this form could have been chosen as the proper shape of the pharaoh's tomb in order to ensure the resurrection of the pharaoh in The Here After. The pyramid's base was always oriented exactly in terms of north-south and east-west. The entrance to the structure faced the Pole Star (Polaris), the one star in heaven that never sets, but remains motionless over the North Pole in the night's sky. This orientation of the tomb's entrance was obviously chosen as a form of magic. Associating the pharaoh with the one truly fixed star in heaven was another way of guaranteeing the pharaoh's enjoyment of eternity.

Another distinctive architectural form of the ancient Egyptians is the obelisk. They were quarried out of pink granite on the southern border of Egypt and were single, continuous and unbroken shafts, four sided and tapering slightly from their base to their top, which terminated in a small pyramid. Modern imitations of the Egyptian obelisk are not monolithic (i.e., consisting of a single stone), but they are assemblages of different pieces of stone. The ancient Egyptians erected them in pairs and had them stand on either side of entrances into temple precincts to form an impressive monumental entrance. They were sacred to the sun god Re and were probably thought to be stone representations of a sunbeam. Consequently, the ancient Egyptian city with the most obelisks was Heliopolis (Sun City in Greek).

Long after the glory days of the ancient Egyptians, their obelisks entered upon a second life, so to speak. Shortly after Egypt was absorbed into the Roman Empire as a province in 30 B.C., following the death of Queen Cleopatra, Roman emperors began hauling obelisks from Egypt and erecting them in Rome. For example, Rome's first emperor (Augustus) brought two obelisks to Rome. One stood in the large open area of the Campus Martius, and the tip of the obelisk served as the gnomon of a gigantic sundial to tell the time. Augustus' other obelish stood in the Circus Maximus, the enormous outdoor facility where the Romans conducted their chariot races, and the obelish served as the turning post at one end of the oval race track. As the result of Roman rulers' enthusiasm for the ancient Egyptian obelisks, the city of Rome today possesses more ancient Egyptian obelisks than any other place, totaling thirteen. One stands today in the center of the Piazza before the Basilica of St. Peter in the Vatican; and the tallest obelisk of all, measuring 105 feet high, stands beside the Church of St. John Lateran in Rome. During the waning years of the Roman Empire when Constantinople (modern Istanbul) had been built to serve as an eastern capital of the Empire, an Egyptian obelisk was brought to the city and erected in the Hippodrome (Constantinople's equivalent to Rome's Circus Maximus), so that the Empire's eastern capital also had such a venerable monument to illustrate its Imperial status. Then during the nineteenth century the cities of Paris, London, and New York received their obelisks, each measuring about seventy feet tall. The one in New

York City stands in Central Park next to the Metropolitan Museum of Art, whence it can be seen through a large window in the museum where the ancient Egyptian collection is on display.

As we have seen in the Epic of Gilgamesh, the poem gives us a very dismal view of the Mesopotamian underworld. This was not the case with the ancient Egyptians, who had a very complex system of beliefs involving the afterlife, only whose basics we can touch upon here. According to their belief system, when a person died, his spirit eventually came before a panel of divine judges in the underworld presided over by Osiris himself. As you will see when you read the excerpt from the Egyptian Book of the Dead (Text #5 in PSWC), the person needed to profess his basic goodness during his life and his avoidance of various wrongful acts. This was accompanied by "the heart weighing ceremony," in which the person's heart, thought to embody his character, was placed in one pan of a set of balance scales. Into the other pan was placed the single feather of ma-at, the Egyptian concept of justice, truth, and order. If the person had lived a fairly good life, his heart would not weigh more than the feather of ma-at, but if the person had done bad deeds, his heart would outweigh ma-at, in which case the heart was removed from the pan and given to a monster to eat. The person's identity was thereby extinguished for good, but if he passed the heart-weighing test, he was allowed to pass on into the Field of Reeds to enjoy an eternal existence that differed little from what he had enjoyed while alive. Thus, the Egyptians had a much more positive view of the afterlife and also thought that it depended upon people's basic morality during their earthly existence.

The Old Kingdom came to an end around 2200 B.C. when the political unity disintegrated and was replaced by rule at the local level. Although we do not know for sure what caused this disruption known as the First Intermediate Period, it seems likely that it resulted from the same drastic climatic change that probably brought down the Sargonid dynasty at about the same time in Mesopotamia. Prolonged drought would have been devastating to Egyptian agriculture; and once the surplus accumulated in the pharaoh's granaries had been consumed, political disunity would have eventually come about when people lost faith in the pharaoh's ability to regulate the flooding of the Nile.

Eventually, however, the prolonged drought ended, and political unity was reestablished by a new dynasty of rulers who lived and ruled from the city of Thebes, located several hundred miles upstream from Memphis in Upper Egypt. Henceforth Thebes served as the capital of the united land. This period, known as the Middle Kingdom (2050-1650 B.C.), carried on the well established traditions of the Old Kingdom, but there have survived from these times various stories written on papyrus that were probably popular Egyptian folk tales. This popular literature therefore flourished around the same time that the Epic of Gilgamesh was composed during the Old Babylonian Kingdom in Mesopotamia. Text #6 in PSWC is an example of this popular literature.

The Middle Kingdom ended in a second period of disunity known as the Second Intermediate Period (1650-1550 B.C.), during which the Egyptians for the first time suffered the indignity of having Lower Egypt overrun by foreign invaders, whom they called the Hyksos. It is still not known whether they brought about the disunity by their invasion, or they simply took advantage of it and moved in to take over once there was no centralized power to keep them out. In any case, the Hyksos came from the east from the area of Palestine, and they were able to establish themselves as rulers over part of Egypt, because they possessed a superior military technology that was just beginning to sweep through the Fertile Crescent and was becoming the standard way for states to wage their wars with one another. The Hyksos had weapons made of bronze, an alloy of copper and tin, and which we shall treat in more detail in the next lecture. They fought in two-wheeled chariots drawn by two or three horses, and in which there rode two warriors, one to serve as the driver, and the other as an archer. The latter was armed with a new kind of bow, a composite bow constructed of horn and wood. It could shoot arrows with much more power than a regular wooden bow; and the chariots were driven around on a battlefield with the archers shooting arrows at the enemy. Eventually, a new dynasty of Egyptian rulers, based in Thebes, led a rebellion against the Hyksos, drove them out of the land, and reunited Egypt once again. This began the last major phase of ancient Egyptian history, the New Kingdom (1550-1100 B.C.). Not only did the Egyptians drive the Hyksos out of their land, but they went on the offensive, conducted numerous campaigns in the Levant (i.e., Palestine and Syria), and established an empire outside the Nile Valley. Hence this period is also known as the Empire, during which many small city-states in the Levant were forced to acknowledge Egypt's superior power and to pay to the Egyptian pharaoh an annual tribute. Egypt therefore enjoyed considerable prosperity from the influx of this new source of wealth and also experienced a noticeable increase in slaves, who had previously been relatively rare in Egypt, but now became more numerous as the result of Egypt's successful wars abroad.

This period of Egyptian history contains the most famous pharaohs. We will therefore devote the remainder of this lecture to surveying them. One of the early rulers of this period was a woman named Hatshepsut. She was one of the very few women to rule as a pharaoh. She began as the regent of her under-age stepson, but then she began ruling in her own right as pharaoh. It is interesting to note that since Egyptian artists for centuries had portrayed all pharaohs as bearded to display their masculine power, this female ruler was represented in art in exactly the same way. She enjoyed a reign of 22 years during the early 1400s B.C. during a period when the Egyptian Empire was well established abroad, and the land was enjoying peace and prosperity. Her reign was most notable for conducting a series of trading expeditions down the Red Sea to a land called Punt, probably somewhere in East Africa and/or the southern tip of the Arabian Peninsula, whence Egyptian traders brought back monkeys, ivory, and various exotic plants that they planted and grew in Egypt. When she was finally succeeded by her stepson, Tuthmosis III, he became Egypt's most glorious conqueror and won a major battle in Palestine at a place called Megiddo, which has been made famous as Armageddon in the last book of *The New Testament*, the Book of Revelation.

In the fourteenth century B.C. occurred the sixteen-year reign of Akhenaten (1352-1336 B.C.), who is well known for his attempt to replace the traditional polytheism of the Egyptian religion with monotheism. The land of Egypt was dominated by two natural phenomena, the Nile and the sun. Akhenaten regarded the sun, represented in art as a solar disk and called Aton, as the one and only god to be worshipped. After all, the sun traverses above the whole earth every day, seeing everything and shedding upon it its life-giving light and heat, which Akhenaten celebrated in a famous hymn. Akhenaten's queen was the equally famous and beautiful Nefertiti, whose bust is world famous and is one of the prized possessions of the Berlin Museum. In order to break away from the established religious traditions, Akhenaten moved the capital from Thebes to a new site further downstream on the Nile, a place called Amarna, where he could build a new city devoted solely to the Aton. The site has been extensively excavated and has provided us with much valuable information about this period of Egyptian history. Although Akhenaten and Nefertiti had six daughters, they did not produce a male heir to succeed to the throne. So, when Akhenaten died, it seems that his religious revolution died with him. The Egyptians went back to worshipping their traditional gods, and Amarna was abandoned in favor of Thebes.

Shortly thereafter the Egyptian throne was occupied by a nine-year old boy, Tutankhamen, popularly known as King Tut. He ruled for about nine years before dying in his late teens. He would probably be a "pharaonic nobody" except that in 1922 the British archaeologist, Howard Carter, discovered his unplundered tomb, whose vast array of possessions has given us a fascinating view of pharaonic splendor.

The last major pharaoh to be considered here is Ramesses II, who enjoyed the second longest reign of any pharaoh, 67 years (1279-1213 B.C.). In the fifth year of his reign he led a large Egyptian army into northern Syria, where he engaged the Hittites in a major battle at a place called Kadesh on the Orontes River. Besides a large force of infantry, the Hittites had 2500 chariots, and the battle must have been the largest fought so far in this part of the world. Although the official Egyptian account portrays the battle as a great victory for Ramesses, it is more likely that he suffered a defeat, because he withdrew from the area right after the battle and in a treaty conceded the region to the Hittites. But of course, Egyptian god-king pharaohs were always portrayed on official monuments as mighty conquerors and victors. In official records they never suffered defeats. Indeed, Ramesses had his supposed victory at Kadesh portrayed in several places throughout Egypt. His long reign witnessed the last glory days of Egypt, and Ramesses was not at all shy in having himself represented in art throughout the whole land. Perhaps his most famous monument is that at Abu Simbel at the very southern edge of Egypt, where he and his queen-wife Nefertari are cut out of the cliff's side as colossal statues. Ramesses succeeded in fathering 79 sons and 59 daughters from a large harim of women; and not many years ago archaeologists discovered a gigantic maze of tombs carved out into a mountainside, which seems to have been where Ramesses' sons were buried. By the time of his death he had outlived many of his children, and it was his thirteenth eldest son who succeeded him on the throne. As we shall see in the next lecture, not long after Ramesses' death Egypt's glory came to a sudden end during the early 1100s B.C. Egypt's decline was part of a much larger phenomenon that destroyed all the major palace centers of the eastern Mediterranean.

LECTURE 4
The Bronze Age

- **2000-1400 B.C.:** Minoan Civilization on the island of Crete.
- **1600-1200 B.C.:** Hittite Civilization in Anatolia and Mycenaean Civilization in mainland Greece.
- **1200 B.C.:** approximate date for the beginning of Widespread destruction of sites throughout the Near East and surrounding areas, resulting in the abrupt ending of the Bronze Age civilizations.
- **Bronze Age:** roughly the second millennium B.C. of the Near East and eastern Mediterranean, named from its metal-working technology (bronze = alloy of copper and tin).
- **Semitic languages:** large interrelated family of languages, including the speech of the ancient Babylonians, Assyrians, Phoenicians, Hebrews, and later Arabs.
- **Indo-European languages:** large interrelated family of languages, consisting of the subgroups of Hittite of ancient Anatolia, Greek, Persian, Sanskrit of ancient India, Latin, Celtic, and Germanic (including English).
- **Phoenicians:** ancient Semitic people of the eastern Mediterranean coast (i.e., modern Lebanon), first great seafarers and merchants of the ancient Mediterranean.
- **Minoan Civilization:** Bronze Age civilization on the island

of Crete, named after the mythical King Minos.

- **Mycenaean Civilization:** Bronze Age civilization of mainland Greece, named after Mycenae (first major palace center discovered by modern archaeologists).
- **Hittites:** Indo-European people, united many diverse peoples of Anatolia under their rule.
- **Sea Peoples:** term in Egyptian texts describing several peoples of the Late Bronze Age responsible for much destruction.

After examining the two earliest civilizations of Mesopotamia and Egypt, we will now study the expansion of civilization into other nearby areas. In this lecture we will survey the Bronze Age, roughly the period from 2000 to 1200 B.C. In doing so we will focus our survey upon three specific civilizations: the Minoan civilization on the island of Crete, the Hittites of Anatolia, and the Mycenaean civilization on mainland Greece. We will also see how during the second half of this period (1600–1200 B.C.) there emerged for the first time an interlocking international system of trade, warfare, and diplomacy. You should notice how the three civilizations that we will survey shared common basic features with those of Mesopotamia and Egypt, and how they also differed, because they had to be adapted to their own specific environments: principally, mountainous terrains instead of great river valleys.

By the middle of the third millennium (c.2500 B.C.) the idea of civilization, pioneered by the Sumerians of Mesopotamia, had begun to spread throughout the rest of the Fertile Crescent, as other peoples living in the area organized themselves into self-governing small communities and began to use a writing system to help them record transactions and to keep track of all sorts of important human activities. For example, about thirty years ago Italian archaeologists uncovered the site of Ebla in Syria, which served as a major ruling and community center for the surrounding region. Among other things the archaeologists discovered the official archives, consisting of thousands of clay tablets. The Eblaites had adapted cuneiform to write their own Semitic language. Ebla was only one of many civilized communities that flourished during the third and second millennia to make the Fertile Crescent a complex patchwork of small and large states, who interacted with one another through trade or warfare.

As we have already seen, by the time that the first two civilizations arose along the major river valleys in Mesopotamia and Egypt, human beings had figured out how to extract certain metals from ore: copper, lead, silver, and gold. They eventually also figured out that when a small amount of tin was added to copper, it produced a metal that was much harder than copper. This alloy was bronze, from which this period of early human history takes its name, because during it all important tools and weapons were made of this metal alloy. It was not until after the end of the Bronze Age that people figured out how to smelt iron and to work it into an even harder metal, thus spawning the beginning of the Iron Age c.1000 B.C. One problem with bronze, however, was the relative scarcity of tin. Copper could be found in abundance in many areas, but this was not the case for tin. As more civilized communities came into existence throughout this region of the world, they all wished to have bronze available in substantial amounts for fashioning their weapons and tools. Thus arose a huge demand for both copper and tin, but since the latter metal was not easily found, the civilized peoples of this area sent out traders and prospectors to find sources of tin, which they often did in relatively remote and distant places inhabited by hitherto uncivilized peoples. This obviously resulted in the establishment of long distant trade routes and different peoples engaging in trade with one another in order to satisfy their need for bronze. Consequently, the idea of civilization itself also spread westward out of the Fertile Crescent and gave rise to the three civilizations that we will survey in this lecture. But before we do, I first wish to point out the importance of the Levantine coast in fostering the trading network that was so characteristic of the Bronze Age. The coastline of modern-day Lebanon has a very narrow hinterland, because it is shut in by the Mountains of Lebanon. The people of this area from early times onwards have therefore found it impossible to support themselves entirely by agriculture and have thus always supplemented their limited agricultural productivity by engaging in seaborne commerce. Since one of their natural resources, growing on the slopes of the Mountains of Lebanon, were large numbers of big cedar trees, they began to trade with both Egypt and Mesopotamia that did not possess such forests and needed these trees for roof beams and other things. Thus, the people of Lebanon, known by the ancient Greeks as Phoenicians, became the earliest important seafaring merchants of the eastern Mediterranean. They organized themselves into several small city-states, such as Tyre, Sidon, and Biblos. Farther north along the coast in what is now Syria arose another very important Bronze Age city-state called Ugarit, which was discovered and extensively excavated by French archaeologists during the period between the two world wars. It faced out onto the Mediterranean and also became a very important trading center in connecting the Fertile Crescent to the larger Mediterranean world. In fact, not far west of Ugarit out into the Mediterranean lies the island of Cyprus, with which Ugarit had very close ties during the Bronze Age, because the island was rich in copper deposits. The island's name, Cyprus, is simply the ancient Greek word for copper.

Farther west of Cyprus is the mountainous island of Crete, measuring 35 miles in width from north to south and 160 miles in length from east to west. It became the home to the first of the three major Bronze Age civilizations that we will survey today. During the third millennium the people of Crete lived in small villages and practiced agriculture and stock breeding (primarily sheep). Then around 2000 B.C. there arose several major palace centers on the island that controlled the surrounding areas, thus forming a civilization characterized by separate city-states, probably ruled by kings. This civilization was unknown to modern scholars until 1900 when the British archaeologist, Sir Arthur Evans, began excavating at the site of Knossos. Since then numerous sites on the island have been extensively excavated, so that we now possess a fairly clear picture of this civilization, which is termed Minoan after King Minos, who according to later Greek myth ruled over the entire island in very early times. After three centuries or so all the palaces on the island except one were destroyed, probably due to earthquake. The one palace center that finally emerged supreme was located at Knossos on the central northern shore of the island. It is therefore conjectured that after a period in which the island was divided among several small kingdoms resulting from the island's mountainous terrain, the whole island was united with Knossos serving as the capital.

Arthur Evans spent much of his life excavating and restoring the ruined palace center at Knossos. It was enormous, spreading out over six acres and in some places had basement areas and an upper floor. The palace consisted of dozens and dozens of rooms, among which were placed open areas to allow light and air to circulate. The rooms would have been used for living quarters, workshops, and storage. The slope of the ground was exploited to develop a system of running water through clay pipes. Many of the inner walls of the palace were decorated with fresco paintings, the most famous of which depicts a man vaulting over the head of a charging bull. It is generally supposed that this formed an important ceremony that was performed in the large inner courtyard of the palace, where it was witnessed by many spectators. It also probably was later remembered in a distorted form in the ancient Greek myth of the Labyrinth of King Minos, the Minotaur, and the heroic exploit of Theseus. According to this story, King Minos conquered Athens and forced the Athenians to send to him each year seven young men and seven young women, who were sent into a maze-like structure called the Labyrinth, haunted by the Minotaur, a man-eating creature with a human body and a bull's head. After years of having their young people feed the savage Minotaur, Theseus, the son of Athens' king, volunteered to go to Crete, where he entered the labyrinth and killed the monster. The rambling nature of the palace at Knossos could have been later reinterpreted as a maze.

Arthur Evans discovered clay tablets in the ruins, but they were written in a script that had never been seen before. Although he was not able to read these texts, Evans could tell that they were written in two different, but somewhat related writing systems. He called one Linear A and the other Linear B. In 1956 a British scholar named Michael Ventris succeeded in deciphering Linear B and discovered that it was an early form of ancient Greek. Linear A still remains unreadable, but since other clay tablets written in Linear B have been found at all the major palace centers of the Mycenaean civilization on the Greek mainland, whereas Linear A is found only at sites on Crete, it is now thought that Linear A was the earlier of the two scripts and was developed by the native inhabitants of Crete to represent their non-Greek *of*

language. Then as Mycenaean civilization arose on the nearby Greek mainland, largely in response to the Minoan civilization on Crete, the Mycenaeans borrowed the writing system of the Minoans and adapted it to fit their own language. Moreover, the presence of Linear B at Knossos is generally interpreted to indicate that during the last phase of its history (c.1500-1400 B.C.) Knossos was taken over by Mycenaeans from the Greek mainland.

As we have seen in the cases of Mesopotamia and Egypt, writing was developed as a necessary means of record keeping. The same applies to the Minoan civilization. Although the Linear A texts still cannot be read, the ones written in Linear B give us valuable information. The texts are all simple accounting records, showing that the palace was an administrative center, taking in surplus produce from farmers and shepherds to be consumed by the palace or shipped out as trading goods to obtain other commodities, such as metals, not available on the island. The Linear B writing system is much simpler than cuneiform and hieroglyphics, because it consists of only 87 symbols, but it is still too complex to be easily mastered and therefore must have been known and used by only a small number of highly trained scribes employed by the palace for keeping its records. Linear B is termed a syllabary, because each of its symbols represents a consonant followed by a vowel (e.g., ko, pa, ti, etc.). It therefore required the scribe to spell all words in a syllabic sequence, whether or not the word was formed of a regular sequence of consonants and vowels. Although 87 signs were easier to master than hundreds of them, the strictly syllabic spelling that it required made it somewhat inexact in its ability to render this early form of Greek precisely. So, although it served well enough for making lists and headings for basic record keeping, it was not sufficiently precise to enable the scribes to produce a Minoan or Mycenaean literature, as we have encountered with the Mesopotamian Epic of Gilgamesh or the Egyptian Book of the Dead. Rather, the Linear B texts simply record the palace's nuts-and-bolts shuffling-around of various commodities.

During the last major phase of the Bronze Age, the so-called Late Bronze Age of c.1600-1200 B.C., there came into being and flourished two other major civilizations: the Mycenaeans of the Greek mainland and the Hittites of Anatolia. Let us first survey the latter. Like so many things involving the

Indo-European → foundation of nearly nearly every modern European language today &

ancient Near Eastern civilizations, the Hittites are a relatively recent discovery. When German archaeologists led by Hugo Winkler began excavating at the Hittite capital in eastern Anatolia in 1906, they discovered the official archives, consisting of thousands of clay tablets written in cuneiform, but in an unknown language. When a Czech scholar deciphered the language during World War I, it turned out to be a language that scholars had never previously encountered, but it belonged to the large family of Indo-European languages. As we have already seen, by the Late Bronze Age the whole Fertile Crescent was occupied by peoples speaking different types of Semitic languages, which belong to the large family of Semitic languages that have originated from the peoples of the Arabian Peninsula. One of the truly great intellectual achievements of nineteenth-century European scholars was the piecing together of a vast amount of linguistic information to construct the Indo-European family of languages: Celtic (including Irish and Welsh), Germanic (including German, Dutch, and English), Baltic, Slavic (including Polish and Russian), Italic (including Latin and its modern-day Romance descendants of Italian, French, Spanish, Portuguese, and Rumanian), Albanian, Hellenic (Greek), Anatolian (including Hittite), Armenian, Indo-Iranian (including Persian and Sanskrit), and Tocharian. All the different modern languages belonging to these subgroups are historically related to one another and ultimately go back to a common ancestor language, Proto-Indo-European. It is generally believed that at some very remote time in the past there existed somewhere in Europe or Asia (probably the area north of the Caucasus Mountains between the Black and Caspian Seas) a population that spoke this language, but as portions of the population moved off into various parts of Europe and Asia, their original Proto-Indo-European language evolved over time in different ways to form the tremendous linguistic diversity exhibited by the whole family of Indo-European languages, stretching from western Europe to southern Asia. Both the Hittites and the Mycenaeans represent the earliest speakers of Indo-European languages recorded in written texts.

Anatolia (also known as Asia Minor) possesses a terrain vastly different from the river valleys of Mesopotamia and Egypt. It is very rugged with mountains that break the land up into a large number of small valleys and

Modern day Turkey

plains. Consequently, in early times the human population in this region did not develop a commonly shared language or culture, but instead, the irregular nature of the geography fostered the development of many small groups of people, each with their own language or dialect and with their distinctive ethnic identity. Accordingly, as traders and metal prospectors from the Fertile Crescent brought the idea of civilization into Anatolia, the Hittites arose as only one of many Anatolian peoples, and they grew up in a tough neighborhood, in which they were obliged to defend themselves from their hostile neighbors or be conquered by them. In fact, the Hittites became so effective militarily that they became the most powerful people of the region and ruled over the other peoples of Anatolia by right of conquest. As they became civilized, they borrowed major features of civilization from the Fertile Crescent, such as writing their language in a cuneiform syllabic script, but they had their own distinctive myths and stories known to us today through their clay tablets. They also had to adapt themselves to an environment very different from the river valleys of Mesopotamia and Egypt; and their human environment required them to become tough warriors or be conquered by their neighbors, but unlike the Egyptians or Mesopotamians, whose peoples had a commonly shared language and culture, the Hittites could not use these things in constructing political unity. Instead, they conquered the different peoples of Anatolia and created a kind of feudal system, in which the ruler of each locale was forced to swear loyalty to the Hittite king, to pay him tribute, and to serve as his ally in war. As you might suspect, the system worked only reasonably well. As long as the local vassal was in fear of the Hittites, he towed the line, but as soon as he saw his chance, he often led his people in rebellion. Consequently, Hittite history is full of ups and downs, as the kingdom was obliged to contend with revolts among its subjects. Nevertheless, by the time that the Hittites arose as a civilized people during the Late Bronze Age (1600-1200 B.C.), they were masters in the techniques of warfare that were becoming standard throughout the Fertile Crescent: namely, the horse-drawn two-wheeled chariot carrying a driver and an archer armed with the composite bow.

In Lecture 2 we first encountered the Hittites as the sackers of Babylon around 1600 B.C. This event testifies to their ability to organize and

Hittites ⇒ really skilled conquerers → environment to which they adapted themselves.

Hittites conquers northern mesopatamia,
Egypt (New Kingdom) conquers southern/
western.

successfully carry out a major military operation over a very long distance. The Hittites, however, reached the pinnacle of their power during the period c.1400-1200 B.C. During the third quarter of the fourteenth century B.C. they came under the rule of their most militarily able king (Suppiluliumas). He succeeded in establishing the Hittites as the rulers over northern Syria. Now remember that the period of the Late Bronze Age (c.1600-1200 B.C.) also coincides roughly with the New Kingdom of Egypt, during which the Egyptians first drove out the Hyksos and then created their own empire in the Levant. As the Hittites under Suppiluliumas descended upon Syria from the north, Egypt was under the rule of Akhenaten, who was so preoccupied with his religious revolution that he paid scant attention to foreign affairs and allowed the Hittites to become Egypt's imperial neighbor and rival. Actual hostilities finally broke out between the two during the early 1200s and culminated in the battle of Kadesh on the Orontes River in northern Syria. This must have been the biggest chariot battle of the Bronze Age. Although Pharaoh Ramesses II claimed victory, he was more likely either defeated outright or fought the Hittites to a draw, because he withdrew to the south right after the battle and conceded the area to the Hittites, who continued to be masters of the region. The battle, however, led the two parties to sign a treaty with each other and to become one another's ally in case of attack by a third party. We happen to possess both the Hittite and Egyptian texts of this treaty, which demonstrates the high degree of diplomacy existing among the major powers of the Late Bronze Age.

2 main rivals 13th century BCE ↓ Hittities and Egyptians

We will now turn our attention to the contemporaneous Mycenaean civilization, which takes its name from Mycenae, the first site of this civilization excavated by the German archaeologist Heinrich Schliemann. Like Crete and Anatolia, mainland Greece is very mountainous, so that the Mycenaean civilization developed as a series of independent small kingdoms ruled from palace centers, which were not nearly as grand as the palace at Knossos. Mycenae and Tiryns were fortified by massive stone walls, suggesting that these small kingdoms were in need of defense against one another, because warfare was an ever-present possibility. Indeed, scenes represented by Mycenaean artists clearly indicate that the elite class of males regularly

* big palace on Cyprus (Manoa)

engaged in hunting wild boars and lions, as well as fighting in war. Mycenaean society therefore seems to have been quite martial. The funerary architecture for the rulers is quite impressive and shows that the Mycenaean rulers could call upon a considerable human labor force and had engineers capable of building very large and difficult structures. The common royal tomb is known as a tholos and is in the shape of a bee hive with a long entrance leading into the domed chamber. The largest of these tombs is at Mycenae itself and is called the Treasury of Atreus. Its entry-way (dromos) is 120 feet long and 17 feet high. The inner chamber is 48 feet in diameter and rises to a height of 43 feet. The domed chamber arises in concentric rings of stone in a technique known as corbeling. At the time that it was built, it was the largest free-standing dome in the world, and it remained so for about 1500 years until the Roman Emperor Hadrian's construction of the Pantheon in Rome. The bodies of the dead were laid out in these tombs and often had their faces covered with a gold mask. Their bodies were surrounded by large amounts of weapons and jewelry fashioned out of precious materials: bronze, gold, silver, and amber, clearly showing that the Mycenaean rulers must have operated a profitable business in trade and/or warfare. In fact, we possess considerable evidence for the far-flung trading of the Mycenaeans in the form of their distinctive pottery, because their large clay storage jars, used to transport various commodities such as wine or olive oil scented with flowers to form a perfume, are found all around the eastern Mediterranean and even to the west in southern Italy and eastern Sicily.

I have already discussed Linear B, which was used at all the Mycenaean palace centers in mainland Greece to keep track of all the goods flowing in and out of the palace, but another very important source of information that we have about international trade during the Late Bronze Age comes from the discovery of two shipwrecks. Both ships date to the last century or so of the Bronze Age (one c.1300 and the other c.1200 B.C.). Both sank off the southwestern coast of Anatolia (Gelidonya and Uluburun) in relatively shallow water (one about 90 feet down, and the other about 150), so that they could be excavated by archaeologists wearing scuba gear. One shipwreck was found and excavated during the 1960s, and the other a generation later during the

1980s, with both expeditions led by the American George Bass, a leading pioneer of underwater archaeology. Although the hulls of the ships had long rotted away, their cargoes still rested on the sea floor undisturbed. One of the ships measured about 30 to 33 feet in length, whereas the other was about 50 feet long. Although both carried a very diverse cargo of numerous goods for trade, their main item was copper. The smaller ship was loaded with one ton of copper, whereas the larger one had six tons. The cargoes also contained lumps of tin about the size and shape of hamburger buns, as well as bronze scrap that was intended to be melted down and recycled into new objects. On board the ships was an assortment of bronze tools and weights of different sizes for conducting trade according to the weights and measures used in the different seaports around the eastern Mediterranean. The cargoes also included ebony logs, Syrian jewelry, a large number of clay oil lamps made in Cyprus, 100 large jars of tree resin used as incense or for embalming, and lumps of blue glass (about the size and shape of hockey pucks) manufactured in Egypt and exported to be melted and shaped into various objects. These two cargoes therefore testify to the existence of a large and flourishing seaborne trade among the different peoples of the eastern Mediterranean during the Late Bronze Age. Although metals figured prominently in this trade, there were numerous other commodities that were exchanged.

This interlocking international system of the Late Bronze Age, which embraced the Mycenaeans, Minoans, Hittites, Cypriotes, Phoenicians, Egyptians, and Mesopotamians, came to a sudden and abrupt end beginning around 1200 B.C. and extending over the early decades of the 1100s. As clearly demonstrated by archaeology, during this time period all major sites from as far west as mainland Greece and as far east as the Euphrates were sacked and destroyed by fire. Something truly catastrophic happened to bring this about, and it still remains a mystery. Egypt alone, protected by its deserts to the east and west, was able to withstand this terrible storm of human destruction; and it is from a temple in Egypt that we possess our only clues about what happened. A hieroglyphic text inscribed on this temple to commemorate the reign of Ramesses III of the early twelfth century B.C. boastfully records how the pharaoh defeated a coalition of invaders, termed the Sea Peoples, when they tried to enter the Nile delta by sea and by land from the east. According to this text, before descending upon Egypt, these people had banded together and had destroyed the Hittite capital and other sites in Cyprus and the Levant. Modern scholars have put forth various theories to explain what happened: a drought causing a massive uprising of starving subjects, the mass migration of foreign peoples like the later Germanic invasions of the Roman Empire, etc. My own theory is that, as had often happened during the Late Bronze Age, some of the Hittites' subjects rebelled; and unlike earlier instances when they were reconquered, the people on this occasion succeeded in defeating and destroying their Hittite rulers, after which they banded together and went on a rampage outside of Anatolia, attacking and sacking all the major palace centers in order to carry off their precious metals and other valuables until there were no easy pickings left, by which time they had succeeded in destroying the well integrated system that had bound together the civilized peoples of the Late Bronze Age.

fire ⟹ destroys several trade posts
some people say it might have
been caused by rebellion of
Hitties.

LECTURE 5
The Ancient Near Eastern Empires

IMPORTANT DATES AND TERMS

- **900-612:** Period of the Assyrian Empire.
- **612:** Destruction of the Assyrian capital Nineveh.
- **626-539:** Period of the Neo-Babylonian Empire.
- **550-330:** Period of the Persian Empire.
- Nineveh: Assyrian capital located near the Tigris.
- **Iranian Plateau:** large arid upland region east of Mesopotamia.
- **Zoroaster** = Zarathustra: early Persian religious leader.
- **Zoroastrian dualism:** good creator god vs. a god of evil, humans must side with good against evil, world ending with final victory of good over evil, concept taken over into Hebrew thought and developed into the idea of God vs. the Devil.

When the palace centers of the Bronze Age civilizations of the eastern Mediterranean were destroyed during the early 1100s B.C., the whole region was plunged into a sharp decline, if not a dark age. Even though Egypt had succeeded in warding off the attacks of the Sea Peoples, it too went into decline and never again enjoyed the political power or cultural vigor exhibited during the New Kingdom. It took several generations for the peoples of the eastern Mediterranean to rebuild; and when they finally did, the cultural and political map of the whole region was quite different from what it had been. One important discovery during this period that spread and affected everyone was

iron

the mastery of the complex technique of repeated smelting and hammering needed to produce iron out of iron ore. The resulting metal was much harder than bronze; and since iron ore was relatively plentiful in many places, iron could be produced in large amounts and at a much lower cost than bronze. Thus, iron metallurgy spread among the civilized peoples, and iron soon became the primary metal used for making tools and weapons. Consequently, the period following the collapse of the Late Bronze Age is often termed the Iron Age by modern scholars. Moreover, the single most important phenomenon that affected the Fertile Crescent and surrounding areas for the next several centuries involved the rise and fall of three great empires: the Assyrian (c.900-612 B.C.), the Neo-Babylonian (626-539 B.C.), and the Persian (550-330 B.C.). They will be the subject of this lecture.

As we have seen, the Babylonians were a Semitic people, who enjoyed great prominence in Mesopotamia during the three centuries of the Old Babylonian Kingdom (1900-1600 B.C.). They had established their capital city of Babylon in central Mesopotamia, where the Tigris and Euphrates nearly touch. During the period covered in this lecture Mesopotamia was regarded as consisting of two parts: Babylonia, the homeland of the Babylonians, comprising the area around and to the south of Babylon itself; and Assyria, the homeland of the Assyrians, consisting of the region of Mesopotamia north of Babylon. The Assyrians and Babylonians regarded each other as kindred peoples, and they spoke the same Semitic language called Akkadian, but they wound up having very different histories. During the period of the Middle and Late Bronze Age (1900-1200 B.C.) the Babylonians were an important people on the international stage in the ancient Near East. The Assyrians, the Babylonians' neighbors just to the north, however, were mostly famous as traders, and they did not emerge as a politically prominent people until after the collapse of the Bronze Age civilizations.

Our earliest major source of information about the Assyrians is a law code dating to the eleventh century B.C. Although it was part of the ancient Near Eastern legal tradition, it offers a very interesting contrast to Hammurabi's law code, because the Assyrian text contains numerous harsh punishments for violating its various provisions: so many lashes with the whip, cutting off the

Babylonians → Conquerors
Assyrians → traders.

annotation at top: ✱ Assyrians may have been given harsh punishments

hand, cutting off the ears, gouging out the eyes, death by impaling, etc. It therefore appears that even before the Assyrians became the conquerors of the Fertile Crescent so feared for their savagery and terrifying treatment of their enemies, they were harsh and violent in dealing with one another.

Another important difference between the Assyrians and the Babylonians lay in the nature of the lands in which they lived. As we have already seen, southern Mesopotamia possessed no forests or stone, so that its inhabitants used mud brick for building and clay tablets for writing. The homeland of the Assyrians, on the other hand, had abundant stone for quarrying and building, and the Assyrian kings exploited this resource and used it for constructing several major palace complexes that survived in good condition under mounds of wind-blown sand until uncovered by modern archaeologists. In addition, the Assyrian kings were so proud of their conquests that they had them illustrated by skilled craftsmen in the form of reliefs on the walls of their palaces. We therefore possess today a rich artistic record of the Assyrian Empire. The Assyrian kings accompanied these reliefs with cuneiform texts narrating their deeds (primarily their conquests) in such a detailed year-by-year fashion that for the first time in the history of the ancient Near East we can construct an absolute and solid chronology of events. Text #7 in PSWC is a translation of the royal chronicle of King Ashurnasirpal (883-859 B.C.), which gives you a very good picture of how these kings saw themselves and wished to be seen.

annotation in right margin: Text #7 PSWC

As the first of these three great empires, the Assyrian was very important in laying down the general pattern of conquest and rule followed by the other two. The Assyrians developed a well organized military system: a large infantry force armed with iron weapons and supported by chariots and bowmen. They mastered the logistics of supply, so that they could conduct long and distant campaigns with large forces; and they also developed the standard techniques of siege-craft by which fortified towns and cities could be captured: battering rams, mining to loosen the foundations of a wall, scaling ladders, and wheeled siege-towers to bring attackers right up to the top level of an enemy's wall. They also perfected the techniques of terrorizing their enemies and subjects. Impaling a person's body upon a stake was a common form of execution, and the body was left on the stake to rot and to serve as a graphic reminder of what might await the living if they defied the Assyrians. In one palace relief King Esarhaddon (680-668 B.C.) is shown holding a rope in each of his hands that are attached to rings put through the noses of two conquered kings, who were thereby humiliated and demeaned as if they were simply the abused canine pets of the mighty king. Assyrian texts indicate that palaces and their environs were "decorated" with the dead bodies and severed heads of enemies and rebels. One palace relief shows King Ashurbanipal (668-627 B.C.) sitting on a throne in his royal garden, and dangling from a tree and hanging just above the top of a table before the king is a human head, as if he is feasting his eyes upon a treasured trophy.

Both in their official royal art and chronicles the Assyrian kings projected the image of all-mighty conquerors, whose cruelty was a testimony to their irresistible power. They regarded themselves as the deputy of the supreme Assyrian sun god Ashur, from whom the Assyrians took their name. The kings therefore felt fully justified in all their actions and clearly relished recording all their conquests in great and gruesome detail, just like a modern-day professional athlete listing all the particular statistics of his career on the playing field. When not engaged in conquests, the Assyrian kings had themselves portrayed in their reliefs as relaxing by hunting and killing lions. These animals, still inhabiting this region of the world and not yet hunted to extinction, were kept inside enclosed royal hunting grounds, so that they would be available when the king wished to hunt and kill them. Of course, even this activity was part of the royal official ideology, because the all-mighty king of the Assyrians spent part of his leisure time in hunting down and killing the monarch of the animal kingdom.

Shortly after 900 B.C. the Assyrian kings embarked upon their military campaigns that ultimately resulted in the Assyrians ruling over the entire Fertile Crescent. Once conquered, the people of an area became a district of the Assyrian Empire, ruled over by a loyal native of the region or by an Assyrian governor. They were forced to pay a heavy annual tribute to the Assyrian king. This was on top of a very heavy price that the people had paid in resisting the Assyrian conquest. In addition to people having been killed in

Assyrians → conquered in 612 BCE
by their once friendly neighbors/
the Babylonians/allies

the fighting, many others were rounded up and marched off into slavery along with thousands of their herd animals. Skilled craftsmen in a conquered district were routinely removed from their homes and brought back to the Assyrian capital to place their artistic skills at the disposal of the king and the ruling class. In some instances, as in the case of the northern kingdom of Israel, in order to break local resistance, the Assyrians deported a sizable portion of the population and forced them to settle down among loyal subjects, while the Assyrians repopulated the abandoned area with their own people. In short, the Assyrians operated their empire in a very predatory manner and in ways that disregarded the feelings of their subjects.

The pinnacle of Assyrian power occurred during the period c.750-630 B.C., followed by their sudden and unexpected downfall. The year 626 B.C. marked the beginning of the end when Babylon revolted. At first the Assyrians had treated their kindred Babylonians as brothers and friendly allies, but as the former became masters of the whole Fertile Crescent, the Babylonians were treated no better than any other subjects. Consequently, the Babylonians were eager to revolt and to create their own empire. When they had risen in revolt twice before, they had been defeated and ruthlessly punished, but now their rebellion coincided with the uprising of another conquered people; and the two rebellions, combined together, eventually succeeded in bringing down the Assyrian Empire. The other rebellious people were the Medes, the speakers of an Iranian language (Indo-European), who inhabited the mountainous northwestern area of Iran just east of Assyria. Thus, faced with not just one, but two major rebellions to their east and south, the Assyrians were placed on the defensive. Eventually the Medes and Babylonians formed an alliance and began coordinating their actions against their common enemy. This culminated in their siege of the Assyrians in their capital city of Nineveh, which was captured and destroyed in 612 and never again reoccupied. So ended the Assyrian Empire, whose downfall was celebrated by many oppressed peoples throughout the Fertile Crescent, including the Hebrews of Judah. One of the smaller books of *The Old Testament* is *Nahum*, which was composed at this time and gloats over how Yahweh, the god of the Hebrews, had finally punished the Assyrians for their wicked ways.

We now come to the second of the three great ancient Near Eastern empires, the Neo-Babylonian, so called in order to distinguish it from the earlier Old Babylonian Kingdom. Of the three empires that we are surveying in this lecture, the Neo-Babylonian was the shortest (626-539 B.C.) and is also the most poorly documented. The latter results in large measure from the fact that we do not possess, as we do in the case of the Assyrians, the impressive remains of royal palaces richly adorned with narrative reliefs, nor do we have cuneiform texts spelling out in great detail all the deeds of the Neo-Babylonian kings. But suffice it to say that the Babylonians now stepped into the imperial shoes previously occupied by the Assyrians; and they inherited and employed the same basic military and political techniques and practices in conquering, controlling, and exploiting the peoples of the Fertile Crescent.

The most famous king of the Neo-Babylonian Empire was Nebuchadnezzar (604-562 B.C.), well known from *The Old Testament* as the conqueror of Jerusalem in 586 and responsible for the Babylonian captivity of the Jews (586-539 B.C.). During his reign Babylon enjoyed its greatest prosperity, power, and elegance. The entire city was surrounded by an enormous brick wall to protect it from enemy attack. The wall was so huge that two chariots could pass one another along its top surface. Although the mud brick remains of Babylon are not much to look at now, the Ishtar Gate is quite extraordinary and gives us a glimpse at how grand Babylon must have been at this time. After it was uncovered by German archaeologists, they carefully took it apart, shipped it back to Germany, and reassembled it in all its glory in the Berlin Museum, where it now stands as one of the museum's most impressive exhibits. The bricks have been fired with a blue or yellow glaze and have been so arranged as to form the shapes of yellow lions, bulls, and dragons imposed upon a blue background. These latter creatures were standard ancient Near Eastern symbols of power. The Ishtar Gate takes its name from the fact that it was along the road leading from this gate that one came to the Babylonian temple of Ishtar. The entry-way of the gate is flanked by two towering walls, also constructed of the same beautifully glazed brick and terminates in two colossal sculptures, winged lions with human heads.

Another impressive monument of Babylon was an enormous ziggurat called Etemenanki, which meant "Foundation of Heaven and Earth." Only its bare foundation has been uncovered by modern archaeology, but according to a cuneiform text that describes the structure, its base measured about 300 feet square, and its height was also 300 feet. It probably consisted of seven layers. The number seven was important to the Babylonians, because it represented the five planets observable with the naked eye (Mercury, Venus, Mars, Jupiter, and Saturn) along with the sun and moon; and from these heavenly bodies the Babylonians fashioned their seven-day week, which was eventually adopted by other ancient peoples and passed on to us today. It is likely that this ziggurat inspired the Biblical tale of The Tower of Babel, recounted in *Genesis* 11.1-9.

Located near this ziggurat was a massive temple called Esagila, in which stood an enormous statue of the god Marduk, the chief god of the Babylonians. Like the Etemenanki, only the bare traces of the foundations have been revealed by modern archaeology. The shrine was the central focus of the most important religious celebration of the Babylonians. It was termed Akitu and was observed every year in the spring to mark the beginning of a new year. The festival lasted for twelve days, and everyone participated in its ceremonies. People begged Marduk for forgiveness and hoped for his blessings. Even the king was required to humble himself. One aspect of the celebration was the public recitation of the Babylonian Creation myth known as *Enuma Elish*, in which Marduk was described as destroying the monster Tiamat, and from her body and the primordial waters the god fashioned the entire universe.

We now come to the third of the ancient Near Eastern empires, the Persian (550-330 B.C.). The Persians were kindred to the Medes. They shared a common culture and language, the latter being Ancient Iranian. As we have already seen in this lecture, the Medes inhabited the mountains of northwestern Iran, whereas the Persians dwelled in the mountainous areas of southwestern and southern Iran. Before the establishment of the Persian Empire both the Medes and Persians were a relatively simple, but extremely tough and hardy people, who eked out an existence by farming and herding animals in an unforgiving mountainous environment. Following their defeat of the Assyrians, the Medes emerged as a major player on the international stage. While the Babylonians became the new masters of the Fertile Crescent, the Medes enjoyed political and military dominance in the region to the north, as well as over their kindred Persians to their south. But around 550 B.C. the tables were turned. After the various Persian mountain tribes were united under Cyrus the Great, the founder of the Persian Empire, he led them in a revolt against the Medes, defeated them in battle, and forced the Medes to acknowledge him as their ruler. Next, Cyrus led the Medes and Persians into Anatolia, where they spent a few years in conquering the whole area right down to the eastern shore of the Aegean Sea, along which many Greeks now dwelled and thus became subjects to the Persians. Finally, Cyrus turned his attention to the big prize: Babylon, which fell into his hands in 539 along with the Babylonian Empire. So, by the end of his reign (530 B.C.) Cyrus had carried out an extraordinary conquest, which exceeded both the Assyrian and Babylonian Empires, because not only did it comprise the Fertile Crescent, but it included a large portion of the Iranian Plateau as well as all of Anatolia.

Cyrus the Great Could be a God

Cyrus now found himself cast into the traditional mold of a great ancient Near Eastern conqueror by some of the people whom he had just subdued. For example, the Babylonians viewed him as having been appointed by their supreme god Marduk to rule over the world. Similarly, the Jews in *The Old Testament* portrayed Cyrus as being chosen by Yahweh to end the hideous Babylonian Empire and to usher in a more benevolent rule of the nations, as witnessed by Cyrus' releasing the Jews of Babylon from their captivity and allowing them to return to Judah. Moreover, Cyrus' birth and youth were given their appropriately marvelous pedigree, like that attributed to Sargon. According to this tale, when the king of the Medes had a dream in which it was foretold that his daughter and a Persian prince would produce a child who would someday overthrow him, he ordered that the newborn infant be exposed in the wilderness to die, but of course, like Sargon, he did not die, but he was taken in by a local shepherd, so that Cyrus grew up and realized his great destiny by overthrowing the king of the Medes and then founding the Persian Empire.

Cyrus was succeeded on the Persian throne by his son Cambyses (530-522 B.C.), who conquered Egypt and added it to the Persian Empire. Under the next king, Darius the Great (521-486 B.C.) the Persian Empire reached its greatest territorial extent, stretching into central Asia as far as the Aral Sea and including Afghanistan and Pakistan, the latter being the Indus Valley of the Indian subcontinent. As the ruling Persian elite adapted themselves to lording it over numerous, more civilized peoples, they developed a new lifestyle that blended the simplicity and toughness of mountain tribesmen with the luxurious and refined ways of their civilized subjects. Like the Assyrians before them, the Persians brought skilled craftsmen from their subject peoples into the Persian heartland and put them to work in building fine palaces in which to live. Noble Medes and Persians began wearing elegant clothes and displayed their wealth by innumerable objects made of silver and gold, but they also prided themselves on being a simple, honest, and warlike mountain people. As a result, they never did adopt the civilized practice of recording things in writing. They left all that record-keeping stuff up to their highly skilled subjects. Consequently, we now possess very few written Persian texts; and most of our knowledge about the Persians and their history comes from Greek historians who wrote about them.

Although the Persians inherited from the Assyrians and Babylonians siege-craft and punishments such as impaling and crucifixion, they proved to be more tolerant rulers, probably because they began their empire as a not fully civilized people ruling over more civilized ones. Persian toleration is particularly well documented in the realm of religion. As soon as Cyrus the Great became master of Babylon and learned of the fate of the Jews being held there in captivity, he gave them permission to return home and to practice their religion as they saw fit. We possess a text from Egypt in which Cambyses authorized the restoration of a cult to an Egyptian god; and there is a Greek inscription from Anatolia in which Darius threatened his Persian governor with severe punishment if he did not respect the local traditional worship of the Greek god Apollo. As long as people obeyed the law, paid their tribute to the Persian king, and did not rebel, the Persians allowed their subjects to live, work, and worship in their traditional ways. religious

The Persians largely followed the lead of the Assyrians and Babylonians in how they organized their empire. It was divided up into a large number of districts, each corresponding to a nation or major ethnic group. They were called satrapies (satrapy in the singular) and were ruled over by a noble Persian or Mede who bore the title of satrap. Then within each satrapy there existed a feudal network of native rulers at the local level who answered to the satrap. Each year the satrapy had to pay its assigned tribute to the Persian king, and the total sum from the whole empire amounted to more than 13,000 talents of silver. A talent was a measure of weight, approximately sixty pounds. The annual tribute was a truly phenomenal sum of money. The tribute was formally offered to the king in an important spring ceremony held at Persepolis in the Persian heartland. King Darius the Great had built this magnificent palace complex to serve as a ceremonial staging center to display Persian grandeur and power. Workers had first constructed a gigantic platform onto the side of a mountain, and they had then erected buildings on the platform, including a large audience hall, in which the king sat enthroned every spring to receive representatives from all the satrapies, who knelt before him and offered him their annual tribute. Access to this mountainside platform was gained by two colossal staircases built on either side and designed to accommodate people on horseback.

In order to keep in contact with all parts of his vast empire, the Persian king received information in two ways. If the message was a very simple one, such as yes or no, or victory or defeat, it could be communicated very quickly by fire signals flashed from high point to high point across the satrapies. Other, more complex messages, delivered orally or in writing, were carried along the rough roads of the empire by a kind of pony-express service. The Greek historian Herodotus (VIII.98) describes it as follows: "Along the whole line of road there are men (they say) stationed with horses, in number equal to the number of days which the journey takes, allowing a man and horse to each day; and these men will not be hindered from accomplishing at their best speed the distance which they have to go, either by snow, or rain, or heat, or by the darkness of night. The first rider delivers his despatch to the second, and the second passes it to the third; and so it is borne from hand to hand along the whole line." Part of this passage has been taken over by the U.S. Postal Service to be its motto.

The final aspect of the Persian Empire that we need to survey is its religion. Like so many other ancient peoples, the Persians were initially polytheists and believed that the world, nature, and human affairs were governed by a large host of different divinities. Then around 600 B.C., before the establishment of the Persian Empire, there arose a major religious reformer, Zarathustra, or Zoroaster, as he is better known by the name bestowed upon him by the ancient Greeks. Zoroaster's religion (known as Zoroastrianism) taught that there were two principal divinities who governed the world: a benevolent creator-god known as Ahura Mazda (Wise Lord) and his evil opponent named Ahriman. These two divine powers have been and always will be locked in struggle until the end of time when there will be a final judgment, and good shall totally triumph over evil. All the evil in the world (including diseases and death) is the work of Ahriman, and it is the duty of all right-minded people to worship the one and only good god, Ahura Mazda. Zoroastrianism was popular among the Persians and was probably well known throughout much of the Persian Empire. In fact, many historians of religion think that the Jewish idea of Satan, which does not emerge until very late in *Old Testament* literature during the Persian period, resulted from Jewish thinkers being influenced by Zoroastrian cosmic dualism. Zoroastrianism continued to be widespread among the Persian population up to the seventh century A.D. when Iran was conquered by the Arabs, shortly after Muhammad's death. Islamic persecution of Zoroastrians thereafter succeeded in greatly diminishing their numbers, so that today there are only about 150,000 Zoroastrians living in Iran and India.

LECTURE 6
Hebrew History

- **1000-965:** Reign of King David.
- **965-930:** Reign of King Solomon.
- **721:** Capture of the northern kingdom of Israel by the Assyrians, and the deportation of the ten tribes.
- **586:** Capture of Jerusalem by the Babylonians.
- **586-539:** Babylonian captivity of the Jews.
- **Phoenicians:** Semitic people of the Levantine coast, closely related in speech and culture to the Hebrews.
- **Philistines:** non-Semitic people from the Aegean, occupied the Palestinian coast, early opponents of the Hebrews.
- **Jerusalem:** town of Judah chosen by King David to be his capital.
- **Judah and Israel:** the smaller southern kingdom and larger northern kingdom of the Hebrews.

In this and the following lectures we will examine respectively the history and religion of the Hebrews, the ancestors of the Jews. In doing so we will place into a broad historical context many stories and ideas of *The Old Testament*, which is one of the cornerstones of the Western tradition. Indeed, the single most important legacy for Western civilization passed on to us from the ancient Near Eastern civilizations that we have thus far been studying is Judaism, the religion of the Hebrews, who arrived on the scene about two thousand years after the beginnings of civilization, and out of the already existing cultural traditions they fashioned their own distinctive culture, including their monotheistic religion that has become so influential. The modern nation of Israel is quite small and roughly corresponds to the land inhabited by the Hebrews in very early times. It is about the size of the state of New Jersey, and we could put 37 Israels inside the state of Texas, but the people who lived there in ancient times developed a religion that in terms of its impact upon history has vastly exceeded the small size of the country itself.

In this lecture I will set forth the basic historical outline of the Hebrew people as we understand it from the various books of *The Old Testament*. At various points I will also tie these events into the larger historical framework that we have constructed in the previous lectures concerning the civilizations of the ancient Near East. But I must point out at the outset that we do not reach fairly solid historical grounds concerning the Hebrews until we come to the period of the early Iron Age, around the tenth century B.C. Before that time the stories contained in *The Old Testament* cannot be given historical credence. They are stories that were popular among the Hebrews in later times. They were told to entertain and explain things and were not written down until centuries after they had supposedly occurred. Consequently, there is much modern scholarly disagreement and debate as to how much, and what parts of these stories contained in the early books of *The Old Testament* can be trusted as possessing any historical truth. My intention is not to challenge anyone's faith in *The Bible*, but since this is a history course, I wish to place the history and religion of the Hebrews in its proper historical context.

According to *The Old Testament*, the Hebrews had as their ancestor a man named Abraham, who came from the Mesopotamian city of Ur. He formed a covenant or binding contract for himself and his descendants with Yahweh, the god of the Hebrews, according to which Yahweh would favor his chosen people and ensure that they prospered in return for their exclusive worship of him. To serve as a seal and constant reminder of this binding contract, Abraham established circumcision among his descendants. Abraham left his native city of Ur and traveled to the new land promised and given to him and his descendants by Yahweh, and there he established himself and was

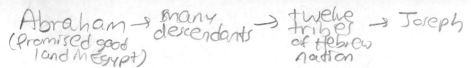

Abraham → many descendants → twelve tribes → Joseph
(Promised good land in Egypt) of Hebrew nation

eventually buried at the town of Hebron. Now if Abraham actually existed and did some or all of these things, modern scholars reckon that he must have lived some time during the first half of the second millennium B.C.

Abraham and his wife Sarah had a son named Isaac, and he and his wife Rebekah had the twin sons Esau and Jacob. The latter was later renamed Israel, and from his two wives, Leah and Rachel, and from their two slave women, Dilhah and Zilpah, he had twelve sons, who became the ancestors to the twelve tribes of the Hebrew nation. One of them was Joseph. When the other brothers became jealous of Joseph because he was favored by their father, they conspired against him and sold him to merchants who happened to be passing through their land. They took him to Egypt, where he was sold into slavery, but because of his extraordinary abilities he became a high ranking member of the pharaoh's government. Then when a famine struck the land of the Hebrews, Israel's sons traveled to Egypt to purchase grain. There they unexpectedly found their brother Joseph, who invited all his relatives to relocate to Egypt, where they could avoid famine. Thus began the Hebrew experience in the land of Egypt, and with this event ends the first book of *The Bible, Genesis*.

The second book of *The Bible, Exodus,* tells the story of how the Hebrews at first enjoyed the pharaoh's favor because of Joseph, but as they prospered and increased in numbers, they became the objects of jealousy, resentment, and fear, so that a later Pharaoh issued the order to have all the newborn babies of the Hebrews slain in order to reduce their numbers. One infant, however, named Moses, escaped this fate. After he had been placed in a basket and set adrift on the Nile River, he was discovered among the bull rushes by the daughter of the pharaoh, who took him in and raised him. Moses therefore, like Sargon, grew up to realize his destiny of leading his people out of Egypt and back toward their promised land. As they traveled through the Sinai Desert, Moses encountered Yahweh on Mount Sinai, where he received from God the Ten Commandments and thus became the lawgiver of his people. Moses, however, died before the Hebrews re-entered their promised land. It was under the leadership of Joshua that the twelve tribes resettled the area in their own districts after conquering its inhabitants. At this point, as described in the book of *Judges*, the Hebrews lived separately in their twelve tribes and were ruled over by a series of charismatic leaders and heroes termed judges.

There now arrived on the scene a people called the Philistines, who occupied the coastal area and settled five towns: Askelon, Ashdod, Ekron, Gath, and Gaza. We are now approaching more solid historical grounds, because the Philistines were probably among the Sea Peoples mentioned in the Egyptian records of Ramesses III as the ones responsible for destroying the palace centers of the Late Bronze Age. They seem to have come from the island of Crete and must have settled the Palestinian coast around 1150 B.C. In fact, the modern name Palestine is simply an altered form of their name. Once established in this coastal area, the Philistines began waging war upon the Hebrew tribes, as they attempted to take over more land; and at first they enjoyed success, because they had weapons made of iron, which the Hebrews did not yet possess. Eventually the period of the judges came to an end when the Hebrew tribes asked their last judge, Samuel, to appoint over them a single king to unite them and to lead them in battle against their Philistine enemy. Samuel reluctantly agreed and chose Saul to be the first king of the Hebrews. In order to formally designate Saul as the legitimate ruler, Samuel performed a ceremony in which he anointed the head of Saul with a holy oil, thus making Saul the messiah or "the anointed one," which in later times was translated into Greek as *Christos* (i.e., Christ). Henceforth the Hebrew term messiah was used to designate the legitimate king of the Hebrews or Jews.

According to the Biblical tradition, Saul ruled for 22 years and led the Hebrews with varying success and was finally killed in battle. During his reign he had given his daughter Mikal in marriage to a shifty character named David, who was a war lord with his own following, sometimes cooperating with Saul and other times opposing him, depending upon how it best suited David's self-interest. Saul's son Ishbaal (also called Ishbosheth) ruled for only four years, and then David became the next king. Once again, according to the Biblical tradition, David and his son Solomon, who succeeded him, each ruled for forty years. Since forty is a figure often used in *The Bible* to specify a period of days or years to mean a long time, we cannot accept these figures as strictly accurate. Nevertheless, if we accept the basic idea that both David and Solomon enjoyed relatively long reigns, and if we reckon that David's reign began somewhere around 1000 B.C., then we can construct the following chronology that may be roughly accurate:

- **1026-1004:** reign of Saul → *less of a like warlord.*
- **1004-1000:** reign of Ishbaal
- **1000-965:** reign of David → *David was a war-like king (Jerusalem)*
- **965-930:** reign of Solomon

Dating the end of Solomon's reign to 930 B.C. can be confirmed by Egyptian records that inform us of an Egyptian military campaign into the Levant, which is mentioned in *The Bible* as having occurred shortly after Solomon's death (see *I Kings* 14).

With David, we are probably standing at the dawn of Hebrew history, but I must add that there are many modern scholars who regard David as largely (if not entirely) mythical. This position is well justified, because no other figure in *The Old Testament*, except for Moses, attracted more attention and had more stories told about him. There is obviously much about the later Davidic tradition in *The Bible* that is clearly fictional and is simply the product of inventive story-tellers, so that the historical waters concerning him have definitely been muddied. But after we discard the majority of these stories as entertaining and sensational fictions, there still probably remain a few basic facts about his reign.

According to *The Old Testament*, David captured the stronghold of Jerusalem from the tribe of the Jebusites and decided to make it the capital from which to rule. He is portrayed as a great conqueror, who subdued the surrounding peoples and made the Hebrews a major player among the other states of this region. This basic outline is likely to be true, but we should not exaggerate the power of the Hebrew people at this time. They were rather small and were simply one of many Semitic peoples living in this area. But we should also realize that their prominence at this time makes sense, because it occurred before the rise of the Assyrian Empire that eventually conquered this whole area and thus rendered all peoples relatively insignificant.

Like David, Solomon figured so large in the later Hebrew tradition that much of what is recorded about him cannot be accepted as true. He was portrayed (in a very exaggerated sense) as a mighty monarch, ruling a rich and prosperous kingdom, and having hundreds of wives and concubines. According to the Biblical tradition (which is probably true on this point), he was responsible for building the first great temple in Jerusalem to house the Ark of the Covenant, and which served as the central house of worship for the Hebrew Yahweh. In order to carry out this major building program, Solomon had to impose taxes upon his subjects' labor and the produce of their fields. By the time that his reign ended, there was so much resentment over these taxes that the Hebrews begged Solomon's son to reduce their burdens, but when he replied that he intended to make them even greater, there was a tax revolt that caused the Hebrew kingdom to split into two parts: the northern kingdom of Israel composed of ten tribes, and the southern kingdom of Judah consisting of the other two tribes and including Jerusalem. Henceforth each kingdom was ruled by its own royal line of monarchs. Israel

The northern kingdom was much larger and possessed much better farmland than Judah. During the 800s B.C. it enjoyed considerable prosperity and had its capital at Samaria. Ahab was one of its most prominent kings, during whose reign we first encounter conflict between monotheism and polytheism. According to the Biblical tradition, the Hebrews were supposed to worship only Yahweh, but their Semitic neighbors, the Canaanites, Phoenicians, and others, were polytheists and worshipped a large number of gods. It is very clear both from the writings of the later prophets and from archaeological findings that many of the early Hebrews were not strict monotheists, but they worshipped Yahweh along with other gods popular among the Semitic peoples of the area. As we will see in the following lecture, strict monotheism was developed by a relatively small number of religious thinkers, the prophets, who eventually succeeded in having their theology adopted by the Hebrews as a whole. During the reign of Ahab we encounter the earliest prophetic figures, Elijah and Elisha. Unlike later prophets such as Isaiah, Jeremiah, and Ezekiel, they did not write down any of their ideas; and what *The Bible* says about them is clearly derived from later oral tradition that portrayed them as wonder-working shamans. But one thing that we can probably say for certain about them is that they were monotheists and insisted upon the sole worship of Yahweh. This brought them into conflict with Ahab, because like other monarchs of this period, he had several wives from the different surrounding tribes in order to establish alliances. This policy, however, as the prophets always realized, was very detrimental to monotheism, because foreign wives introduced their polytheism into the royal court and thus undermined the exclusive worship of Yahweh. This was most famously illustrated by Ahab's wife Jezebel, who came from the Phoenician city of Sidon, and whom the Biblical tradition hated for her polytheism. When Ahab died, tensions between the monotheists and polytheists exploded into violence. The former were led by Jehu, who seized power, executed the sons of Ahab, and killed Jezebel.

The Assyrians were now becoming powerful throughout the Fertile Crescent; and as we see from the so-called Black Obelisk of the Assyrian King Shalmaneser III (858-824 B.C.), Jehu of Israel was forced to acknowledge the superior might of the Assyrians by kneeling before their king. Jehu and his successors on the throne of Israel must have been vassals of the Assyrians and paid them tribute for about a century. Then around 722 or 721 B.C. the Assyrians invaded Israel, captured Samaria, and destroyed the kingdom by carrying off a substantial portion of the population and resettling the area. What actually became of the deported Hebrews has always been and is still a mystery, thus creating the notion of the ten lost tribes of Israel. The surviving remnant of the Hebrew people were now the inhabitants of Judah, from which they received their name, the Jews. Twenty years later in 701 B.C. the smaller and poorer kingdom of Judah came close to suffering the same fate as Israel. In that year the Assyrian King Sennacherib invaded the land. Here is what he actually records about this campaign in his royal records:

Taken from *Ancient Near Eastern Texts Relating to the Old Testament*, ed. James B. Pritchard, third edition (Princeton 1969) 288.

As to Hezekiah, the Jew, he did not submit to my yoke. I laid
siege to 46 of his strong cities, walled forts, and countless

small villages, and conquered them by means of well-stamped earth-ramps and battering-rams brought near the walls with an attack by foot soldiers, using mines, breeches as well as trenches. I drove out 200,150 people, young and old, male and female, horses, mules, donkeys, camels, big and small cattle beyond counting, and considered them slaves. Himself I made a prisoner in Jerusalem, his royal residence, like a bird in a cage. I surrounded him with earthwork in order to molest those who were leaving his city's gate. Thus I reduced his country. His towns which I had plundered, I took away from his country and gave them over to Mitinti, king of Ashdod, Padi, king of Ekron, and Sillibel, king of Gaza. Thus I reduced his country, but I still increased the tribute and the presents to me as overlord which I imposed upon him beyond the former tribute, to be delivered annually. Hezekiah himself, whom the terror-inspiring splendour of my lordship had overwhelmed and whose irregular and elite troops which he had brought into Jerusalem, his royal residence, in order to strengthen it, had deserted him, did send me, later, to Nineveh, my lordly city, together with 30 talents of gold, 800 talents of silver, precious stones, antimony, large cuts of red stone, couches inlaid with ivory, nimedu-chairs inlaid with ivory, elephant-hides, ebony-wood, boxwood and all kinds of valuable treasures, his own daughters, concubines, male and female musicians. In order to deliver the tribute and to do obeisance as a slave he sent his personal messenger.

One of the reliefs in Sennacherib's royal palace shows the town of Lakhish, one of the 46 captured during this campaign, being assaulted by the Assyrians with a siege tower. These events occurred while Hezekiah was king of Judah, and the prophet Isaiah lived. *The Old Testament* gives its own version of these events and confirms the Assyrian royal annals concerning the siege of Jerusalem and Hezekiah being forced to pay a very heavy tribute to

Sennacherib. The amounts of gold and silver listed here would have been enormous for the small and relatively poor kingdom of Judah and underscore what we have already seen regarding the predatory nature of the Assyrian Empire. In fact, the Biblical account indicates that in order to pay this tribute, the temple of Solomon had to be stripped of its various decorations made of precious metals. Although Jerusalem itself was not captured, the kingdom had been severely humbled and crippled by the tribute, the loss of many smaller towns, and the deportation of people and animals. Thus, while Assyria enjoyed the pinnacle of its power during much of the seventh century B.C., the Jews under the rule of Manesseh (697-642 B.C.) were forced to worship the gods of the Assyrians in Yahweh's temple in Jerusalem. But as Assyria rapidly declined during the reign of Manesseh's grandson Josiah (639-605 B.C.), the latter was able to rid the temple in Jerusalem of such a polytheistic abomination and to carry out a major religious reform, in which Yahweh alone was to be worshipped in the Jerusalem temple.

Judah did not long enjoy its liberation from the Assyrian Empire, because, as we have seen, the Babylonians immediately emerged as the next empire throughout the Fertile Crescent. It was during these years that the prophet Jeremiah lived and warned his fellow Jews of the impending disaster. In 597 B.C. Nebuchadnezzar invaded Judah and forced it to become his vassal. In order to guarantee its loyalty, he carried off a number of Jews to be held in captivity in Babylon to serve as hostages. Among these Jews was the prophet Ezekiel. When the king of Judah foolishly formed an alliance with Egypt in order to protect himself against the Babylonians, Nebuchadnezzar returned with his army, captured Jerusalem in 586 B.C., destroyed it as a functioning urban center, demolished the temple built by Solomon, and carried off Judah's most highly skilled and educated members to Babylon. This began the so-called Babylonian captivity or exile of the Jews that lasted nearly fifty years (586-539 B.C.). What remained in Judah was the peasant farmers, left to their own devices, while the Jewish elite, including its most important religious thinkers, were forced to accommodate themselves to an entirely new environment. Nevertheless, this difficult period of Jewish history turned out to be very productive for them in the long run, because in order to retain their traditional beliefs and worship of Yahweh, the Jews in exile had to steel themselves against the attractions of Babylonian polytheism. This was largely accomplished by insulating themselves with a highly complex and comprehensive code of laws and religious practices, which were later all attributed to Moses, because they resulted from Jewish interpretations of the Ten Commandments.

When Cyrus the Great became master of Babylon in 539 B.C., he gave the Jews permission to return to their native land and to live their lives as they wished. By this time there had arisen in Babylon a sizable population of Jews. Some did in fact go back to Judah, but others stayed in Babylon, because they were by now well adjusted to life in the big city. Those who did return found a land that was still shattered from the Babylonian conquest and sacking of Jerusalem. Thus, when in 520 B.C. King Darius of Persia granted the Jews permission to rebuild Solomon's temple that Nebuchadnezzar had destroyed, they possessed such meager resources that they were able to build a structure that was a mere shadow of its previous glory.

Our last two detailed glimpses of Hebrew history during the Persian period are offered by the Biblical books of *Nehemiah* and *Ezra*. According to the former, Nehemiah was a Babylonian Jew who had risen into the governmental hierarchy of the Persian Empire. When he learned that his fellow Jews in Judah had still not succeeded in getting back on their feet, he persuaded the Persian king to appoint him governor of Judah; and during the years 444-432 B.C. Nehemiah personally oversaw the reconstruction of Jerusalem, so that it once again became a well functioning urban and administrative center for the surrounding area. Then in the next generation (397 B.C.) Ezra led several thousands of Jews from Babylon back to Judah, and they brought with them a written body of law that had been governing their lives. This text is generally supposed by modern scholars to have been the first five books of *The Old Testament* (*Genesis, Exodus, Leviticus, Numbers,* and *Deuteronomy*). Armed with such an authoritative text, Ezra soon established himself as a priest-king, who established a new covenant between Yahweh and the Jews by persuading the latter to accept his text of the so-called Mosaic law as a charter and constitution by which their lives henceforth would be

397 BC → founding of the Judaism religion

governed. It is at this point that we can date the beginning of Judaism as a well organized and delineated system that became integral to the lives of the Jews in Judah.

LECTURE 7
Hebrew Religion

IMPORTANT TERMS

- **prophets:** long succession of Hebrew religious leaders, outspoken critics of social injustice, responsible for developing Jewish monotheism and ethics.
- **Sheol:** shadowy underworld of the early Hebrews, resembling the dismal underworld of the Mesopotamians.

In this lecture we will examine how the Hebrews developed their own distinctive religion (Judaism) by adopting and adapting many aspects of ancient Near Eastern culture to fit with their particular world view. We will not be examining Judaism from the perspective of religious studies or metaphysics. The ultimate truths contained within Judaism are matters of personal religious faith that have nothing to do with this course. My approach is simply that of a historian interested in looking at our available data and trying to make sense out of it by using the standard methods of historical analysis.

The first major point that I wish to make is that *The Hebrew Bible* (or *Old Testament*) is not a single book. It is a collection of many books composed by different people with varying perspectives and intended to address different issues. In fact, these writings were written over a period of about six centuries (c.750-150 B.C.). Rather than thinking of *The Hebrew Bible* as a single book, we should regard it as a library of books, a highly select library of books chosen

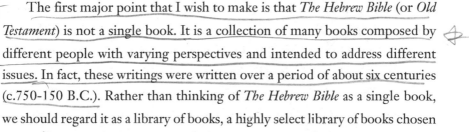

out of a much bigger collection of religious literature. Over time these particular books came to be especially prized by Jews, because they best expressed Jewish beliefs. In some instances the notion of *The Hebrew Bible* as a highly select library of religious literature does not do justice to the complexity of the matter: for although most of the individual books of *The Old Testament* were written by a single author, there are cases in which a book, such as *Isaiah*, had its text extended by two different authors writing at two later times than the original author. The most complex example of multiple authorship is encountered in the first five books (*Genesis, Exodus, Leviticus, Numbers*, and *Deuteronomy*), collectively termed The Torah. Modern scholarly study of the language and content of these books has established that they were written and rewritten by at least four different authors over the course of two or three hundred years. It should therefore not be surprising that we encounter different views and attitudes expressed throughout these writings.

The next major point that I want to examine is how the Hebrews adopted and adapted already existing ancient Near Eastern traditions and incorporated them into their own religious system and world view. We can see this most clearly when we compare and contrast some of the readings contained in PSWC. We should remember that the earliest civilizations of Mesopotamia and Egypt came into being more than two thousand years before the Hebrews arrived on the scene (c.1100 B.C.). By the time that they did, the ancient Near East had developed a well established pattern of culture of which the Hebrews became a part; but like all other peoples of this region, they created their own unique cultural identity by shaping many of the widely accepted traditions in their own way. You must have noticed the basic similarity between the Sumerian King List and the first chapters of *Genesis*. Both of these texts exhibit the same view about the remote past: namely, that in the beginning humans lived much longer lives than they did in later times when the author was writing. As time progressed, humans lived shorter and shorter lives. This pattern expressed the notion of decline from an initial state of perfect (or nearly perfect) human existence to the author's own troubled times. The ancient Greeks formulated the same theme in terms of a succession of four early ages of mankind, named after metals: the golden age, the silver age, the bronze age, and finally the iron age, each being worse than its predecessor. It was only during the Early Modern Period, which we will cover at the very end of this course, that people in Western Europe developed the contrary notion of progress: namely, that things become better for humans as time advances. Today we take the notion of progress for granted, because technology and science continue to advance right before our very eyes and have a major impact on our lives, but this was not at all the case for the first several thousands of years of human civilization, when progress was so slow that it was not discernible. On the contrary, most people tended to idealize the past and to think that they, in contrast, were living in the worst of times.

Another similarity that we find in the readings in PSWC is between the legend of Sargon and the story of the baby Moses. We should also add that Cyrus the Great, the founder of the Persian Empire, had his own biography formulated in similar terms. Moreover, when we come to the myth of the foundation of ancient Rome in Lecture 12, we will see the same pattern used to describe the beginning of the Roman state with its foundation by the twins Romulus and Remus: i.e., twin infants placed in a basket in a river to drown, but rescued and raised to realize their unusually important destiny. Consequently, when a historian, such as myself, finds this pattern applied to historically important personages, the conclusion to be drawn is not to regard the stories as actually factual, but to see them as the products of a commonly shared tradition or pattern of popular thinking, in which a really important person was so designated by a suitably impressive birth and upbringing.

The most obvious parallel between ancient Near Eastern literature and *The Hebrew Bible* is, of course, the flood story. We first encountered it in Lecture 2 as part of the Epic of Gilgamesh dating to the Old Babylonian Kingdom (c.1900-1600 B.C.). The Biblical version is described in Genesis. Although these accounts tell basically the same story, it is important to see how they differ, because these differences reveal how the Hebrews adopted a common ancient Near Eastern story and fitted it into their own way of looking at things, especially in how they viewed the divine. In the Mesopotamian account the flood occurs, because mankind has become so numerous and noisy on the Earth that the gods in heaven have no peace. Enlil, the chief of the gods, therefore decides that mankind must be destroyed. This is a rather trivial explanation for the flood. In *Genesis*, however, Yahweh decides to wipe out mankind, because they had become very wicked. Thus, the Biblical account views this event from a moral perspective. In the Mesopotamian version, once the fury of the storms is released, even the gods are terrified and flee into the highest part of heaven and crouch down in fear like trembling dogs. This is not a very flattering view of divinity. No such thing is attributed to Yahweh in the Biblical account. Then toward the very end of the Mesopotamian story, when Utnapishtim emerges from the boat, he erects an altar and performs a sacrifice; and when the gods in heaven smell it, they descend to earth like flies. This again is not a very flattering view of divinity. Then when Enlil realizes that a few people have survived the flood, he becomes angry, and the gods begin to quarrel among themselves. It finally ends with Enlil relenting and even bestowing immortality upon Utnapishtim and his wife. We have a much more exalted view of the divine in the Biblical account. When Yahweh smells the sacrifice performed by Noah, he does not descend to Earth, but he makes a series of pronouncements, which form the first covenant between himself and mankind. Yahweh states that he will never again destroy mankind in this way. He commands Noah and his sons to go forth and replenish the Earth and to exercise dominion over all its creatures. Then after additional provisions involving the blood of animals and mankind, Yahweh states that the sign of this binding covenant will be the rainbow.

The next covenant that we encounter in *The Bible* is the one made between Abraham and Yahweh, when the Hebrews are designated as Yahweh's chosen people. The perpetual reminder of this binding covenant is circumcision, which was in fact quite common among other ancient Near Eastern peoples. Among the Hebrews, however, it was given this very special meaning. The other famous story involving Abraham is Yahweh commanding him to sacrifice Isaac, which, of course, is countermanded when Abraham is about to kill his son. The story has been much discussed over the centuries. It clearly reveals Abraham's absolute obedience to Yahweh, but what else does it mean? How might it be understood in the larger context of ancient Near Eastern culture? Now we do know that the Hebrews' Semitic neighbors, the Canaanites and

Phoenicians, actually did engage in the practice of sacrificing their small children. Archaeologists have discovered sacred sites (known as tophets) stacked with large numbers of small clay urns containing the burned remains of very young children. In addition, there are passages in *The Bible* in which the prophets protest against Hebrews doing the same in imitation of their neighbors (see *Jeremiah* 7.31-32). So, what all might this mean? Perhaps the story of Abraham nearly sacrificing Isaac was designed to give the Hebrews the following message. Your neighbors do in fact sacrifice their very young children to their gods, but Yahweh is different. He is not a cruel god and does not demand that you offer him your children in sacrifice. If this was the story's intended meaning, it would provide us with an example of how the Hebrews reacted against a common practice of their neighbors, rejected it, and did not adopt and adapt it into their culture. By doing so, they were defining themselves as differing from their neighbors.

There are three other matters that allow us to compare the Hebrews with general features of ancient Near Eastern culture. One of these is law. There are many striking similarities between Hammurabi's law code and what we encounter in The Hebrew Bible. This is especially clear with provisions that embody the principal of retaliation (*lex talionis*), in which the law insists upon doing unto the perpetrator of a crime what he has done unto his victim. For example, in Hammurabi's law code someone who broke the bone or put out the eye of a noble was to have his bone broken or his eye put out, but if the victim were a peasant, then the person paid a fine; and if the victim were a slave, the fine was reduced by half. This is the principal of retaliation tempered by the class system, whereas in *The Hebrew Bible* there is no such tempering: "life for life, eye for eye, tooth for tooth, hand for hand, foot for foot, burning for burning, wound for wound, stripe for stripe" (*Exodus* 21.23-5). Another striking similarity that is in both legal systems is that it was permitted for a man to have children by a slave and to acknowledge them as his rightful offspring in order to make sure that he would have children to succeed to his property and to care for him in his old age. Moses, of course, was supposed to have obtained the Ten Commandments from Yahweh himself on Mount Sinai. The idea of human law having a divine origin is a common one. Thus, on the stone pillar that contains the cuneiform text of Hammurabi's law code the Babylonian king is shown receiving a staff and ring from the Mesopotamian sun god Shamash, the god of justice, as emblems of his authority to institute his law code.

In surveying the civilizations of Mesopotamia and Egypt we discovered that the two peoples had rather differing views of the afterlife. As it turns out, what we find in *The Hebrew Bible* seems to agree with the rather pessimistic Mesopotamian view. There are only a few places in which *The Old Testament* mentions *Sheol*, the Hebrew word for the underworld, but it was a place of murky existence after death, like the dark and dreary place described in the Epic of Gilgamesh. It was not until many centuries later with the rise of Christianity that the Jewish tradition adopted from the mystery religions of the contemporary Hellenistic culture (see Lectures 11 and 16) the possibility of a happy afterlife. During the period that we have covered so far (c.1000-400 B.C.) the Hebrews really did not concern themselves much with this issue. Their religion focused upon the here and now and how people were to conduct their lives and worship Yahweh properly.

Lastly, before moving on to my next major theme, let me repeat something from the close of Lecture 5. Many modern historians of ancient religion think that the concept of Satan or the Devil, which does not enter the writings of *The Old Testament* until the Persian period (550-330 B.C.), was adopted by the Jews from Zoroastrian cosmic dualism, the good creator-god Ahura Mazda vs. the evil Ahriman.

The single most important way in which Judaism differed from other ancient Near Eastern religions was its strict monotheism, the belief that there existed one and only one god, eternal, all-powerful, and the creator of the universe. All other religions of the ancient Near East (except for Zoroastrian dualism and the brief revolution carried out by Akhenaten of Egypt) were polytheistic and conceived of their divinities in anthropomorphic terms. Strict monotheism was a concept developed by a long line of Hebrew religious thinkers, whom we refer to collectively as the prophets, and about whom we will speak at greater length below. They were the ones responsible for insisting that the Hebrews worship Yahweh and him alone, and that all other divinities were false and did not exist. For example, a passage in *Isaiah* (44.6-20) ridicules the idea of people fashioning a god's statue out of wood and precious metals and then worshipping it. The one and only true god is invisible and has no human-like form. He is all pervasive and omni-present, being both the beginning and the end.

Hebrew belief

We need to realize, however, that this exalted view of god was not self-evident to all writers of *The Hebrew Bible* or to all the Hebrews. It was a notion that developed over time through the thinking of many prophets; and while it was being developed and refined, many ordinary Hebrews worshipped other gods along with Yahweh, against which the prophets strongly protested. In the previous lecture it was pointed out that according to the evidence that we have, Elijah and Elisha of the ninth century B.C. seem to be the earliest prophets who preached monotheism, but in doing so, they ran afoul of King Ahab of Israel, who apparently had no trouble in worshipping other divinities. Ahab was certainly not alone among the Hebrews in this regard at that time. As a result, there arose the earliest known major division among the Hebrews involving polytheism vs. monotheism. This conflict resulted in a political revolution in Israel following Ahab's death. Jehu, who led the monotheists, had Ahab's sons and his Phoenician wife Jezebel killed in order to stamp out supporters of polytheism, and then he became the next king of Israel and promoted monotheism.

*9th cent. B.C.
Elisha
is
Elijah*

Now when we look carefully at the text of *The Hebrew Bible*, we seem to come upon passages that indicate earlier anthropomorphic views of Yahweh that eventually gave way to the exalted concept of a transcendent divinity in the writings of the later prophets. For example, in the Creation story in *Genesis* God is portrayed as saying "let us create man according to our own likeness and image." If man and God have the same likeness, then God, according to the writer of this verse, must have been viewed as anthropomorphic. Similarly, when God discovers the disobedience of Adam and Eve in the Garden of Eden, he is described as walking through the garden in the cool of the day, as if he were a man with legs and feet. Then just before the great flood the sons of God are said to have consorted with women and produced a race of giants, which again suggests that the sons of God were anthropomorphic. But when we come to *Exodus*, Yahweh has no such human-like attributes. He makes himself known to Moses through the marvel of a burning bush that is not consumed by the fire. God is not this burning bush, but he has chosen this medium in order to catch the attention of Moses. Similarly, in *Job*, when there is finally an encounter between Job and God, the latter speaks to Job through a whirlwind. He does not take on a human form; and when he rebukes Job for questioning his judgments, he portrays himself as a being truly incomprehensible by mere human intelligence, as having always existed, even before the existence of the universe, which he created. It therefore appears likely that the earliest Hebrew conception of Yahweh was anthropomorphic, but the prophets replaced it with a much more exalted view of divinity, which was not the least anthropomorphic.

The record of history demonstrates that polytheistic systems have had very little, if any, difficulty in tolerating one another, because one polytheistic people usually had no trouble in equating their gods with other divinities worshipped by another polytheistic people. Consequently, the historical record contains few instances of one polytheistic system being intolerant of others. This is not the case, however, with monotheism. Since it acknowledges the existence of only one divinity, there is no room to compromise with polytheism. Accordingly, since the Jews and Christians were the only monotheists in the ancient Mediterranean world and were surrounded by polytheists, early Jewish and Christian history was characterized by conflict between these two incompatible systems of belief. In fact, one result of this conflict was a prohibition on intermarriage between the two groups. Many monotheists from the Biblical prophets onward urged their fellow monotheists not to marry polytheists, because it opened the door to monotheism being watered down and no longer being real monotheism. Moreover, since monotheism did not tolerate polytheism or allowed itself to be merged into a polytheistic system, the exclusionary nature of monotheism tended to protect it from being absorbed into a competing religious system. As a result, monotheism bestowed upon both Judaism and Christianity a much greater chance of surviving. So, from the perspective of historical analysis, it is not surprising that these two religions outlasted ancient polytheistic systems and survived into modern times.

We will now end this lecture by examining a few of the more important themes found among the writings of the prophets. First of all, despite their name, we should not think of these people as glorified fortune tellers, interested in predicting future events. For the most part, they were more akin to social critics than to gypsies armed with crystal balls and tarot cards. They came from all walks of life and felt the strong urge to speak out against immorality, corruption, and various abuses that they saw around them in society. They sincerely believed that God was calling upon them to be his spokesmen in pointing out this sinful behavior and urging people to mend their ways, because as Yahweh's chosen people, they were bound by their covenant with him to live their lives according to his laws. All the prophets firmly believed that God worked his will through the historical process. Accordingly, as Assyria and then Babylon arose to power throughout the Fertile Crescent during the eighth and seventh centuries B.C., they urged the Hebrews to cultivate justice and piety. Otherwise, they would incur the wrath of Yahweh, who would use the Assyrians or Babylonians to punish his sinful people. Consequently, when the Assyrians did indeed destroy the northern kingdom of Israel in 721 B.C., and when the Babylonians later in 586 B.C. destroyed Jerusalem and carried a portion of the Jewish population into captivity, the prophets regarded these events as clear proof of what they had been saying. It is also worth noting that the prophets had differing ideas about sin. The earlier prophets, such as Amos, thought in terms of collective sin, guilt, and punishment, so that if only a portion of the Hebrew population happened to be sinful, Yahweh would punish the entire nation. Later prophets, however, such as Ezekiel, put forth the idea that Yahweh did not hold the children responsible for the sins of the parents, but that people were accountable only for their own sins.

Finally, we may be able to adduce two significant historical factors that helped to shape the overall message of these prophets. They were constantly pointing out shortcomings in their society and preaching that the rich and powerful must not exploit the poor and weak. They insisted that everyone should behave toward one another justly. Perhaps one factor that contributed to this constant and powerful prophetic message was the nature of the land itself. Although it was a very small piece of real estate, it contained four distinct regions that produced very different local lifestyles and economies: the coastal plain in the west, the central highlands, the well watered Jordan Valley in the east, and the desert to the south. As a result, there were people with differing ways of life crammed together into this small space and forced to live with one another. The problem was made even more acute by the fact that most people had just barely enough to get by. Consequently, the margin between surviving and experiencing hard times was very small. This fragile situation was aggravated by the Assyrians and Babylonians, because their imposition of tribute upon this poor land affected all its inhabitants; and as usually happens in such instances, the rich did their best to shift the burden downward upon the poor, onto the people who could least afford it. As a result, the land itself and the predatory nature of the great empires may have been important factors in shaping the prophets' constant demand for justice, which has continued to reverberate through all subsequent centuries to our own day.

LECTURE 8
Greece During the Archaic Period

IMPORTANT DATES AND TERMS (ALL DATES ARE APPROXIMATE)

- **1100-800 B.C.:** Dark Age in mainland Greece, following the collapse of Bronze Age Mycenaean Civilization.
- **800-500 B.C.:** Archaic Age of Greece.
- **Trojan War:** most important of the Greek myths, ten-year war between Trojans and Greeks, caused by the abduction of Helen of Sparta by Prince Paris of Troy, ending with Troy's destruction by means of a wooden horse concealing warriors inside.
- **Homeric Poems *(Iliad and Odyssey):*** written long after the supposed events described, gods interacting with mortals, men of heroic bravery, embodying values of Greek society.
- Nature and effects of geography upon Greek political development.
- Nature and cultural importance of the Greek alphabet.
- Nature and cultural importance of the Homeric poems.
- **polis (plural = poleis)** = Greek term for city-state.
- **Importance of Greek colonization:** spreading Greek people with their language and culture, established Mediterranean economic system.
- **Anaximander:** geocentric universe, cylindrical Earth, first world map.

- **Pythagoras:** mathematics used to describe nature, musical scale as mathematical ratios, pythagorean theorem.
- **Democritus:** atom = indivisible unit of matter, atomic theory.
- Early Inscription upon a Greek Vase

The invention of the Greek alphabet exercised a profound influence upon the development of Greek culture by enabling far more people within the society to become literate. One of the most striking illustrations of this phenomenon is revealed by a very simple inscription scratched onto a Greek vase dated to the late 700s B.C. The vase was discovered at Athens and was apparently awarded as a prize for a local dancing contest. The use of Greek writing in such an ordinary context marked a major departure from the uses of writing in the civilizations of the ancient Near East. The inscription simply reads:

"The man who now of all dancers performs most nimbly"

We have now completed our survey of the ancient Near Eastern civilizations. In this lecture we will begin our survey of the ancient Greeks and Romans by examining the very beginning of Greek civilization in order to contrast it with the ancient Near East. This lecture will cover what we call the Archaic Period of Greek history, 800-500 B.C. The term "archaic" comes from a Greek word (*arche*) meaning "beginning," and it refers to the fact that this period represents the beginning or formative phase of ancient Greek culture.

We have actually dealt with the early Greeks in connection with the Bronze Age, when we surveyed the Hittite, Minoan, and Mycenaean civilizations in Lecture 4. As you may remember, the Mycenaean civilization flourished on the Greek mainland during the Late Bronze Age (1600-1200 B.C.); and we know from the clay tablets discovered in the palaces that the people of this civilization spoke an early form of Greek. Moreover, the overall pattern of this civilization closely resembled what we encounter elsewhere at this time in the eastern Mediterranean area: palace centers ruling over a large surrounding region, extracting surplus commodities (largely agricultural products) from the population in the form of taxes, engaging in international trade to obtain raw materials and manufactured goods (bronze, amber, glass, gold, silver, etc.), and using a writing system to keep track of the countless number of transactions resulting from these exchanges. Thus, in this sense the Mycenaean civilization of the Bronze Age represents a Greek variation of the overall pattern of Bronze Age life. This civilization on the Greek mainland was swept out of existence by the sudden destruction of the Bronze Age sites shortly after 1200 B.C. By c.1100 B.C. Greece had declined into what modern historians call the Greek Dark Age, which lasted until about 800 B.C. This period of approximately three hundred years is termed a dark age, because we know very little about it, and because civilization as represented by the palace centers disappeared, and people lived in small simple villages. Since writing in the Linear B syllabary had been exclusively a function of the record-keeping habits of the Mycenaean palaces, all knowledge of writing disappeared from among the Greeks of the Dark Age along with those palaces. Our knowledge of these centuries derives from archaeology, which shows that the Greeks lived very simple lives, practicing farming and animal-herding while living in small villages. Then around 800 B.C. the Greeks began to experience population growth that triggered economic and political changes that gradually transformed their entire culture and made them once again a civilized people. At the beginning of this Archaic Period the various peoples of the ancient Near East were already at a higher level of civilization and served as the Greeks' teachers in becoming civilized. Although the Greeks began as eager students to learn from their civilized neighbors, they soon surpassed their teachers, and by the close of the Archaic Period they had gone beyond what their teachers had accomplished, and the Greeks were well on their way to creating the world's first modern-looking civilization.

When we look at a geographical map of the Greek mainland, two things are quite obvious. One is that the land is very mountainous, and the other is that given its long peninsulas, bays, and gulfs, it has a very long coastline with respect to its area. These two geographical features played a very important role in how Greek civilization developed. The mountainous nature of the terrain broke up the land into numerous small areas separated from one another by the mountains. Consequently, when at the beginning of the Archaic Period the Greeks began to outgrow their small village life and organized themselves into larger communities, they did not form themselves into a unified nation, although they were united by the same language and culture. Instead, the geography encouraged the Greeks to form themselves into a large number of relatively small communities, each of which governed its own affairs. The Greeks used the word *polis* to describe such a self-contained community, and the word is usually translated into English as "city-state." It is from this word that we derive "politics," which simply means "affairs of the polis." The *polis* became such a normal feature of Greek social and political life that they considered it as resulting from our very nature as human beings. As we will see in the next lecture when we examine Aristotle's treatise on politics, he made the famous remark that "man is by nature a creature of the *polis.*"

Besides exercising a profound influence upon the political development of the Greeks, the land's mountainous nature and long coastline produced another important consequence for Greek history. Since the land was not rich and fertile for agriculture like the major river valleys of Mesopotamia and Egypt, it was not easy for a large population to support itself simply by farming the land. The coastline, however, provided easy access to the sea and encouraged the Greeks to become seafarers and to engage in trade as a way of increasing and diversifying their economic opportunities.

Once the Greeks took to the sea and began trading with their neighbors, they encountered the more civilized peoples of the ancient Near East and began learning things from them. Their earliest cultural lesson was to be reacquainted with the notion of writing. At the very beginning of the Archaic Period (800-750 B.C.) the Greeks created the world's first true alphabet by borrowing and adapting the writing system of the Phoenicians. The latter had a script consisting of 22 letters to represent the various consonants of their Semitic language that was closely related to ancient Hebrew, but since there were no letters used to express vowel sounds, this writing system, although rather simple, was not a true alphabet. The Greek language possessed so many vowel sounds that it was necessary for the Greeks to devise letters for them in order to have a writing system that could spell words unambiguously. Once they carried out this necessary adaptation, they had a true alphabet, and it is hard to overestimate the impact that it had on the overall cultural development of the ancient Greeks. Since the writing system involved only 24 letters, it was easy to learn, and knowledge of it spread very quickly and involved a much larger portion of the Greek population than what we encounter in the ancient Near East, where the complicated cuneiform and hieroglyphic systems were known to only a very small fraction of the inhabitants. In fact, this difference between the Greeks and the other peoples of the eastern Mediterranean might go a long way in accounting for the extraordinary cultural revolution carried out by the Greeks during the Archaic Period. Modern studies of the human brain have shown very clearly that it grows and develops in response to stimuli and learning. Like a muscle, the more we use it, the more it grows and increases its ability to perform complex operations. Learning how to read and write are very complicated tasks that require the brain to grow and adapt in order to do them. Consequently, if one population has many more members than another with the ability to read and write, it would probably become more advanced, simply because it could harness far more collective brain power.

At the beginning of this lecture is a short text that has been found engraved upon a large Greek pot. It dates to about 740-720 B.C. and comes from a man's grave in Athens. The Greek text in translation simply reads: "the man who now of all dancers performs most nimbly." It is generally thought that this pot had been given to the deceased as a prize when he distinguished himself in some sort of dancing event. It is therefore equivalent to an inscribed plaque or trophy that people today would receive to honor their achievement in sports, music, or the like. The thing that is so striking about this short text is its very ordinariness, suggesting that writing at this early part of the Archaic Period was already common and widespread. The text's ordinariness is typical of our own modern times, in which reading and writing are extremely common, but this was not the case at this time in the other ancient Near Eastern civilizations.

Not long after the Greeks devised the world's first true alphabet, writing was used to create their first two great works of literature, the Homeric poems of *The Iliad* and *The Odyssey*. Although the Greeks of later times thought that both these epics had been written by a man named Homer, we do not know if this was so. It is possible that two different people wrote the poems, but whoever he or they was or were, these poems could not have been composed without the use of writing. During the Greek Dark Age there had flourished a small class of highly skilled story tellers who entertained people by reciting in poetic verse from their prodigious memories myths of the Greek gods and heroes of the past. Early on in the Archaic Period (probably 750-700 B.C.) someone or someones, drawing upon this rich oral poetic tradition, assembled much of this material into the literary masterpieces of *The Iliad* and *The Odyssey*. We have already encountered the notion of heroic epic in the guise of the Epic of Gilgamesh; and there are features shared by the Mesopotamian and Greek epics. But the latter are much longer, tell far more complicated stories, and develop their characters far more realistically and convincingly, so that *The Iliad* and *The Odyssey* still rank today among the great works of world literature. Both poems concern parts of the Greek myth of the Trojan War. Here is the basic storyline of the myth. When Paris, a prince of Troy (located on the Hellespont in northwestern Anatolia) seduced and ran off with Helen, the queen of Sparta and reputed to have been the most beautiful woman then alive, the kings of the various Greek communities banded together under the leadership of Agamemnon, king of Mycenae, and sailed to Troy to force the Trojans to return Helen to Menelaus her husband. But when the Trojans refused, a ten-year war ensued. After countless vicissitudes and numerous great heroes being killed in battle on both sides, the war finally ended with Troy's capture and destruction through the stratagem of the wooden horse full of armed Greek warriors. *The Iliad* tells the story of only part of the Trojan War and largely focuses upon the heroic exploits of the greatest Greek warrior, Achilles, who at the end of the poem kills in battle the bravest of the Trojan warriors, Hector, one of the sons of King Priam. Achilles was so angry with Hector for having killed his best friend Patroclus that he refused to ransom Hector's body, so that it could be properly buried by his fellow Trojans. Text #9 in PSWC is an excerpt from *The Iliad* describing how King Priam came to the Greek encampment with divine assistance in order to obtain the body of his dead son. It is a truly fine piece of writing and gives you a sample of these magnificent works of literature.

PSWC#9

The other Homeric epic, *The Odyssey,* deals with the adventures of Odysseus following the capture of Troy. When the Greeks finally achieved victory, the kings from the various states proceeded homeward, and many of them ran into difficult weather and other adversities to make their homecoming less than easy. Odysseus, the king of the island of Ithaca, fared the worst in this regard: for he and his fellow Ithacans were blown off course repeatedly and wound up having many hair-raising and deadly encounters with strange people, such as the one-eyed man-eating Cyclops, the enchantress Circe who changed men into swine, etc. Finally, after ten years of wandering, Odysseus returned to Ithaca, the sole survivor of all those from Ithaca who had sailed off to Troy. After ten years of war and ten more years of wandering, Odysseus landed in Ithaca only to find his wife Penelope and his palace besieged by the young nobles of the island, who had been trying to force the queen to choose one of them as her new husband, so that he could become the next king of Ithaca. The poem ends with Odysseus, concealing his true identity in the disguise of a beggar, succeeding in killing all the young nobles and regaining both his wife and kingship. The Homeric poems encapsulated so much that was characteristic of ancient Greek culture that they served as a kind of *Bible* to the Greeks. Not only did they portray the gods of Olympus as the Greeks understood them, but they embodied the values of competition and striving for excellence. Besides the Homeric epics, during the second half of the Archaic Period there flourished a large number of poets: Archilochus of Paros, Tyrtaeus of Sparta, Alcaeus and Sappho of Lesbos, Solon of Athens, Theognis of Megara, Xenophanes of Colophon, etc. Although we now possess only portions of their poetry, the fragments that we do have give us many interesting glimpses into contemporary Greek life and personal experiences.

When we turn to the arts, we encounter a similar situation in which the Greeks first were eager pupils of the ancient Near East and then surpassed them. Since the land of Greece was blessed with deposits of marble, they had an excellent material for building their temples and developing the art of sculpture. During the first half of the Archaic Period Greek art was largely an imitation of the traditions current in the ancient Near East. For example, Greek sculptors adopted the Egyptian manner of representing the human form, especially when standing: the person holding the body fully erect and rigid, legs held together (but with one foot slightly forward of the other), arms straight down along the sides. But the Greeks then began to portray the human body in more natural poses, and they were especially keen in representing the young male naked athletic form, because to them, the well developed body of a young man was truly beautiful; and by the close of the Archaic Period Greek sculptors had so carefully studied human anatomy that they were able to represent the human form with amazing realism. The two bronze-cast statues, known as the Riace Bronzes and dating to the Classical Period, display the male human body in very precise exactitude.

Although there have not survived fine paintings from this period, we do possess numerous vases that are beautifully decorated and give us a sense of the power and beauty of Greek painting. At the very beginning of the Archaic Period Greek potters were simply adorning their pottery with lines, arcs, and circles, but they soon adopted the ancient Near Eastern habit of representing animal and human forms; and then by the end of the Archaic Period Greek vase painting had become a highly refined art.

One of the most important phenomena of the Greek Archaic Period was colonization. Since the land of Greece was relatively poor for agriculture, the Greeks soon began to suffer overpopulation, which they remedied by sending out people to establish colonies in other parts of the Mediterranean. As you can see from a map, the Greeks colonized the northern Aegean, all around the coast of the Black Sea, the eastern part of Sicily, the southern coast of Italy, and the southern coast of France. Establishing a colony began as a small venture on the part of a Greek city-state. After deciding that it was necessary to send out part of its population to form a colony, a voyage of exploration had to be undertaken in order to locate a suitable site. Notice that the Greeks did not found colonies in the eastern Mediterranean, because those areas were already occupied by highly civilized people who could and would have prevented them from establishing a colony in their midst. Instead, the Greeks settled areas that were sparsely inhabited or had people whom the Greeks could push aside. The first phase of the colony involved a relatively small number of people, but once the site was secured, more people were brought in, so that by the end of the Archaic Period these colonies had grown and were flourishing communities, just like their mother-cities back in Greece. Once a colony was established, it became a new *polis*, so that colonization spread this form of life along with the Greek language and culture.

One important result of Greek colonization was that it brought the Greeks into contact with many different peoples throughout the whole Mediterranean and made them realize that Greece was simply a small part of a much larger and complex world. By the end of the Archaic Period there had emerged the earliest Greek philosophers or scientists, who were interested in exploring and explaining the world around them in logical and rational terms. As we have seen, the ancient Near Eastern civilizations primarily relied upon myth in order to come up with explanations for life's mysteries. For example, in the Epic of Gilgamesh the peculiar phenomenon of the snake rejuvenating itself by shedding its skin is explained by a snake eating the marvelous plant obtained by Gilgamesh from the bottom of the sea. The Greeks too had a highly developed mythology, but they eventually outgrew this mode of thinking and replaced it with a modern-looking rational approach to things.

The term philosopher comes from a Greek word meaning "lover of wisdom," and the earliest philosophers were more akin to modern scientists than what we would consider today to be philosophers, because what interested them was not ethics, but the natural world surrounding them with all its mysteries. One of the earliest Greek philosophers was a man named Anaximander, who is supposed to have been the first person to make a map of the entire world as the Greeks understood it at the time. This was his way of using logic to put together into a coherent picture all the geographical data that the Greeks had accumulated as the result of their seafaring, trading, and colonizing. He also speculated on the nature of the Earth and its position within the universe. He postulated that the Earth was shaped like a cylinder poised motionless at the center of the universe with all the other heavenly bodies revolving around it; and that the Greeks inhabited part of the Earth that formed one of the flat circular ends of the cylinder. Eventually, other Greek thinkers figured out that the Earth must be spherical, and some even postulated that the sun, not the Earth, was at the center of things.

Another early Greek philosopher was Pythagoras, most famous today for the Pythagorean theorem in geometry, which was, by the way, one area of mathematics fully developed by the Greeks of the Classical Period and illustrating their rigorous use of logic. While playing around (or experimenting) with the standard Greek stringed instrument, roughly corresponding to our modern-day guitar, Pythagoras figured out that attributes of the musical scale could be expressed in exact mathematical terms of ratios. This led him to the important conclusion that numbers were in everything, that is, natural phenomena could be explained or described by using mathematics.

A third Greek philosopher with whom we will end this lecture was Democritus. Like so many of these early thinkers, his curiosity was boundless, and he inquired into virtually everything, but he became most famous and important for one particular idea that he developed involving the nature of matter, a question that had puzzled and continued to puzzle Greek philosophers. Why were there so many different substances in the world, and how did they change from one thing to another? Democritus answered these questions with his atomic theory. He postulated that if we took any type of matter and could cut it into smaller and smaller pieces, we would eventually reach the point at which the material could no longer be subdivided. These indivisible pieces of matter he termed atoms from the Greek meaning "uncuttable." He further postulated that there must be certain basic types of matter, what today we call elements, and that they combined in different proportions (i.e., compounds) to form all the different things that surround us.

In conclusion, the Greeks during the Archaic Period carried out an extraordinary cultural revolution. By developing the world's first true alphabet and by using it to compose great works of literature, they advanced from being an illiterate people living in simple villages to form a highly sophisticated civilization, as exemplified in the realism of their sculpture and in the rationalism of their early philosophers.

LECTURE 9
Greek Political Ideas and Practice

IMPORTANT TERMS AND CONCEPTS

- **Polis:** Greek city-state, its public affairs termed politics.
- **Aristotle:** great Greek philosopher, author of important analytical treatise on politics, "man is by nature a creature of the polis."
- **three-part division of the polis:** elected officials, citizen assembly, and advisory or deliberative council.
- Greek theory of the three basic forms of constitutions (three good and three bad): monarchy or kingship (just rule by one person), tyranny (unjust rule by one person), aristocracy (good rule of the few best), oligarchy (corrupt rule of the few, usually those of property), polity (balanced rule by a large segment of the *polis*), democracy (irresponsible rule of the masses).
- Aristotle's conclusion of ensuring political stability by entrusting the constitution to the middle order of citizens.
- **Athens:** polity-democracy, involving large numbers of citizens in public affairs, all issues decided by majority vote in the citizen assembly, fostering individualism and self reliance.
- **Sparta:** conquest of Messenia, reduction of Messenians to Helot slaves, military training for Spartan citizens, fostering obedience to the state, citizen assembly but more restricted

authority with powers given to two kings, five annually elected ephors, and the gerousia of thirty noble elders.

Since this second part of the course will be devoted in large measure to the political history and ideas of the ancient Greeks and Romans, from whom we derive many of our own basic ideas about political institutions, we will lay the foundations in this lecture by describing the most fundamental ideas of Greek political thought. First, I will summarize and explain the excerpts from Aristotle's *Politics* comprising Text #10 in PSWC. Then I will describe the constitutions of Sparta and Athens, about which we know more than any other Greek states.

You will probably find that the readings from Aristotle's *Politics* are the most difficult ones that you will encounter in PSWC. I will therefore summarize the major conclusions that Aristotle reaches in these passages. First of all, Aristotle was a pupil of Plato, one of the other two great Greek philosophers whom we will study to some extent. Aristotle was born in 384 and died in 322 B.C. He therefore lived during the later part of the Classical Period of Greek history. He possessed without a doubt one of the greatest minds of all time. If he were living today, he certainly would win the Nobel Prize in some field. Aristotle had the real knack of being able to study any subject or complex phenomenon, to accumulate all the relevant and seemingly random data associated with it, and then be able to put it all into a logical order and to see patterns and how they were related to one another to form a whole. His intellectual curiosity was boundless, and over the course of his life he wrote treatises on virtually everything; and much of his work was so convincing and authoritative that it formed the bedrock of Western thought up to the sixteenth century, when finally experimental science began to disprove some of his ideas.

Our word politics comes from a Greek word, *politika*, which simply means "affairs of the *polis*." To the Greeks, politics and their life in their city-states were inseparable. Aristotle wrote *The Politics* at a time when the Greeks had worked out their city-state form of political life and had devised numerous constitutional configurations, with their histories having demonstrated that some systems were more stable than others. By looking back upon the histories of all the Greek city-states, Aristotle sifted through a huge pile of empirical political data, from which he arrived at his various conclusions in *The Politics*. Unlike Plato, whose philosophical writings are in the form of dialogues with different parts spoken by a number of characters and always composed in a highly readable and entertaining way, Aristotle wrote in the form of the impersonal essay, in which he moves from point to point with rigorous logic. As a result, his writings often require careful and slow reading in order to follow his thoughts.

As he usually does, Aristotle in these excerpts starts from the most basic idea and builds things up from there. He first observes that men and women are by nature inclined to join together to form binding unions that we call marriages, and which are essential for the begetting and raising of children. This leads to the creation of the family or household with husband, wife, children, and slaves. But since this unit can rarely do everything to satisfy all of its needs, families are inclined to group together into villages, but since even villages can usually do no more than to satisfy basic human needs, they tend to grow into larger associations that can provide the necessary environment for humans to reach their full potential by living a good life, by achieving happiness, and by having sufficient leisure to pursue excellence in many activities. It is this larger association of humans that the Greeks called the *polis*; and since this association arises out of the natural needs and impulses of human nature, Aristotle reaches a conclusion that is probably the most quoted line from *The Politics*: "man is by nature a creature of the *polis*." The last two words, *zoon politikon*, meaning "creature of the *polis*," are often wrongly translated as "political animal."

Having arrived at the conclusion that humans are by nature designed to organize themselves into *polis-like* communities, Aristotle next asks what are the different ways in which the affairs of a polis can be arranged. He observes that governments are of three types: by one, by a few, or by the many. The Greeks termed government by one person monarchy, by a few people aristocracy (rule of the best), and by the many polity. He next points out that all three types share the feature that they govern for the common good of the entire community, but as often happens in human affairs, in reality they often fail to do so; and instead, they govern to suit the interest of those in power. He therefore makes a distinction between good forms and perverted forms of government, so that there are six different classifications that he makes.

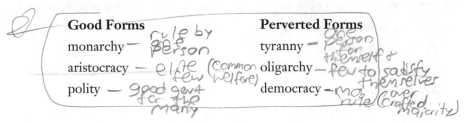

Good Forms
monarchy — *rule by one person*
aristocracy — *elite few (common welfare)*
polity — *good govt for the many*

Perverted Forms
tyranny — *one person for themself*
oligarchy — *few to satisfy themselves*
democracy — *maj over rule (crafted majority)*

Thus, monarchy is just rule by a single person, but tyranny is rule by one person who governs in his own self-interest and not for all his fellow citizens. Similarly, aristocracy is government by an elite few, good people who rule for the common welfare; but oligarchy is government by a few who rule to satisfy their own needs and purposes. Although today we regard the term democracy as a very positive political label, Aristotle instead uses it to characterize what we would call mob rule, irresponsible government by the majority; whereas he employs the word polity to mean good government by the many. Notice that this word is almost identical to *polis* itself and therefore signifies that the citizens (*politai*) of the community are in charge of their own affairs.

After reaching these conclusions and setting forth these basic definitions, Aristotle poses the important question. How should we go about forming a government in order to ensure the greatest stability. Here again, Aristotle draws upon the rich and varied history of the Greek city-states to see general patterns and to arrive at an answer to this question. This was, in fact, a very important question, because over the course of Greek history there had been countless instances in which governments of city-states had been overthrown through violent revolutions and civil wars. After noting that a community's population usually consists of three classes, a wealthy element, a poor element, and a middle element between the other two, he proceeds to characterize each element according to its political suitability. For the most part, he observes, the wealthy turn out not to be the best people to run a government, because by their upbringing and lifestyle many of them see themselves as better than others, and this causes them to behave arrogantly. In addition, given their wealthy status, many are prone to be overly concerned with acquiring more riches. The poorest element is likewise flawed, but for different reasons. Many of them are so ground down and lacking in resources that they are often not well educated and are habituated to petty criminality. On the other hand, the middle class, possessing sufficient resources, tends less toward the arrogance of the wealthy and is more disposed to listen to reason. Thus, of the three classes, the middle element is best suited by nature to govern and to be governed. Consequently, one can best ensure political stability within a community if the middle class is entrusted with the larger share of power and decision making.

This final conclusion is quite remarkable, because when we apply it to the political history of peoples and nations world-wide, we find that it is true. If a society has a substantial middle class, and if that middle class has a major say in the governmental system, the society is likely to enjoy much more political stability than others not so constituted. So, for example, the United States has the largest and most prosperous middle class of any society in all of human history, and this middle class has an important political role through our representative republic. It is this socio-economic and political circumstance that best accounts for the fact that we have abided by our written constitution for over two hundred years. On the other hand, if we look at under-developed countries, we generally find that they rarely have a sizable middle class. Instead, they usually have a small wealthy class and a very large poor class with not much in between. Such societies usually have political systems characterized by oppression, distrust, and class-envy and class-warfare. Our written constitution is truly a magnificent document, but it would be meaningless if our society did not have the large middle class to serve as a stabilizing element, as Aristotle would have it. Many countries have had and do have equally wonderful written constitutions, but they have failed to live up to them, in part because their societies do not have the necessary social and economic systems to go along with the institutions and ideas embodied in their constitutions.

Now that we have worked our way through these fundamental ideas and conclusions of Aristotle, we will examine two particular Greek governmental systems, those of Sparta and Athens. Now please note that both these peoples were Greek, but they had very different histories, organized their political affairs quite differently, and thus wound up with populations that were rather different in their values and chief characteristics. But before looking at Sparta and Athens, we need to note that just as Aristotle has a three-fold classification of governments (by the one, by the few, or by the many), so Greek city-states had constitutions consisting of three parts: a citizen assembly (the many), elected officials or magistrates (one chief executive element), and a deliberative council(the few). Despite this common pattern, there was tremendous variation from state to state in terms of the powers enjoyed by these three parts of the government; and the way in which the powers and duties were distributed determined whether the city-state's constitution was a government of the one, the few, or the many.

Sparta had a rather peculiar history during the Archaic Period. The initial Spartan population lived in a valley in the southern Peloponnesus, the Eurotas Valley. As this population grew and was in need of more land, it satisfied this need not through colonization, but by warring against the neighboring Messenians to the west. During this First Messenian War (735-715 B.C.) the Spartans eventually succeeded in conquering the Messenians; and instead of making them Spartans on equal terms with themselves, they reduced them to a kind of slavery, took over their land, divided it up into sections to be shared out among Spartans, and forced the Messenians (henceforth known as Helots) to work the land as serfs for their Spartan masters. After about two generations the Messenians rose up in revolt to regain their freedom, but after thirty years of fighting in the Second Messenian War (650-620 B.C.) the Spartans again subdued the Messenians. But this time the conquest was accompanied by a major political and military reorganization of the Spartan state that gave it its famous form. In order to guard against another Helot uprising, the Spartans instituted a rigorous military training system for all its male citizens, beginning at the age of seven and going up to twenty. Young Spartan males were not given much book learning, but instead, were made physically fit, capable of enduring hardship, and trained in the use of weapons and military drill. Rather than having a male citizenry consisting of farmers and shop keepers who were periodically called up for military service as an amateur citizen militia as was the norm in other Greek city-states, the Spartan state had an adult male citizenry that constituted a class of professional warriors, so that in the event of another Helot revolt the Spartans would be well prepared to put it down.

The Spartan political constitution was designed to reflect and to be in harmony with this military system. All Spartan men who made it through the rigorous military training became members of the Spartan voting assembly; and since they were the ones who did the fighting, they had the power to declare war and to make peace by majority vote. This was Sparta's element of the many. The citizen assembly also elected each year five men called ephors (overseers or supervisors), who exercised considerable power and formed a major part of another component of the constitution, the elected officials or magistrates.

This executive branch of the Spartan government was further composed of two other figures, the two Spartan kings. Most Greek city-states at a very early time had been ruled by kings, but during the Archaic Period monarchy was abolished, and kings were replaced by annual officials elected by a citizen assembly. In Sparta, however, the early monarchy was not abolished, but was greatly reduced in power and absorbed into the constitution in a drastically altered form. But rather than having a single king from a royal family, for some reason that even the Spartans themselves in later times did not know, they had not one, but two royal families; and at any particular time there were two kings of Sparta, one from each royal family. They held their position for life, and their chief function was to lead Spartan armies in the field in wartime. Aristotle therefore characterized the Spartan kings as hereditary generals. These two kings and the five annually elected ephors served as the chief officials or magistrates of the Spartan state.

The third part of the Spartan constitution, its element of the few, was its deliberative body, which in Greek city-states served the purpose of debating issues and formulating policies to address them. These deliberative bodies also often exercised important judicial powers and could act as a kind of supreme court. In Sparta this body was the gerousia. It was composed of thirty men, the two kings and 28 others. The latter had to be at least sixty years old. Once they were elected by the assembly, they held their office for life. The gerousia took its name from the Greek word *geron*, meaning "old man." Although we are not exactly sure what all its powers were, we do know that it was quite powerful and worked closely with the ephors to decide things and to carry them out. In fact, the Spartan government was largely controlled by the two kings, five ephors, and gerousia, so that we can conclude that Sparta, despite its citizen assembly, had a government of the few. Whether it should be called an aristocracy or an oligarchy, depends upon how one views the quality of the government itself. In any case, the whole Spartan system laid great stress upon obedience, soldier-citizens hearkening to their superiors, and loyal service to the state.

Another aspect of the Spartan system that we need to mention is the Peloponnesian League. During the last decades of the Archaic Period (550 B.C. onwards), as Sparta emerged as the most militarized state in Greece, other Greek city-states of the Peloponnesus formed alliances with Sparta, in which both parties agreed to assist one another in times of war. This alliance system is termed the Peloponnesian League and was responsible for further amplifying Spartan power and prestige and making Sparta the recognized military leader in the Greek mainland during the subsequent Classical Period.

As we will now see, the Athenian system of government was quite different, although it also had three basic parts, corresponding to those of Sparta. During the Archaic Period Athens had gone through a very complex political and constitutional history. At a very early date Athens seems to have replaced monarchy with a form of aristocracy that lasted from the early seventh to the middle of the sixth century B.C. Then in 546 B.C. an ambitious aristocrat named Peisistratus seized control of the state and made himself sole ruler. Since he was not regarded as a legitimate monarch or king, he was termed a tyrant. He and his two sons (Hippias and Hipparchus, who succeeded their father as tyrants) ruled Athens for 36 years, 546-510 B.C. When Hippias was finally overthrown, there was a power struggle in Athens between two groups: one led by Isagoras, who wanted to reestablish some form of aristocracy; and the other group headed by Cleisthenes, who wished to form a more broadly based government. Cleisthenes eventually got the upper hand in the struggle and organized the Athenian democracy.

All adult male Athenians were members of the voting assembly, which, as in Sparta, declared war, made peace, and elected officials; but it also had many other powers that the Spartan assembly did not have. In fact, the Athenian assembly met every nine days and could be called into other emergency sessions. All public matters, big and small, had to be voted on by this assembly. Thus, Athenian democracy was based upon the idea of popular sovereignty, and that the ordinary Athenian citizen possessed enough commonsense to be a good judge in deciding all affairs concerning the Athenian state. In contrast to the obedience fostered by the Spartan system, the political culture of Athens promoted self reliance and individual resourcefulness.

I will not bother to describe in any detail the various elected Athenian officials forming the government's executive element. Suffice it to say that they existed, as they did in all Greek city-states; and they had their specified powers and duties. Given the supreme power of the Athenian assembly, these elected officials were clearly subordinate to it. The deliberative body of the Athenian democracy was called the boule. Although it corresponded to the Spartan gerousia of thirty members, it was very different and reflected the difference between the two political systems. It was composed of 500 members, who held their office for only one year. The way in which these 500 members were chosen was rather complicated. The whole Athenian population was divided into ten parts, and each year each of these ten parts chose its fifty members to represent it in the boule. These fifty people were chosen through a complex system of nomination and the use of the lot. The idea was to obtain a cross-section of the Athenian population; and since the position was held for just one year, it allowed a considerable number of Athenians over the course of time to serve the state and to gain valuable hands-on experience in public affairs. This was all part of the Athenian democratic ideology. Since the boule was the state's deliberative body, it was always in session to discuss any and all matters needing to be addressed. In a sense the boule was the sub-committee of the assembly, and its members formulated possible policies and solutions, but the boule did not have the power to implement any of them. Rather, whenever the assembly was convened, the boule made a report to the assembly in order to inform the Athenians what issues needed resolution, and the boule might even make suggestions, but it was up to the assembly to decide what to do, often after the assembly had held its own debate. It is therefore quite obvious that Athens had a government of the many.

I will end this survey of the Athenian constitution of the Classical Period by describing one of its most peculiar features. Today we use the term ostracism to mean shunning, that is, to punish people by avoiding them and not interacting with them socially, so that they are excluded from a particular group. In ancient Athens ostracism was part of the political system, and here is how it worked. If the Athenians were deeply divided over some issue and were having a difficult time in resolving the controversy, they could do so by resorting to ostracism. First, the assembly had to decide that they wished to hold an ostracism; and if it did, a day was appointed for it. On that day at least 6000 Athenians had to show up to vote. If this minimum number of voters was met, then each person present was given a small piece of broken pottery (*ostrakon*) on which he scratched with a metal stylus the name of the leading politician whom he most disliked. Whoever received the largest number of votes was obliged to leave Athens for ten years, which usually succeeded in destroying the man's political career; and if he had been on one side of the controversial issue (as was likely), it was the one that lost out.

Athens and Sparta are only our two best known Greek systems of government. The Greeks, of course, lived in several hundreds of relatively small communities that had a similar three-fold division among their political institutions. One common feature was that a sizable portion of the citizens in each community was politically active in varying degrees; and the relatively high degree of political freedom enjoyed by the Greeks in their city-states goes far in explaining why they were so successful in creating such a sophisticated culture and literature that has been so influential in the formation of the Western tradition.

LECTURE 10
The History of Classical Greece

- **500-336 B.C.:** Classical Period of Greece.
- **480-479 B.C.:** Xerxes' invasion of Greece.
- **431-404 B.C.:** Peloponnesian War between Athens and Sparta and their allies.
- **399 B.C.:** trial and execution of Socrates.
- **338 B.C.:** Battle of Chaeronea.
- **Herodotus:** father of history, author of the Persian Wars.
- **Thucydides:** the scientific historian, author of the History of the Peloponnesian War.
- **Thermopylae:** battle between Greeks and Persians in which 300 Spartans fought and died to a man.
- **Salamis:** decisive naval battle in which the Greeks with much fewer ships defeated the Persians.
- **Xerxes:** Persian King who invaded Greece, symbolic of despotic caprice.
- **Melian Dialogue:** brutally frank discussion between Athenian generals and the leaders of the small island of Melos, representing the naked power of Athenian imperialism.
- **hegemony** = "leadership:" goal of the more powerful Greek city-states to attain military preeminence, the struggle for which led to weakness and stalemate.

- **Macedonia:** large but backward kingdom on the northern confines of Greece.

This lecture will cover the years 500-336 B.C., the history of Classical Greece, which falls rather neatly into five phases: the period of the Persian Wars, the rise of the Athenian Empire, the Peloponnesian War between Athens and Sparta, the struggle for hegemony, and the rise of Macedonia under King Philip II.

The first of these five periods, the Persian Wars, lasted twenty years, 499-479 B.C. We know quite a bit about these events thanks to the survival of the historical account of the earliest Greek historian, a man named Herodotus and often called the father of history. When we covered the three great empires of the ancient Near East in Lecture 5, we ended with the Persian Empire, established by Cyrus the Great (550-530 B.C.) and extending over Iran, the Fertile Crescent, Egypt, and Anatolia. We know about the early history of the Persian Empire, because they have been recorded in the historical account of Herodotus. There has survived almost nothing in the form of informative historical writing from the Persian themselves. When Cyrus conquered Anatolia, his conquest included several Greek city-states along the western coast, so that the Greeks of the Aegean area were divided between those subject to Persia and those who were still independent and were governing their own affairs. Thus, one of the principal themes of Herodotus' history is political freedom enjoyed by many Greeks vs. political slavery endured by others under the rule of Persia and its king. This can be illustrated by the first three selections from Herodotus as Texts #11A-C in PSWC. We will consider here the first two and then touch upon the third momentarily. The first selection fits very nicely with the excerpts from Aristotle's *Politics* treated in the previous lecture. This first passage from Herodotus narrates what happened when the second Persian king, Cambyses, the son of Cyrus, died. Several high ranking Persian nobles met and debated whether they should continue the monarchy or replace it with a different form of government. Herodotus describes this meeting as if it had been one in which Greeks were debating the advantages and disadvantages of the three different kinds of government: by the one, by the few, or by the many. The first man argues against monarchy, because they have just witnessed how a monarch (Cambyses) can become a tyrant. Instead, this man urges that they form an aristocracy in which they would be the leading members. The second man outlines how aristocracies often behave as corrupt oligarchies, and he therefore suggests that they establish a democracy, the form of government with the fairest sounding name. Lastly, Darius characterizes democracy as nothing more than the irresponsible rule of the rabble, and he argues that the best form of government is monarchy with the best man in charge. He therefore urges that they continue the tradition of their ancestors. Of course, Darius not only wins the debate, but he succeeds in arranging that he be the one chosen as the next king.

The second passage from Herodotus describes how the Athenians defeated their hostile neighbors around 510 B.C. They had just overthrown a tyranny that had ruled over them for 36 years and had just won back their political freedom. When the neighboring states realized that the Athenians were no longer a submissive people, but were ready and willing to exert their independence, they joined together and attacked Athens in the hope of defeating the Athenians and keeping them beaten down. Instead, as Herodotus describes, the Athenians defeated them, so that Herodotus concludes this episode with his remark that nothing is greater than political freedom, because while the Athenians were under the thumb of a tyrant, they were no better than others, but as soon as they became a free people, they became the best among the Greeks.

In 499 B.C., after living under Persian rule for nearly fifty years, the Greek city-states of western Anatolia rebelled in an attempt to regain their independence. The revolt lasted about five years. After initial successes, the Greeks were slowly defeated and reconquered as the Persians mobilized their superior military strength and brought it against the rebels. Since Athens had lent support to the revolt at its very beginning, Darius, the Persian king, decided that he should first punish Athens for its intervention and then carry out a conquest of mainland Greece itself. Therefore, in 490 B.C. a Persian army sailed across the Aegean and landed on Athenian soil at a small town called Marathon that was 26 miles from Athens. The Athenians sent messengers to Sparta to ask for assistance, and in the meantime they placed all their able-bodied men under arms and marched out to Marathon. Before the Spartans arrived, a battle developed between the two sides in which the Athenians succeeded in defeating the larger military force of the Persians, who then withdrew and sailed back home. Before Darius could mount an even larger expedition, he died and was succeeded on the Persian throne by his son Xerxes, who eventually got around to organizing a massive invasion of Greece. So, in the spring of 480 B.C. a gigantic Persian army and navy began moving from Anatolia, across the Hellespont with the aid of a pontoon bridge built by the Persians, around the northern Aegean coast, and finally upon Greece itself from the north.

The third passage from Herodotus in Text #11 of PSWC comes from his account of Xerxes' advance. One of the wealthiest men in the Persian Empire graciously entertained Xerxes and his army as it passed through his neighborhood. Obviously, this pleased Xerxes very much until the man made a request of the king: to allow him to keep one of his sons from the expedition in order to stay behind to take care of him in his old age. This so infuriated Xerxes that he ordered the son to be executed. To Herodotus, this displayed the capricious and arbitrary nature of Persian kingship, and that no matter how rich or powerful a person in the Persian Empire might be, he was always under the rule of the king and was no better off than a slave.

Since the Persians were advancing with a numerically superior army and navy, many Greek communities thought that it was foolish to resist, and they therefore simply surrendered to them, but both Athens and Sparta decided that despite the long odds, they would fight to the end and not submit. Sparta was joined in its decision by its various allies of the Peloponnesus, and there were a few other states who also placed themselves under Spartan leadership to form an anti-Persian league of Greek states. In order to have any chance to defeat the Persians, the Greeks realized that they had to engage the Persians in narrow or confined places where their superior numbers could be largely nullified. Consequently, the first fighting occurred in northern Greece at two nearby places: Thermopylae and Artemisium. The former was a narrow pass where the mountains nearly came down to the sea coast, so that a much smaller body of soldiers could keep the vast Persian army from advancing farther. This is where one of the two Spartan kings, Leonidas, chose to block the Persian advance; and he and his body of 300 Spartans and about 4000 other Greeks were quite successful until the Persians learned from a local inhabitant that there was a pass over the mountains just to the west, by which they could lead a portion of their forces and then attack the Greeks from front and rear. Once they did this, the Greeks were surrounded by superior numbers and died to a man. At the same time the two navies encountered one another not far off in the confined waters between the mainland and the island of Euboea, a place called Artemisium from the fact that the place had a temple to the goddess Artemis. Like the fighting at Thermopylae, the navies engaged for several days, and eventually the superior numbers of the Persians prevailed and forced the Greeks to withdraw to the south.

The Greeks now had to devise a second line of defense. As the Persians stormed southward into Greece and overran the land of the Athenians, the Greek navy took up a position on the small offshore island of Salamis, where the Persians, confident in victory, engaged the smaller Greek navy in the restricted waters between the island and the mainland. This time, however, the Greeks delivered a crushing defeat upon the Persians and all but destroyed their navy. At this point King Xerxes, who had thus far accompanied his army and navy, decided to go back home, but he left the best part of his army under the command of one of his generals named Mardonius, who, after wintering in northern Greece, renewed the fighting in 479 B.C. By now the Greeks were smelling blood and becoming hopeful of victory. Some states, which had so far been sitting on the fence to see how things turned out in order to be on the winning side, joined the Greek cause. Thus, when the big battle came at Plataea just north of Athens, the two armies were probably about the same size; and although the Persian infantry archers were initially quite effective in inflicting losses on the Greeks, once the two armies closed for hand-to-hand combat, the Persian archers were no match for the ordinary Greek infantryman, protected with a shield, helmet, and wielding a thrusting spear. The Persian army was largely destroyed, and Mardonius was killed. The vast army and navy of Xerxes, so hopeful and confident of victory, were defeated and destroyed by a coalition of Greek states, who had banded together to defend their land and freedom. It was a stunning victory for the Greeks and was integral to the confidence felt by the Greek people during the Classical Period.

We now come to the second phase of the Classical Period, the years 479-431 B.C., characterized by the rise of the Athenian Empire. As soon as the Greeks secured their victory over the Persians, the other Greek states of western Anatolia rebelled for a second time from the Persians, because they too wanted to have their freedom back. But in order to make sure that Persia did not try to reconquer them, they sought assistance from the Greeks of the mainland. When Sparta indicated its unwillingness to be their leader in the long term because they always had to keep a close watch on their Helot population, the Athenians stepped forward and took over the role as leader against the Persians. This made perfectly good sense at the time, because Athens had the largest navy, and naval power would be needed to maintain the independence of the Aegean islands and coastal areas. Accordingly, representatives from the different islands and coastal communities met on the centrally located island of Delos and exchanged oaths of allegiance to support one another against their common Persian enemy. This alliance system is therefore known as the Delian League and was headed by Athens. Each state agreed to supply men, money, or ships each year to provide a strong naval defense against Persia. Over the next few years naval expeditions led by the Athenians defeated the Persians until the latter finally gave up on trying to regain control of these areas. But when the members of the Delian League, thinking that their freedom and security were well established, decided to slack off in contributing men, ships, or money, they found that they had the Athenian navy bearing down on them and forcing them to live up to their agreement. Consequently, within a short period of time, what had begun as a voluntary association of free states, evolved into what we call the Athenian Empire, in which superior Athenian naval force was used to keep smaller states to remain in the Delian League and to keep making annual contributions to Athens. Since most states decided that it was less irksome to give money rather than ships or men, the Athenian state began taking in sizable sums of money that they used to increase the size of the Athenian navy and thereby to make Athens even more powerful with respect to its allies or subjects. In addition, the Athenians began to use the surplus funds from this annual tribute to beautify Athens itself by building temples, the best known one of which is the Parthenon. As a result, Athens at this time enjoyed tremendous power and prosperity with its most gifted and talented politician, Pericles, wisely guiding the affairs of the democracy. Furthermore, due to its growing wealth Athens became the cultural magnet of the Greek world. The Greeks were now developing various branches of literature, such as historical writing, many different forms of poetry, drama (both comedy and tragedy), philosophy, and oratory. The latter was the art of argumentation and persuasive public speaking, which, given the nature of political life in Greek city-states, was extremely useful in addressing citizen assemblies and juries in the law courts. Many of the ablest practitioners of these arts now flocked to Athens, where they encountered an appreciative audience and persons willing and eager to pay them to be educated by them. As a result, this period of Greek history was a golden age for Athens.

We now come to the third phase of the Classical Period, the years 431-404 B.C., the Peloponnesian War between Athens and Sparta. As we have already seen, before Xerxes' invasion of Greece, Sparta was the dominant military power in mainland Greece, and it headed an alliance system that we call the Peloponnesian League, because most members of this alliance were located in the Peloponnesus. But once Athens arose to power with its transformation of the Delian League into the Athenian Empire, the Greek states of the mainland and the Aegean area were largely divided into one of two camps: either the Peloponnesian League or the Athenian Empire. Moreover, given the fact that Greek states were often at war with their neighbors, small conflicts of this sort eventually succeeded in dragging Athens and Sparta into a head-to-head confrontation and all-out war, the Peloponnesian War of 431-404 B.C., which is well documented for us by the greatest Greek historian, Thucydides. His masterful and moving account of this great war still ranks today among the finest works of historical writing.

His account is so impressive, because he was able to describe the particular events of this war in larger universal terms. He operated on the assumption that human nature is the one constant of history, and that in the realm of international affairs people are primarily motivated by three factors: fear, self-interest, and ambition. Thus, his historical account of the Peloponnesian War not only describes the complex events of this particular war, but it does so in such a way as to demonstrate how people behave and make decisions under the pressure of war.

Text #12 in PSWC comprises several excerpts from Thucydides. The first passage introduces the subject to his readers and describe his methods as a historian. Then we come to his description of the debate at Sparta. After some of Sparta's allies lodged complaints about Athenian aggression that they regarded as just causes for war, the Spartans met to deliberate and decide what to do. All these matters were conducted before the Spartan warrior assembly, because as we treated in the previous lecture, it was this body that had the power of declaring war and making peace. Two opposing views were put before the assembly, one by King Archidamus, and the other by one of the five ephors of the year. Although Archidamus did not advocate that their allies' grievances be ignored, he urged that the Spartans proceed cautiously and take their time before rushing into a war that would certainly prove to be a very serious and dangerous enterprise. The ephor, on the other hand, urged that war be declared immediately, because the Athenians had clearly misbehaved and were deserving of punishment. After hearing all the allied complaints and then the two speeches of their king and ephor, the Spartans were called upon to vote, and they decided that the Athenians had violated their treaty with Sparta, and that this was a cause for war. This episode gives us a detailed look at the Spartan government in operation.

As we have seen from our survey of the Athenian government in the previous lecture, the Athenian democracy was, to put it in Aristotle's terms, a government of the many, in which all issues, large and small, had to be brought before the Athenian citizen assembly to be debated and voted on. In Text #12C in PSWC we have an excellent illustration of how in Athens the war effort was micro-managed by the assembly, and how this could lead to vacillation.

Although the Spartan assembly had the power of declaring war and making peace, the Spartan government as a whole was a government of the few: kings, ephors, and gerousia. Thus, what Thucydides describes as having been decided by the Athenian assembly in this passage would have been decided in Sparta not by the assembly of warriors, but by the ephors in consultation with the thirty members of the gerousia.

When the people of Mytilene on the island of Lesbos tried to rebel from Athens, the Athenians learned of it in time to keep the rebellion from getting off the ground. At first, when the Athenian assembly debated what to do to punish Mytilene, a narrow majority voted in favor of killing all the adult males and selling all the women and children into slavery in order to terrorize the rest of Athens' subjects and to convince them not to contemplate rebellion. But after sending out a commander and fleet to carry out this decision, the issue was brought before the assembly for a second time and debated all over again. As Thucydides shows us, Cleon argued in favor of the decision already made and spoke out against trying to conduct a serious war with the assembly second guessing everything in this way. In reply Diodotus argued that it was in the self-interest of the Athenians to execute only the ring leaders of the rebellion and to let the rest of the population of Mytilene off the hook, because if they continued to survive as Athenian subjects, they could keep paying their annual tribute. In addition, wiping out the entire population would, he argued, not be a guaranteed deterrent against future rebellions. It only guaranteed that when a community did rebel, they would fight to the bitter end, because they knew that total extinction was what awaited them if they failed. The Athenians now reversed their earlier decision and sided with Diodotus; and luckily for the people of Mytilene, the ship carrying the news of the changed decision succeeded in arriving before the Athenian commander had begun to carry out his first orders.

The Peloponnesian War lasted for twenty-seven years and went through many ups and downs and through different phases. Early on it looked as if the Athenians would succeed in using their superior naval power to bring Sparta to its knees, but Athens lost its ablest leader, Pericles, who was one of many Athenian victims of a deadly epidemic that broke out in Athens at the

loss of Pericles ⇒ changes the war

beginning of the war due to the overcrowded and unsanitary conditions in the city, resulting from the rural population fleeing from the enemy's invasion of the countryside and seeking the protection of the city walls. As might be expected of such a long war, it proved to be very destructive in terms of human life, resources, and public morality. Thucydides' account shows how the grinding pressure of the war corroded morality and decency on both sides, because it accustomed them to resort to violence to solve problems and to reach their goals. This unwholesome situation is best illustrated by Text 12D in PSWC, the so-called Melian Dialogue. In 416 B.C., about halfway through the war, the Athenians decided that the small island of Melos, which up till then had been neutral, was an embarrassment to Athenian naval supremacy. The Athenians therefore sent out a fleet with orders to give the Melians two choices: either submit and become tribute-paying members of the Delian League, or face total extinction. When the representatives of the Athenians met with the officials of Melos, they engaged in a brutally honest interchange of ideas. The Athenians justified their harsh measures by pointing out that they were not inventing a new kind of international law of the jungle. It had and would always be like that. The powerful do what they can, and the weak suffer what they must. This trumped any appeals to decency that the Melians put forth; and when they asserted that Sparta would come to their assistance, the Athenians pointed to their naval supremacy and observed that the Spartans would decide what to do, not in the interest of the Melians, but in terms of their own self-interest. In the end, the Melians valiantly decided to resist Athenian aggression, but sad to say, the latter prevailed, and the Athenians did what they said: they killed all the adult male Melians, sold the women and children into slavery, and occupied the island for themselves.

Although the events of the war showed the Athenians to be bold and enterprising, as we might expect of a political system that placed trust in the judgment of the ordinary citizen, Athenian boldness and enterprise sometimes went too far and became rash and foolish in making major miscalculations. Another weakness in the Athenian conduct of the war lay with its leadership, because its leading politicians often played politics with the war and persuaded the assembly to adopt measures for political, rather than strategic and military reasons. In the end, Sparta decisively defeated Athens, destroyed its navy, and deprived it of all its subjects. So ended Athenian power, prosperity, and optimism of the mid-fifth century.

We now come to the fourth phase of the Classical Period, the years 404-360 B.C., what we can term the struggle for hegemony. The latter term comes from a Greek word simply meaning "leadership." It is applied to this period, because Greek political and military affairs during this period were largely dominated by a struggle between several major states, as each one attempted to establish itself as the leading power on the international stage. Sparta, of course, had emerged victorious from the Peloponnesian War, but Greek international affairs had always resembled a game of king of the mountain. As soon as one state became dominant, others banded together to pull it down in an attempt to elevate themselves. Thus, Spartan supremacy lasted about ten years, and then it was challenged by a coalition of four states, including Thebes and Athens, but the ensuing war, the so-called Corinthian War of 394-386 B.C., finally ended with Sparta reasserting its dominance, which lasted another fifteen years until 371 B.C. While Athens had been trying to reestablish its naval power, its neighbor immediately to the north, Thebes, emerged as a major power with its land army. Finally, in 371 B.C. near the small town of Leuctra west of Thebes a larger Spartan army was decisively defeated by a smaller Theban one. The Thebans followed up their unexpected success by invading the Peloponnesus. They not only liberated the Helots and formed them into the new anti-Spartan state of Messenia, but they won over other allies and reduced Spartan power to a mere shadow of what it had been. But just as in the game, king of the mountain, Athens and other states now joined Sparta to oppose Thebes. After more years of confused fighting, Theban hegemony sputtered to an end in 362 B.C. when the battle at Mantineia in the Peloponnesus north of Sparta resulted in stalemate instead of a victory for either side. Thus, competition, which had always been an integral part of Greek culture and had served to encourage the Greeks, both individually and collectively, to achieve their best, proved to be all too destructive when pushed to its fullest in the realm of international affairs.

We now come to the fifth and final phase of the Classical Period, the years 360-336 B.C., the rise of Macedonia under its king, Philip II, the father of

Alexander the Great. Situated on the northern frontier of Greece, Macedonia was a sizable area, much larger than most Greek city-states, but it had always been a cultural, political, and military backwater, ruled over by kings, which the more highly developed Greeks in their city-states to the south regarded as a primitive and backward form of government. The land was surrounded by very hostile non-Greek tribes to the north, east, and west, who were constantly attacking or poised to invade Macedonia. Moreover, since the land possessed large forests of fine trees suitable for ship building, the Athenians during the fifth century B.C. had kept Macedonia weak and under their thumb, so that they could obtain all the ship timber that they needed. Then during the first part of the fourth century, while the Greeks were involved in their wearisome struggle for hegemony, Macedonia was plagued by both internal and external problems: assassinations and intrigue at the royal court and attacks and invasions by hostile neighbors. When Philip became king in 360 B.C., the Macedonians had just suffered yet another terrible defeat at the hands of the Illyrians, and Philip's older brother, the Macedonian king at the time, was even killed in battle. It therefore looked as if Macedonia would keep to its earlier sorry path of defeat and weakness. But this was not what happened. Just the opposite. During his reign of twenty-four years Philip totally transformed Macedonia and made it the leading power in the Balkan Peninsula. The giant, slumbering on the northern fringe of Greece that had been stepped on and kicked around by its neighbors, now became the greatest power of the region. The achievement is a powerful testimony to monarchy when exercised by a very capable and single-minded individual.

First, Philip used his considerable skills as a diplomat to patch up things, at least for the time being, with different enemies. This bought him valuable time to carry out his first really important act as king. This was a complete reorganization of the Macedonian army. For the first time in its history he organized a well trained infantry force to go along with the effective aristocratic cavalry. Once he had his new army equipped and trained, he turned the tables on the Illyrians and defeated them. He then secured and extended the other boundaries of his kingdom through additional victories. As he was busily engaged in building up his power and resources, a golden opportunity came his way. Of course, another war was raging to the south among the Greek city-states, the so-called Third Sacred War. When the Thessalian Greeks, who lived along Philip's southern border, invited him into an alliance to assist them and other states in this war, Philip accepted the invitation. It gave him entry into the affairs in Greece to the south. By 346 B.C. Philip had succeeded in using both military force and diplomacy to bring this war to a conclusion in such a way that he was now a major power player. He spent the next few years in carrying out more campaigns in the non-Greek borderlands of his kingdom, so that for the first time in its history Macedonia was the clear master of its neighbors, rather than the other way around. By now Athens, led by its greatest orator Demosthenes, realized that Macedonia was rapidly becoming its equal, if not its superior, and could endanger its importation of grain for the city by disrupting Athens' control of sea routes. Thus, in order to check the growing Macedonian menace, Demosthenes persuaded other Greek states to join Athens in a coalition. The final showdown was the battle of Chaeronea in 338 B.C. in which the Macedonians and their Greek allies defeated the coalition led by Athens and Thebes. The victory granted hegemony to Macedonia. Philip used the position to organize the states of Greece into the League of Corinth, in which all states swore allegiance to Philip, declared war upon Persia, and appointed Philip to be the general of a combined Greek and Macedonian army to invade the hated and feared Persian Empire.

The past forty years or so had demonstrated to the Greeks that the Persian Empire was largely a paper tiger. Its king possessed fabulous wealth, but revolts in Egypt, Phoenicia, Cyprus, and Anatolia indicated that not all was well inside the empire, and that the Persian government was not terribly effective in dealing with these revolts. As a result, many Greeks had been dreaming of establishing Greek unity and then destroying and plundering their old hated rival, but rather than achieving this goal on their own, it was their Macedonian neighbor to the north that had forced them to unite and would be leading the invasion of the Persian Empire.

In the spring of 336 B.C., just as Philip was sending the first military forces into Anatolia to begin the invasion, he staged in the Macedonian capital a huge public ceremony to mark his rise to power and to celebrate the wedding of his daughter. He planned that as soon as this big event was over, he would leave and join his forces in Anatolia. Unfortunately for him, as he was striding along in a parade without his body guard around him, a disgruntled Macedonian noble ran out of the crowd of spectators, struck him down, and killed him. Philip was succeeded on the Macedonian throne by his twenty-year old son, Alexander; and it was he, rather than Philip, who led the Greek and Macedonian conquest of the Persian Empire.

LECTURE 11
The Hellenistic Age

- **336-323 B.C.:** Reign of Alexander the Great.
- **323-31 B.C.:** The Hellenistic Period.
- **167-164 B.C.:** Jewish Maccabaean Revolt from the Seleucid Empire.
- **164 B.C.:** First celebration of Hanukkah.
- **31 B.C.:** Battle of Actium, resulting in Queen Cleopatra's suicide and Rome's annexation of Egypt, the last independent Hellenistic kingdom.

New Kingdoms and Cities

Ptolemies of Egypt	Alexandria in Egypt
Seleucid Empire	Antioch in Syria

New Cultural Concepts and Configurations

- **syncretism** = blending together
- **mystery religion:** initiation into religious mysteries, promise of personal salvation, death and resurrection of a divine figure.

- Egyptian cult of Isis and Serapis.
- Hellenistic Science
- **Euclid:** consolidation of Greek geometry.
- **Archimedes:** simple machines, displacement and floatation in liquids (eureka!).
- **Eratosthenes:** member of the Museum in Alexandria, calculated the circumference of the Earth.

Hellenistic Greece 323-31 BC

In this lecture we shall survey the very large period of the Hellenistic Age. It begins in 323 B.C. with the death of Alexander the Great and lasts for nearly 300 years. It ends with the battle of Actium in 31 B.C., fought between the Romans and Egyptians, the former under the command of Octavian (soon to be renamed Augustus and Rome's first emperor) and the latter commanded by Queen Cleopatra and Mark Antony. At that time the last independent Hellenistic kingdom, Ptolemaic Egypt, was absorbed into the Roman Empire, thereby melding the Hellenistic Age into the history and culture of the Roman Empire.

We ended our coverage of the Classical Period of Greece with the rise of Macedonia under Philip. After raising Macedonia for the first time to the level of a major power and making it dominant over Greece, Philip was poised to lead a combined army of Greeks and Macedonians against the tottering Persian Empire when he was assassinated in 336 B.C. He was succeeded on the Macedonian throne by his twenty-year old son Alexander. Since the latter had grown up while his father was shaping the Macedonian army into a truly magnificent fighting machine, Alexander came to the throne with a knowledge of everything that there was to know about the military, and he added to this a true genius in generalship. Thus, he and the Macedonian army formed an unbeatable combination.

Before carrying out Philip's plan to attack Persia, Alexander had to spend two years in putting down rebellions that had arisen after Philip's assassination. He therefore did not begin his invasion of the Persian Empire until 334 B.C. The Greeks had long known that Persia was relatively weak, despite its immense size and vast wealth, but the Greeks had not succeeded in uniting in order to eliminate Persia as a threat to their independence. Instead, the Greeks

It takes Macedonia to finally unite a coalition to defeat Persia.

had been too busy in fighting wars among themselves in order to achieve hegemony over one another. Greek unity was finally accomplished only through superior Macedonian force.

Soon after crossing the Hellespont into northwestern Anatolia with a combined force of Greeks and Macedonians (probably numbering about 40,000), Alexander encountered a regional Persian army at the Granicus River in the spring of 334 B.C. After defeating them, he proceeded down along the western coast of Anatolia, liberating the various Greek cities from Persia, after which he struck inland to secure his control of the interior. His second major battle came in the fall of 333 B.C. at Issus along the northern Syrian coast, in which he defeated a much larger Persian army under the command of the Persian king himself (Darius III). Alexander then moved down along the coast, receiving the cities into surrender and needing to capture two by sieges (Tyre and Gaza). He then crossed the Sinai Peninsula along its northern coast and entered Egypt, where he was greeted as a liberator, because the Egyptians had never been happy under Persian rule. Alexander was regarded as a new pharaoh. While there, he founded a new city called Alexandria at the western edge of the Nile delta on the Mediterranean coast. It soon became very large and prosperous, exporting vast quantities of Egyptian grain and bringing in all sorts of commodities from other places throughout the Mediterranean. Alexandria became one of the largest Hellenistic cities and one of the most important Mediterranean seaports, which it still is today.

Conquers Egypt & new pharaoh.

After leaving Egypt, Alexander moved eastward into the heartland of the Persian Empire. In the fall of 331 B.C. he again encountered the Persian king with a much bigger army just east of the Tigris River at a place called Gaugamela, where he again won a smashing victory. This opened up the whole area to him. After moving south and receiving Babylon into surrender, he moved southeastward, took over the two Persian centers of Susa and Persepolis, and then moved north to secure the Median capital of Ecbatana, located in the mountains of western Iran. He then marched further eastward into the eastern areas of the Persian Empire, where he was occupied for a few years in very hard fighting, as the people strongly resisted conquest, but he eventually subdued the area.

He then crossed the Hindu Kush Mountains into the Indian subcontinent into what is now Pakistan. He fought his last major battle at the Hydaspes River, a tributary of the great Indus. He and his army descended the river in a large fleet, conquering the various tribes as they went. When they reached the mouth of the river at the coast of the Indian Ocean, he sent part of his forces back to Mesopotamia by ships, so that they could conduct a voyage of exploration along the coast and into the Persian Gulf. Alexander led the rest of his army overland. He then spent the last two years or so of his life in the area of Mesopotamia and Persia, making all sorts of arrangements for his new empire, but in June of 323 B.C. he fell ill in Babylon and died just short of the young age of 33, probably from malaria or some other disease.

Alexander's conquest of the Persian Empire had broken down the barrier between the Greek world and the civilizations of the ancient Near East, and it ushered in this new period of history that we call the Hellenistic Age, characterized by the blending together of these two very different cultural traditions. The term "Hellenistic" comes from the Greek word *Hellenisti*, which means "to speak in Greek." The term Hellenistic signifies that during this period of history many people living throughout the lands conquered by Alexander adopted Greek as their first or second language, although they were not biologically connected to the ancient Greek people. This widespread phenomenon therefore testifies to the dominance of Greek language and culture that came to prevail in these non-Greek areas.

Since Alexander died before being able to make proper arrangements for the succession to his throne, his various generals soon fell to fighting over parts of his vast empire, which comprised Macedonia, Greece, and what had been the Persian Empire. This fighting involved one war after the next and dragged on for about forty years. When the dust finally settled around 280 B.C., Alexander's vast empire had broken up into three major kingdoms: the Macedonian homeland under its own line of kings (the Antigonids); Egypt under a dynasty established by Ptolemy, one of Alexander's generals; and the area of Syria, Mesopotamia, and Persia under the Seleucid dynasty, founded by Seleucus, another of Alexander's generals.

gov't => three branches
king was executives

As a result, this whole area now took on a new political configuration. Monarchy now became an important feature of the political landscape, but not the simple monarchy or tyranny of single city-states known to the Greeks of the Archaic and Classical Periods. These monarchs were powerful figures and ruled over large areas, but within these kingdoms there were numerous communities or city-states that had their own local governments with the typical Greek three-part system of assembly, deliberative body, and elected officials. Besides the big three monarchies of Antigonid Macedonia, Ptolemaic Egypt, and Seleucid western Asia, there were a few other smaller kingdoms, such as Pergamum of western Anatolia, Bithynia situated around the Sea of Marmora, Pontus along the southern shore of the Black Sea, and Cappadocia and Armenia of eastern Anatolia. There also flourished a large number of independent city-states; and in mainland Greece two major leagues of such states (the Etolian and Achaean) came together for mutual defense against the powerful monarchy of Macedonia. In addition, the island Republic of Rhodes emerged as an important player in international affairs due to its flourishing maritime commerce and substantial navy that served to keep the eastern Mediterranean safe from piracy. The existence of these three large monarchies and a large number of other smaller kingdoms, leagues, and states ensured that major and minor wars were almost constantly being fought, as these different states formed and reformed alliances with or against one another.

The new ruling dynasties of the three big kingdoms were Macedonian and required a large bureaucracy to run things. The official language of government now became Greek, and there was now an exodus of skilled Greeks from their homeland into the conquered eastern areas to staff the governmental bureaucracies. There now developed a two-level society in what had been the Persian Empire: a Greek and Macedonian ruling class with Greek as their language, and the native population with their own traditions and language. In addition, the Hellenistic kings founded numerous cities, organized along Greek lines; and they invited Greeks to come populate them in order to Hellenize or make the surrounding areas as Greek as possible. The two biggest success stories in this regard were Alexandria in Egypt founded by Alexander himself and the city of Antioch on the northern coast of Syria.

Hellenistic → blending of Greek
Age and Near Eastern
cultures

Modern historians use the word syncretism to characterize the Hellenistic Age. It derives from a Greek word meaning pouring or blending together, and it refers to the blending of the two different cultural traditions: Greek and ancient Near Eastern. This resulted in new cultural formations.

Syncretism is best illustrated in the area of religion. Greek religious and philosophical ideas melded with local and regional Near Eastern traditions to create a set of so-called mystery religions, which conformed more or less to the same pattern, in which the central myth involved the death and resurrection of a divine being, such as Adonis of Syria or Attis of Phrygia. The central myth of the religion was shaped into a sacred drama, in which the story of the myth was acted out; and initiates into the mystery religion either observed or participated in these sacred dramas, so that their association with the religion's central mystery of life and resurrection ensured that the initiate would enjoy a happy afterlife.

These mystery religions received their name from the fact that they taught a profound religious mystery to their followers, the mystery of life after death; but they were also so called because their mysteries were supposed to be kept secret from non-initiates. These religions were totally private: that is, they were not part of the various states' official public religion and festivals. People could choose either to join or not to join them. Virtually every major area of the Hellenistic world produced its own version of a mystery religion, so that taken together, they all formed a kind of homogeneous religious culture, which, as we will see in Lecture 16, was important in the formation of Christianity: for the latter can be seen as the historical product of traditional Judaism being Hellenized and transformed into a mystery religion with Jesus as a dying and reviving god at its center.

One of the most popular mystery religions of the Hellenistic world came from Egypt. In Lecture 3 we touched upon the myth of Isis and Osiris in connection with early Egypt and the Egyptians' belief in enjoying a happy afterlife. In Hellenistic Egypt the old myth of Osiris dying and coming back to life through the magical spells of Isis was blended with elements of a well-known Greek mystery religion involving the goddess Demeter and her daughter Persephone to form a modified religious system that was thereby acceptable to both the Greeks and native inhabitants of Ptolemaic Egypt. Osiris was now renamed Serapis; and given the dominant role played by Alexandria in Mediterranean trade, the cult of Isis and Serapis was soon exported throughout the Hellenistic world and became very popular outside of Egypt, because most people regarded Egypt as the oldest civilization, and they therefore had great respect for its religious traditions.

The religious syncretism of the various polytheistic peoples of the Hellenistic Period occurred peacefully, but this was not the case with respect to the monotheistic Jews. Their reaction to the growing dominance of Greek culture and its religious and philosophical ideas was very complex, varying from full acceptance to outright rejection and everything else in between. Many Jews left their small and poor homeland and traveled to many of the Hellenistic cities, especially to Alexandria in Egypt and Antioch in Syria, where they sought job opportunities offered by these gigantic cosmopolitan communities. This resulted in the so-called *diaspora* or the scattering or dispersal of the Jews into the larger Hellenistic world. By the late 200s B.C. both Alexandria and Antioch had large Jewish minorities living in them, and many of these Jews spoke only Greek. Consequently, in order for these Greek-speaking Jews to read their traditional sacred literature, the various books of *The Old Testament* were now translated from Hebrew into Greek; and this Greek translation of *The Bible* is known as the Septuagint from the Latin word for seventy, because 72 Jewish scholars were supposed to have carried out this translation. The Septuagint therefore symbolizes the success that Hellenistic culture had in penetrating Jewish culture.

Although many Jews were willing to adopt aspects of Greek culture in varying degrees, others were offended by it and wanted nothing, or little, to do with it, in part because strict monotheism is exclusionary and rather intolerant and is incompatible with polytheism. The clash of these two different religious traditions occurred most violently in 167 B.C. Antiochus IV, the ruler of the Seleucid Empire, had just completed subduing rebellious parts of his empire; and in order to try to establish some degree of uniformity by which to unite the different peoples of his kingdom, he imposed upon all his subjects a standardized form of polytheism. All the polytheistic inhabitants of Antiochus' culturally diverse kingdom had little difficulty in accepting this form of worship, but as we see from Text #14 in PSWC, this was not the case for some of the monotheistic Jews in Judah. When the king's emissaries attempted to install polytheism in Judah, they met with strong resistance, resulting in an uprising led by a man named Judas Maccabaeus. After a few years of fighting, the Jewish rebels succeeded in driving the agents and supporters of Antiochus IV out of Judah. After purifying the temple in Jerusalem from the pollution of polytheism, they rededicated it and marked this important event of hard-won religious independence with the new festival of Hanukkah.

Over the next two generations following the death of King Antiochus IV, the vast Seleucid Empire slowly disintegrated until the area of Mesopotamia and Iran came under the rule of a new dynasty, the Parthians of northern Iran. As we will see in the next lecture, by that time the Romans had emerged as the dominant power of the whole Mediterranean. In 168 B.C. they had conquered and ended the Antigonid monarchy of Macedonia; and although still nominally independent, the other major Hellenistic kingdom, Ptolemaic Egypt, remained weak and subservient to Rome until finally in 30 B.C. a Roman army under the command of Octavian (soon to be renamed Augustus) entered Egypt and annexed it as a province of the Roman Empire. In addition, during the first half of the first century B.C. the Romans extended their power eastward from the Mediterranean coast to the Euphrates River, so that the latter then became the frequently contested border between the Romans and the Parthians until the Parthians themselves fell from power during the 220s A.D. Thus, much of the Hellenistic world, resulting from Alexander's conquest of the Persian Empire, was eventually absorbed into the empire of the Romans.

As we have seen, the Greeks during the Archaic and Classical Periods had developed a very sophisticated culture and literature, and they continued to make significant advamces in the areas of mathematics and science during the Hellenistic Period. The one area of mathematics in which the Greeks excelled was geometry. They had been developing this branch of mathematics logically and systematically from Pythagoras onwards. In fact, Plato regarded geometry as so essential in training his students how to think logically that over the

#1 area of mathematics ⇒ geometry. (Euclid)

doorway into his school in Athens (the Academy) it was written, "Let no one ignorant of geometry enter here." By the close of the Classical Period the Greeks had thoroughly developed this area of mathematics, so that one of the first major intellectual achievements of the Hellenistic Age (around 300 B.C.) was the publication of a book by Euclid in which he set forth systematically the whole body of Greek geometry, beginning with the five basic postulates and working out the theorems one after the other through rigorous logic.

Although the Greeks were ingenious in developing Euclidian geometry, they did not advance nearly so far in other areas of mathematics, in part because like the Romans, they had a very cumbersome system of mathematical notation that made the performance of calculations not all that easy. Our present simple system of ten numbers in base ten harks back to the Arabs, who in turn obtained it from the Indians; and once the people of Western Europe adopted this much simpler system of mathematical notation from the Arabs around 1200, modern mathematical progress began to take off.

Nevertheless, despite the inadequacies of the Greek mathematical notation, there was one man who seems to have come close to developing calculus. This was Archimedes (287-212 B.C.). Many stories are told about him to illustrate his genius. He lived in the city of Syracuse on the island of Sicily and was employed by his king to design all sorts of machines to ward off attackers to keep Syracuse secure. He was apparently a real genius in using simple machines, such as pulleys and levers, in devising various things. He is supposed to have made a machine that enabled him to drag an entire ship onto land by turning a crank. This was based upon the principle of moving a heavy weight through a short distance by exerting a small force through a long distance (i.e., turning a crank around and around and around). He was so masterful in constructing such devices that he is alleged to have boasted, "Give me a place to stand, and I will move the Earth."

Archimedes was once given a very difficult problem to solve. The king had given a goldsmith a certain weight of gold out of which he was to fashion a crown. When the crown was finished, the king wanted to know if the goldsmith had cheated him by replacing some of the gold with another cheaper metal, such as lead or copper. Was there a way that Archimedes could figure out whether the crown was pure gold without harming the crown in any way? After pondering this puzzle for a long time, Archimedes finally hit upon the solution when he stepped down into a bath tub in a public bath. As he watched his body displace the water, he suddenly realized the solution to the problem: he could measure the volume of the crown by seeing how much water it displaced when submerged; and by already knowing its weight he could figure out the density of the material and then check to see if it was the same as the density of pure gold. If not, then the metal of the crown was not solid gold. Archimedes was so excited by his sudden intellectual discovery that he ran out of the public bath (supposedly without stopping to put his clothes back on) shouting "Eureka! Eureka! = I have found it! I have found it!"

In recent years a stunning discovery in the form of a lost ancient Greek text has emerged, testifying to Archimedes' extraordinary genius. Around 1990 a family in France realized that they were in possession of an old Greek book of some sort. Their family had owned for a long time a Medieval religious text written on many pages of parchment, but they now discovered that the Medieval text had been written on top of something else. During the Middle Ages it was not uncommon for parchment of one book to be recycled as writing material for another, because parchment was expensive and not easy to come by. Thus, sometimes a scholar in need of writing material would take a book that he no longer wanted, did his best to scrape away the writing, and then wrote his new text on top of it. Such an erased and reused text is known as a palimpsest. It eventually emerged that this text owned by the French family had once been a book of Archimedes written in Greek and even containing diagrams.

Once discovered, the Archimedes Palimpsest came onto the market and was auctioned off for two million dollars. The wealthy purchaser then generously donated the text to The Walters Art Museum in Baltimore, Maryland, where it is now being studied by a team of scholars. The underlying Greek writing is very difficult to read, and experts are using all sorts of high technology (viewing the text with different kinds of light) in order to reconstruct the text letter by letter and word by word.

The text may eventually tell us how Archimedes was able to perform extremely complex calculations to come up with the best (up until then) value for Pi and to determine the area or volume of objects with curved edges or surfaces. Today these calculations are performed through the process of integration in calculus. Archimedes may have devised his own method that was similar to integration in calculus developed a little more than 300 years ago by Newton and Leibnitz.

Finally, we come to Eratosthenes and his calculation of the Earth's circumference. Early on in the Hellenistic Period the king of Egypt founded an important institution of higher learning. It was called the Museum, taking its name from the nine Muses of Greek mythology, nine minor divinities who each presided over one of nine different areas of literature. The Museum was a place where the greatest thinkers and scholars of the age lived under the patronage of the Egyptian king. They received a salary and were given leisure to explore their ideas and write them up in books. These scholars were poets, historians, literary critics, philosophers, mathematicians, geographers, and astronomers. Eratosthenes was one of these scholars with interests in many areas. At one point he was even the director of the Museum. In any case, he succeeded in applying some simple geometry to figure out the circumference of the whole Earth.

From various observations the Greeks had long known that the Earth was a sphere; and Aristarchus of Samos, an astronomer of the early third century B.C., had even placed the sun, instead of the Earth, at the center of the solar system. But the Greeks had no idea how big the Earth was until Eratosthenes figured it out. He learned from travelers that several hundred miles south of Alexandria on the southern border of Egypt there was a town called Syene, where at noon on the summer solstice the sun was directly overhead and shone straight down into a vertical well. He knew that when it was noon on the summer solstice in Alexandria, the sun appeared to be directly overhead, but it was actually a bit to the south and therefore cast a shadow slightly to the north. He realized that the angular distance of this shadow from the vertical represented the angular distance between Syene and Alexandria on the circumference of the Earth. Thus, by knowing the actual distance between Alexandria and Syene, Eratosthenes was able to figure out the entire circumference of the Earth through a simple ratio: angular distance between

Alexandria and Syene is to 360 degrees what the mileage between Alexandria and Syene is to the Earth's circumference.

In conclusion, the Hellenistic Age, stemming from the conquest of Alexander the Great, was a period of political diversity, large bureaucratic monarchies with numerous communities governing their own local affairs. It was also an age marked by the spread of the Greek language and cultural syncretism, resulting in the formation of mystery religions and stimulating people to advance further the arts and sciences already developed to a very high degree by the Greeks of the Classical Period.

LECTURE 12
Rome's Rise to Mediterranean Dominance

IMPORTANT DATES AND TERMS

- **753-509 B.C.:** Rome's Regal Period, characterized by the rule of kings and Rome's growth from a small village into a sizable city of central Italy.
- **509-264 B.C.:** Period of the Early Republic, characterized by Rome's development of its major political institutions and its conquest of peninsular Italy.
- **264-133 B.C.:** Period of the Middle Republic, characterized by Rome's great overseas wars of conquest.
- **Livy:** Roman historian, important source of information for the Regal Period and the early and middle Republic.
- **Romulus and Remus:** legendary twin founders of Rome.
- **consuls:** two elected every year for leading armies.
- **senate:** major political institution for debate and guiding the state, composed of members from elite families.
- **tribunes:** ten elected every year to watch over other officials, to convene the citizen assembly for public business, armed with veto power (veto = "I forbid").
- **dictator:** constitutional official, appointed for maximum term of six months to handle some crisis.
- **Polybius:** Greek hostage in Rome, author of a history narrating Rome's rise to Mediterranean dominance, describing

the Roman Republic as a mixed constitution.

- **Carthage:** Phoenician colony of North Africa, major commercial and naval power of the western Mediterranean, great adversary to Rome in three Punic Wars (264-241, 218-201, and 149-146 B.C.).

 We have now finished our survey of Greek history and culture and come to Rome. Roman history falls into three major periods with the latter two being further subdivided. First there is the regal period during which the Romans were ruled by kings, followed by the Republic, and then the Empire. The history of the Roman Republic is usually divided into three parts: early, middle, and late. In this lecture we will cover the three periods of the regal period, the early Republic, and the middle Republic, spanning about six hundred years, 753 to 133 B.C.

Rome is situated on the Tiber River in west-central Italy about fifteen miles in from the sea. As you can see from a map showing the ethnic and linguistic areas of early Italy, this region began as a real patchwork of different peoples. The histories of mainland Greece and of early Italy were rather different. After forming themselves into a large number of relatively small city-states and having the same language and culture, the Greeks never did succeed in uniting themselves into a nation. In contrast, the Romans, who emerged as only one of many peoples in early Italy, succeeded not only in conquering all the other Italian peoples, but by the end of the Republic they had united them all into a Roman nation with all being Roman citizens and having Latin as their common language. This was a truly extraordinary accomplishment and was characteristic of the great organizing skills and practicality exhibited by the Romans throughout their entire history.

As we have seen, the Greeks during the Archaic Period (800-500 B.C.) emerged from a simple village lifestyle and developed their distinctive culture and city-state system of self government. It was during this same period that the Romans likewise progressed from simple villagers to being inhabitants of a well formulated city-state. Since the Romans did not begin to write their history until centuries after they had emerged as a people, we have little to go on concerning their origins except for myths and legends that cannot be given too much credibility. We also have a certain amount of independent archaeological evidence; and according to these latter data, the site of Rome was inhabited by simple farming and herding villagers as early as about 1000 B.C., and finally around 650-600 B.C. the Romans were organizing themselves into a city-state-like community. When the regal period came to an end around 500 B.C., Rome probably had a population of about 30,000 people and was a sizable city-state in comparison to other communities in Italy at that time.

When we turn to the much later stories told by the Romans about their beginnings, we encounter a very colorful series of tales. When the Romans finally got around to trying to piece together their early history, they had rather little reliable information upon which to base their ideas, but they did have a list of annually elected officials (called consuls) that went back to the beginning of the Republic to the year 509 B.C. Before that, they thought, they had been ruled over by a series of seven kings; and they estimated that these kings had reigned about 250 years. So, they figured, Rome must have begun as a community in the year 753 B.C. They therefore believed that the regal period had begun in 753 and ended in 509 B.C. *PSWC #15*

Our single most important source of information concerning Rome's early years is the narrative of the Roman historian Livy, who wrote centuries later at the very beginning of the Principate (30 B.C. to 17 A.D.). But since he is our single most important ancient Roman historian for the periods of the kings and the early and middle Republic, Text #15 in PSWC comprises three passages from his history that illustrate features of Roman history covered in this lecture. The first of these passages is Livy's story of how Rome was founded by the mythical twins Romulus and Remus. Their mother was a priestess impregnated by the god Mars; and after their birth the twins were taken away from her by the local evil king, who ordered that they be exposed in the wild to die. They were accordingly placed in a basket and set adrift on the Tiber River, but instead of drowning and dying, they drifted to the river bank, where they were first nursed by a she-wolf and then taken in and raised by a shepherd. When they became young adults, Romulus and Remus realized their destiny by overthrowing the wicked king, who had attempted to kill them as infants; and after placing their mother's father on the throne to succeed the evil king, they went off to establish their own new community at the site where they had been exposed to die as newborns. But after quarreling, Romulus killed Remus, founded Rome, and became its first king in 753 B.C.

You should recognize that the basic outline of this story is similar to what we have already encountered in other historical contexts. It resembles the story of Sargon, the first great conqueror of Mesopotamia, who after being born to a priestess, was placed in a basket, set adrift on the Euphrates River, and did not die, but was taken in by a stranger, raised, and grew up to realize his great destiny. Of course, a similar tale was told by the Hebrews about their early great leader Moses. The same applies to Cyrus the Great, the founder of the Persian Empire. There were also several similar stories told about different figures of Greek mythology and legend. It is therefore clear that the Romans drew upon this well established folklore in order to fashion a myth worthy of Rome's foundation.

According to the later Romans, after they had been ruled by seven kings, who did much to shape the community into an organized society and fledgling state, the monarchy was ended and replaced by a new form of government that they called the Republic. Just as the Greeks developed city-states with governments consisting of three basic parts, so the Romans devised their Republic with three major divisions resembling those of Greek city-states. One part of the government was an assembly of adult male citizens, who, in return for serving in the army, had the right to vote. They were the ones who declared war and made peace and also elected the various officials. The Roman assembly also possessed the power of legislation. Any matter brought before it that received a majority vote became binding law.

The branch of the Roman Republican system of government, comprising the elected officials, constitutes a large and complex body of names and functions. But in our somewhat simplified survey we will merely concentrate on three particular offices: the consuls, the tribunes, and the dictator. When the Romans abolished the monarchy in 509 B.C., they replaced their king with two annually elected officials called consuls. They were primarily the generals of the Roman state and had the duty to levy military forces and to lead them

fall of
Monarchy
509 BCE
→
replaced by
governing
generals
(consuls)

against Rome's enemies. They were therefore Rome's most important elected officials in the military sphere. Since they were also seen as the highest ranking officials in the state, they served more or less as the heads of state during their term of office; and their two names were used to label the year of their office. Consequently, the Romans were careful to keep a list of the names of these annual officials and used them for dating events.

The tribunes numbered ten, held their office only for one year, and were the civilian counterparts to the consuls. They oversaw various activities in the city of Rome and presided over meetings of the assembly to put proposals to the vote. As the result of this latter function, they played a primary role in the process of legislation. They also watched over the conduct of the other officials. Each tribune possessed a very important power, termed veto, meaning "I forbid" in Latin. Any proposal brought before the assembly by another tribune was subject to veto by another tribune; and unless the veto was withdrawn, the tribune's veto power stopped the matter dead in its tracks. Therefore, in order for much of Rome's public business to be carried out, it required the cooperation or at least the acquiescence of all ten tribunes. Furthermore, if an elected official misbehaved, he could find himself being prosecuted before the assembly by a tribune, who thus acted as a kind of prosecuting attorney with the assembly sitting in judgment as the jury. Given this watch-dog role played by the tribunes, some newspapers in the United States use the term tribune in their name to suggest that they also serve the public interest as watch-dogs over the doings of our government and elected officials.

Although the term dictator is now synonymous with tyrant or despot, it did not have this meaning during the early and middle Republic. Rather, it was a thoroughly constitutional office. Since the two consuls had equal powers, they could obstruct one another. This often served as an important check and balance, but in times of extreme crisis it could also paralyze the state when action was really necessary. Early on, therefore, the Romans devised the office of dictator to avoid such paralysis. When Rome was confronted with a really serious military threat, stalemate between the consuls could be averted by the senate deciding that the situation called for a dictator. After being chosen by the senate and Roman assembly, this man could hold absolute power for no more than six months and was given the job of dealing with the extraordinary emergency. Meantime, the two consuls served under him; and when the dictator laid down his powers, they resumed their positions as the chief heads of state and supreme military commanders. As we will see in the next lecture, by the close of the Republic this office was revamped to give military despots, such as Sulla and Julius Caesar, absolute authority to rule the state indefinitely.

The principal deliberative body of the Roman Republic was the senate. It took its name from the Latin word *senex*, meaning "old man." This therefore resembled the Spartan gerousia that took its name from the Greek word *geron*, also meaning "old man." Both the Roman senate and the Spartan gerousia served as the chief deliberative body of their respective states, but whereas the gerousia was composed of only thirty men, the senate was much larger. When we begin to have more reliable information about the Roman state during the middle Republic, it appears that the senate numbered somewhere around 300 members. They came from the aristocratic families, met in the senate house in the Roman Forum, and were always discussing public business and formulating policies. People became members of the senate as soon as they were elected to a public office by the Roman assembly, and they retained their membership in that body for life unless they were expelled for gross misconduct. Issues discussed in the senate and ratified by a majority vote of senators became decrees of the senate, but they were not binding law. They usually took the form of instructions directed to officials. Although the consuls had considerable latitude in exercising their power and judgment in their conduct of military and foreign affairs, the senate played a very important role in directing their actions and in advising them in what to do. Similarly, the senate routinely passed decrees that directed the tribunes to take a specified matter before the assembly; and if the assembly voted in favor of it, the matter became binding law. Of the three basic components of the Republican government (assembly, elected officials, and senate), the senate can probably be judged to have been the most important, because it served as the major clearing house for all public business, both foreign and domestic; and it coordinated the other two parts of the government by instructing through its decrees what measures the elected officials should take.

During the period of the early Republic (509-264 B.C.) Rome accomplished two very important things. One was that it grew and evolved as a state and developed various political institutions to cope with all of the growing needs of the Roman community, including various offices that we do not have the time to treat in detail. The other important phenomenon of the early Republic was Rome's conquest and organization of Italy. During the fifth century B.C. (400s) the Romans were constantly fighting wars against their immediate neighbors, who were trying to take over parts of Roman territory. But by the end of the fifth century these wars of defense had become wars of offense, as the Romans gained the upper hand and were expanding their land holdings for a growing population. This pattern of territorial expansion continued on throughout the fourth century (300s). Although this expansion was slow going for a long time, once Rome achieved dominance in central Italy around 340 B.C., its expansion really took off in a big way, resulting in Rome's relatively rapid conquest of Italy (except for the large Po Valley in the north) in less than eighty years (340-264 B.C.).

The second excerpt from the Roman historian Livy (Text #15B in PSWC) illustrates this period of conquest. By 295 B.C. the Romans were well on their way to emerging as the great power of Italy, but their growing strength, which threatened the independence of three different peoples (the Etruscans, Umbrians, and Samnites), had forced the latter into a coalition to oppose Rome. This culminated in the battle of Sentinum of 295 B.C. described by Livy. The anti-Roman coalition was such a major threat to the Romans that they carried out what must have been the biggest military levy up to that time for them. Rather than assigning the campaign to only one of the consuls, as they usually did, the Romans instead placed both in command; and as Livy describes, the fighting was so fierce and determined on both sides that not only were there high casualties, but one of the two consuls was killed in battle through a form of self sacrifice in which he vowed his life to the gods in return for them granting victory to the Romans.

By 264 B.C. the Romans had forced all peoples of Italy to become their allies, and Rome was now at the head of a large Italian confederation consisting of three types of people. Central Italy comprised the actual territorial extent of the Roman state inhabited by Roman citizens. Then there were the so-called Latins. As Rome had carried out its conquest of Italy, it had found it important and useful to establish colonies as strategic outposts in frontier areas to secure Roman interests. The people settled in these communities were given a special legal status, a kind of watered-down form of Roman citizenship. All other communities of Italy were forced to sign bilateral treaties with Rome, according to which they had to supply Rome with soldiers and supplies in times of war, but they were otherwise allowed to govern themselves on the local level. This Italian confederation (Roman citizens, Latins, and allies) gave the Roman state manpower resources numbering 700,000 infantry and 73,000 cavalry, which the Romans used to best effect in embarking upon its wars of overseas conquest.

This brings us to the last period of Roman history covered in this lecture, the middle Republic of 264-133 B.C. It was during this period that the Romans carried out their really big wars of overseas conquest that succeeded in making them the ruling power of the Mediterranean area. During the first half of this period (264-201 B.C.) the Romans fought two gigantic wars with Carthage and emerged as the masters of the central and western parts of the Mediterranean, whereas during the second half (200-133 B.C.) the Romans waged wars in the Hellenistic eastern half of the Mediterranean and established their dominance there.

Carthage, located in North Africa near modern-day Tunis, had begun as a colony of the Phoenicians, the ancient Semitic people inhabiting the eastern shore of the Mediterranean, corresponding to modern-day Lebanon. During the Archaic Period of Greek history, as the Greeks were expanding through colonization, the Phoenicians, a seafaring people, had likewise expanded by establishing trading posts and colonies in Sardinia, northwestern Sicily, southern Spain, the northern coast of Africa, and other places of the western Mediterranean. Carthage eventually grew very large through trade and emerged as the leading state of the Phoenicians in the West, but since the Greeks had also colonized the eastern part of Sicily, there had long been fighting between the Greeks and Carthaginians for control over central Sicily, but these wars never ended in any lasting results for the victor, whether Greek

Rome battles Carthage (North Africa) starting in 264 BC → by 128, they control everything

or Phoenician. It was a see-saw struggle until the Romans challenged the Carthaginians for control of the island. This began in 264 B.C, marking the beginning of the First Punic War that did not end until 241 B.C. Both Rome and Carthage were at the pinnacle of their power and resources at this time, so that this war was a truly titanic struggle of two great powers. Much of the fighting involved enormous fleets of oared warships called quinqueremes, each with a crew of 300 men. In fact, it has been estimated that the battle of Ecnomus in 256 B.C. was the largest naval battle ever fought in history in terms of manpower involved, consisting of about a quarter of a million men. Rome eventually defeated Carthage, forced the latter to give up all places in Sicily, and annexed the island as Rome's first overseas province. Shortly thereafter Rome took over the other two big islands of the region, Sardinia and Corsica, and organized them into the second overseas province.

After losing its holdings in Sicily, the Carthaginians decided to expand their empire in southern Spain. Eventually, minor disputes arose between Rome and Carthage and resulted in the outbreak of a second great war, the Second Punic or Hannibalic War of 218-201 B.C. The Carthaginian cause was led very effectively by its great general Hannibal, who after consolidating power in Spain, decided to take the fight directly to the Romans on their own soil. He led his army overland from Spain, across the Pyrenees and southern France, over the Alps, and into Italy. His goal was to defeat the Romans, to cause their allies to rebel, and thereby to deprive Rome of its considerable resources of manpower. He did in fact inflict several stunning defeats upon the Romans during the first three years of the war and caused some of Rome's Italian allies to defect. The Romans therefore soon figured out that they were up against one of the greatest generals of all time, after which they approached and engaged Hannibal far more cautiously. Despite early devastating defeats and defections in the war, which would have caused other Mediterranean states at the time to negotiate a settlement, the Romans displayed their unusual character by persevering and eventually emerging victorious. Their own great general, Scipio Africanus, subdued Spain, invaded Africa, threatened Carthage itself, forced Hannibal to evacuate Italy to return home, and then decisively defeated Hannibal at Zama in 202 B.C. The peace terms of the next year deprived Carthage of Spain and reduced the Carthaginians to an unwilling, but subservient power to the Romans, who now organized Spain into two more provinces. This made Rome the dominant power of the central and western Mediterranean.

Early on in the Second Punic War, when Hannibal was at the peak of his greatest victories, Macedonia had allied itself with Carthage in order to oppose Rome's growing influence in the Adriatic Sea between Italy and the Balkan Peninsula. Consequently, as soon as the war with Hannibal had ended, the Romans turned their attention eastward. Between 200 and 168 B.C. the Romans fought two wars against Macedonia and one against the Seleucid king of western Asia. Rome's victories in these wars established Rome as the dominant power in the Hellenistic East. Following Rome's victory at Magnesia in 189 B.C. the Romans forced the Seleucid king, Antiochus III, to give up all his holdings in Anatolia; and the Roman victory at Pydna in 168 B.C. over the Macedonians so firmly established Roman rule over Greece that the Romans ended the Macedonian monarchy for good, executed many Greek leaders who had favored Macedonia during the war, and rounded up one thousand leading Greeks, and brought them to Rome to be hostages in order to force the Greek states to be obedient to Rome's will.

One of these hostages was a man named Polybius. He was in his early thirties at the time and came from a prominent Greek family. With nothing much to do in Rome, he became friendly with some of the leading politicians of the day and decided to occupy himself by writing a massive history in Greek in order to explain to his fellow Greeks how these Romans, who were still relative newcomers on the world stage, had succeeded in establishing their Mediterranean rule in the rather short time of a century (264-168 B.C.).

Although much of Polybius' history has not survived, we do possess large portions of it, and Text #16 in PSWC has been assigned as reading to accompany this lecture. Polybius devoted one very large section of his history to describe the political, military, and moral institutions of the Roman Republic in order to account for Rome's greatness. He uses the political vocabulary of the Greeks (monarchy, aristocracy, and democracy) to describe the Roman Republic as a mixed constitution with the consuls, senate, and assembly

PSWC #16.

representing these three types of government. He then proceeds to describe the power of each element and to show how they interacted to check and balance one another. His rather abstract analysis can be nicely juxtaposed to Text #15C in PSWC from Livy. This passage is taken from Livy's description of events dating to 211 B.C. during the Second Punic War. From it we can see, as described by Polybius, the Republican system of government in operation. The senate serves as the basic clearing house for all issues relating to the conduct of the war by making decisions and instructing the consuls and others to carry them out. The consuls, of course, are given duties in accord with their function as the state's supreme military commanders. Lastly, we see the tribunes and assembly working together in the prosecution of an official of the previous year charged with cowardice on the battlefield. After both sides present their case, the accused avoids condemnation and the confiscation of his property by going into voluntary exile before the assembly reaches its final verdict.

During the years 149-146 B.C. the Romans fought two major wars: one against Macedonia and the Greeks, and another against Carthage (the Third Punic War). Both areas had long been unhappy with their subordinate position to Rome, and they both now attempted to reassert their independence and survival as free peoples. Rome defeated both adversaries and demonstrated clearly its superior might in 146 B.C. in destroying the cities of Carthage and Corinth. These were calculated acts of terrorism to ensure that the message of Roman might was well received for all future time. These two wars ended with the creation of two more overseas provinces: Macedonia and Africa. Then in 133 B.C. the king of Pergamum, a kingdom in western Anatolia long allied to Rome, died without an heir to succeed him. When it was learned that he had specified in his will that his kingdom was to be taken over by the Romans, the latter received his bequest and organized his kingdom into the seventh overseas Roman province called Asia. Consequently, by the close of the middle Republic the Romans had emerged as the dominant ruling power over the entire Mediterranean with seven overseas provinces: Sicily, Sardinia-Corsica, the two Spains, Macedonia, Africa, and Asia.

As Rome emerged as the dominant Mediterranean power during the middle Republic, Roman society began to be permeated by Greek culture; and as Romans began to learn the Greek language and to read Greek literature, Romans began to develop their own literature written in Latin based upon Greek models. the plots of Greek plays were used as models for both comedies and tragedies performed on the stage in Rome to entertain the public during major religious festivals. Roman senators, proud of their nation's achievements, borrowed the idea of writing history from the Greeks and began composing historical works that narrated Roman affairs from the mythical origin of the community down to the writer's own day. Roman politicians began to use the same techniques of Greek oratory to adorn their own Latin speeches in order to make themselves more persuasive speakers in the senate, before the Roman assembly, and in the law courts. Other Romans engaged in the writing of poetry, both serious epic and humorous satire. In addition, Greek art and architecture began to be employed to beautify Rome. Thus, as Rome established itself as the dominant power over the Greek Hellenistic East, Roman society slowly came under its cultural spell, so that Roman culture and literature began to develop in response to Greek influence. This process, known as Hellenization, continued on into the late Republic and early Principate and eventually led to the formation of a bicultural Mediterranean society, a Greco-Roman culture with the Latin language and Roman culture prevalent in the western half of the Mediterranean and Greek language and culture continuing to be dominant in the eastern Mediterranean.

LECTURE 13
Rome During the Late Republic

IMPORTANT DATES AND CONCEPTS

- 133-31 B.C.: Period of the late republic, characterized by intermittent political violence in Rome and occasional civil wars.
- 44 B.C.: Assassination of the dictator Julius Caesar.
- 31 B.C.: Naval battle of Actium off the northwestern coast of Greece, fought between Caesar's adopted grand-nephew Octavian (later renamed Augustus) and Mark Antony and Queen Cleopatra of Egypt.

(You need not know the dates enclosed within parentheses)

- Cicero: new man, moderate politician, greatest Roman orator and man of letters.
- Julius Caesar: conqueror of Gaul (58-50 B.C.), fought civil war against Pompey and the senate (49-45 B.C.), became Rome's second military despot.

Causes for the Downfall of the Roman Republic

- Highly competitive nature of Roman politics.
- Growing division between rich and poor.

- Close bond between unscrupulous military commanders and their impoverished soldiers.
- Conflict between major military commanders and the Roman government.

In this lecture we will cover roughly 100 years, 133-31 B.C. This is the third and last part of the Roman Republic known as the late Republic. As explained in the preceding lecture, Rome during the early Republic (509-264 B.C.) had developed its Republican form of government and had carried out the conquest and organization of Italy into a confederation of Roman citizens and allied communities. Then during the middle Republic (264-133 B.C.) Rome had waged various overseas wars that resulted in Rome becoming the dominant power throughout the whole Mediterranean area. During the late Republic covered in this lecture we will trace the complex series of events that led to the gradual destabilization and ultimate demise of the Republic itself through political violence that escalated into periods of civil war, ending in military dictatorship. It is worth noting that the demise of the Roman Republic during this period did not result from invasion or conquest by an outside power, but instead, the Romans themselves were responsible for doing it to themselves. As we can see from Reading 16 in PSWC, Polybius, writing at the end of the middle Republic, had praised Rome's Republican system of government for its stability through the checks and balances inherent in its political institutions; and he had also praised the Romans of his day for their good public morals. But within a century of him writing this positive account around 150 B.C., Rome's public morals had declined precipitously, and the Roman Republic was about to collapse through civil war. The history of the decline and collapse of the Roman Republic is therefore a salutary lesson in how a properly functioning political system is always subject to change, and that this change may not be for the good.

Now when we began this second part of the course devoted to ancient Greece and Rome, we did so by examining portions of Aristotle's *Politics* in order to have the proper conceptual framework in which to understand Greek and Roman political history, which forms much of the basis of modern political thought and practice in the Western tradition. We can now draw upon some of those ideas in order to place the complex history of the late Republic into a broader conceptual framework. As you may remember, Aristotle concluded that if you wish to design a constitution to have the greatest stability, you can do so by entrusting the largest share of power to the middle class, because generally speaking, this element of a society will govern a community's affairs with the greatest moderation and reason. We can apply this basic idea to the Roman Republic and can understand, at least in part, why it slowly collapsed, because the various social and economic effects of Rome's expansion during the middle Republic seriously eroded the small farmer class of Roman society, widened the gap between rich and poor, and thus destabilized the political system that Polybius had praised so highly. Rome's assembly of citizens, responsible for electing officials and passing laws, gradually underwent change from a body of law-abiding sensible farmers to an unruly urban mob easily manipulated by unscrupulous and ambitious members of the elite class, who used the votes in the assembly to legitimate the pursuit of their personal goals.

By 133 B.C. Rome was not only the dominant power throughout the Mediterranean, but it had now become a slave-owning society. Victories in war had made the Roman state very rich through war indemnities imposed upon the defeated and through the capture of booty. Part of these riches went into the Roman treasury, but part also came into the hands of Roman commanders and their officers, causing Roman aristocratic families to become quite wealthy. The city of Rome was now growing by leaps and bounds; and as many families left their small farms and moved to the big city to enjoy a more interesting lifestyle and to take advantage of job opportunities, the abandoned small farms were bought up by rich landowners, who created large plantation-like estates worked by slaves, who had also become very numerous through Rome's conquests. These fundamental social and economic changes eroded the class of small farmers, who had long formed a kind of middle class. Their voting in the Roman assembly contributed to political stability, and their service in Rome's armies guaranteed the military's loyalty to the state. Meanwhile, the city of Rome itself was increasingly populated by large numbers of impoverished and poorly educated people, whose voting in the assembly was often determined by increasing levels of intimidation and violence.

In 133 B.C. one of the ten tribunes of the year, an aristocrat named Tiberius Sempronius Gracchus, tried to address the problem of the declining middle class of small farmers by proposing a program of major land reform, by which public land (land owned by the Roman state) would be divided into small allotments and given to individuals in order to rebuild Rome's class of small farmers. Despite its merits, the proposal immediately developed strong opposition from two different quarters. Some Roman politicians opposed the measure, because they did not want Tiberius Gracchus and his political associates to get credit for this program. Secondly, although the land to be redistributed was public land owned by the Roman state, much of it had been rented out to individuals and families for such a long time that the land was now regarded and treated as if it were private property. Thus, many people opposed the measure, because they might wind up losing much of what they regarded as their land. In addition, Tiberius Gracchus did not help his cause in how he dealt with the political opposition. When he proposed the bill before the assembly to be voted on, one of the other nine tribunes blocked the proposal by using his veto; and instead of respecting his fellow tribune's legal power, Tiberius adopted an unprecedented countermeasure by proposing to the assembly that the opposing tribune be voted out of office; and having removed him from office, Tiberius had his agrarian bill passed into law. Tiberius' high-handed action in deposing his colleague from office so angered his opponents that they vowed to prosecute him for misconduct as soon as his annual term as tribune came to an end when he was no longer protected by the immunity of his office; but in order to avoid such prosecution, Tiberius adopted another irregular stratagem by trying to have himself elected to a second consecutive year as tribune, so that he would continue to be immune from prosecution for another year. As far as we can tell, this was something that a Roman tribune had never done before. The political climate in Rome became so polarized over these matters that when the assembly met for the tribunician elections, violence broke out between the supporters and opponents of Tiberius Gracchus, resulting in the murder of Tiberius and 300 other people. This was the first instance in which civilian blood had been shed in Rome involving political disputes, and it indicated that all was not well with the Republic.

Ten years later in 123 B.C. Tiberius' younger brother, Gaius Sempronius Gracchus, followed in Tiberius' footsteps by embarking upon a very ambitious legislative program as tribune. His laws were designed to address other problematic issues facing the Roman state and succeeded in gaining him a large following. Other politicians, however, not to be outdone, put together a similar legislative program and eventually succeeded in undermining Gracchus' popular support. This situation revealed an unhealthy political pattern: the willingness of elected officials to advance themselves by pandering to the voters. During a highly contentious assembly some Gracchans killed an attendant of one of the two consuls; and when Gracchus and his supporters fled and took refuge in the temple of Diana on the Aventine Hill in Rome, the senate declared a state of emergency and authorized the consul in Rome to take whatever measures were necessary to restore order. When the Gracchans refused to lay down their arms and surrender, they were attacked, and large numbers were killed, including Gaius Gracchus himself.

Throughout the remainder of the late Republic political violence of this sort erupted periodically and contributed to the destabilization of the government, as groups ignored hallowed traditions and legal procedures and resorted to violence to attain their goals. If a few people within a stable political system ignore long accepted practices and proceed down this road of illegality and violence, and if they are soon joined by others in such pursuits of power, and if this trend is left unchecked and is not stopped and reversed to restore the previous stable state of affairs, then the political system is likely to continue to degenerate until it becomes totally unworkable. That is what eventually happened to the Roman Republic, and the political turmoil resulting from the careers of Tiberius and Gaius Gracchus was only the opening chapter in a long and complex story of political degeneration.

The next generation witnessed the emergence of two other factors that led to the first outbreak of actual civil war and the establishment of a military dictatorship. One factor was the fierce rivalry between two prominent military

political conflict b/t prominent military leaders

leaders, Marius and Sulla. Roman politics had always been a rough-and-tumble game among members of the aristocratic families, but it had always been a game fought out within certain limits and with all participants agreeing to the rules, which kept their conflict from harming the political system. But as disregard for laws and traditions continued to erode public morals, the rivalry among aristocratic leaders began to exceed the bounds of earlier accepted behavior and became increasingly violent and damaging to the Republic. The other factor contributing to the Republic's further destabilization involved changes in military recruitment. During the closing years of the second century B.C. (107-101 B.C.) Marius emerged as Rome's greatest general of the day by bringing two difficult wars to a successful conclusion. The first of these wars took place in Numidia, a large desert area in North Africa west of the Roman province of Africa and roughly corresponding to modern-day Algeria. After various ups and downs under three previous commanders, Marius ended this war in Roman victory in 105 B.C., but one of his subordinate officers, named Sulla, also played an important role in the final victory by orchestrating the actual capture of the king of Numidia; and when Sulla promoted his achievements at the expense of Marius, the latter became the former's implacable enemy. Marius' second great war was against two Germanic tribes, the Cimbri and Teutones, who migrated from their homeland west of the Rhine, crossed into the western parts of the Roman Empire, and even threatened to invade Italy itself. Marius destroyed these two large tribes in battles fought in 102 and 101 B.C.

When Marius recruited soldiers for these campaigns, he broke with Roman precedence by allowing destitute citizens to volunteer. As time was to show, this change enabled powerful and prominent members at the top of the political system to develop strong bonds of loyalty with large numbers of Roman citizens at the bottom of society; and this bond in the hands of an ambitious and unscrupulous military leader could be manipulated to enlist military power successfully against the leader's political enemies.

But before these two new factors fully exhibited themselves for the first time, Rome had to first contend with another terrible crisis, a war with its Italian allies. During the early and middle Republic the Romans had been generous in extending Roman citizenship to other people of central Italy; and during the middle Republic the other Italian communities had been relatively happy with their status as Rome's allies. But by the late Republic these allies had become desirous of Roman citizenship, because now that Rome was the dominant power of the whole Mediterranean, Roman status had become quite prestigious and valuable. Moreover, since the Italian allies had done much to help Rome in the acquisition of its empire, they felt that they should be rewarded by being given Roman citizenship. Although the issue was taken up by different Roman politicians, they could not win the support of a majority vote in the Roman assembly, because many Romans did not wish to share their privileged status with their Italian allies. With each failure to gain Roman citizenship, the Italians became increasingly impatient and annoyed with what they regarded as their inferior status. Finally, in 91 B.C. one of the tribunes, Marcus Livius Drusus, once again took up this cause, but when his polarizing actions resulted in his assassination, many of the Italians decided that it was time to secede from Rome and to form themselves into their own republic. When Rome learned of these plans, it declared war upon the allies. This brought about the Social War of 90-88 B.C. This war takes its name from the fact that the Romans termed their allies *socii*. Since the Romans and their allies had been fighting alongside one another for generations and had developed a highly effective military system, the Social War was an extremely bloody and violent one. Not long after it began, the Romans realized that they had been shortsighted in not granting Roman citizenship to the Italians, and they passed a series of laws that gradually extended this status to all Italians: first by giving it to those who had not taken up arms against Rome, then to those who laid down their arms within a certain period of time, and finally to any and all combatants. The war therefore ended only when Rome gave the Italians what they wanted. Henceforth, all Italy was now Roman. Local communities saw to their own affairs, but Rome served as the capital of a Roman nation that comprised Italy.

On the very heels of this awful and bloody war came Rome's first period of civil war, resulting from the two new factors outlined above. Just as the Social War was winding down, another one arose on Rome's eastern frontier in Anatolia when Mithridates, an independent king of that area, posing as a liberator of peoples from Roman rule, invaded the Roman province of Asia and carried out a systematic massacre of all Romans and Italians residing in the province. When Sulla was elected to the consulship for 88 B.C., he was assigned the command of this war; but as he was gathering his forces and preparing to sail from Italy, Marius schemed to have the Roman assembly vote to take the command away from Sulla and to have it given to himself. When Sulla learned of this, he addressed his soldiers and persuaded them to follow him against Rome itself in order to vindicate his claim to the command. So, for the first time in Roman history a Roman general led his army against Rome itself; and this action was an outgrowth of the slow decline in public morality, the growing disrespect for the law, the increasing trend to resort to violence to settle disputes, and the willingness of soldiers to obey their commanders instead of being loyal to the state.

Sulla seized control of Rome and reinstated his right to the Mithridatic command, after which he departed for the war. As soon as he was out of Italy, Marius, who had gone into hiding in North Africa, returned to Italy, rounded up a large following among his veterans, attacked Rome as if it were an enemy city, defeated all opposition, and then proceeded to carry out a massacre of all of his enemies by having gangs of assassins roaming about to hunt these people down. *Military disagreement over a small war motivates Sulla to dictator*

Meanwhile, Sulla conducted the war against Mithridates, chased him back into his own kingdom, and negotiated a peace settlement. By the time that Sulla was ready to return to Italy, Marius was dead of old age, but the government was still in the hands of Marius' partisans and Sulla's enemies. Consequently, in order to return, Sulla landed in southern Italy with a massive army and fought his way to Rome; and once he had control of the city again, he assumed the office of dictator. As we saw in the previous lecture, the office of dictator had been created at the beginning of the Republic and was a legal and constitutional office employed by the Romans in times of extreme crisis, but the Romans had not resorted to this office for quite some time. Sulla now revived this office and gave it a new meaning by using it to legalize his seizure of power through military force. Nor did he limit his tenure of the office to six months, but to as long as he wanted. He thereby made the office into what we today consider dictatorship to be.

Like Marius, Sulla carried out massacres of his enemies, but he did so in a more organized way through what were called proscriptions. This involved the formal posting in the Roman Forum of the names of people who could be killed with impunity, followed by the confiscation of their property, part of which was used to reward the murderers. In addition, in order to gratify many of his veterans, Sulla confiscated the property of thousands of people who had opposed him and distributed their land and possessions to his veterans. As a result, the decade of the 80s was a terrible one for Italy and Rome, ravaged as they were by the Social War and then the civil war and violence carried out by Sulla and Marius.

Sulla was dictator for less than three years, 82-79 B.C., during which he carried out numerous reforms in an attempt to strengthen the political institutions of the Republic and to try to make sure that the Republic could function without the violence that had been troubling it from the time of the Gracchi. When Sulla felt reasonably confident that he had done all that he could do along these lines, like a traditional Roman dictator, he voluntarily laid down his extraordinary powers, went into retirement, and allowed the Republic to resume functioning. But within a generation civil war broke out once again and eventually brought about the final death of the Republic: for Sulla's legal and constitutional reforms could not restore Roman public morality to the high state at which it had stood before the Gracchi, as described by Polybius. Indeed, within a decade of Sulla's retirement many of his reforms had been swept aside, as ambitious politicians, eager to capitalize upon Sulla's unpopularity, won public approval by having the Roman assembly repeal his measures. So, by 70 B.C. the turbulent game of Roman politics had largely reverted to what it had been before Sulla's reforms. Moreover, by 61 B.C. one of Sulla's young supporters, Pompey, had become Rome's current military leader by successfully concluding a series of wars during the 70s and 60s B.C. But when Pompey found himself strongly opposed by others wishing to maintain Republican traditions, he allied himself with two other unscrupulous and ambitious aristocrats, who were eager to use their alliance with Pompey to become his equals and rivals. These two men were Crassus and Julius Caesar, and the First Triumvirate (meaning a group of three) is the term used by modern scholars to describe this political coalition.

After succeeding in their first goal to get Julius Caesar elected consul in 59 B.C., Caesar used his office, accompanied with the necessary violence provided by Pompey's loyal veterans, to have various measures passed through the Roman assembly to benefit all three members of the First Triumvirate. By doing so, Julius Caesar created many enemies, who vowed to prosecute him for his misdeeds. But before they could do so, Caesar left Rome and assumed his military command in Gaul (modern France), where he was busy for the next eight years (58-50 B.C.) in conquering various Celtic tribes, adding new areas to the Roman Empire, developing his skills as a military commander, fashioning an army loyal to himself, and enriching himself and all his friends through war booty, large portions of which were used back in Rome for bribing people to support Julius Caesar.

At this point we need to examine the career of another leading figure of this time, Cicero. Unlike Marius, Sulla, Pompey, and Caesar, Cicero came to prominence not through military service, but by his extraordinary ability as a public speaker. He was also what the Romans called a new man, a person who was the first member of his family to run for public office in Rome rather than being from a well established aristocratic family whose members could count upon a large hereditary following of supporters. Cicero had to build up his political support from scratch, and he did so through his extraordinary talent as a public speaker. In fact, he was Rome's greatest orator. As a young man, he became famous as Rome's best courtroom trial lawyer; and after being elected to lower public offices, he used his speaking ability to gain even further renown by his speeches made before Roman assemblies. Not only was he a masterful public speaker, but he was a very prolific writer; and due to the survival of many of his writings, the years 65-43 B.C. are the best documented years of Roman history, because we now possess many of his courtroom speeches, speeches delivered before Roman assemblies or in the senate, treatises on oratory and philosophy, but especially his letters. During his public career he was constantly receiving letters or writing them to other people in order to stay informed about all aspects of Roman politics. When Cicero died, his secretary rounded up all these letters, numbering about 950, and had them published; and since they survived into modern times, they give us a nearly day-by-day account of Roman politics for the years 65-43 B.C.

PSWC #17

Text #17 in PSWC comprises four excerpts from this vast and rich Ciceronian material to illustrate the immorality, lawlessness, violence, and rowdy nature of Roman politics at this time. The first item shows how criminal trials had become susceptible to bribery. The second passage demonstrates that violence had also become a standard element in public meetings. The fourth text describes how the streets in Rome during much of the 50s B.C. were the scenes of combat fought out by two rival political gangs, finally resulting in the death of one of the gang leaders, rioting in Rome, and the burning-down of the senate house. Recall that one hundred years earlier Polybius had praised the Roman system of government for its stability and the Romans for their high public morality.

After exercising a virtual strangle-hold on the Republican government for several years, the First Triumvirate by the late 50s B.C. was coming apart. In 53 B.C. Crassus was killed in battle while trying to win military glory by waging a war against the Parthians in Mesopotamia. Thereafter, Caesar's enemies in Rome worked on Pompey and slowly persuaded him to join the side of the Republicans against Caesar, whom Pompey began to fear as his principal rival. Thus, by 50 B.C., as Caesar's command in Gaul was coming to an end, Caesar found himself in a difficult dilemma. On the one hand, he could be an obedient citizen of the Republic, lay down his military command, return to Rome, and take his chances in facing his political enemies in court for his misdeeds as consul in 59 B.C. On the other hand, he could try to defend himself and his ambition by refusing to give up his military command and by waging a civil war against his enemies. Given the sorry state of affairs in Roman politics at this time, we should not be surprised that it was the latter choice that Julius Caesar decided upon. Consequently, in early 49 B.C. Caesar began a civil war by invading Italy. The next four years (49-45 B.C.) witnessed fighting in all areas of the Roman Empire. Early on, in 48 Pompey was defeated in the battle of Pharsalus in northern Greece, after which he fled to

Egypt, where he was immediately murdered in order for the young Egyptian king to try to gain Caesar's favor. Caesar eventually emerged victorious from these years of civil war; and like Sulla before him, he used the office of dictator to legalize his position as military despot of the Roman state. Also like Sulla, Caesar used his power to make many changes in Roman government and society, but unlike Sulla, Caesar had no intention of laying down his dictatorial powers and going into retirement. He intended to replace the Republic with his own brand of autocracy. According to one ancient source, Caesar said that by giving up his dictatorship Sulla showed that he did not know his political ABC's. In early 44 B.C. Caesar was made dictator for life, but there were still many who were not reconciled to his murder of the Republic, and they made sure that his life-long dictatorship was going to be very short in duration. These staunch Republicans, led by Brutus and Cassius, formed a broadly based conspiracy and assassinated Caesar on March 15 that same year. But contrary to their expectations, the Republic did not simply spring back into existence, because by then Caesar had amassed such a huge following that it rivaled that of the state itself. Therefore, what ensued was a stand-off between the Republicans and the Caesarians, which soon developed into another round of civil war, culminating in the battle of Philippi in 42 B.C. and resulting in the death of the Republican cause with the deaths of Brutus and Cassius.

In November of 43 B.C., prior to the Philippi campaign, the three leading Caesarians of the day, Mark Antony, Lepidus, and Octavian, though initially suspicious of each other, formed an alliance against the Republicans and had it legalized by the Roman assembly passing a law that conferred upon these three men the same dictatorial powers as previously enjoyed by Sulla and Caesar. This three-man dictatorship is known today as the Second Triumvirate. They began their ruthless regime by reviving Sulla's practice of proscriptions and authorized the assassination of several thousands (including that of Cicero on December 7 of 43 B.C.). They did so to accomplish two goals: to destroy supporters of the Republic and to use their confiscated property to enrich their soldiers and thereby to make them loyal to themselves rather than to the state.

Once the Republicans were eliminated through proscriptions and the battle of Philippi, the three dictators divided up the Roman Empire among themselves. Mark Antony, initially the most prominent of the three, took control of the eastern half of the empire and embarked upon a war against the Parthians to win military renown and to avenge Crassus' death and defeat. Lepidus and Octavian divided the western areas between themselves; and Octavian, the twenty-one year old grand-nephew and adopted son of Julius Caesar, was given the most difficult task of trying to put the shattered pieces of Italy back together again. What eventually emerged out of this division probably surprised most contemporaries. Rather than drowning amid all his difficulties and youthful inexperience, Octavian slowly restored order in Italy, stripped Lepidus of his western holdings, and succeeded in consolidating his power over the entire western half of the empire. Meanwhile, Antony's Parthian war foundered, and his sexual and emotional involvement with Cleopatra, the last ruler of Ptolemaic Egypt, allowed Octavian to stigmatize Antony as a weak Roman who had fallen under the magical spell of an eastern enchantress. As had happened before with Marius and Sulla, and then with Pompey and Caesar, these two men were not content with only half of the Roman Empire. They both aspired to having the whole thing. Thus, on September 2 in 31 B.C. the forces of both sides encountered one another in the form of two gigantic navies at Actium on the northwestern coast of Greece. Octavian's generals defeated the forces of Antony and Cleopatra, who fled from the battle and returned to Egypt, where in August of the following year (30 B.C.), with Octavian in hot pursuit, they committed suicide. Octavian then annexed Egypt as a Roman province and emerged victorious as the unchallenged master of the entire Roman world. He was now faced with the same problem as Sulla and Caesar before him. Now what should he do? His solution was different from both Sulla's and Caesar's, but in a sense it was a combination of the two. Rather than restoring the Republic or trying to replace it with a dictatorship, Octavian created a new and lasting form of government that we call the Principate. It was a form of monarchy dressed up in Republican forms. It guaranteed Octavian's supreme position through a collection of constitutional powers, but at the same time it attempted to mollify widespread Republican sentiments in Roman society by preserving Rome's Republican institutions and practices.

LECTURE 14
The Roman Principate

IMPORTANT DATES AND TERMS

UNLESS OTHERWISE INDICATED, ALL DATES ARE A.D.

- **31 B.C.-68 A.D.:** Julio-Claudian dynasty of emperors, derived from two great noble families of the Roman Republic.
- **69:** Year of the Four Emperors, characterized by civil war fought among several claimants to the imperial throne following the death of Nero without an heir to succeed him.
- **69-96:** Flavian dynasty of emperors, a family originating from a typical small town of central Italy.
- **96-192:** Antonine dynasty of emperors, derived from several prominent provincial families of Spain and Gaul.
- **193-235:** Severan dynasty of emperors, derived from prominent provincial families from North Africa and Syria.
- **Augustus:** Julius Caesar's grand-nephew and adopted son (Octavian), first Roman emperor, founder of the Principate.
- **Principate:** form of monarchy, thinly disguised in the constitutional forms of Republican institutions, based upon control of Rome's military forces.

Once Octavian emerged as the supreme figure in the entire Roman Empire after defeating Antony and Cleopatra in the battle of Actium in 31 B.C., he

was faced with the difficult problem of what to do next. He had now become
the third man in fifty years to achieve total mastery of the Roman state. Sulla,
the first man to march on Rome and to seize control of the state through civil
war, had revived and redefined the office of dictator to give himself a kind of
legalized tyranny. He had held supreme power for about two years, had carried
out numerous reforms in an attempt to ensure against future violence and
turmoil in the Roman state, and then had voluntarily resigned from his
dictatorship to allow the Republic to resume functioning. Unfortunately,
within a decade all his reforms had been swept aside, and the old game of
seditious and violent politics had resumed, eventually leading to the rise of
two powerful dynasts: Pompy and Julius Caesar. Their rivalry had led to
another destructive round of civil war and to Julius Caesar emerging
victorious. Like Sulla, Caesar had assumed the office of dictator, but unlike
Sulla, Julius Caesar had concluded that the Republic was dead, and he decided
to be dictator for the rest of his life. He succeeded in enjoying his supreme
power very briefly, because a large number of aristocrats, who were still
wedded to the notion of a thriving Republic, formed a conspiracy and carried
it out against Julius Caesar on the infamous ides of March. Caesar's
assassination had plunged the Roman state into another round of civil war
between Republicans and others who were intent upon replacing Julius Caesar
as Rome's next despot. When the leading Republicans were either slaughtered
through proscriptions or killed in battle, Mark Antony and Octavian had
divided the Roman world between themselves and had then fought one last
round of civil war for complete mastery. Octavian now had before him the two
unsuccessful examples of Sulla and Julius Caesar, and his redefinition of his
supreme position differed from both. He avoided altogether the office of
dictator, which by now had become synonymous with tyranny.

After Octavian took various measures to end the irregularities of the recent
period of civil war and to restore law and order, the senate in 27 B.C. rewarded
Octavian by bestowing upon him the honorific name of Augustus, by which
he was henceforth known as Rome's first emperor. Having before him the
recent example of Julius Caesar's assassination carried out by aristocrats
committed to Republicanism, Augustus proceeded very cautiously over the

next decade in trying to find the proper balance between his supreme position in the Roman state and the still strong Republican traditions cherished by many Romans. Since Augustus was in fact a consummate politician and diplomat, he eventually succeeded in acquiring a set of constitutional powers granted to him by the senate and people that secured his dominance by law, while at the same time the hallowed traditions and practices of the Republic were left in place. The senate continued to exist and serve as Rome's chief deliberative body. The assembly of citizens continued to convene to elect tribunes, the consuls, and other Republican officials. But over this Republican structure of government presided a kind of constitutional monarch, who controlled the military forces and enjoyed various legal powers that made him the unchallenged master of the Roman state. This political solution resulted in the formation of a new form of government that modern scholars term the Principate, deriving its name from the Latin word *princeps*, meaning chief or first citizen, because the Roman state was now headed by one man who wielded nearly absolute power.

The Principate was a blending of two rather distinct forms of government: monarchy and Republicanism. While Augustus enjoyed various powers that maintained his preeminence in the Roman state, all offices and practices that had characterized the Roman Republic continued to exist as well, so that the Roman government was now a two-part system: the *princeps* (also known as the emperor) with his own very large administrative staff for carrying out all his duties and functions, and another large governmental apparatus consisting of the senate and aristocrats who held the various Republican offices. By the close of Augustus' reign (14 A.D.) Rome's voting assembly of citizens had gradually disappeared, and its function had been replaced by the senate, so that the emperor and the senate formed the two major elements in this new governmental scheme. In the end, however, the emperor was by far the senior partner in this new political two-part system, and the senate and Republican officials represented the junior member of this partnership. But given Augustus' extraordinary tact and ability in things political, he was successful in exercising his powers judiciously and cooperating respectfully with the senate and elected officials so as not to transgress Republican traditions or to behave despotically. Augustus also had the good fortune of living a very long life, not dying until 14 A.D. at the ripe old age of 76 when there were living very few people who could personally remember the Roman Republic as it existed before the last period of civil war and the establishment of the Principate. Therefore, by the time of his death Augustus had succeeded in creating a kind of constitutional monarchy dressed up in the trappings of the old Republic.

This lecture will survey the 265 years of the Roman Principate from 31 B.C. to 235 A.D. In keeping with the central theme of this second part of the course, the political ideas and practices of the Greeks and Romans, we will examine the strengths and weaknesses of the Principate as a political system. First, we need to notice that these 265 years of the Principate comprised four different dynasties of emperors, and the geographical origin of these dynasties is an important indicator in the overall success of the Roman Imperial system in accommodating the different peoples of the Roman Empire. By the end of the Republic all inhabitants of Italy were Roman citizens; and during the first two centuries of the Principate people in the provinces gradually adopted Roman ways and were given Roman citizenship as well. This process of Romanization was completed in the year 212 A.D. when the emperor issued a decree granting Roman citizenship to all inhabitants of the Roman Empire except slaves. As this process of Romanization progressed, leading citizens from the different provinces succeeded in becoming members of the senate, so that this body gradually became representative of all areas of the Roman Empire, and we can see the same pattern of gradual inclusiveness in the position of the emperor.

The first of the four dynasties of the Principate, the one founded by Augustus, lasted for about a century from 31 B.C. to 68 A.D. It is termed the Julio-Claudian dynasty, because it resulted from the intermarriage of the Julian and Claudian families, both of whom were among the most ancient aristocratic lineages of the Roman state, going back to the very beginning of the Republic. The second dynasty, the Flavians, 69-96 A.D., did not come from the old aristocracy of Rome and the Republic. Instead, this family came from ordinary small-town Italy and thus represented a shift away from the old established aristocracy of Rome itself. The third and fourth dynasties, the Antonines (96-192 A.D.) and the Severans (193-235 A.D.), did not even originate in Italy, but from the provinces, thereby showing how, as the Principate progressed, the political system succeeded in absorbing a wider and wider circle of people into itself and making them a part of the establishment. The Antonines came from two provincial families who had intermarried, one from southern Gaul (France) and the other from southern Spain. The Severans also came from two provincial families, one from North Africa and the other from Syria. Thus, the progression of these four Imperial dynasties testify to the great success of the Roman political system in bringing in new members and making fully Romanized insiders of people who had once been non-Roman provincial outsiders. It was this spirit of inclusiveness that made the Roman Empire such a long lived success story. We should also note that the Principate succeeded in granting the inhabitants of the Roman Empire a long period of peace and prosperity. In fact, Western Europe has enjoyed no longer period of peace than when it was part of the Roman Principate.

Another way in which to assess the political success or failure of the Principate is to examine it in terms of monarchy and tyranny, the Greek political terms used to characterize respectively good and bad governments by a single person. History has shown very clearly that hereditary monarchy is the one form of government that is most easily corrupted, because it only requires one person to become corrupt in order to ruin the whole system; and hereditary succession is a very chancy business, because there is no guarantee that a good ruler will beget an offspring who will turn out to be as capable as the parent. As we shall see in our survey, the history of the Roman Principate demonstrates this all too clearly. The succession of Rome's emperors also shows that the Principate often worked best when an emperor had no biological heir but had to resort to adoption to have a successor. Adoption allowed the emperor to choose someone of obvious experience, good character, and sound judgment. In addition, since emperors served for life, the only way to remove a bad emperor from power was through conspiracy and assassination, which on two occasions (68-69 A.D. and 193-197 A.D.) plunged the empire into periods of civil war.

By the time that Augustus died in 14 A.D., he had outlived several members of his family whom he had designated at different times to be his successor. He was eventually forced to adopt his stepson Tiberius and make him his successor. When Tiberius became emperor, he was in his fifties and had enjoyed a long and distinguished career as a government administrator and military general in several successful campaigns, but he simply did not possess the extraordinary political and diplomatic skills of Augustus that made him such a success in dealing with senators. In fact, Tiberius soon wearied of the political game of tactfully balancing his great powers against Republican traditions and practices. He therefore retired to a charming little island in the Bay of Naples south of Rome (Capri), where he continued to be emperor by conducting all his official business through the commander of his praetorian guard. The latter were the military forces kept in Rome to serve as the emperor's body guard and also as a kind of security force to maintain law and order. This situation played into the hands of this commander, a man named Sejanus, who was unscrupulous and ambitious and used his unique connection with Tiberius to elevate himself higher and higher until he entertained the hope of becoming the next emperor. He had even secretly conspired to poison Tiberius' only son in order to increase his chances of following Tiberius on the imperial throne. Sejanus' rise was halted only by Tiberius finally realizing what a threat Sejanus had become, and Tiberius was forced to have him arrested, tried for treason, and executed along with many of his adherents. This is a clear example of what can happen when too much power is entrusted to the wrong person. Sejanus' rise and downfall blighted Tiberius' reign.

When Tiberius died in 37, he had to adopt a nephew to succeed him. This man was Caligula (37-41). He was in his mid twenties at the time and had not acquired the necessary training and experience to make him a mature and competent emperor. Since Tiberius had been a really tight-fisted ruler, the Roman treasury had an enormous surplus when Caligula became emperor, but within a few months all the money was gone, because Caligula spent it all on lavish public entertainments to please the people in Rome and to make himself popular. But as soon as the money was all spent, Caligula became a tyrant. He had rich people executed on trumped-up charges in order to confiscate their

Caligula → 3rd emperor
bankrupts the
empire → tyrannical
fundraising methods

property, and he imposed all sorts of taxes to raise money. As a result, Caligula became extremely unpopular and hated, and the resentment eventually resulted in a conspiracy that led to his assassination in 41, so that he had a very short reign of just four years.

Caligula's tyranny clearly reveals a weakness in the Principate, but so does his assassination, because the only way in which a tyrannical emperor could be removed from office was not by some legal procedure, but through the risky business of assassination. As soon as he was dead, the senate convened and debated whether they should abolish the Principate and bring back the Republic in all its glory, but their debate was rendered meaningless when the soldiers of the praetorian guard proclaimed Caligula's uncle Claudius to be the next emperor. He was about fifty years old at the time, was well educated, and turned out to be a competent and conscientious ruler. He died in 54 when his fourth wife poisoned him, so that her young son by an earlier marriage (Nero) could become Rome's next emperor instead of Claudius' own son. Claudius' death by poisoning at the hands of his wife reveals a common trait of hereditary monarchies world-wide. When great power is enjoyed by a single person, the members of the monarch's family often engage in the most unfamilial behavior, including killing one another, so that they can enjoy supreme power. Nero was Rome's first teenage emperor and was not at all prepared to take on the weighty responsibilities required of an emperor. Nevertheless, despite his youthful inexperience, the empire functioned well for several years, because Nero at first was happy to let his mother and other competent and experienced persons oversee the running of the government, while Nero simply enjoyed himself in pursuits typical of his age. He enjoyed driving chariots as fast as possible, and he underwent serious musical and singing training in order to become a celebrity on the Roman stage. He even enjoyed being a kind of gang leader. As described in Text #18A in PSWC from the great Roman historian Tacitus, Nero led his own gang of toughs out on the dark streets of Rome at night in order to have fun in mugging people. The other passage from Tacitus (Text #18B in PSWC) is even more revealing about the possible effects of absolute power. After about five years, when Nero began to regard his mother as an irksome nag, he decided to fix the problem simply by having her murdered. It was arranged to look as if it had been an accidental drowning, but when things did not go as planned, Nero had to pretend that his mother had been executed, because she had been caught plotting against him. Although few believed it, no one was courageous or stupid enough to challenge the all-mighty emperor on the matter. Consequently, people went along with the lie, and it taught Nero that he could literally get away with murder or anything else.

In 64 a fire broke out in Rome at the Circus Maximus, the enormous outdoor facility where the Romans staged their chariot races. The fire raged out of control for several days and wound up destroying a huge part of the city. As the Romans were recovering from this disaster, Nero took advantage of it by seizing a large piece of real estate in the heart of the city that had been devastated, and upon it he built a gigantic, magnificent, and expensive palace called The Golden House. It so angered people that many began to suspect that Nero had actually ordered the fire to be set, so that he could indulge himself in this way, thus giving rise to the story (doubtless false) that Nero fiddled while Rome burned.

By 68 Nero had become so unpopular that he was driven from power by revolts in the provinces. When he committed suicide before his enemies could lay their hands on him, the Julio-Claudian dynasty came to an end. There then followed a year of civil war as four different military commanders fought among themselves to become the next emperor. When the dust finally settled, the Flavian dynasty had emerged, and Rome was now ruled by an elderly, well experienced man named Vespasian, who had the difficult task of restoring financial health from the ruins of Nero's reign and the civil war. One thing that Vespasian did to curry popular favor was to tear down Nero's lavish palace and to build over it a facility designed for public use and entertainment. This was the famous Colosseum, the place where the Romans staged their gladiatorial shows. Vespasian died in 79 and was succeeded first by his older and then his younger son. The older, named Titus (79-81), had assisted his father during the last years of Nero's reign in putting down a revolt of the Jews in Judea, ending in the capture of Jerusalem and the destruction of the magnificent temple erected by King Herod the Great during the reign of

Augustus. In keeping with Roman tradition, Titus celebrated his victory over the Jews with a victory parade in Rome, what the Romans called a triumph. To commemorate his victory permanently he erected an arch, the Arch of Titus, that still stands in Rome today, decorated with reliefs illustrating the triumphal procession.

Vespasian's younger son, Domitian (81-96), was a capable administrator of the empire, but he was not the most tactful person and eventually alienated many of the senatorial class, who came to fear him. This climate of suspicion resulted in Domitian falling victim to a conspiracy that ended the Flavian dynasty. The conspirators, however, were careful to make plans to have someone to place on the imperial throne immediately so as to avoid the outbreak of civil war. The new emperor was a man named Nerva (96-98), an aged senator without any children. Due to his childlessness, one of his first acts was to mollify the military by adopting as his son and successor a man named Trajan (98-117), who was middle-aged and well respected by the soldiers. Nerva and Trajan began the series of five good Antonine emperors, whose dynasty ended with its sixth bad member. It is no accident that this succession of five good emperors was brought about through a series of adoptions, whereas the sixth bad emperor who ended this dynasty had come to power as the result of being the biological son of the preceding emperor.

Trajan was very successful in governing the empire efficiently and effectively, and he also conducted successful wars in frontier areas. From one of these wars against Dacia (roughly modern Rumania) he enriched the Roman state by the capture of large amounts of silver and gold, which were used to lay out a large and lavishly built Forum or marketplace in Rome, Trajan's Forum, at one end of which he had erected a huge column measuring 100 feet high and decorated on its outside by reliefs spiraling from bottom to top that through its sequence of scenes narrated the events of the Dacian War. In order to have enough space for this large public area, thousands of workmen had to chip away at a rocky hill (125 feet high), and out of its cut-away face they fashioned a large semi-circular vertical surface, out of which they constructed a series of about 150 shops in six levels to form a gigantic shopping mall, where almost everything manufactured or traded in the Roman Empire could be purchased. Consequently, for the next 300 years Trajan's Forum was about the nicest place in Rome for people to do their shopping.

Since Trajan, like Nerva, wound up being childless, he adopted the son of a cousin to succeed him. This was Hadrian (117-138). Both he and Trajan's family came from southern Spain. By the time that Hadrian became emperor, he had held an impressive series of important governmental posts and was well experienced in both administration and military affairs. In addition, he was very well educated, probably Rome's most educated and learned emperor. Since he possessed such a keen curiosity about everything, he decided not to sit in Rome and to govern the empire from there through his network of subordinates, instead, he went on tour, spending many years of his reign in traveling through all parts of the empire, combining business and pleasure by sight-seeing and supervising at first-hand the regional and local affairs in the various provinces.

There still stand in Rome today two impressive monuments from Hadrian's reign. One is the Pantheon that Hadrian is supposed to have designed himself. It is still one of the great monuments of all time. It was intended to be a temple dedicated to all the gods worshiped by the Romans, hence the building's name. Although it is now largely a huge tourist attraction, it is technically a church. Its main entrance resembles a large ornate Greek temple, but this merely leads one into the structure itself, which is in the shape of an enormous octagon surmounted by a gigantic hemispherical dome with a circular opening at the top, measuring thirty feet in diameter. The hemisphere is an architectural wonder, free standing and measuring more than 140 feet in diameter. At its base it is very thick and composed of strong heavy material for bearing the weight of the whole structure, but as it ascends, it becomes thinner and is composed of increasingly lighter material.

The other Hadrianic structure is Hadrian's Tomb, a very large monument in the shape of a cube surmounted by a cylinder and embellished with all manner of refinements. From the Middle Ages onward it was incorporated into the fortifications around the Vatican to defend the popes from enemy attack, and it has been altered in various ways over the centuries. It is now known as the Castel Sant'Angelo and houses the Italian Stock Exchange among other things.

Since Hadrian too was childless, he was succeeded by his adopted son Antoninus Pius (138-161), whose family came from southern Gaul. Although the ancient sources about him are rather meager, it is clear that he was a very decent man, considerate of others, and a conscientious ruler, whom Marcus Aurelius greatly admired and regarded as an ideal emperor to be imitated. Once again, since Antoninus Pius was childless, he used adoption to place Marcus Aurelius (161-180) into position to succeed him. During his early years Marcus Aurelius became interested in philosophy and especially admired the writings and teachings of the Stoic philosopher Epictetus. As we can see from his *Meditations* (Text #19 in PSWC), Marcus Aurelius attempted to put his philosophical learning into actual practice even when he was the all-powerful ruler of the Roman Empire. It is interesting to note that early on in his own life, before becoming a famous philosopher, Epictetus had been a slave, so that teachings of a former slave exercised a profound influence upon the most powerful man in the Roman Empire. The emperor's serene and serious majesty is beautifully portrayed in his famous equestrian statue that has survived.

For the past sixty years or so the Roman Empire had been enjoying peace and prosperity watched over by able emperors. Marcus Aurelius was the last in the succession of the five good Antonines, but since Germanic tribes along the Danube frontier of the Roman Empire were now threatening war and invasion, Marcus Aurelius was obliged to spend much of his reign in this area as he personally supervised Roman military operations that eventually proved successful in holding back these tribes. Like Trajan before him, Marcus Aurelius erected a column in Rome to commemorate his military successes in defending the empire. But unlike the previous Antonine rulers, Marcus Aurelius and his wife had several children, so that the imperial succession for the first time in over eighty years actually involved biological inheritance instead of adoption. Accordingly, when Marcus Aurelius died on the Danube frontier in 180, he was succeeded by his young son Commodus, who unfortunately repeated the same pattern as Nero. Since Commodus was at first surrounded by capable persons appointed by his father, the empire continued to run smoothly, but eventually the character of Commodus' reign changed as these people went into retirement and were replaced by less competent individuals, and as Commodus himself grew older and became more assertive. Commodus' primary preoccupation, however, was to become a great gladiator, which filled the serious minded members of the ruling class with loathing and disgust. This led to distrust and mutual suspicion, which eventually resulted in a conspiracy to poison Commodus at lunchtime on December 31 of 192. When he went off to take a nap and awoke vomiting instead of dying, the conspirators persuaded Commodus' wrestling coach to go into his bedroom and finish the job by strangling him.

Commodus' death ended the Antonine dynasty and led to a period of civil war similar to what had happened after Nero's death. Eventually the Severan dynasty emerged with its first member being Septimius Severus (193-211), a man from North Africa and married to a very capable woman, Julia Domna, from Syria. This dynasty witnessed the twilight of the Principate. The relatively peaceful conditions along Rome's Rhine and Danube frontiers slowly disappeared as Rome's neighbors became increasingly hostile. Septimius Severus added to this problem by embarking upon an ill-advised war against the Parthians on Rome's Euphrates frontier, which involved the Romans in many decades of unsuccessful and costly fighting. He commemorated his victories by erecting a magnificent triple arch in the Roman Forum that still stands there today. He and his son Caracalla (211-217) abandoned all tact in dealing with the senate and its cherished Republican traditions. Instead, they relied blatantly upon military force to keep themselves in power and to carry out their plans. According to one ancient source, when Septimius was on his death bed, he advised his two sons to rule in harmony, to enrich the soldiers, and not to bother with anything else. His two sons, however, hated each other; and within a few months Caracalla killed his own brother in their mother's presence. Then when Caracalla complained to his commander of the praetorian guard that many Romans were unhappy with what he had done, the man, Papinian, one of Rome's greatest legal scholars, frankly and honestly replied, "fratricide is a hard thing to justify." Caracalla rewarded Papinian's frankness by having this eminent jurist executed. Caracalla soon reaped the reward of his own brutality by falling victim to assassination; and the Severan dynasty staggered along for another seventeen years (218-235) under two more members of the family. The more obvious and unsavory role played by the military in the affairs of this dynasty is seen clearly from the fate of its last member, Severus Alexander (222-235): for when he displayed his inability to deal adequately with one of Rome's enemies on the Rhine frontier, some of his officers, regarding him as militarily ineffectual, formed a conspiracy and murdered him.

As we will see in Lecture 17, with the ending of the Severan dynasty the Roman Empire was plunged into a period called the Military Anarchy (235-284), a period of extraordinary turmoil and chaos that nearly caused the total collapse of the Roman Empire. Consequently, the Severan dynasty marked the end of the Principate, its relative peace and prosperity, never to be seen again. Moreover, this brief survey of the political history of the Roman Principate has demonstrated the strengths and weaknesses of hereditary monarchy, as well as the need for a society to have persons of good character and judgment in positions of extraordinary power.

LECTURE 15
Society and Economy of the Roman Empire

IMPORTANT TERMS AND CONCEPTS

- **Roman Frontier:** Hadrian's Wall, Rhine, Danube, Euphrates, North African desert.
- **Roman Army:** professionalism, size, distribution, role in promoting Romanization and the growth of towns.
- **Romanization:** adoption of Latin language and Roman culture.
- **Romance Languages:** Latin > Italian, French, Spanish, Portuguese, Rumanian.
- Latin-speaking West vs. Greek-speaking East.
- **slavery:** permeating all levels of society, freed slaves became Roman citizens, upward social mobility very common.
- **Town life:** local government, basic amenities (aqueducts, public baths, theater, library, gymnasium, stadium).
- **Pompeii:** typical town of central Italy, buried 79 A.D. by volcanic eruption, frozen in time to reveal daily life.
- **Family Life:** nuclear family, hard living conditions, evidence of epitaphs.

I will begin this lecture by quoting and commenting upon two passages from Roman poets who lived during the time of Augustus, because these quotations nicely sum up the great civilizing success achieved by the Roman Empire during the Principate, whose political history we surveyed last time. The first quotation comes from the greatest Roman poet, Vergil, and it is probably the most quoted part of all his writings. The lines contrast the great intellectual, artistic, and literary achievements of the Greeks with the extraordinary success of the Romans in organizing and operating a vast empire that comprised numerous different peoples.

> "Others shall cast the breathing bronze more softly. So I do believe. They shall draw living countenances from marble. They shall plead cases better. They shall map the paths of heaven with the compass and shall speak of the rising constellations. You, Roman, remember to rule people with your empire. These shall be your arts. Add civilization to peace. Spare the conquered, and war down the proud."

The second quotation comes from the poet Horace, a contemporary and friend of Vergil, and it elegantly expresses the indebtedness that the Romans had to the Greeks in developing their own distinctive literature by borrowing and adapting the literature of the Greeks.

> "Conquered Greece captivated its fierce conqueror and introduced the arts into the rustic land of the Latins."

As we have seen, the Romans during the middle Republic (264-133 B.C.) first conquered the central and western Mediterranean areas before taking over the eastern Mediterranean that comprised the Greek Hellenistic culture. When the Romans established their power over the western areas, most people in that region were still living in a semi-civilized tribal state. As time progressed, these people developed Romanized ways, including town life and the Latin language, so that during the Principate the western half of the Roman Empire became Roman and Latin in terms of its culture and language, whereas the eastern half of the Roman Empire, which had long been Greek in culture and language, remained so. Thus, the Roman Empire during the

Principate was characterized by a Greco-Roman culture with a Latin West and a Greek East.

The success of Romanization in the western half of the empire is evident from the survival into modern times of the Romance languages. When the Roman Empire finally fell apart during the fifth century, it obviously disrupted the communication between different regions; and as populations became isolated from one another, their common Latin language changed and developed along different lines, so that in the course of centuries what had been a single language of the Romans developed into five different, but interrelated languages that we term the Romance languages: Italian, French, Spanish, Portuguese, and Rumanian. The first four are spoken today in western Europe in what had once been a large part of the western Roman Empire, whereas Rumanian is the only Romance language located in what had been the eastern half of the empire. This is because the Emperor Trajan added that region to the Roman Empire as the province of Dacia; and since it lay north of the Danube and outside the zone of Greek language and culture, the inhabitants adopted Latin, not Greek, as their language. We can therefore see that the Roman Empire, though it passed out of existence 1500 years ago, continues to have an important impact upon the languages of Europe still spoken today.

In addition, by the time the Romans embarked upon their conquest of the Mediterranean during the middle Republic, Greek culture had become the principal and prestige culture of the eastern and central Mediterranean; and the Romans began to come under its influence, so that during the last two centuries B.C. talented Romans borrowed the basic literary forms of the Greeks (poetry, historical writing, drama, philosophy, etc.) and produced their own rich body of Roman literature written in Latin verse and prose. We have already encountered the historical writings of Livy and Tacitus, the two most important Roman historians of the Republic and Principate respectively. Cicero, whom we have also encountered, was Rome's greatest orator during the late Republic and composed numerous works on philosophy, political thought, and the art of rhetoric. Vergil, from whom I have just quoted, composed a monumental epic poem entitled *The Aeneid*,

Cicero → Rome's greatest Orator

which told the story of how Aeneas, one of the few Trojan survivors from the Trojan War, after years of wandering eventually made his way to central italy and became the ancestor of the Roman people. In writing this epic poem Vergil was heavily influenced by the two great Homeric poems of the Greeks, *The Iliad* and *The Odyssey*. As the western provinces became Romanized during the first two centuries of our era, Latin literature was further enriched by authors from Spain, Gaul, and North Africa. Taken together, all these developments demonstrate the truth summed up in the two quotations from Vergil and Horace.

The Principate established by Augustus proved to be relatively stable and gave the inhabitants of the Roman Empire peace for a very long time. In fact, this area enjoyed the longest period of peace in all of its history. If you travel today throughout western Europe, the eastern Mediterranean, or the northern part of Africa, you are likely to come upon remains of structures built during this time period. The Roman Empire took in a vast area, an area that now comprises about thirty different nations. One thing that Augustus did was to establish rational and defensible frontiers for the empire. In Europe the two great rivers of the Rhine and Danube served as barriers between the empire and warlike Germanic tribes. Everything west of the Rhine and south of the Danube belonged to the Roman Empire. In the east the Euphrates River was the boundary between the Roman and Parthian Empires. The latter were a people who had replaced the Seleucids as the rulers of Mesopotamia and Iran, and during the Principate they occasionally fought wars with the Romans for control of border areas. The southern boundary of the Roman Empire was the desert of Africa. The Romans succeeded in developing the region along the Mediterranean coast of Africa into a prosperous civilized region.

In order to keep this enormous area secure from outside attack or invasion, the Romans stationed a large, well trained army at strategic points along the frontiers. This military was highly professional and in many ways resembled modern armies, the main difference, of course, being the lack of modern technology. The Roman Imperial army comprised thirty legions and an equal number of auxiliary forces. Each legion numbered about 5000 men, and all legionaries had to be Roman citizens. The auxiliary forces, on the other hand, were composed of non-Roman provincials, and an equal number of them served alongside the legionary forces. The total number of people serving in the Roman Imperial army was about 350 thousand, and the forces were stationed where they were thought to be needed to guarantee the security of the frontiers, with the heaviest concentration being along the Rhine and Danube. The second heaviest concentration of these forces lay along the eastern frontier with Parthia.

Besides protecting the empire from outside attack, the Roman Imperial army also played an important role in the empire's society and culture. At the beginning of the Principate these forces were stationed in areas that were largely devoid of Roman citizens and culture, but the presence of Roman soldiers in these regions over time succeeded in Romanizing the people of these areas. In addition, one important consequence of serving in the auxiliary units was the gradual Romanization of the non-Roman provincial soldiers. In fact, if an auxiliary soldier succeeded in completing his required thirty years of military service, he received as part of his discharge benefits the legal status of a Roman citizen, and this same status was granted to his wife and children. As a result, in the course of time the Roman Imperial army served as an important mechanism in Romanizing a significant portion of the population. Furthermore, the concentration of soldiers along the frontiers promoted the growth of towns and cities in these areas, because the army units consumed enormous amounts of food and other things, which prompted the surrounding population to develop their economy to service the needs of the soldiers, and this led to the growth of town and city life that was characteristic of Roman civilization. In fact, if you look at a map of Europe and locate all the modern cities along the Rhine and Danube, virtually every one of them goes back to a Roman military encampment of the Principate.

One of the few additions made to the Roman Empire after Augustus was England as the Roman province of Britain, conquered by the Emperor Claudius. In order to establish a secure and defensible frontier, the Emperor Hadrian oversaw the construction of a wall, 84 miles long, stretching across northern England. Hadrian's Wall measured fifteen feet high and was ten feet thick. It was fronted by an enormous ditch and guarded by forts and watch

PSWC #20

towers at regular intervals along its entire length. Portions of this fortification still survive today. Of course, the presence of Roman military forces promoted Romanization in the province, which included the development of town life and the spread of Latin. Text #20A in PSWC is a very interesting and revealing document. It is a short Latin text written on a thin piece of wood, dating to about 100 A.D. and discovered not too many years ago in northern England not far from Hadrian's Wall. It is a simple note written by the wife of a Roman soldier and is addressed to her sister, who was also married to a Roman soldier in a nearby settlement. In the text the one sister invites the other to come with her family to celebrate her birthday on September 11. It therefore gives us a glimpse into the life and family activities of ordinary Romans.

Besides the Roman Imperial army, another important institution of Roman society was slavery. We have touched upon slavery in connection with other civilizations. It has existed in virtually all pre-industrial societies, because given such societies' very low level of technology, slavery was necessary as a way of mobilizing human labor in order to get things done. Slavery was an integral part of Roman society, and one would have encountered slaves at all social levels and in all facets of the economy: performing very hard and dangerous work in mines or workshops, working on the large agricultural plantations of the wealthy, working alongside ordinary farmers and shop owners who were prosperous enough to afford a slave or two, and working as domestics in many households. The Roman emperor would have been the biggest slave owner of all, with thousands working for him in many capacities and in all areas of the Roman Empire, with many of them enjoying considerable status and influence. It was very common in Roman society for masters to free their slaves, and in Roman law a freed slave automatically became a Roman citizen. Consequently, freed slaves became another important element in the growing numbers of Romans in the Roman Empire, and many of these freed slaves became quite successful. In fact, we possess numerous inscriptions, either as epitaphs or local public decrees, in which a freedman celebrates and advertises his success story as a businessman and/or respected pillar of his community. This can also be illustrated by Text #21 in PSWC. It comes from a novel written during the reign of Nero, *The Satyricon* of

PSWC #21

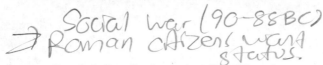
Social War (90-88 BC)
→ Roman citizens want status.

Petronius, in which a former slave briefly tells the story of his life to impress his dinner guests: how he began life as a slave, obtained his freedom, went into business for himself, and made a killing in shipping, so that he became fabulously wealthy and wound up living in a mansion like a king. Although this fictional character is exaggerated for comic effect, he nevertheless represents a common phenomenon of Roman society, the rags-to-riches success enjoyed by many Roman slaves.

As we have seen in connection with our survey of the history of the late Republic, the Romans granted citizenship to all their Italian allies as a result of the so-called Social War (90-88 B.C.), so that Italy became a Roman nation. During the first two centuries of the Principate Roman citizenship was slowly granted to people who lived outside of Italy in the provinces, sometimes to individuals and other times to entire communities, as they became fully Romanized and desired to be incorporated into Roman society, culture, and the political system. By the close of the Principate (212 A.D.) this pattern of gradual Romanization and granting of citizenship had progressed so far that the Emperor Caracalla completed it by issuing a decree that bestowed Roman citizenship upon all free inhabitants of the empire.

It has been estimated that the population of the Roman Empire during the Principate was somewhere around sixty million. This is a very large number, but the population inhabiting this area now is far larger, because most regions in this area now are industrialized and have a much higher population density than pre-industrial societies like that of the Roman Empire. Probably about 80% of the Principate's population would have lived on small farms, much like the heavily rural United States of the nineteenth century. The rest of the population would have lived in towns and cities, whose growth and proper functioning the Romans promoted all across the empire by ensuring that each community possessed at least the basic amenities: an abundant supply of fresh water, a reliable food supply, roads and bridges, temples for worship, public baths, gymnasia and libraries, theaters, stadia, and other public buildings for commerce and government. The Romans were excellent engineers and built structures that were not only designed to serve the needs of ordinary people, but were also impressive and elegant. During the first century B.C.

they discovered how to make concrete, and this building material gave them tremendous flexibility in constructing large and complicated structures.

On the other hand, the Roman government itself was quite small and unobtrusive compared to our modern gigantic national governments with their numberless government programs for everything under the sun, operated by an enormous bureaucracy and funded by an Everest-size mountain of tax money. During the Principate most government took place at the local level with each town or city having its own magistrates, council of leading men, and citizen body. Text #20B in PSWC is revealing in this regard. It is an inscription from a wealthy woman's tomb in a town south of Rome. The text indicates that the woman donated to her community a large sum of money that was to be invested, so that the interest earned could be given out as monthly welfare payments to 100 girls and 100 boys. There was no governmental welfare program. With few exceptions, social assistance was provided at the local level by private organizations or by wealthy benefactors, such as the woman profiled in this text. Pompeii → a city in time.

Perhaps the single most detailed illustration of Roman Imperial town life comes from Pompeii, a town located on the beautiful Bay of Naples south of Rome and at the foot of Mt. Vesuvius. On August 24 of 79 A.D. Mt. Vesuvius erupted and buried the entire city in a deep layer of ash. The city was never reoccupied. For nearly 300 years (since the 1730s) excavations have been conducted at this site, which informs us moderns as if it were a gigantic time capsule, an entire town frozen in time.

When uncovered, the walls of buildings still contained private graffiti and public announcements, of which you have a few examples in Text #20C in PSWC. Early on in their excavations archaeologists discovered that there were hollow pockets in the ground where a human body, a dog, or the like had been buried by ash, but over time as the ash stayed in place, the organic remains slowly deteriorated and were washed away. Thus, by pouring liquid plaster into these pockets and letting it harden, they were able to reproduce in surprising detail replicas of these dead bodies.

But far more important are the countless artifacts and buildings. Modern tourists can stroll down the ancient sidewalks and streets, looking inside shops and private homes. The inner walls of the latter were often painted in various designs or with scenes, and their floors were often decorated with mosaics, which was an art developed by the Romans.

We will now end this survey of life in the Roman Principate by examining the evidence of tombstones or epitaphs, thousands of which have survived. As you can see from the samples presented in Text #20D in PSWC, they allow ordinary people of the distant past to speak to us directly about what they did during their lives, what they believed to be awaiting them after death, and how deeply they mourned for the loss of their loved ones. Like modern-day Western society, Roman society was based upon the nuclear family: husband, wife, and children. For most families life would have been rather hard and would have required them all to work and to work together in order to get by. They did not have cars for easy transportation, or washers and dryers for doing their laundry, or microwave ovens to cook their food. All these things had to be done the old-fashioned hard way with human labor only slightly relieved and assisted at times by animal labor. The emotions expressed in these epitaphs also indicate that family life was more or less what we moderns experience today: love and close companionship between spouses, and affection between parents and children. The epitaphs also show us what they believed about the possibility of an afterlife. Many people thought that their spirits would be descending into an underworld, where they would happily spend the rest of eternity, but others expressed agnosticism on their tombstone or outright disbelief in life after death.

Since many of these epitaphs specify the age of the deceased at the time of death, they give us a large body of data useful in estimating the average life expectancy. Before the development of modern medicine and good preventive health care, which we take for granted, all societies, including that of the Roman Principate, experienced high rates of infant and child mortality, and infections of almost any sort could take people away at virtually any time in their lives. Thus, although we know of many instances in which Romans lived into their seventies or eighties and even into their nineties, getting to that ripe old age was far rarer then than it is today. In fact, when we add up the ages at death to come up with an average life expectancy, the figure thus calculated is about 32 years, less than half of what it is now in the United States. Consequently, although we can see many similarities between the lives of people then and now, such as a commonly shared emotional atmosphere of the nuclear family, there are also some differences resulting from the vastly different technologies of a pre-industrial vs. an industrialized society. As the result of a much shortened life expectancy, the trauma caused by the deaths of loved ones would have affected the lives of the members of this pre-industrial society far more than most of us today.

LECTURE 16
Christianity in the Roman Empire

IMPORTANT DATES AND TERMS (ALL DATES ARE A.D.)

- **32:** Approximate date for the death of Jesus.
- **312:** Conversion of Constantine.
- **391:** Imperial edict forbidding all forms of Pagan worship.
- **395:** Permanent division of the Roman Empire into eastern and western halves with their own emperors.
- **syncretism** = blending together.
- **mystery religion:** initiation into religious mysteries involving the myth of a dying and reviving divine figure to ensure personal salvation.
- **cult of Isis and Serapis:** syncretic religious cult from Egypt, produced during Hellenistic Period and very popular in Roman Imperial times.
- **Messiah** = Greek Christos, "anointed one:" God-sent leader to defeat Judaism's enemies and to establish a supreme Jewish kingdom on earth.
- **Christian salvation:** original sin of all mankind inherited from Adam and Eve as the result of their disobedience of God; redemption made possible by the sacrifice of Jesus; salvation through faith in the resurrection.
- **orthodoxy:** correct religious belief as determined by the Roman government.

- **heresy:** unacceptable religious belief as decreed by the Roman government.

We are now beginning the third quarter of this course, and one of the major themes will be Christianity. This lecture will examine the origin of Christianity and its gradual spread and acceptance throughout the Roman Empire. In doing so, we will treat these matters not in terms of religious faith, but from the perspective of historians, who attempt to explain religious developments as the outgrowth of social and cultural factors.

First, we need to recognize that Christianity was part of a much larger religious culture that was characteristic of the Hellenistic world. If you recall, when we surveyed the Hellenistic world in Lecture 11, we found that one of its chief characteristics was syncretism, the blending together of the Greek and ancient Near Eastern cultural traditions to form a hybrid culture. In explaining this I used the area of religion to demonstrate Hellenistic syncretism, because perhaps our best illustration of syncretism is the phenomenon of Hellenistic mystery religions.

There were several mystery religions that arose and flourished from Hellenistic times on into the Roman Empire. They usually shared the common feature of having a central divinity who suffered death and then resurrection. This myth was then translated into symbolic rituals either witnessed or enacted by initiates, so that the central divinity was identified with the initiate, who was thereby given the promise of ever-lasting life after death. When we surveyed ancient Egypt in Lecture 3, we looked at the cult of Isis and Osiris. The latter was thought to have died and then was brought back to life through the magical spells of his wife Isis to become ruler of the dead, while his son Horus succeeded to his throne as ruler of the living. In Hellenistic times this cult was modified slightly to fit with Greek religious ideas, and Osiris was renamed Serapis. The mystery religion of Isis and Serapis spread from Egypt and became quite popular throughout the eastern Mediterranean.

A mystery religion was so-called, because it involved the teaching of myths and doctrines concerning the ultimate mystery of what happens to us after

Judaism ⟹ originally did not believe in afterlife ⟹ mystery religions influence that

death. But they were also called mystery religions, because initiates were bound by oath not to reveal the religion's doctrines to non-initiates. These different mystery religions formed the overall religious culture in which Christianity originated and then spread.

Secondly, it is important to understand the nature of Judaism during later Hellenistic times and the Roman Principate, c.200 B.C. to c.100 A.D. If we could travel in a time machine back to that period, we would find that Judaism was not one religion, but many different variations of a common religious tradition, somewhat like today with the different brands of both Judaism and Christianity. When we looked at early Judaism in Lectures 6 and 7, we traced its development down through the period of the Persian Empire (550-330 B.C.), and I pointed out that the early Jews had little interest in the afterlife. There are a few references in Old Testament literature to Sheol, an underworld to which people's souls descended after death, but it was not a place of happiness or joy. The souls existed there in a shadowy and vague way, resembling what we encountered in the Epic of Gilgamesh. This situation began to change as Judaism came under the influence of the larger Hellenistic religious culture with its mystery religions and their doctrines of a dying and reviving god that promised worshippers a happy afterlife. As a result of these influences, some Jews began to entertain the idea that the afterlife was something rather different from the shadowy Sheol, but instead, it resembled the eternal existence promised by the Hellenistic mystery religions. Consequently, Christianity in that sense can be viewed as Judaism's Hellenistic mystery religion, because it involved the death and resurrection of its central divine figure (Jesus), and the resurrection was central to the believer's salvation.

Let us now turn to the Jewish notion of the Messiah. This is a Hebrew word that simply means "the anointed one." The term was later translated into Greek as Christos, so that Christ is a word indicating that his followers regarded Jesus as the Messiah. The word refers to the practice of using a holy oil to anoint the head of a king of the Hebrew people in a kind of coronation ceremony. Saul was the first person to be chosen as king over all the twelve Hebrew tribes to lead them against the Philistines, and the judge Samuel used holy oil to anoint Saul to symbolize that Saul was Yahweh's chosen one to rule over his chosen people. Such anointing continued with the other kings until the two royal lines were exterminated, when the northern kingdom of Israel was wiped out by the Assyrians in 721 B.C., and then the southern kingdom of Judah was conquered by the Babylonians in 586 B.C.

The idea of the messiah reemerged as an important idea among the Jews at the time of the Maccabean Revolt in the 160s B.C. When the Seleucid King Antiochus IV tried to establish polytheistic practices in Judah, many Jews rose up in rebellion to defend their traditional monotheism. They succeeded in driving out agents of the Seleucid Empire from their land and to reestablish their former ceremonies, which they commemorated with the celebration of Hanukkah. This religious revolution was also accompanied by a political one, in which a new dynasty of Jewish kings (the Hasmoneans) emerged to rule over Judah. At first some regarded the new ruler as God's messiah, but as these rulers showed themselves to be all too flawed, the idea of the messiah took on a more august religious interpretation. According to this view, at The End of Days God would send his messiah to lead the Jews in a world conquest that would usher in a kind of universal Jewish Empire and Utopia. Thus, the messiah was henceforth often viewed as a powerful military leader, but there were others who saw him in more religious and mystical terms, because they associated him with The Last Judgment in which there would be a resurrection of all the dead and then God's judgment of both the living and the resurrected dead, with the condemned being consigned to Gehenna, the lake of fire (hell), and the approved being elevated to heaven or to the earthly paradise now established by God and the messiah. All these ideas were current in Judaism before, during, and after Jesus' lifetime.

Another, somewhat related development in Judaism at this time involved a group known as the Zealots. When the Romans first became the dominant power in the eastern Mediterranean, they were content to allow the Jews to be ruled over by their own kings, who were themselves subservient to Rome as client kings. The most famous of these client kings of Judah (or Judea, as the Romans called it) was Herod the Great, who ruled during the years 37-4 B.C. He was succeeded in Judea by one of his sons, Archelaus, but in 6 A.D. Augustus deposed him, because the Jews had come to hate him. But rather

kings were subservient to Rome → god switch causes rome to tax the Jews than replacing him with another Jewish client king, Augustus decided to join Judea to the larger province of Syria and to place Judea under the administration of a Roman official with the title prefect. Part of this change involved the Romans taking a systematic census of the population and then imposing Roman taxation on the people. This did not sit well with a small number of Jews, because as they saw it, God's people and God's land should not be subject to the power or taxation of a non-Jewish people. Those who opposed Roman rule and taxation on these grounds came to be known as Zealots from a Greek word indicating that they were extremely devoted or zealous in their strict monotheism. As the decades of the first century passed, this group became larger and began to carry out terrorist attacks upon Romans and their Jewish sympathizers in Judea. They finally became so powerful that they persuaded their fellow Jews to rebel against Roman rule in 66 A.D. The uprising was crushed after four years of fighting, ending with the Roman capture and destruction of Jerusalem along with the magnificent temple built by Herod the Great. The only part of this structure that survived destruction was the so-called Wailing Wall.

The idea of the messiah had actually played an important role in this Jewish revolt, because many Jews then believed that they were living during The End of Days, that God would soon send them the messiah, and that The Last Judgment was not far off. In fact, while Jerusalem was being besieged by the Romans in 70 A.D., many Jews inside the city were expecting that God would miraculously intervene to rescue them and destroy the Roman forces. In addition, our most important source of information on Jewish history for this period, a man named Josephus, tells us of two messianic figures during the 40s and 50s A.D. They claimed to possess miraculous powers and attracted large followings in Judea until they were eventually apprehended and executed.

Let us now finally turn to Jesus himself. Virtually all that we know about him comes from the four Gospels of *The New Testament*: *Matthew, Mark, Luke, and John*. An entire field of academic study has evolved out of the examination of these works in order to try to reconstruct an accurate picture of what Jesus did, and how he viewed himself. The modern scholarly consensus is that the four Gospels were written during the period 70-100 A.D., and that none of them was composed by a person who had personally known Jesus. *Mark* was the first of the Gospels to be written, probably around 70 A.D. and therefore about forty years after the crucifixion. *Mark* is the shortest and the simplest of the four Gospels. *Matthew* and *Luke* were probably written next; and as can be seen from a side-by-side comparison of Mark with Matthew and Luke, the latter two works largely reproduced the text of Mark along with additional material. Since these three Gospels have much in common, modern scholars refer to them as the synoptic Gospels, synoptic being a Greek word meaning "viewed together." *John* was probably written last and is rather different from the other three in both its content and theology, but all four have their own characteristic themes and different interpretations of Jesus and his mission. There are so many stories and sayings associated with Jesus in the four Gospels that it is difficult to come up with a biographical and religious picture of the man with which everyone agrees. Modern scholars of *The New Testament* have worked hard to devise objective analytical methods in order to sort the material into likely-historical and unlikely-historical categories, so that a reliable reconstruction can be obtained. Nevertheless, differences of opinion still abound, thus resulting in differing reconstructions and interpretations.

In any case, one theme that runs throughout much of the Gospel material is the idea that The End of Days is at hand. Jesus therefore may have accepted this idea and might have even regarded himself as the messiah who was to usher in the messianic age (see Text #22C in PSWC). Indeed, Paul believed that he would live to be part of The Last Judgment (see *Romans* 13.11, *I Thessalonians* 4.13-17, and *I Corinthians* 7.29-31).

Another theme that runs throughout the Gospel material involves the Pharisees, one of the major groups within Judaism at the time. Like many other Jews of the day, they were attempting to live holy lives; and their main concern was to do so by making sure that they were in strict compliance with the law of Moses, which they interpreted in a very legalistic manner, so much so that many at the time did and today do regard what they did as splitting hairs and nit-picking. One of their primary preoccupations was the observance of the sabbath every seven days when Jews were commanded to rest and to refrain from all forms of work. Now, if a farmer's sheep happened to fall into a pit on the sabbath, was it work for the farmer to pull his sheep out of the pit, or did he have to wait until the sabbath had ended? See *Matthew* 12.11-12. Jesus apparently had little patience with such legalistic hair-splitting and stated that the sabbath had been made for man, not the other way around. Many of his sayings seem to oppose legalistic interpretations and enjoined people instead to live in accordance with the spirit of the law of Moses, not to become bogged down with countless strictures that regulated their every move and action (see Text #22B in PSWC). If they simply loved God with all their hearts and their neighbors as themselves, all the rest would take care of itself (see Text #22A in PSWC).

According to *Luke* (3.1-23), Jesus was about thirty years old when he began his public ministry that coincided with the activity of John the Baptist, which Luke dates to the fifteenth year of the reign of the Emperor Tiberius (september 28-September 29 A.D.). Since according to *John*, Jesus' activities seem to have been spread over three years, he may have died sometime around 32 A.D. His end came when he decided to come to Jerusalem to observe the Passover. In fact, it was such an important Jewish festival that at that time of year Jerusalem was jam packed with Jews from all over the Roman Empire; and since the huge crowds often spawned disturbances, the Romans always stationed a small force in the city to watch and to keep the peace. The synoptic Gospels indicate that when Jesus came into the temple, he was outraged to see how commercialized it all was, with hundreds (if not thousands) of people buying lambs for sacrifice. He is said to have overturned the tables of the money-changers and preached to the crowd (see Text #22D in PSWC). If so, this certainly would have brought him onto the Roman and Jewish priestly radar screen as someone potentially dangerous and needing to be watched. Eventually, he was arrested, tried and convicted, and then executed. It makes good historical sense that the Romans had him executed as a trouble-making messiah and potential king of the Jews.

Not long after his execution, the rumor spread that Jesus had actually arisen from the dead, and it was this resurrection that now became central to Christianity: for Jesus' death and resurrection were now viewed by his followers in terms similar to a Hellenistic mystery religion, because Jesus was

[handwritten at top: Some Jews resisted the death of Jesus b/c Jesus was not the messiah that Jews described of.]

now regarded as the son of God, who had taken on mortal form, and by his death he had taken on all of mankind's burden of sin stretching back to the original disobedience of God by Adam and Eve in the Garden of Eden. People could now obtain their eternal salvation through belief and faith in Jesus as their savior.

The fifth book in *The New Testament, The Acts of the Apostles,* is our best source of information about the spread of Christianity during its first thirty years after the crucifixion. Since Jesus and his disciples had been Jews and had lived as Jews, the first Christians also regarded themselves as Jews, and that Jesus had been their messiah. As a result, at first they began to work among their fellow Jews in trying to convince them of this fact and to persuade them to adopt Jesus as their savior; and although some Jews joined this new movement, most Jews rejected it, largely because what Jesus had done did not fit at all well with the common Jewish idea of the messiah. Jesus had not been a powerful military figure. He had not led the Jews in victory over the other nations. He had simply been the son of a lowly carpenter from the one-horse town of Nazareth in Galilee, and then he had been executed ignominiously by the Roman authorities.

Accordingly, after meeting with modest success among their fellow Jews, but finding that many non-Jews were interested in this new-fangled religion, the apostles turned most of their attention into this latter direction, so that the early Christian movement soon divorced itself from Judaism. The apostles first established small fledgling groups of Christians in the various towns and cities of the Greek eastern half of the Roman Empire before doing the same in the Latin west. The movement began at the bottom of society and slowly worked its way up. Many poor people were attracted to Christianity because of its stress upon charity, an attribute that it had inherited from the prophetic tradition of Judaism: for as we have seen, the prophets of *The Old Testament* had constantly rebuked the rich and powerful for abusing the poor and weak. Christians were urged to donate what they could afford in order to help out fellow Christians who were in need.

Another very important attribute that Christianity inherited from Judaism was its strict monotheism. This had both positive and negative consequences.

[handwritten at bottom: messiah, giving, respect, monotheism]

On the one hand, as in the case of Judaism itself, it was probably responsible more than anything else in guaranteeing the long term survivability of the religion. On the other hand, strict monotheism made Christianity incompatible with the polytheistic religions of the Roman Empire and soon produced the phenomenon of religious persecution. Different polytheistic religions of the Roman Empire had no trouble in getting along with one another, because they simply equated one set of gods with another. Thus, when the Roman state wanted its gods to be worshipped and respected by the other peoples of the empire, the latter obliged, but it was a very different matter for the monotheistic Christians, who either denied the existence of other gods or regarded other peoples' polytheistic gods as demons and the agents of the Devil. As a result, when Christians were asked to participate in the usual religious activities of their town or city or of the Roman Empire itself, they either had to swallow their discomfort and go along with the crowd or to risk being singled out as atheists through their non-conformity.

We now come to the four readings that comprise Text #23 in PSWC. The first passage comes from the historian Tacitus and describes a persecution of Christians in Rome itself in the year 64 A.D. after the great fire that had destroyed much of the city. Since Nero took advantage of the fire by building an enormous and lavishly rich palace complex in the heart of Rome, many people in the city wrongly suspected that Nero had actually started the fire, but in order to turn suspicion away from himself, Nero decided to fasten the blame for the fire upon the newly arisen and poorly understood group of Christians. Consequently, many of them were arrested and subjected to horrible deaths as a form of public entertainment.

At this point, however, our evidence for the spread of Christianity disappears until we come to the second of these four readings (Text 23B in PSWC). It is an exchange of letters between a provincial governor, Pliny the Younger, and the Emperor Trajan, dating to 112 A.D. Pliny had recently been obliged to interrogate Christians and to punish any who persisted in their faith and refused to make token offerings to the gods of the Roman state. Since Pliny was unfamiliar with the whole matter of Christians, he wrote to Trajan to find out if he had acted correctly. Trajan replied that Pliny had acted properly, but he hastened to add that although being a Christian was illegal and worthy of punishment, Pliny should not seek them out, but if they were brought to his attention, he would need to enforce the law. Thus, the exchange informs us that at this time it was illegal to be a Christian, probably because the Roman state viewed it as a form of sedition, since Christians refused to acknowledge the gods of the Roman state.

This exchange of letters is also important in demonstrating the sporadic nature of persecution. In fact, there was no systematic attempt to persecute Christians throughout the whole empire until the middle of the third century. Before that time, persecution was a local phenomenon. Its overall nature can be neatly summed up by quoting Tertullian, one of the early Christian writers (c.200), who wrote that whenever there was a flood, drought, earthquake, famine, or epidemic, the cry went up, "Christians to the lions!" What this means is that when an area was struck by some disaster of nature, many of the people attributed it to divine wrath and figured that since there were Christians in their midst who were not worshipping the traditional gods, the gods were angry on that account. Consequently, Christians had to be sought out and either forced to worship the gods or executed for their atheism. Then and only then would the gods relent and stop harming the community with the local disaster.

When we look at the third of these four readings (Text #23C in PSWC), we see that the flip side of persecution was martyrdom. It is likely that when Christians began to be persecuted anywhere, many of them simply knuckled under for the time being in order to avoid bodily harm or death, but often there were a brave few who refused to give in and openly embraced their deaths. In this third text a Roman provincial governor interrogated several Christians and asked them repeatedly if they were in fact Christians, and he even urged them to give up their silliness so as to save their lives. He verbally cut them off when they tried to explain that they were not seditious dangerous people; they obeyed the laws and respected the emperor, but they worshipped one and only one god. In the end, when the governor could not persuade them to recant, he ordered them to be taken away for execution. As in the case of other convicted criminals, many victims of persecution died in the local arena as a form of public entertainment; and the Christian view was that these martyrs had suffered a fate similar to that of Jesus, so that when they died, they were instantly elevated to heaven and glorified for what they had done. During these early years of Christianity it was believed that when a person died, he went to sleep and remained in that state until The Last Judgment, at which time he would be resurrected, judged, and then either elevated to heaven or condemned to hell. Consequently, Christians who suffered death by martyrdom were thought to be rewarded for their self-sacrifice.

There were two periods when the Roman state attempted to carry out a systematic persecution of Christians. The First Great Persecution occurred during the years 250-260 during the time of the Military Anarchy when the Roman Empire was being invaded in the east and along the Rhine and into Gaul, to such an extent that it looked as if the empire might actually collapse. The rationale for the persecution was basically what it had always been, but this time, it was applied to the whole empire. Since the Romans believed that they had acquired their empire in part due to divine favor, the disasters of the Military Anarchy convinced many that these troubles resulted from divine displeasure, which was caused by so many inhabitants not worshipping the gods. Thus, the Emperor Decius ordered that everyone in the empire had to come before a local official and to show his or her acknowledgement of the state's gods by some token gesture of worship: pouring out a small libation of wine, offering incense on an altar, or eating a small portion of meat from a sacrificed animal. People who did this were then issued a certificate, showing that they had done this. Anyone who was found without a certificate and refused to engage in some token form of worship was subject to punishment: death in the arena or serving out a sentence of hard labor in the mines.

The Emperor Valerian, however, (253-260 A.D.) decided instead to target the Christian leaders by depriving them of their social status in Roman society and by confiscating the properties owned by groups of Christians. Valerian's son and successor, Gallienus (260-268), called off the persecution, because he had far more difficult problems to face and did not need to be distracted by it. Christians then enjoyed about forty years of peace with the Roman government until in 303 the Second Great Persecution was begun by the Emperor Diocletian. It lasted eight years and resulted from the same official reasoning as the earlier persecution, but it was again called off by the government, partly because it was not easy to enforce, and partly because by now many non-Christians were familiar enough with Christianity and Christians that they did not believe that Christians were atheists or disloyal subjects of the Roman Empire. Indeed, persecution was often counterproductive. As Tertullian had written earlier (c.200), the blood of the martyrs was the seeds for the church: for the deaths of martyrs often attracted as many people to Christianity as they repelled.

In 312, on the heels of the Second Great Persecution, Christianity scored its first really big break with the Roman government. At that time two would-be emperors were contending for control of the western half of the Roman Empire: Constantine and Maxentius. The latter ruled Italy and Rome, whereas the former was master of Britain and Gaul. In order to challenge Maxentius, Constantine invaded Italy and marched on Rome. The two met in a big battle just north of Rome at the Mulvian Bridge. According to one contemporary source (see Text 23D in PSWC), on the night before the battle Constantine had a dream in which he was instructed to place the chi-rho symbol on his soldiers' shields if he wanted to win. The chi and rho were the first Greek letters of Christos, and they were written so that the X (chi) was vertically bisected by the P (rho). When Constantine defeated Maxentius and became master of the western half of the Roman Empire, he concluded that the god of the Christians must be a powerful being, and he would henceforth worship him.

For centuries Roman generals had been seeking divine support on the eve or even during the course of battles, but all these earlier instances had involved polytheistic gods, who simply received a nice temple in Rome for their assistance. It was far otherwise when it involved the exclusive, intolerant monotheistic deity of the Christians. Immediately following his conversion to Christianity, Constantine issued an edict guaranteeing universal religious toleration for all religions. This was intended to safeguard Christianity from further persecution, so that it was now legal to be a Christian. But within the space of just eighty years (311-391) Christianity rapidly went from a persecuted religion to one that was being favored, promoted, and encouraged by the Roman government, and governmental power was increasingly used to persecute all forms of polytheism along with Christian heresies, i.e. forms of Christianity not officially approved by the Roman state.

The ancient sources for this period give the impression that virtually the entire population of the Roman Empire embraced Christianity over the course of the fourth century, but the results of modern scholarship tell a very different story. It seems likely that at the time of Constantine's conversion to Christianity in 312 no more than ten percent of the empire's population was Christian, and the figure may be much less than that. This means that in 312 the Roman Empire was by no means on the verge of becoming fully Christian. In addition, by the year 391 when the Emperor Theodosius issued his blanket ban on all forms of paganism, probably about half of the empire's population were Christian, and the demographic distribution of Christians was quite uneven. Christians were largely concentrated in the towns and cities, whereas they were scarce in the countryside, where most of the empire's population resided; and Christians would have been more numerous in the Greek-speaking eastern provinces than in the Latin West. It therefore appears likely that governmental power from the top played an important role in how and why Christianity became dominant in Roman society during the fourth century.

In 325 Constantine presided over the very first universal (or ecumenical) church council, the Council of Nicaea. It brought together a large number of Christian bishops from all over the Roman Empire in order to resolve an important doctrinal dispute concerning the nature of the holy trinity (God the father, God the son, and the Holy Spirit) that had arisen in recent years. This council set an important precedent for future rulers interested in settling other theological controversies. The result was that the state placed its stamp of approval upon one particular variety of Christianity, and all other interpretations were condemned and branded as heretical and worthy of suppression by the state. Therefore, as Christianity became part of the governmental establishment, there arose a clear distinction between Christian orthodoxy (straight opinion) and heresy (choosing, i.e. choosing not to follow the right way).

Christianity was lucky in that Constantine was one of the most long lived emperors of all time (306-337), so that he was able to preside over a slow

Christianizing of the Roman government. In addition, Constantine established a dynasty of Christian sons to follow him on the imperial throne for another 24 years (337-361). Constantine and his successors were extremely generous in using state funds to build magnificent churches and to do other things to promote Christianity and to discourage polytheism, but for about sixty years (312-370) polytheism, though discouraged by the government, was often left alone. After Constantine, the only pagan to sit on the imperial throne was Julian, who ruled for less than two years (361-363), during which time he attempted to revive paganism and to suppress Christianity, but with his death in battle against the Persians in Mesopotamia, the line of Christian emperors resumed and remained uninterrupted. From 370 onwards the emperors pursued a much more aggressive anti-pagan policy and looked the other way when Christian vigilantes demolished and burned down pagan temples. Finally, in 391 the Emperor Theodosius issued a decree that banned all forms of pagan worship. Henceforth the Roman state would tolerate only orthodox Christianity as defined by the state.

LECTURE 17
The World of Late Antiquity

IMPORTANT DATES AND TERMS

- **235-284:** Military Anarchy of the Roman Empire, characterized by near collapse of the Roman Empire due to foreign invasions, Persian resurgence, and numerous internal military revolts.
- **284-337:** Reigns of the Emperors Diocletian and Constantine, characterized by reunification and drastic reorganization of the Roman Empire.
- **284-395:** Period of Late Antiquity.
- *395:* Final division of the Roman Empire into eastern and western halves.
- **410:** Alaric and the Visigoths sack Rome.
- *476:* Abdication of Romulus Augustulus, last Roman emperor of the West.
- **Constantinople:** founded by Constantine in 330, new capital of the eastern half of the Roman Empire.
- **Goths and Vandals:** Germanic tribes that invaded the Roman Empire.
- **Attila:** King of the Huns (434-453), ravaged central region of the Roman Empire.

This lecture will survey the last 300 years or so of the Roman Empire, roughly 235-568. This last major period of Roman history is called either Late

Antiquity or the Later Roman Empire. It falls into three parts: first, the Military Anarchy of about fifty years (235-284), then the period of Late Antiquity proper (284-395), and then a period during which the eastern and western halves of the Roman Empire begin to go their separate ways with the western half slowly disintegrating under the incursions of the various Germanic tribes, who carved their own kingdoms out of the Roman Empire. This last period had its beginning in 376 and lasted for nearly two centuries, finally ending with the arrival of the Langobards (Long Beards) or Lombards in northern Italy in 568.

If you will recall, Marcus Aurelius (161-180) spent much of his reign on the Danube frontier, supervising military operations against various hostile tribes in order to keep that sector of the empire safe from invasion. He succeeded quite well in that goal, but the pressure on the northern Rhine-Danube frontier continued to be a problem and gradually became worse during the Severan dynasty (193-235), the last of the four dynasties of the Principate that we have already surveyed in Lecture 14. In that sense the Severan dynasty can be viewed as transitional from the good times of the Principate proper and the much more troubled times of the Later Roman Empire.

Toward the end of the Severan dynasty, however, there arose a second major threat to the Roman Empire. This was the rise of the New Persian Empire during the 220s. As you may remember, around 100 B.C. the Seleucid Empire, the Asian portion of Alexander's vast conquests, finally collapsed. The area of Mesopotamia and Iran then came under the rule of a new ruling dynasty, the Parthians, who then became Rome's eastern neighbors for the next 300 years with the Euphrates River serving as the boundary between their two domains. During the Principate there were occasional wars fought between the Romans and the Parthians, but this sector of the Roman frontier became far more problematic with the rise of the New Persian Empire. This dynasty overthrew and replaced the Parthians; and since they came from the same southern region of Iran from which the rulers of the earlier Persian Empire had come (550-330 B.C.), they saw themselves as resurrecting the glory and pride of that earlier period and wished to extend their rule over what had once been the entire Old Persian Empire. Thus, during the third century the rulers of the New Persian Empire pursued a very aggressive policy against Rome, as they attempted to conquer the eastern provinces of the Roman Empire. Consequently, during much of the third century the Romans found themselves being attacked simultaneously along their northern and eastern frontiers.

These attacks proved to be very destabilizing and sent the Roman Empire into a tail-spin that we call the Military Anarchy. When the last Severan emperor, Alexander Severus (222-235), disappointed many of his soldiers in how he was dealing with the German threat along the Rhine, he fell victim to an assassination plot formed by his officers; and since there was no other member of the Severan dynasty to replace him, the assassination spelled the beginning of this tail-spin down into near collapse. Soon many areas of the Roman Empire were being invaded and ravaged by enemies. Germanic tribes crossed the Rhine and plundered Gaul. Another Germanic people, the Goths, who were living around the Black Sea, built ships and carried out raids all around the Aegean; and the Persians overran Syria and Anatolia. Since the Roman central government was unable to provide adequate defense against these attacks, the people in these threatened regions were often forced to mobilize their own military response in order to defend themselves. This occasionally prompted powerful leaders in these regions to go one step further in laying claim to the imperial throne itself, or they were often viewed as potential threats to the ruling emperor. This situation led to civil wars being fought out among these contenders and rivals as they were also having to deal with the very acute problems of foreign invasion. Both problems led to a rapid turn-over of emperors, as many fell victim to assassination or death in battle. As a result, the empire, already under serious threat externally, found itself destabilized even more by these internal difficulties.

In order to deal with these problems, the Roman Imperial government had to increase the size of the military. This in turn increased the need for higher taxes to pay for a larger military system. This added a greater economic burden upon the inhabitants of the Roman Empire. In addition, in order to have enough money to pay the soldiers, the Roman government issued more and more coins, but since they ran out of silver and gold, they began issuing large quantities of copper coins plated in silver to make them look like solid silver coins. The government in fact issued such large numbers of these devalued coins that it soon resulted in runaway inflation, which proved to be very devastating for everyone living in the Roman Empire. Moreover, as the government had to rely increasingly upon the soldiers in the army to defend itself, and as contenders and rivals for the imperial throne tried to win support with the army by promising the soldiers more and more in the way of pay, the soldiers became harder to control and often turned upon the civilian population in taking from it what they wanted and needed.

In 260, the chronological midpoint of the Military Anarchy, the Roman Emperor Valerian was not only defeated by the Persians, but he was captured and taken prisoner and died in captivity. He was the only emperor in all of Roman history to suffer such a fate. Things finally began to turn around for the better during the reign of Aurelian (270-275), who first restored Roman rule over the eastern provinces and then did the same in the west, but then he fell victim to assassination, so that there was another nine years of several emperors succeeding one another until things finally were restored to order with the accession of Diocletian (284-305). His reign and that of Constantine (306-337) can be taken together as forming an important watershed in the reorganization of the Roman government. When we compare the governmental system of the Principate with that of the Later Roman Empire, it is hard to believe that the latter grew out of the former, because they are so very different. The Principate had a rather simple and small government, basically consisting of just two levels, the relatively small government of Roman provincial administrators and the local governments of the towns and cities. When Diocletian and Constantine finished reorganizing everything, the government of the Later Roman Empire had four different levels, each with their own sizable bureaucracy. The whole empire was divided into four large regions called prefectures. They in turn were subdivided into twelve smaller areas called dioceses, which in turn were divided into more than one hundred even smaller areas called provinces; and then at the very bottom there was the government of the local towns and cities. All this restructuring

Late Roman Empire government was much larger and less efficient than previous one.

was done, of course, in the name of greater efficiency and control. As you might expect, however, what it produced was a vastly enlarged and much more expensive government that was actually much less efficient because of the vast size of the bureaucracy. In addition, given the continuation of economic hard times, it was often not easy for the ordinary person to have the government administer justice and do other things that it was supposed to do. It was not at all uncommon for people to have to bribe government officials to do what they should have been doing as part of their regular job. Widespread corruption therefore placed yet another burden upon the inhabitants of the Later Roman Empire.

As part of their attempt to create a highly centralized government that controlled everything, Diocletian and Constantine issued decrees in which they required people to remain in their various occupations, so that the empire's economy would be adequately serviced by farmers, carpenters, metal workers, shop keepers, etc. In short, the restructuring of the government resulted in the creation of a kind of totalitarian system in which the government tried to take over, operate, and manage about everything, either directly or indirectly. But given the conditions of ancient communications, it turned out to be a rather inefficient and ramshackle totalitarian system. Nevertheless, it did restore order and unity to the empire and gave it another century or so of life, during which, as we saw in the preceding lecture, Christianity arose to become the only religion officially tolerated by the government. Yet, as I have studied this period, I have often wondered whether the inhabitants of the Roman Empire might have been better off if it had collapsed during the Military Anarchy, because the reorganization of the Roman government imposed a very heavy burden upon its people.

Perhaps the single best illustration of the nature of the governmental system at this time is Diocletian's decree on maximum prices, issued in 301. Since inflation was still out of control, Diocletian decided to fix the problem by this decree, which established limits on what people could charge for goods and services in the marketplace. Of course, the decree utterly failed to fix the inflationary problem, because it did nothing to address the actual cause of inflation: namely, the government issuing larger quantities of relatively worthless coins. The decree simply ordered that all goods and services not be sold above specified limits, while the underlying economic forces kept driving up the prices of everything. Consequently, the decree quickly resulted in even more misery and unrest, as people tried to avoid selling their products at an economic loss by exchanging them in an underground economy or black market, and as the government proceeded to do its best in punishing them for disobeying the law. As a result, the decree was soon withdrawn, but it reveals very clearly the basic mindset of the government during this period. Emperors, like too many of our own governmental officials today, seem to employ child-like magical thinking. Such people, both past and present, think that they can establish control over anything and everything simply by issuing an executive order or passing a law, as if merely saying that something will be so will make it so. In fact, as the historical record demonstrates, governmental interference into the marketplace, more often than not, produces unintended consequences, which are usually worse than the problem that the government is trying to fix. The economic forces of the marketplace are just as inexorable as the laws of physics or chemistry. A government might be able to use its power to withstand them for a short time, but like the tide turning and rushing in again, the fundamental laws of economics will eventually reassert themselves, no matter what the government wants or expects. For example, if you place something in a pressure cooker and turn up the heat, you can keep the cooker under control for a while by forcing down the lid with more weight, but if you keep applying the heat, it will eventually result in an explosion.

As we have seen, one of the most important trends of Late Antiquity was the Christianization of the Roman Empire. Another important development was the emergence of cities other than Rome to serve as imperial capitals. Given the threat of invasion across the frontiers, the emperors often spent most of their time in cities near these threatened areas. In fact, many emperors spent very little, if any, time at all, in Rome itself. Antioch in Syria, located near the frontier with the Persians, was often where the emperor stayed. There were various cities along or near the Rhine and Danube that also served as the imperial court. In addition, the problems of the empire were now so large that it was not uncommon for an emperor to have a brother, son, or other close *divisions of east/west Rome ⟹ easier to govern.*

relative assist him by having them each take half of the empire (western and eastern) to govern. This division of the empire into western and eastern halves became final in 395 when Theodosius died, leaving his two sons in charge of the two halves. From that point onward the two areas slowly went their own way historically. The western half disintegrated under invasions and settlement by Germanic tribes, and the eastern half of the empire continued on for another thousand years and evolved into the Byzantine state, although throughout its history the inhabitants of the Byzantine civilization continued to call themselves Romans.

This trend toward alternative imperial capitals and the growing division between east and west are well illustrated by Constantinople. The Greeks of the Archaic Period had first founded this city as a colony named Byzantium in 657 B.C., but in 330 A.D. Constantine officially designated it as his eastern capital; and the city was renamed in his honor. It was situated on a very defensible peninsula of the Bosporus, the strait between Anatolia and Europe; and it commanded the Golden Horn, a large curving bay (seven miles in length) suitable for receiving a high volume of trade from all over the Mediterranean. Moreover, in keeping with his conversion to Christianity, Constantine planned this city to be entirely Christian, with many magnificent churches, but no temples to pagan deities. Since the emperor himself lived there, the city grew and became large and prosperous and continued to be the capital of the Byzantine Empire long after the Roman Empire in the west ceased to exist.

Despite the problems of governmental inefficiency, corruption, and excessive control, the Later Roman Empire enjoyed relative peace and prosperity for slightly more than a century (284-395); and during this period the Romans were able to keep their foreign enemies largely at bay. The latter situation, however, began to change in 376 with the arrival of the Huns. Their collision into the Ostrogoths set in motion a series of movements, like the scattering of billiard balls, that eventually caused the collapse of the western half of the Roman Empire. Very little is known about the Huns, because they have left behind no written evidence about themselves. We only have relatively brief descriptions and accounts in Greek and Roman writers of this period.

The Huns were a nomadic people, probably an offshoot of the Turks, who, we will see, produced two other major disruptions in Western Civilization: the Seljuk Turks of the eleventh century, and the Ottoman Turks of the fourteenth and fifteenth centuries. In fact, from the eighth century B.C. onward there were occasional westward migrations of nomadic peoples from central or northeastern Asia that caused major disruptions among the civilizations of western Asia and eastern Europe. The huns were not farmers, but stock breeders, mostly of cattle; and they roamed about on the vast ranges of Asia to provide suitable grazing for their animals. Their families traveled about in wagons with their small quantities of personal goods. The males of the population virtually lived on horseback from the time that they could walk. They were therefore highly expert horsemen and used bows and arrows with equal expertise for hunting and waging war.

For reasons that we still do not understand, the Huns migrated westward, and in 376 they fell upon the Ostrogoths (eastern Goths) in the area of the Black Sea. The Ostrogoths in turn fled south and thus forced their southern neighbors, the Visigoths (western Goths), up against the lower Danube that separated them from the Roman Empire. When the Visigoths sought permission to cross the Danube and to seek refuge inside the Roman Empire, the imperial government granted them permission, but the Visigoths were so numerous that the Romans could not adequately cope with the refugee problem. Soon there were merchants selling commodities to the Visigoths at grossly inflated prices, because the items were in short supply. This created resentment and hostility between the Visigoths and Romans, which eventually prompted the former to take up arms against the latter. Thus, in 378 the two fought a huge battle at Adrianople, in which the Visigoths crushed the Roman army and even killed the emperor. Then over the next twenty years or so the Visigoths remained in the area south of the Danube and carried out raids upon Roman towns and cities of the Balkan Peninsula. When they had picked that whole region rather clean, they turned their attention to the west. Under the leadership of King Alaric they crossed the Alps and descended into Italy, raiding and plundering as they moved southward to Rome. When the people of Rome refused to open their gates and to pay a huge ransom in order to be left alone, the Visigoths in 410 captured the city and plundered it for three days. The Visigothic sack of Rome, the nominal capital of the empire, shocked the inhabitants of the empire and was only the beginning of many more bad things to come.

The Visigoths eventually left Italy, plundered their way across Gaul, and took up their final residence in southern and southwestern Gaul and part of Spain. Their westward movement, however, had also resulted in other Germanic tribes crossing into the Roman Empire: for in order to mount a defense of Italy against the advancing Visigoths, the Roman government removed all its forces from Roman Britain and also recalled forces from along the Rhine. Eventually, the Germanic tribes of the Angles and Saxons of Denmark and northern Germany began raiding the southern and eastern shores of Britain and then pushed back the native Celtic and Roman population to the west as they took over the land for themselves. Roman rule in Britain disappeared. The Germanic language of the Anglo-Saxons is the ancestor of modern English; and both designations, English and England, derive from the tribal name of the Angles.

While the Visigoths were rampaging through Italy, other tribes were taking advantage of the demilitarized situation along the Rhine. The Vandals crossed the Rhine, pillaged Gaul and Spain, and crossed the Strait of Gibraltar into North Africa. Their notorious reputation as destructive raiders is still with us today, because we still use the term vandal to refer to someone who destroys other people's property. The Vandals carved out a vast new area in which to live. It included the southern area of Spain, so that in later times it was known as Andalusia, an altered form of their tribal name. But they also occupied all of North Africa from the Atlantic to Carthage, with the latter serving as the capital of their African kingdom. From there they took to the sea and carried out attacks upon Italy and the islands of the central Mediterranean: Sicily, Sardinia, and Corsica. In 455 they captured Rome and plundered it not for three days as the Visigoths had done in 410, but for three weeks; and when they finally loaded up their ships with plunder and sailed away, part of their booty included the wife of the recently deceased Roman Emperor of the west and her two daughters. At that point imperial rule in the west basically ceased to exist. There was a series of imperial claimants for the next twenty years, but they controlled only Italy and other small parts of the west that had not yet come under the rule of Germanic chieftains. Finally, in 476 the last emperor of the west, Romulus Augustulus, was forced to abdicate, so that this date is often regarded as marking the end of the western half of the Roman Empire. At this point the king of the Ostrogoths became the ruler of Italy.

The Germanic tribe of the Franks also took advantage of this confusion and carved out a kingdom in what had been the Roman provinces of Gaul. In fact, the Merovingian and Carolingian kings of this Frankish Kingdom lasted more than 500 years (c.450-987), thereby becoming the most long lived of all these Germanic kingdoms. Moreover, the Franks became so dominant in this region that they lent their name to it: Franks > France.

Around 435 or so the Huns came under the rule of their most famous and most feared king, Attila. By this time the Huns had settled down in the plain of what is now Hungary. Not only did this area provide their cattle and horses with abundant pasturage, but it placed them in a suitable position from which they could threaten and carry out raids upon the Danubian provinces of the Roman Empire. The Huns sacked towns and cities, killed anyone who resisted, carried off others as slaves, and took whatever there was of value. In order to keep these attacks from occurring, the eastern emperor in Constantinople often agreed to pay Attila large sums of gold, but finally Attila rounded up his thousands of horsemen and infantry and moved west. He crossed the Rhine and entered Gaul. His arrival resulted in the last big battle in the Roman west. Since the Huns were viewed as everyone's enemy, both the Romans and the Germans living in this area united against them. The battle of the Catalaunian Plain in 451 was a bloody one, but basically ended in a draw. Attila retreated back across the Rhine, invaded Italy the next year, destroyed the city of Aquileia at the head of the Adriatic Sea, but then died in his sleep in the year after that (453); and with his death the coalition of different tribes that he had held together fell apart, and the Huns disappeared from history.

By 500 the Ostrogoths migrated into Italy, and their king became ruler both of his German subjects and of the native Roman inhabitants. The last major movement of a Germanic tribe occurred in 568 when the Langobards crossed the Alps and took over the northern Po Valley of Italy for themselves. Part of this region, Lombardy, is still known by an altered form of their name.

In conclusion, over the course of about two hundred years (376-568) Germanic penetration into the western half of the Roman Empire weakened and destroyed the imperial government and completely redrew the political and demographic map of that whole area.

↓ Germanic tribes destroy the western Roman Empire by 568.
→ Visigoths. (Spain)
(Vandals)
⇒ Huns (Atilla)
=) gave free movement to these tribes in their conquest
⇒ Anglo-Saxons
→ England
⇒ Franks (France)

Western Europe During the Dark Age

IMPORTANT DATES AND TERMS

- **432:** Patrick begins his missionary work in Ireland.
- **481-511:** Reign of King Clovis among the Franks.
- **450-750:** Dark Age of Western Europe, also known as the Early Middle Ages.
- **Merovingian Kingdom:** Frankish Kingdom of Gaul.
- **Clovis:** first great Frankish king, converted to Christianity.
- **Gregory of Tours:** author of *The History of the Franks* (lived 538-594).
- **wergeld:** "man money" paid according to Germanic law, varying in amount according to the offense and the person injured or killed.
- **St. Patrick:** youth of Roman Britain, enslaved among the pagan Irish, escaped, returned to convert the Irish to Christianity (lived 385-461).
- **Angles and Saxons:** Germanic tribes that invaded England and supplanted both Celtic and Roman culture.
- **Beowulf:** early Anglo-Saxon epic poem, combining Germanic traditions with Christianity.

This is the first of three lectures that will survey the three major cultures that came into being to replace the cultural unity of the Roman Empire. Since the previous lecture examined the world of Late Antiquity and the disintegration of the western half of the Roman Empire brought about by the invasions of the Germanic tribes, this lecture will look at western Europe in the period following these invasions.

Modern historians view Western Europe as having entered upon a very different period of history when the Roman Empire gradually passed out of existence over the course of the fifth century. They term this new period the Middle Ages or Medieval history. It can be thought to begin c.450 and to end with the beginning of the Renaissance c.1350. In this lecture we will survey the first part of this period, the Early Middle Ages, covering the years c.450-750; and we will do so by concentrating primarily upon the culture of Gaul (France) and the British Isles. But notice that the title of this lecture is "Western Europe during the Dark Age." Many historians today (especially Medieval historians) would object to the use of the term "dark age" in describing this period because of its negative connotation, but the term is well justified in order to emphasize the great cultural discontinuity resulting from the disappearance of the western half of the Roman Empire and the emergence of the various Germanic kingdoms. The economy of the Roman Empire had provided its inhabitants with a large number of mass-produced commodities of relatively high quality, much like what we have today in our own modern society: bricks of standardized size and uniformity for building houses, pottery for as shipping vessels, tableware, and cooking. In addition, the literacy rate in the Roman Empire seems to have been fairly high for a pre-industrial society. The Germanic invasions changed all of this. It brought about a system's collapse that resulted in a drastic drop in the level of western Europe's material and literate culture for several centuries. The invasions also destroyed the complex system of political ideas and institutions that had long characterized the public lives of the ancient Greeks and Romans. The term "dark age" can therefore be properly applied to this period for this and one other reason: because we have relatively few sources of information about this period.

By 500 the cultural geography of western Europe was vastly different from what it had been a century before. The provinces of the Roman Empire no longer existed, but in their place now stood various Germanic kingdoms ruled over by chieftains or kings. The complex political institutions of the Roman Empire had also disappeared, replaced by a primitive form of Germanic tribal kingship. As we will see in Lecture 21, this form of tribal leadership was further elaborated over time and eventually evolved into the Medieval system of feudalism. The population of western Europe now consisted of two rather distinct elements: the native inhabitants of the Later Roman Empire, and the members of the various Germanic tribes. These two groups were initially quite distinct from one another, because they spoke different languages and lived according to different cultural traditions, including very different ways of diet and dress. Over the course of the next several centuries there gradually came into being a new culture formed out of three different cultural traditions: the remnants of the civilized culture of the Later Roman Empire, the primitive warlike culture of the Germanic tribes, and the religious culture of Christianity. Our survey in this lecture will trace the very beginning of the process of synthesis (especially of the latter two cultural traditions).

But before we actually begin our survey, I wish to point out an interesting aspect of this period. From the twelfth century onward one aspect of popular culture in France and England was a series of stories told about King Arthur and his knights of the round table at Camelot. Did King Arthur actually exist, or was he merely the creation of later story tellers? If there does exist a kernel of historical truth at the heart of the Arthurian legend, it probably goes back to the events of the Anglo-Saxon invasions of Britain around 500. One of our few contemporary sources for this period is a British monk named Gildas, who wrote a treatise entitled *The Downfall and Conquest of Britain (De Excidio et Conquestu Britanniae)*. In it he mentions a leader of the native inhabitants, a man with the good Roman name of Ambrosius Aurelianus, who rallied people against the invaders and won an important victory over them in 516 at a place called Mount Badon. According to Gildas, the victory brought about a long period of peace. Some modern Medieval historians think that this man represents the historical kernel that grew into the Arthurian legend of later centuries. After the invading Angles and Saxons had overrun the eastern and central areas of Britain, the native Celtic population were pushed westward and continued to live in the districts of Cornwall and Wales. It was among these people that the Arthurian legend originated and grew, at first as a source of cultural pride in opposition to the victorious Angles and Saxons. But by the twelfth century the stories of King Arthur had become part of the contemporary Medieval culture involving ideas of chivalry, knights jousting on horseback in shining armor, and courtly romance that would have been totally alien to the people of Britain in the early sixth century.

We now begin our survey proper by comparing and contrasting the legal systems of the Later Roman Empire and the Germanic kingdoms. As we have already seen in the case of Hammurabi, law codes can reveal many things about a past society. By the fourth century of our era the Romans had developed a very complex and sophisticated system of law with an enormous legal literature. During the Dark Age in western Europe this legal system was replaced by the simple and primitive legal customs of the Germanic tribes. For example, one way in which legal disputes could be settled among people from the Dark Age onwards involved ordeals, tests that were thought to ferret out the truth with divine assistance. In Ordeal by Water a Christian priest was first summoned to bless a river, stream, pond, or large vessel of water in order to assure that God was present and witnessing the proceedings. The accused was then immersed; and if he floated, he was thought to be guilty, because the blessed water had rejected him due to his guilt; whereas if he sank, that was taken to be God's judgment of his innocence, because the water had received him. In Ordeal by Boiling Water a person was required to reach into a kettle of boiling water to retrieve a stone; and after a certain amount of time the person's injured hand was examined. If it was healing normally, the person was judged to be innocent; whereas if the hand appeared not to be healing properly, the person was judged to be guilty. Similarly, in Ordeal by Hot Iron the accused was forced to pick up a red hot piece of iron and to hold it as he walked a prescribed distance. After several days the person's hand was examined to see what condition it was in. If it appeared to be healing properly, the accused was thought to be innocent, but if the hand was becoming infected and not healing as it should, that was regarded as a sign of the person's guilt. In Ordeal by Combat the litigants agreed to settle their dispute by taking up weapons and fighting it out. Whoever emerged victorious was thought to be in the legal right, because God had empowered him to overcome his opponent. Another idea central to Germanic legal customs was *wergeld*, meaning "man money." In numerous cases in which one person victimized another by theft, robbery, or bodily harm, the delinquent had to pay his victim a fixed amount in compensation. The amount of the payment varied considerably, depending upon the presumed value of the victim within the tribe. For example, in the case of murder the amount paid to the relatives of a king's retainer was thrice what it was for other people. On the other hand, the *wergeld* for a young or middle-aged adult was higher than those of children and the elderly, because adult men and women were valued by the tribe, because the former could serve as warriors, and the latter could bear children, whereas males and females of tender or elderly years could do neither.

One of our few sources of information for western Europe during the Dark Age is the historical account of Gregory of Tours. His life spanned much of the sixth century among the Franks. Text #24 in PSWC consists of several excerpts from his historical narrative, which usually goes by the name of *The History of the Franks*. In the preface to the work Gregory complains that during his lifetime knowledge of writing had virtually disappeared. This is stark testimony as to the destructive effects that the Germanic invasions had had upon the culture of western Europe. It had caused the near extinction of reading and writing. About the only people with any knowledge of reading and writing in western Europe for the next several centuries were the very few members of the priestly order in the Roman Catholic Church, because they were expected to be able to read the Latin text of *The Bible* and other relevant Christian literature. As Gregory writes in his preface, given this sorry state of affairs in Gaul during his day, he had decided to set down in writing an account of events, so that knowledge of them would be passed on to posterity; but he also apologizes for his writing style, because he is acutely aware that the Latin of his day was a far cry from what had been written and spoken in this area before the Germanic invasions.

As bishop of Tours, Gregory was a pious Christian; and one of the big differences between his historical writing and that of the Roman Empire is its religious orientation. As mentioned already, one of the three important cultural ingredients that went into the formation of Medieval culture was Christianity, and we see this very clearly in Gregory's writings. Historical writing among the ancient Greeks and Romans focused upon human beings and their communities and states engaged in the affairs of this world. But with the rise of Christianity, this humanist world view in the writing of history was replaced by a God-centered one in which the historian had as one of his principal themes the spread of Christianity and the demonstration of the faith's truth through the performance of miracles. In fact, in addition to writing his ten books on *The history of the Franks*, Gregory also composed seven books of miracles; and his historical account is full of stories involving the supernatural: miracles performed by God and bad things caused by the Devil.

Gregory's Christian interpretation of history is clearly seen in his account of King Clovis (481-511). Gregory describes how Clovis came to abandon his traditional Germanic gods and to embrace Christianity. After marrying Clotilda, a princess of the neighboring Germanic kingdom of the Burgundians, his new wife, who was a Christian, began nagging him to adopt her faith, but Clovis resisted until one day during a bitterly contested battle Clovis called upon the Christian god for aid; and when he was victorious, he decided to be baptized as a Christian along with thousands of his soldiers. In fact, all of Gregory's historical narrative from beginning to end is cast in the framework of Christianity. It begins by summarizing Biblical history from Adam and Eve and going through all the traditions found in *The Old Testament*, and then charting the gradual progress of Christianity from Roman times up to his own day.

Besides illustrating the shift from a humanist to a God-centered world view, Gregory's history also offers us interesting glimpses into the warlike and rough-and-tumble nature of Germanic society at this time. Germanic kingship was based upon the ability of the king to lead his warriors successfully in battle. He was not simply a general or commander, but was expected to wield his battle axe and other weapons quite effectively along with his soldiers. Although he was respected and honored by his men due to his superior leadership, he was in some degree just one of the boys; and when there was a division of the spoils after victory, the king received his portion by lot along with everyone else, although as their king, he could make special requests.

Clovis in fact was one of the important figures of this period, because he laid the foundations for the emergence of France. He was the first significant king in the Merovingian dynasty of Frankish kings who ruled for about 300 years (450-750). Through his conquests and devious brutality (see Text 24B in PSWC) he succeeded in making the Franks the dominant Germanic tribe in this region of western Europe, and he chose the town of Paris to serve as his kingdom's capital. His conversion to Christianity and its imposition upon his subjects also began the very slow process of Christianizing the Franks and beginning the synthesis of the Germanic and Christian traditions.

We will now travel across the English Channel and devote the remainder of this lecture to the British Isles. In 385 Britain was still a province of the Roman Empire and had not yet begun to experience the invasions of the Angles and Saxons. In that year there was born in Roman Britain a child whom his parents named Patricius. We know him today as Saint Patrick. As a young man of sixteen years, he was kidnapped and carried off to Ireland, where he was sold into slavery. Now, Ireland had never been part of the Roman Empire. It was inhabited by a Celtic population, divided up among numerous small tribes ruled over by local chieftains, who were often fighting with one another and carrying out cattle raids. Patrick served as a slave shepherd in Ireland for six years, usually tending animals all by himself, forced to survive in the fields with little clothing, food, or shelter. Although his parents had raised him as a Christian, he did not begin to take his faith seriously until he was forced to draw upon his own inner strength during these lonely years of his life when prayer functioned as about his only source of spiritual strength.

Patrick eventually succeeded in escaping slavery. He made his way to the coast, was received aboard a ship, and returned to his native Britain. He now decided to devote the rest of his life to God. He therefore was accepted into Holy Orders and was educated as a priest. Then at the age of 47 in the year 432 he decided to return to the place of his enslavement in order to bring Christianity to the Irish; and he was actively engaged in this missionary work until his death in 461. He succeeded in converting many of the Celtic chieftains to Christianity, and they in turn began to abolish their pagan practices and to persuade or force their subjects to become Christian as well.

As the Irish became increasingly Christian during the Dark Age that we are surveying today, something really remarkable happened. While the attributes of civilization were being destroyed by the Germanic tribes in Britain and across the English Channel on the European continent, the Irish for the first time became well acquainted with reading and writing and did much to keep the light of literate culture burning while it was being extinguished elsewhere in western Europe. As part of their Christianization, Irish priests learned how to read and write. They established monasteries that were the centers of Irish literate religious culture. Literate monks spent much time and effort in producing books to make sure that works of literature would be passed on to the next generation. Of course, since the printing press would not be invented until 1450, producing a book at this time required a person to copy out the entire text by hand, a slow and arduous process. Moreover, the Irish rendered their books into works of art by decorating their covers and pages with designs, gilding, and ornate and multi-colored lettering. This type of book form is today termed an illuminated manuscript, of which we still possess many beautiful examples.

As the Christian tradition and its accompanying literate culture took root in Ireland during the sixth century, Irish monasteries began sending out missionaries to Christianize Scotland, England, and across the English Channel to parts of the European continent: for although England and western Europe had ben Christianized in part during the closing years of the Later Roman Empire, much of this was swept away and undone as the result of the Germanic invasions, so that the population in many areas had to be reconverted. Irish priests played a very important role in this process of re-Christianization, as well as the reintroduction of literate culture to the rest of western Europe through their establishment of numerous monasteries that served as important centers of learning and book production. As we will see in Lecture 21, Irish missionary activity of the sixth and seventh centuries was instrumental in laying the foundations for the Carolingian cultural revival of Charlemagne.

We will end our survey of the basic cultural patterns of western Europe during the Dark Age by examining the earliest major document written in Anglo-Saxon or Old English, the ancestor to the modern English language.

This is the epic poem of *Beowulf*, probably composed around 700 toward the end of the Dark Age and revealing evidence of the early synthesis of the two rather different Germanic and Christian cultural traditions: for the central hero, the warrior-king Beowulf not only possesses the warlike leadership of a Germanic chieftain, but in keeping with the Christian tradition of humanity, he does not direct his hostility against other humans, but against monsters who embody evil and the Devil. Moreover, the poem contains no mention of the traditional Germanic gods, but it does allude to the monotheistic Christian god, as well as to the story of Cain and Abel. The poem falls neatly into two distinct parts, the second of which is set out as Text #25 in PSWC. I will briefly summarize the epic in order to illustrate many features that typify the culture that created this work of literature.

The poem begins with a Danish chieftain building a feasting hall for himself and his warriors. The Danish setting reminds us of the origin of the Angles and Saxons from Denmark and northern Germany. In the evenings the chieftain and his men gather there to feast and drink while they are entertained by a minstrel, who sings songs of heroic deeds. But their nightly feasts are disturbed by a monster named Grendel, who emerges from a nearby lake, breaks into the feasting hall while the warriors are asleep, and carries some off to be eaten. Finally, Beowulf and his band of warriors arrive to save the day. During the first night Beowulf lies awake and succeeds in fighting with Grendel and killing him. This is followed by great celebration, but during the following night Grendel's mother emerges from the lake and carries out another raid upon the feasting hall. On the next day Beowulf and others go to the nearby lake, into which Beowulf plunges fully armed. After descending into the cave of the monster, the two engage in fierce combat; and after breaking his own weapon, Beowulf eventually kills the monster by using a sword of another hero that he finds in the cave. To the surprise of the others, who are still waiting anxiously on the lake shore, Beowulf emerges to the surface with the severed head of the monster, which they carry in celebration back to the feasting hall, where Beowulf is honored that evening with new songs that describe his deeds. Beowulf and his band of warriors then return home.

Now the second half of the epic begins, and it is fifty years later. Beowulf is an aged king, but he is called upon once more to protect his people by killing a devilish monster. A man comes upon a cave, in which a dragon is sleeping amid his vast treasure of plundered valuables. The man secretly removes some of it and departs, but when the dragon awakens and discovers that part of his treasure has been stolen, he goes on a rampage, destroying everyone and everything around him with his fiery breath. Beowulf and his band of warriors come to the rescue, but the dragon is so frightening that despite their oath-bound duty to follow their king even to death, all the warriors flee into the forest to hide while Beowulf takes on the dragon all by himself. As they are locked in mortal combat, one of the warriors, Wiglaf, is so shamed by their desertion of Beowulf that he emerges from the forest and joins in the fighting, but by then the dragon has bitten Beowulf. Nevertheless, the two men succeed in killing it. As Beowulf is dying from his wound, he orders that the dragon's treasure be placed before him, so that he can see what all his exploit has won. After heaving the carcass of the dragon into the sea from a cliff, the warriors proceed to give Beowulf a fitting hero's burial, just like what we find at the end of Homer's *Iliad* with the burial of Hector. After cremating Beowulf's body on a pyre, around which horsemen ride in his honor, they bury his ashes near the sea and erect over the spot a huge earthen mound, so that people in after times will see it and know that beneath it lies the remains of a mighty hero.

LECTURE 19
The Byzantine Civilization

- **330:** Refoundation of Byzantium as Constantinople by the Emperor Constantine.
- **395:** Final division of the Roman Empire into eastern and western halves.
- **527-565:** Reign of the Emperor Justinian.
- **1204:** Capture of Constantinople by the crusaders.
- **1453:** Capture of Constantinople by the Ottoman Turks.
- **Justinian and Theodora:** most famous imperial couple of the Byzantine Empire.
- **Digest of Roman Law:** Justinian's comprehensive codification of Roman law.
- **Greek Fire:** secret weapon used to defend Constantinople.

In this lecture we will survey more than one thousand years of Byzantine civilization, beginning with the establishment of Constantinople in 330 and ending with its capture by the Ottoman Turks in 1453. The Byzantine civilization represents the long term survival of the eastern half of the Roman Empire. While the empire's western half collapsed under the Germanic invasions and sank to a much lower level of culture, the Greek east managed to survive and maintained the high cultural standards of Greek and Roman civilization. After we survey the rise of Islam and the general characteristics of the Islamic world in the following lecture, we will return to western Europe and trace its development from the Dark Age up to the Early Modern Period, but as we do so, we will again encounter both the Byzantine and Islamic civilizations when we examine the history of the crusades.

As we saw when we looked at the period of Late Antiquity, by the fourth century the Roman emperors were spending very little, if any, time in Rome, because they needed to be near or at the frontier in order to deal with serious foreign threats. Thus, the emperors established their courts in various cities as the situation required. Constantine made the decision to designate one particular city to serve as the imperial capital of the eastern half of the Roman Empire. This was the Greek city of Byzantium that had been founded as a colony in 657 B.C. and had thus enjoyed a history of nearly one thousand years. After considerable remodeling to serve its new function, the city was finally officially dedicated as Constantinople (Constantine's city, today's Istanbul) on Monday May 11, 330; and it henceforth served as the imperial capital for the eastern half of the Roman Empire.

This city was chosen by Constantine largely because of its location. It was not too far from the lower Danube, one of the two important frontier zones for the Greek east. It was situated on a peninsula on the European side of the Bosporus, the strait between Europe and Anatolia, where the Black Sea and Sea of Marmora meet, the latter flowing into the Aegean Sea. This peninsula made the city highly defensible, especially after a set of three massive walls had been constructed from sea to sea. Although the city was threatened numerous times by various enemies, it was able to hold out against them until the walls were finally breached in 1453 by the Ottoman Turks with the use of gunpowder and a gigantic cannon. In addition, the site was blessed with an enormous harbor, stretching in a curve for seven miles, the so-called Golden Horn, along which there were numerous docks and warehouses for importing and exporting goods of all sorts.

From the outset Constantine designed the city to be thoroughly Christian with many fine churches, but with no pagan temples. It was equipped with all the refinements and amenities commensurate with being an imperial capital. It always had a large and varied population; and as already noted, while western

Europe was sinking into the Dark Age and losing much of the cultural refinement characteristic of the Roman Empire, Constantinople continued those cultural traditions and represented the height of culture in the entire Mediterranean area. When the Emperor Theodosius died in 395, he left behind two young sons, Honorius in Italy and Arcadius in Constantinople. At this point the two halves of the Roman Empire began their slow drifting apart to their very different historical destinies. Although the Visigoths and Huns both ravaged and devastated the Balkan lands of the Byzantine east, they eventually moved westward and proved to be even more destructive in the Latin west.

The Emperor Justinian (527-565) is often viewed as the last Roman emperor of the ancient world and the first Byzantine emperor. His reign is noteworthy in several respects. First of all, we know a great deal about his reign, because a contemporary, Procopius, wrote a lengthy and detailed historical account of this period. Procopius was writing his history in Greek at the same time that Gregory of Tours was writing his *History of the Franks* in Latin, but the two works are worlds apart. Gregory's account reflects the near disappearance of high culture in the west, as well as the emergence of a new God-centered world view that focuses upon the spread of Christianity and the performance of miracles to demonstrate the validity of the one true faith. Procopius' history, on the other hand, is a continuation of the high standards of historical writing begun by Herodotus and Thucydides and maintained by other Greek writers during the Hellenistic and Roman periods.

One of the principal themes of Justinian's reign and of Procopius' history is the former's attempt to reunite the Roman Empire by conquering the areas in the west lost to the Germanic invaders. Justinian succeeded in toppling the Vandal kingdom in North Africa and reestablishing imperial rule there, but when he embarked upon a similar goal for Italy, he ran into a much more difficult situation. Throughout his reign he consumed considerable manpower and financial resources in trying to defeat the Ostrogoths, but the latter proved to be very formidable adversaries. The tide of war ebbed and flowed back and forth between the two, as each side gained and lost various areas. The city of Rome was captured and recaptured by both sides on several occasions. This resulted in the city suffering progressive damage and depopulation, so that by the end of Justinian's reign the city had lost almost all of its huge population, large areas had become abandoned, and Rome was a mere shadow and ghost of what it had been; and it remained in this deteriorated, neglected, and largely abandoned state for about 900 years, until it began to be rebuilt by the various popes during the Renaissance of the fifteenth and sixteenth centuries. Thus, by the close of his reign, Justinian's efforts to reunite the empire had little to show for all the effort, but the Byzantines did establish control over some parts of Italy (the Greek area of the south and the city of Ravenna in the northeast) and the island of Sicily.

Perhaps the single most important lasting achievement of Justinian's reign was his codification of Roman law. Over the course of the previous one thousand years the Romans had developed a very sophisticated system of law; and during the period of the Principate there had flourished an entire scholarly discipline devoted to the study of Roman law with learned jurists, as they were called, like modern law professors, writing books on all aspects of the law and teaching this material to their students. In addition, the workings of the Roman Imperial government produced massive amounts of law in the form of emperors' decrees and judicial decisions. Since there had never been an attempt to codify all this vast and varied material, by the time of Late Antiquity Roman law was a mountain of overlapping and sometimes conflicting evidence. Since Justinian thought that the reunification of the empire could be assisted by establishing a standardized system of law, he appointed a commission of legal experts and gave them the daunting task of compiling a definitive codification of the law. After several years of work, they succeeded in producing *The Digest*, a kind of legal encyclopedia. It was organized to facilitate easy use by lawyers and judges. The whole work was divided into fifty books, with each book devoted to one specific major part of the law. Each book was then further subdivided into titles, each of which dealt with a discrete subcategory; and the titles were arranged in a logical order so as to move through the whole topic of the book in a step-by-step fashion.

Since Latin had always been the language of Roman law, *The Digest* was written in Latin, but since Greek was the language of the Byzantine Empire, the work was soon translated into Greek and became the foundation of law in the Byzantine Empire. Copies of the Latin text were brought to Italy in the hope that *The Digest* would become the legal basis of a reunited empire, but this did not happen. But what did happen began to unfold 500 years later and has had significant consequences for the overall legal history of Western civilization.

In the year 1061 there was discovered in northern Italy a Latin text of *The Digest*, which had been lying neglected for centuries. Western Europe, however, was now at a stage at which it could appreciate this complex system of Roman law. As we will see in a later lecture, this period marked Western Europe's slow intellectual reawakening, as witnessed by the establishment of the earliest Medieval universities. Moreover, since some areas of Western Europe were beginning to develop into embryonic nation-states, the latter had a need for a system of law that was much more sophisticated than those that had grown out of Germanic customs. Consequently, *The Digest* soon became one of the major objects of scholarly study in the Medieval universities; and as students were taught Roman law, they began to employ its concepts and practices in the legal work of their own countries. Thus, Roman law gradually became the basis for the legal systems of all the continental European countries.

Another enduring monument of Justinian's reign is the Church of Holy Wisdom (Hagia Sophia). It still stands today in Istanbul, but is now a museum. The floor plan of the structure is that of a Greek cross, a cross with cross-bars of equal length and intersecting at their midpoints. The area of their intersection is surmounted by an enormous dome, measuring 102.5 feet in diameter and rising to a height of 181.5 feet. Although the dome is not nearly as large as that of the Pantheon in Rome erected during the reign of Hadrian (117-138), it is still very large and quite impressive. Its mere construction testifies to the Byzantine continuation of the extraordinary engineering skills developed by the ancient Romans. In contrast, a structure of this nature could not have been built at this time in the Latin west, where the Germanic invasions had almost entirely obliterated Roman civilization.

The last significant aspect of Justinian's reign to be touched upon is his wife Theodora. She began life at the bottom of society and rose to be empress. Her father worked as the bear keeper in the Hippodrome in Constantinople.

This was the huge stadium in which chariot races and other public entertainments were staged, including various events involving wild animals, such as bears. Theodora's mother was an acrobat, who performed in the Hippodrome. As a young woman, Theodora followed in her parents' footsteps by also performing in the Hippodrome as a strip-tease performer, and this is how she came to Justinian's attention. He was so captivated by her that he decided to make her his wife, but the law stood in the way. This was a law enacted by Rome's first emperor, Augustus, which forbade anyone of the senatorial class to marry people of low social station, which included prostitutes and actresses. Justinian prevailed upon his uncle, who was emperor at the time, to change the law, so that he and Theodora could be married. Not only was she beautiful and sexy, but more importantly, Theodora was very intelligent and capable. She was Justinian's closest and most trusted advisor and partner in ruling the Byzantine Empire. Justinian loved her dearly throughout their marriage; and when she predeceased him (in 545 probably due to breast cancer), he mourned for her until his own death.

We must now skim quickly through the remainder of Byzantine history. The Persians were the eastern neighbors of the Byzantines along the Euphrates frontier; and the two empires were frequently engaged in wars that resulted in only minor changes along their borders. Then in the seventh century Byzantium's foreign affairs became far more complicated and threatening due to the arrival of two new peoples: the Avars and the Arabs. The Avars were a nomadic people, who, like the Huns, originated in central or eastern Asia and migrated westward. They, along with the Slavs, occupied the area around the Black Sea and even crossed the Danube to overrun much of the Balkan Peninsula, parts of which they eventually took away from the Byzantine Empire. Following Muhammad's death in 632 the Arabs attacked both the Persians and the Byzantines. The Persians were thoroughly defeated and lost their whole empire to the Arabs. The latter also defeated the Byzantines in Syria and followed up their success by overrunning Syria, Palestine, Judea, Egypt, the rest of North Africa, and even Spain. They therefore deprived the Byzantine Empire of all its provinces south of Anatolia. Thus, what had formed the southern half of the Roman Empire now became part of the new Islamic Empire, which we will survey in the following lecture.

By the early eighth century the Arabs were attempting to capture Constantinople itself by naval attacks. This brings us to another interesting feature of Byzantine civilization, its secret weapon known as Greek fire. It was the only major scientific or technological innovation that the Byzantines devised throughout their long history. For its time, Greek fire was high-tech in Mediterranean warfare and played an important role in keeping Constantinople from falling into enemy hands. In fact, the Byzantine emperors classified the making of Greek fire as a state secret, so that none of their enemies could use it against them. Greek fire was a crude flame thrower, usually mounted on ships. It consisted of a highly flammable liquid being pumped through a cannon-like tube and then ignited. The liquid had several ingredients: petroleum, naphtha, quick lime (calcium oxide), and saltpeter (potassium nitrate). Greek fire remained unchallenged as a high-tech weapon until the thirteenth century, when it then began to give way to gunpowder. The latter, invented by the Chinese, was developed for military use by the Mongols, who then spread the technology as they conquered Asia and parts of eastern Europe.

During the tenth and eleventh centuries Byzantine emperors succeeded in expanding the size of their empire at the expense of the Slavs, but then the arrival of the Seljuk Turks led to major territorial losses. Like the Huns and the Avars, the Seljuk Turks were a nomadic people, who migrated westward across Asia and caused disruption in both the Byzantine and Islamic Empires. In 1071 the Seljuk Turks defeated the Byzantines in the battle of Manzikert in eastern Anatolia. This defeat resulted in the Byzantines losing much of the interior of Anatolia to the Turks, and this deprived Constantinople of its most valuable source of military manpower and tax revenues. Consequently, the battle of Manzikert began the decline of the Byzantine Empire that finally ended in the Turkish capture of Constantinople in 1453.

As we will see in Lecture 26, the Turkish menace and capture of the Holy Land brought about the crusading movement of Western Europe: for the crusades were initially intended to assist the Christian Byzantines against their non-Christian Turkish enemies and to win back the Holy Land in order to keep the area open to religious pilgrims. At the time of the First Crusade that began in 1096, Alexius was the emperor of the Byzantine Empire (1081-1118). We are well informed about his reign due to the survival of a historical account written by his oldest child, his daughter Anna. The work is entitled *The Alexiad* and is unique in being written by a woman. Anna was the oldest of seven children. She loved and admired her father, but when he died, she and her brother fought to succeed him. Anna thought that as the oldest child, she should rule the empire, but the next oldest, her brother John, thought that he, as the oldest male child, deserved to be the next emperor. When John emerged victorious from the power struggle, he had his oldest sister packed off to a convent, where she lived out the rest of her life as a nun, but she used her free time to write *The Alexiad*. The work, written in Greek, is most interesting in giving us a detailed picture into court life and the complex foreign affairs of the Byzantine Empire. Anna does not refer to her people as the Byzantines, as we do today. Instead, she calls them the Romans, because they saw themselves as directly descended from the Romans of the Roman Empire. Among other things, Anna gives us a fascinating account of the First Crusade from the Byzantine perspective. She uses the term Celts to refer to these crusaders from western Europe, whom she portrays as semi-civilized uncouth people, never to be trusted. Calling the crusaders Celts harks back to Polybius, the Greek historian of the middle Republic of Rome, because when he was writing in the second century B.C., the Celts were a semi-civilized warlike people who occupied much of western Europe, and who often plagued both the Greeks and Romans with their predatory raids.

As we will see when we survey the history of the crusades in Lecture 26, despite their shared Christianity and common Turkish and Arab enemies, the Byzantines and crusaders had just as much to divide them and to set them at odds with one another. Their mutual distrust and animosity grew with each crusading campaign, finally culminating in the Fourth Crusade of 1202-1204. After arriving in Constantinople, the crusaders decided that instead of setting out against the Islamic Infidel farther to the east, they would simply capture Constantinople itself, which they did. The imperial family fled into exile, and for the next 57 years (1204-1261) the crusaders occupied and ruled Constantinople. They plundered the great city of its artistic treasures and anything else of value. At the same time the Venicians, the seafaring merchants of northern Italy, took advantage of Byzantine weakness and established trading posts and networks throughout the eastern Mediterranean and Black Sea in order to expand their commercial empire. When in 1261 the Byzantines finally succeeded in driving the crusaders out of Constantinople and reestablishing control, their empire had suffered major damage and had been seriously weakened. Constantinople itself had also suffered severely from a major fire and never again regained its splendor, opulence, and large flourishing population.

During the fourteenth century the Turks of Anatolia began to pose a really serious threat to the Byzantines. From 1302 to 1453 the Turks, now led by a new line of rulers known as the Ottomans, nibbled away at the Byzantine Empire, until they had overrun all outlying areas except Constantinople itself. In 1331 and 1337 the Turks captured respectively Nicaea and Nicomedia, the last two important Byzantine possessions in Anatolia, located on the southern shore of the Sea of Marmora. The great epidemic of the bubonic plague of 1348-50 and an earthquake of 1354 further weakened the Byzantine state and enabled the Turks to establish an European bridgehead by occupying the Gallipoli Peninsula, from which they gradually overran Thrace, the only area now controlled by Constantinople.

Although the city had successfully withstood numerous enemy attacks over the centuries due to its use of Greek fire and its massive fortifications across the neck of the city's peninsula, the Ottoman Turks finally captured Constantinople in the spring of 1453. by using a gigantic cannon to chip away at the walls. A German engineer was commissioned by the Turkish monarch to manufacture this weapon. It was made of bronze and measured 27 feet in length. The barrel was eight inches thick and had a bore of two and a half feet. It could hurl a projectile of about 1300 pounds for about a mile; and it required sixty oxen to move it into position. It began its assault on April 6 of 1453 and could be fired only once every two or three hours. Nevertheless, after many days of constant bombardment the cannon succeeded in doing its work, so that Turkish soldiers were able to enter the city and capture it on Tuesday May 29. The last Byzantine emperor (Constantine XI) fell amid the fighting, and many women and children were led off into slavery. Indeed, Constantinople was now emptied of its Byzantine population through slaughter and enslavement and lay virtually unoccupied for a time until it was repopulated by the Turks. The victorious Ottoman sultan immediately declared Justinian's magnificent Church of Holy Wisdom to be an Islamic mosque. Thus ended the long history of the Byzantine Empire, and so began the Ottoman Empire that ruled over the eastern Mediterranean for the next four and a half centuries, right up until World War I.

Having surveyed Byzantine history, we will wrap up this lecture by touching upon the most notable features of Byzantine culture. One of its most important contributions to the larger Western tradition was its preservation and passing-on to posterity of the rich and sophisticated literature of their Greek ancestors from Homer onwards. Much of ancient Greek literature that we have today probably would have been lost if the Byzantines had not been in existence for all those centuries.

The other major legacy of the Byzantines relates to Christianity and consists of two distinct parts. Since the Greeks had invented philosophy, it is not surprising to find that the Byzantines used philosophical speculation to develop and refine Christian theology. This was accomplished in large measure through the periodic convening of ecumenical councils, in which bishops were called together to iron out hotly contested theological differences. The first of these ecumenical councils was held by Constantine at Nicaea in Anatolia in 325 to settle a controversy over the nature of the holy trinity. As other similar councils met generation after generation (such as Ephesus in 431 and Chalcedon in 451), various aspects of Christian theology were agreed upon and became accepted as official Church doctrine. Since learned Christians of the Latin west tended not to be as philosophically inclined as those of the Greek east, it was the latter who made the most significant contributions to Christian theology. Moreover, although the highest ranking priest in the Greek east was the bishop or patriarch of Constantinople, all Christians of the Byzantine Empire accepted the supremacy of the pope in Rome up until 1054, at which time the pope and the patriarch of Constantinople excommunicated one another, thus causing the division between the Roman Catholic Church of the Latin west and the Greek Orthodox Church of the Greek east. But before that split, during the seventh and eighth centuries the intellectual superiority of Greek eastern Christianity had resulted in some of its bishops serving as pope.

Byzantine Christianity also played an important role in the further spread of the faith. As the various Slavic peoples of eastern Europe interacted with the superior culture of Constantinople, the latter sent out among them Christian missionaries, who eventually succeeded in converting them to Christianity; and since these peoples had no previous tradition of reading and writing, the missionaries used their own Greek alphabet to develop a Slavic writing system. Consequently, much of eastern Europe today practices Christianity according to the Greek Orthodox tradition of Byzantium; and the Cyrillic alphabet for writing Russian takes its name from a Byzantine Christian missionary named Cyril, who, along with his brother Methodius, were Christian missionaries among the Slavs during the 860s and translated the holy scriptures into Old Church Slavonic.

LECTURE 20
The Islamic World

IMPORTANT DATES AND TERMS

- **610-632:** Religious mission of Muhammad.
- **661-750:** Umayyad dynasty of Damascus.
- **750-1258:** Abbasid dynasty of Baghdad.
- **Qur'an:** sacred book of Islam.
- **Ka'ba:** shrine in Mecca, containing sacred meteoric stone, object of the Islamic religious pilgrimage (hajj).
- **caliph:** supreme ruler of the Islamic world.
- **assassins:** Islamic dissidents willing to murder.
- Arabic numbers and algebra.
- **status of women:** polygamy, veiling, seclusion in the house.
- **slavery:** women concubines, males castrated to serve as eunuchs.

This lecture will survey about 600 years of Islamic history. After touching upon the origins of Islam, we shall treat the general features of the Islamic world during its first two major dynasties: the Umayyad (661-750) and the Abbasid (750-1258). This will cover nearly the same chronological ground that we went over in the previous lecture in connection with the Byzantine civilization.

Islam originated among the Arab tribes of the western Arabian Peninsula. The Arabs were a Semitic people, speaking a Semitic language related to other Semitic languages that we touched upon in connection with ancient Mesopotamia: for Semites had migrated out of the Arabian Desert into the

Fertile Crescent to such an extent that the whole area eventually became totally Semitic in language.

Like virtually all other ancient peoples whom we have studied, the Arabs were initially polytheistic and were organized into separate tribes. They lived a hard existence in trying to survive in a rather harsh environment. The Arabs along the western edge of the Arabian Peninsula supplemented a lifestyle of nomadism and warfare with trade, because from very early times there developed a long distance trade route down along the Red Sea to East Africa and the southern tip of the Arabian Peninsula: for in these regions there grew trees that produced very fragrant resins (myrrh and frankincense) that were highly valued by the ancient Near Eastern peoples. These substances were used in religious rites and for embalming human bodies. Mecca came into being at roughly the midpoint of this trade route. It therefore served as a way-station for traders, as well as an important religious center for the surrounding Arab tribes. The principal shrine in Mecca was the Ka'ba, a temple that housed a black stone venerated by the Arabs, because it was thought to have fallen from heaven. It has therefore been conjectured that the stone might have been a meteorite.

Muhammad was born in the year 570, five years after the death of the Emperor Justinian. During his early adult years he was one of many merchants in the vicinity of Mecca, but when he was forty years old in 610, he had his first major religious experience, in which he believed that he had been visited by the angel Gabriel. It was from such mystical experiences that he fashioned the new religion of Islam, a large portion of which derived from Judaism. His knowledge of the latter religion resulted from the fact that there were many Jewish traders either living in or constantly passing through Mecca.

Islam took from Judaism the idea of strict monotheism, but it also accepted the notion of a Devil, and that both God and the Devil were served by hosts of lesser spiritual beings. Like the later form of Judaism and Christianity, Islam had as part of its belief system the idea of a Last Judgment, in which there would be a resurrection of the dead with the damned being consigned to a hell of seven levels and the blessed being elevated to heaven. Like Jesus and the prophets of *The Old Testament*,

Muhammad also insisted upon people treating one another humanely and being charitable toward the poor.

Muhammad viewed himself as standing in the long line of Biblical prophets, but that he represented the final culmination of the prophetic tradition. Jesus was seen as being one of Muhammad's prophetic predecessors. Thus, both Judaism and Christianity were seen as imperfect forms of religion, whereas Islam was the final stage of this religious tradition perfected by Muhammad.

For the first twelve years of his religious mission (610-622) Muhammad remained in Mecca and had rather limited success in winning converts to his new religion. This situation abruptly changed when he was invited to come to Medina, located 210 miles north of Mecca. There a sizable portion of the population embraced Islam and regarded Muhammad as their political and religious leader. Once Muhammad was established in Medina, he led them in a war against Mecca, consisting of raids and attacks that disrupted the trade upon which Mecca relied. Finally, in 630 Muhammad captured Mecca and imposed his religion upon its people. The Ka'ba was now cleansed of all polytheism and was rededicated as the central shrine of Islamic monotheism. By the time that Muhammad died two years later in 632, he had succeeded in uniting the Arab tribes for the very first time through the zeal of religious faith. In 651, nineteen years after Muhammad's death, the Qur'an was composed by collecting all the utterances of Muhammad that people could remember. They were 114 in number, were organized according to their length, and henceforth served as the sacred text of Islam.

When Muhammad died in 632 without any male offspring, the recently united Arab tribes had to confront for the first time the question of who would be the successor (caliph) to Muhammad's authority. They eventually agreed to be led by Abu Bakr, one of Muhammad's earliest converts and most respected followers, but there were other Muslims at the time who thought that the position of caliph should go to Ali, Muhammad's closest male relative, a cousin and husband of his daughter Fatima. Over the course of the next several decades this original dispute concerning the succession intensified. It gradually took on an important religious difference among Muslims, and it eventually developed into the fundamental split between Sunni and Shia sects. The former emerged as the majority of Muslims, and the latter the minority. Over the centuries the Shia sect has produced numerous radical and extremist movements against the Sunni majority. For nearly 30 years (632-661) the succession to Muhammad's authority, known as the caliphate, was held by four men. Then in 661, following the assassination of Ali, Muhammad's cousin and son-in-law, the fifth successor or caliph established the Umayyad dynasty that for the next 89 years (661-750) ruled over the rapidly expanding Islamic Empire from its capital at Damascus in Syria.

Within a century of Muhammad's death (632-732) the Arabs carried out the conquest of a vast area and brought into being the Islamic Empire. They invaded Mesopotamia and Syria at about the same time. The former was part of the Persian Empire, and the latter formed part of the Byzantine state. Not only did the Arabs defeat the Persians, but they totally ended their rule and soon found themselves in possession of the civilized and flourishing areas of Mesopotamia and Iran. Similarly, after defeating a Byzantine army in 636 at the Yarmuk River near the Sea of Galilee, the Arabs overran all the southern provinces of the Byzantine Empire: Syria, Phoenicia, Judea, and Egypt, thus confining the Byzantine civilization to the areas of Anatolia and the Balkan Peninsula. Following these initial conquests, the Arabs extended their sway both eastward and westward: eastward into central Asia and becoming masters of what are now the Islamic nations of Afghanistan and Pakistan; and westward from Egypt across North Africa to the Atlantic. In 698 the Arabs captured Carthage and shortly thereafter reached the Atlantic coast. Then in 711 they crossed the Strait of Gibraltar, quickly overran Spain, and even crossed the Pyrenes Mountains into southern France until finally checked in 732 by Charles Martel in the battle of Poitiers. Thereafter Charles Martel, his son Pepin, and his grandson Charlemagne rolled back the Arab advance into Europe by securing southern France and Spain north of the Ebro River for Western Christian Europe. But for the next several centuries most of Spain was part of the Islamic Empire and formed an important cultural borderland between the Christian and Islamic worlds, through which aspects of Islamic culture gradually made their way into western Europe.

By the year 750, what had been the Roman Empire, which had embraced all lands surrounding the Mediterranean Sea, had been reconfigured into three distinct cultural areas: the Germanic kingdoms of western Europe, the Byzantine civilization of the eastern Mediterranean, and the Islamic Empire embracing the entire southern half of the Mediterranean area. As already stated, during the earliest period of Arab expansion the Syrian city of Damascus served as the empire's capital for the Umayyad dynasty. But as the Islamic conquest penetrated farther east into central Asia, a new capital city was established at Baghdad in 762 on the western bank of the Tigris in Mesopotamia and was the residence of the Abbasid dynasty. The overall political structure of this vast empire was rather simple. It was basically the Arab tribal organization writ large. The supreme ruler was the caliph, an Arabic word meaning "successor" and referring to the notion that the caliph had succeeded to Muhammad's leadership of the Islamic world. Theoretically, he exercised control over the entire empire, but given its vast size and the limitations of communication in those days, practicality modified political theory by each major region being ruled by its own ruler. For example, in the course of time Egypt came to be ruled by its own monarch residing in Cairo, Tunisia by its ruler in Tunis near the site of Carthage, Morocco by its ruler at Fes, and southern Spain (Andalusia) by its ruler at Cordoba. In this sense the political organization of the Islamic Empire mirrored that of the Old Persian Empire (550-330 B.C.) that had been founded by Cyrus the Great and his hardy mountain tribesmen from southern Iran. Both peoples had begun as the semi-civilized inhabitants of a hard land, who had carried out a rapid conquest of a much more civilized region; and in order to govern it, they had simply imposed an expanded form of tribal leadership upon it. In the next lecture we will encounter a similar phenomenon in the Frankish Kingdom concerning feudalism, which in large measure was the simple leadership of the Germanic tribes elaborated and expanded in order to encompass a greatly enlarged population and territory.

At the time that the Arabs emerged from the Arabian Peninsula and embarked upon their conquests, their society was largely egalitarian, even for women. This was a function of the harsh conditions of the Arabian Desert.

But with the establishment of the Umayyad caliphate at Damascus earlier social equality began to be replaced by social hierarchy, as a small ruling elite adopted the traditional trappings, pomp, and court ceremony typical of great Near Eastern monarchies. Just as had happened centuries earlier with the ruling elite of the Old Persian Empire, the original simplicity and relative equality of tribesmen were superceded by an all-powerful monarch surrounded by noble courtiers, whose ambition and rivalry were the constant source of political intrigue and executions, greed, and oppression of ordinary people. This dichotomy of a ruling elite, on the one hand, and of the ordinary people, on the other, soon began to play an important role in defining the division between Sunni and Shia Muslims. Muhammad had exercised both political and religious authority; and in fact, Islam never did (nor does it today) recognize a clear division between these two spheres of society. Nevertheless, as the umayyad caliphs became increasingly absorbed in the pomp and grandeur of their court, they tended to neglect religious matters and were viewed by many as not representing the justice and ethical values of Islam. Consequently, the old dispute over the succession that had arisen in the early years after Muhammad's death now took on an important factor, which was crystalized by the Umayyad massacre of Husayn and his followers in 680 at Karbala on the Euphrates (in modern Iraq). Husayn was the son of Ali and Fatima, the cousin and daughter respectively of Muhammad, and thus the grandson of the great prophet. Henceforth, there gradually arose within Islam the Shia sect that was opposed to the Sunni, characterized by the former regarding the latter as spiritually and religiously corrupt and therefore needing to be overthrown and replaced by a true successor to the combined political and religious authority of Muhammad. It eventually became believed that the Shia victory over Sunni Islam would come about when "the rightly-guided one (the *mandi*)" would someday emerge to bring this about. As you may recognize, this latter notion closely resembles that of the Jewish messiah that was current in Judaism in Roman times, and which, as treated in Lecture 16, led to the powerful Zealot movement within Judaism and brought about the failed Jewish revolt against Roman power during the years 66-70.

The first great success achieved by the Shia sect came in 750 when it lent its support to an uprising against the Umayyads, whose defeat in battle was followed by a wholesale massacre of the family with only one member escaping to Cordoba in Spain, where he founded a new Umayyad dynasty. Nevertheless, when the new Abbasid dynasty established itself in power further east in Baghdad (founded in 762), its rulers soon turned their backs on the religious fervor of the Shia sect and found it far more convenient to follow in the path of the Umayyad Sunni caliphs. The Abbasid rulers' primary focus was the political sphere, and they fostered the development of a class of priests, known as the *ulema*, who became the recognized experts in interpreting Islamic law and religion. Yet, despite its failure to achieve supremacy through the Abbasids, the Shia ideology, splintered into numerous groups, has continued to be responsible for centuries of resistance, unrest, and uprisings against the Sunni majority within the Islamic world. This trend is illustrated by Text #26 in PSWC. The reading is a passage from Marco Polo and describes a radical terrorist group of Syria, who trained and sent out assassins to kill persons regarded as enemies of the faith. It is from this group that we derive the name assassin. They took their name (Arabic *hashishin*) from the drug (hashish) that was used to recruit them.

When the Islamic Empire came into existence, the Arabs formed a very small ruling minority over a vast non-Islamic population, many of whom were members of societies culturally superior to the Arabs. This situation resembled the one in which the founders of the Old Persian Empire had found themselves; and like the early Persians, the Arabs initially adopted a sensibly tolerant policy toward their non-Arab and non-Islamic subjects in allowing them to continue on as before in their established ways. But as time progressed, Arabic, the language of the ruling minority, gradually spread among the general population and eventually became the common language of the whole Islamic Empire. In addition, Islam was slowly adopted by non-Muslims as their religion, because it was the faith of the ruling class, who regarded it as the only true religion. Nevertheless, there continued to exist throughout the Islamic world minorities of Jews and Christians, and even of Zoroastrians in Persia. Since Muslims viewed Jews and Christians as following imperfect and premature forms of the one true religion perfected by Muhammad, the Islamic government allowed them to continue in their faith, but Zoroastrians did not enjoy such toleration. They were persecuted and had their sacred writings destroyed. Consequently, the Zoroastrians shrank considerably in numbers, so that today they number in the hundreds of thousands, not millions; and their two sacred books, *The Gathas* and *The Avesta*, are not complete. On the other hand, Jews and Christians did not enjoy complete freedom within Islamic society, but they were subject to various legal disabilities. They were not allowed to own weapons or a horse in order to prevent them from organizing themselves militarily against the Muslim population. Jewish and Christian men could not marry Muslim women and thereby deprive the one true religion of its female worshippers and childbearers. Nor could Jews or Christians testify in court against a Muslim. Beginning around 800, as Islamic society began to emerge with its own culture and attendant confidence, rulers throughout the empire issued decrees requiring Jews and Christians to publicly identify themselves as non-Muslims by their dress. This took a variety of forms, depending upon the region. In Persia, for example, where there was also a sizable Zoroastrian population, members of the three non-Islamic faiths were required to wear clothing of a certain color, one for each of the religions. In another area Jews were required to wear two distinctive patches, one on their hats and one on their shirts or coats. One law specified that Jewish women had to wear one black and one red shoe.

As already noted, by 800 there began to emerge a distinctive Islamic civilization. By that time the descendants of the rough Arabs of the desert had adapted themselves to the urban civilized culture of their subjects; and during the 800s and 900s numerous ancient Greek works, such as Euclid's *Elements of Geometry*, medical treatises by Hippocrates and Galen, the astronomical work of Claudius Ptolemy, and the philosophical writings of Plato and Aristotle, were translated into Arabic and stimulated what can be called a golden age of Islamic scholarship that endured until c.1200. Greek philosophy was taken over by Islamic intellectuals and used to develop Islamic theology, just as we saw in the previous lecture concerning Christian theology in the Byzantine civilization. Arab learning continued and built upon the Greek science of astronomy by making important observations, so that still today certain prominent stars in the heavens go by their Arabic names; and astrophysics uses Arabic terms, such as azimuth and zenith, in its technical vocabulary.

The one area of learning in which Arab scholars made their most significant contribution was mathematics. As we have seen, the Greeks of the Classical Period developed the marvelously logical system of Euclidian geometry, but with the exception of a few towering intellects such as Archimedes, the cumbersome method of arithmetical notation used by the ancient Greeks and Romans prevented them from making major strides beyond plane geometry. As the result of their commercial interaction with the Indians of southern Asia, the Arabs adopted from them a very simple and useful arithmetical notation, consisting of only ten symbols, the digits one through nine with a zero. We know this system today as arabic numbers. Armed with this system, Arab scholars developed a new area of mathematics that is still known by its Arabic name, algebra. The Medieval people of Western Europe continued to use the clumsy system of Roman numerals for several centuries, but finally, during the twelfth century, as Western Europe was experiencing the intellectual reawakening of the High Middle Ages, the system of Arabic numbers was slowly adopted; and once it became widely accepted, it enabled Western European scholars to forge ahead steadily in developing modern mathematics that has played such a crucial role in the development of Western science and technology (see Lecture 34).

Another important cultural borrowing of the Arabs was paper. The idea of making a writing material out of vegetable matter (in this case rice pulp) was pioneered by the Chinese. The Arabs borrowed the idea from them and thus manufactured and used paper as their principal writing material. Since it was much easier and cheaper to produce than the parchment and vellum used in Medieval Europe, book production in the Islamic world far exceeded that of Western Europe until the middle of the fifteenth century when the European invention of the printing press, coupled with Europeans borrowing the notion of paper from the Arabs, enabled Western Europe to equal and then to vastly exceed the Islamic world in both the volume and variety of book production.

Since the enormous area of the Islamic Empire embraced a tremendous variety of ecologies and environments, and since, like the Roman Empire, its unity facilitated the trading of commodities over long distances, the Islamic world contributed to the spread of localized items of food and made them part of the empire's diet, whence they spread to Western Europe. Sugar was a plant native to the island of New Guinea in the Indian Ocean. Thence it made its way to India and then to Persia. Once the latter area became part of the Islamic Empire, sugar began to be grown in many other areas that were sufficiently wet and warm to support it. Sugar therefore slowly became a standard element in the Islamic economy and diet, to such an extent that our words sugar and candy both derive from Arabic. Similarly, lemons, oranges, and coffee, all of whose words derive from Arabic, were transplanted from their native habitats and propagated throughout the whole Islamic Empire. The coffee plant, for example, had been indigenous only to East Africa. By the High Middle Ages Western Europe had become familiar with all these products through trade and interaction resulting from the crusades. Then, when Western Europeans discovered the New World, sugar and coffee quickly became staples in the Western diet, when these products began to be grown on large plantations in the Caribbean and Central and South America.

Finally, there are two major interrelated aspects of Islamic society worthy of comment: slavery and the status of women. As we have seen, slavery was a common institution in ancient societies, and this was no exception in the Islamic world. As was the case in the Roman Empire, slaves could be found in all areas of Islamic society and its economy, but given the vast geographical extent of the Islamic Empire, its slave trade involved a full range of skin colors: whites from the Slavs of eastern Europe, blacks from Africa, browns from India, and yellows from China. Moreover, the peculiar institution of Islamic polygamy resulted in two sexualized aspects of slavery. Toward the end of his life, after he had become the greatly revered founder of Islam, Muhammad displayed his special standing among the Arabs by accumulating four wives, one of whom he took at the tender age of nine years. To further advertise his special status, he kept his wives secluded indoors and required them to be veiled whenever appearing in the presence of others. It was not until long after

Muhammad's death during the Abbasid dynasty that religious scholars decided that polygamy had not simply been the privilege of the religion's founder, but that it was permissible for all Muslim men.

Stories from the pre-Islamic period of Arab society indicate that women initially enjoyed relative equality with men. This is not at all surprising, because we find the same phenomenon in the early period of many societies, when the harsh realities of human existence require men and women to work hard and to cooperate and interact quite openly. But with the advent of a more settled and stable lifestyle and the emergence of an elite class centered in towns and cities, early societies often used the special treatment of women as a sign of refinement and a way in which the well-to-do could advertise their superior status to others. Thus, as far back as the eleventh century B.C. there were provisions in the Assyrian law code that required respectable women to be veiled when in public, whereas prostitutes were to be unveiled; and any female who went about unveiled was to be regarded as a prostitute; and adult males of a woman's family could be harshly punished if a female relative went about unveiled. Other texts indicate that the veiling of women in public was a common practice in the cities of the Near East. In this respect, the Islamic custom of veiling and secluding women can be viewed as part of a larger cultural phenomenon, whereby the rough Arabs of the desert adopted the ways of their civilized subjects. Polygamy, however, was an Islamic innovation.

Obviously, not all Muslim men had the necessary wealth to support more than one wife, but those who could quite often did, going up to the legal limit of four, as Muhammad had done. On the other hand, it was very common for female slaves to be purchased to serve their masters as concubines, not as wives, so that the legal limit of four wives could be exceeded. Given the multi-racial nature of the Islamic slave trade, there developed a sliding scale of value attached to concubines based upon their skin color, with the fairest skin being most highly prized and the darkest assigned the least value. Moreover, since well-to-do Muslim households usually included several adult females whose sexual services were reserved for the husband-master alone, male eunuch slaves were very common, because their inability to engage in sexual intercourse made them safe as domestic servants. Thus, one grisly aspect of the Islamic slave trade involved the castration of young males. Rather than simply having their testicles amputated (without the benefit of anaesthetic, of course), the common practice was to remove all male genitalia: testicles, scrotum, and penis; and many young males so mutilated died and did not survive the operation to become eunuch slaves.

The Abbasid dynasty came to an abrupt and sudden end as the result of military defeat and slaughter. In 1256 a Mongol army crossed the Oxus River (modrn Amu Darya) that formed the boundary between the arid region of central Asia and the northeastern region of the Islamic Empire. After laying waste to the land and its population in their usual destructive manner, they either captured the fortresses of the sect of the assassins in the mountains south of the Caspian Sea, or they forced them to surrender; and the extremists who dwelled in them were either exterminated or released. In any case, their power vanished. Then in early 1258 the Mongols defeated a Muslim army just east of the Tigris, captured Baghdad, slaughtered a large portion of its population, left the city in ruins, and ended the Abbasid dynasty.

LECTURE 21
The Age of Charlemagne

IMPORTANT DATES AND TERMS

- **450-750:** Merovingian line of Frankish kings.
- **768-814:** Reign of Charlemagne.
- **800:** Coronation of Charlemagne as Emperor Augustus.
- **814-840:** Reign of Louis the Pious.
- **Bede:** early English Christian scholar, author of *Ecclesiastical History of the English Nation* (lived 673-735).
- Carolingian < Carolus Magnus, Latin name for Charlemagne (Charles the Great).
- **Feudalism:** the network of power relationships between lords and vassals created by oaths of fealty and homage that defined the political and military structure of the Frankish Kingdom.
- **Manorialism:** the social and economic system of Medieval Europe in which peasants were bound to estates (manors) to work the land for their lords on large self sufficient farms.
- **Einhard:** biographer of Charlemagne, using Suetonius' *Lives of the Caesars* as his literary model.
- **Carolingian Minuscules:** lower-case letters of the alphabet, enabling copyists to write more text onto the page of a manuscript.

A Military Summons (804-811)

(Taken from *University of Pennsylvania Translations and Reprints*, Volume VI, by D. C. Munro [Philadelphia 1900] pp.11-2)

In the name of the Father, Son and Holy Ghost. Charles, most serene, August, crowned by God, great pacific Emperor, and also, by God's mercy, King of the Franks and Lombards, to Abbot Fulrad.

Be it known to you that we have decided to hold our general assembly this year in the eastern part of Saxony, on the river Bode, at the place which is called Strassfurt. Therefore, we have commanded you to come to the aforesaid place, with all your men well armed and prepared, on the fifteenth day before the Kalends of July, that is, seven days before the festival of St. John the Baptist. Come, accordingly, so equipped with your men to the aforesaid place that thence you may be able to go well prepared in any direction whither our summons shall direct; that is, with arms and gear also, and other equipment for war in food and clothing. So that each horseman shall have a shield, lance, sword, dagger, bow and quivers with arrows; and in your carts utensils of various kinds, that is, axes, planes, augers, boards, spades, iron shovels, and other utensils which are necessary in an army. In the carts also supplies of food for three months, dating from the time of assembly, arms and clothing for a half-year. And we command this in general, that you cause it to be observed that you proceed peacefully to the aforesaid place, through whatever part of our realm your journey shall take you, that is, that you presume to take nothing except fodder, wood and water; and let the men of each one of your vassals march along with the carts and horsemen, and let the leader always be with them until they reach the aforesaid place, so that the absence of a lord may not give an opportunity to his men of doing evil.

Send your gifts, which you ought to present to us at our assembly in the middle of the month of May, to the place where we then shall be; if perchance your journey shall so shape itself that on your march you are able in person to present these gifts of yours to us, we greatly desire it. See that you show no negligence in the future if you desire to have our favor.

In the previous three lectures we have surveyed the three distinct cultures that came into being to replace what had been the unified civilization of the Roman Empire. Let us take a few moments to compare these three cultures. The Byzantine civilization, of course, was the continuation of the eastern half of the Roman Empire; and as such, it could be considered the most advanced and sophisticated of the three, with Constantinople representing the height of urban culture for several centuries. The Arabs began as rough desert tribesmen and traders, who created a vast empire through the rapid conquest of much more civilized peoples, but by the ninth century they had adopted the cultural sophistication of their subjects and were creating their own highly advanced Islamic culture, so that they were generally on a par with the Byzantines, both of whom inherited philosophy, medicine, geometry, and other arts and sciences from the Greeks of the ancient world. In contrast, western Europe had lost much of its Roman civilization and for centuries was characterized by the relatively primitive culture of the Germanic invaders. Indeed, during the period of the crusades (c.1100-1300) both the Byzantines and the Muslims regarded the crusaders from western Europe as hardly better than savages in comparison to themselves. Yet, at this very same time, which historians term the High Middle Ages, western Europe was beginning to experience an intellectual reawakening, as seen in the foundation of numerous Medieval universities (see Lecture 29). By this time the Islamic world had reached its zenith in terms of its cultural creativity and henceforth made very few important discoveries or innovations. In 1453 the Byzantine civilization ceased to exist altogether, while in western Europe the Italian Renaissance had begun to revolutionize Western civilization as a whole. From that point onwards Western Europe has continued to advance in terms of economic growth, technology, science, religious toleration, and political pluralism. Thus, as we note the relative cultural backwardness of western Europe during the Early and Central Middle Ages, it is important to remember that western Europe eventually caught up with the Byzantine and Islamic civilizations and then surpassed them. In fact, the radicalism in the contemporary Islamic world results in part from the fact that at one time it was more culturally advanced than western Europe, but while the former has stagnated, the Western tradition has emerged supreme on the world stage in virtually all areas of human endeavor.

In this lecture we return to western Europe and will spend the remainder of this course in tracing its history throughout the Middle Ages up to the Early Modern Period. This lecture, entitled The Age of Charlemagne, will treat the eighth and part of the ninth centuries, but let us first recall a few things from our survey of Western Europe during the Dark Age (Lecture 18) in order to establish historical continuity between these two periods.

As we saw, Ireland had played a very important role in the history of western Europe during the Dark Age by adopting Christianity and its attendant literate culture as the latter was rapidly dying out in the other parts of western Europe. By the seventh century Irish monasteries were sending missionaries out to Scotland, England, and to the European continent to Christianize or re-Christianize the peoples of these areas; and as they did so, they established or reestablished and promoted reading, writing, and book learning among the clergy. As we will see, one important feature of Charlemagne's reign was his attempt to carry out a cultural revival, which in large measure was the expansion of a process already begun by the Irish tradition of Christian learning.

Perhaps the single best illustration of this whole phenomenon is the career of the Venerable Bede (673-735). He was a native of Anglo-Saxon Britain; and at the age of seven he was given by his parents to a local monastery to be a monk for the rest of his life. This was a common practice during the Middle Ages. Families with too many mouths to feed often reduced the stress on the family's limited resources by giving one of their children to a monastery or church to be raised as a monk or clergyman. As was customary, the older monks taught Bede how to read and write; and as he grew up and read the books belonging to the monastery, he became quite learned and distinguished himself as one of the few scholars of this period. He wrote commentaries on parts of *The Bible*, but he is most famous today for his *Church History of the English Nation*. As we saw in the case of Gregory of Tours, Bede's historical perspective was a Christian one. His historical account traced the progress of Christianity as it was adopted by the various petty kings of Anglo-Saxon

Britain. In addition, when dating events, Bede did so in reference to the birth of Jesus and used the Latin phrase *Anno Domini*, meaning "in the year of the Lord," which we still use today in its abbreviated form A.D.

We will now move across the English Channel to the Frankish Kingdom. As we have seen, the Franks were one of several Germanic peoples who carved out a kingdom for themselves inside the crumbling Roman Empire. Their first dynasty of kings are known as the Merovingians, who ruled for 300 years (450-750), coinciding with the period of the Early Middle Ages. Of these kings the most famous was Clovis (481-511), who converted to Christianity, established the town of Paris as his kingdom's capital, and made the Franks the strongest people of this region through his military campaigns. As time passed, the power of the Frankish monarchy became fragmented and dispersed as the result of two different factors. Instead of passing the royal power onto a single son, it was the Frankish tradition to divide the realm among all the king's sons. Besides causing the kingdom to become fragmented, such division also often resulted in warfare between the different regions. Thus, for example, Clovis divided his kingdom into four parts among his four sons, but three of them soon died, so that the kingdom was reunited under the last surviving son; but when he died with four sons, the kingdom was once again divided into four parts. Another factor that tended to disperse and dissipate royal power was the king's need to maintain support among his nobles by rewarding them with portions of land. Consequently, in the course of time there arose within the Frankish Kingdom aristocratic families that were powerful and influential due to their large land holdings and leadership in war.

By the eighth century the most important of these nobles was the Carolingians, who took their name from Carolus, the Latin form of Charles, one of the personal names commonly used by them. The dominance of this aristocratic family was firmly established by Charles Martel (Charles the Hammer) when he led the Franks to victory over a Muslim army in 732 at Poitiers in western France. The Arabs had crossed the Strait of Gibraltar in 711, had quickly overrun Spain, and had added it to their Islamic Empire. They had then followed up this success by crossing the Pyrenes and had seized control of several towns of southern and southwestern France. Charles Martel's victory at Poitiers checked further Arab expansion in western Europe. In fact, Charles Martel's son, Pepin, who succeeded to his father's position as mayor of the palace of the Merovingian king, led the Franks in other victories that deprived the Arabs of their holdings north and east of the Pyrenes. In 750 the Merovingian line of kings came to an end when Pepin, the father of Charlemagne, pushed the king aside, sent him off to a monastery to be a monk for the rest of his life, and then took over the powers of king for himself. Thus began the Carolingian dynasty of Frankish kings that endured until 987; and it is with this Carolingian dynasty that we can date the beginning of the Central Middle Ages (750-1050).

At the time that Pepin established himself as king of the Franks, the pope was having major troubles with the Lombards in northern Italy. By 600, with the disintegration of the Roman Imperial government in the western half of the empire and in Italy itself, the Pope in Rome moved into this power vacuum and began to emerge as the political ruler of much of Italy, as well as serving as the religious leader of all Christians, both east and west. But since the Germanic tribe of the Lombards ruled over the Po Valley of northern Italy, conflict between them and the pope to the south eventually arose, thus obliging the pope to cast about for an ally. Since the Byzantine emperor was too far away in Constantinople and had his own troubles to deal with, the only other obvious ally was the Frankish Kingdom. Pepin gladly received the pope's overtures, because he was interested in obtaining the pope's approval of his seizure of power. Consequently, in order to consolidate their alliance, the pope traveled to the Frankish Kingdom and personally crowned Pepin as king. Pepin in turn invaded northern Italy, defeated the Lombards, and secured the pope from the Lombard threat. He also handed over to the pope a series of small areas in central and northern Italy for him to rule; and they were henceforth known as the Papal States, over which the popes exercised authority for the next 1100 years until 1871, when the various kingdoms and states of Italy were united to form the modern nation of Italy. Since then the popes have been political sovereigns only over the very small area of the Vatican, while being the religious rulers of the entire Roman Catholic Church throughout the whole world. Indeed, one important aspect of Medieval history was the pope's exercise of political power in Italy along with his religious authority, because the former gave the popes the status of Medieval kings and often brought them into conflict with other monarchs.

When Pepin died in 768, he was succeeded by his son Carolus or Charles; and since he became the greatest conqueror in western Europe at that time, his Latin name, Carolus Magnus (Charles the Great), is commonly rendered today as Charlemagne. Like his father, he continued to be a staunch ally of the pope; and amid his numerous military campaigns he invaded northern Italy, defeated the Lombards, ended their rule of northern Italy, and reasserted the pope's claim to rule the Papal States. Accordingly, on Christmas day in 800 the pope in gratitude crowned Charlemagne as emperor (i.e., Augustus) when the latter happened to be visiting Rome. In later times this event became an important precedent for the Holy Roman Empire, as the ruler of what is now Germany sought to enhance his position by receiving the sanction of the pope, while the popes in turn claimed the exclusive right and power to crown these rulers as emperors.

The relationship between the Carolingian kings and the popes illustrates the complex and tangled nature of politics and religion during the Middle Ages. As we have seen, the popes were not merely heads of the Christian Church, but they were political rulers in their own right; and as Medieval history demonstrated time and time again, Christianity often suffered from this combination of religious and political power, because many popes devoted an inordinate amount of their efforts to their political responsibilities and ambitions to the detriment of their religious duties. On the other hand, Medieval kings did not simply regard themselves as secular rulers, but as important religious leaders as well. Since they saw themselves as having been placed in power through divine Providence, many monarchs took their duties as Christian kings as seriously as their strictly political ones. Most of the time their goals coincided with those of the pope, but on some occasions the two were at odds with one another; and it was this curious conflict between kingly and papal power that characterized much of the history of the Middle Ages.

There were very few years of Charlemagne's reign (768-814) in which he was not carrying out a military campaign to secure or to extend the borders of his realm. He was in fact so successful militarily that he created an enormous kingdom that embraced much of western and central Europe, extending from the Ebro River in northern Spain to the Elbe River in Germany. In keeping with his self image as a Christian monarch, he forced defeated pagans to be baptized. In order to govern his vast empire, Charlemagne created an administrative structure that slowly developed into feudalism, the political and military system typical of much of Medieval Europe. Charlemagne divided his empire into about 600 districts called counties and appointed counts to watch over them. They were supposed to provide their district with protection from outside attack and to hold court to settle disputes. Within each district there was a similar delegation of authority with each locale placed under its own leader. These smaller areas in later times were often dominated and protected by a castle, and the lord of the castle was known as a castellan. These local leaders were answerable to the count. The area of the local leader was further parceled out as manors or farms and entrusted to persons who were obligated to serve their local lord on horseback as knights in time of war along with his own band of followers, who fought on foot.

This vast pyramidal network was held together through personal relationships created by feudal ties. The feudal lord (i.e., the superior party in the relationship) granted a fief to his vassal (the inferior partner in the relationship). The way in which this relationship between lord and vassal was created was as follows. The vassal, usually kneeling before his lord, swore oaths of homage and fealty. The latter was an oath of loyalty or fidelity, whereas homage (from the Latin word *homo* meaning man) referred to the vassal's swearing that he would be his lord's man, to serve him in war and peace. The fief was a piece of land. It could be as large as an entire county or as small as a single farm. It was entrusted by the feudal lord to the vassal to tend, enjoy, and protect. He was expected to maintain order within his fief; and in return for receiving its produce and revenues, the vassal was obligated to render his lord military service. Thus, instead of the abstract notion of the state characteristic of the ancient Greek and Roman world, political power, the administration of justice, and military service in Medieval Europe were defined and exercised through this vast network of personal bonds. This system was simply the elaboration of the personal nature of political and military leadership that had characterized the early Germanic tribes even before their entry into the Roman Empire. Its ultimate basis was the war band, as we encountered in *The Epic of Beowulf*, in which the chieftain gathers around him a personal following of warriors due to his prowess in battle and his ability to reward his warriors with land, captives, and other forms of booty. As the Frankish Kingdom grew under the Merovingian and Carolingian kings, the personal relationships between leaders and followers were gradually expanded and extended into different levels; and by the High Middle Ages many of the positions within this network had become hereditary and were passed on to members within the same family, so that this structure eventually evolved into a class system of hereditary noble titles.

Frankish feudalism was entirely based upon who had possession and the use of land. By Charlemagne's time the vibrant town life that had characterized the economy, society, and culture of the Roman Empire had largely vanished. During the Central Middle Ages the vast majority of the Frankish population were serfs, who differed from the slaves of the Roman Empire by not being owned by a master, but by being legally bound to the agricultural estate on which they had been born, and on which they were obligated to live and work for the person who happened to have possession and use of the estate as his fief. This Medieval system of social and economic organization is termed manorialism and is derived from the word "manor," which was the usual term applied to a large plantation-like estate. Text #28 in PSWC is a document entitled *Capitulare de Villis*, which was issued by Charlemagne's son Louis the Pious to serve as a basic guide for operating manorial estates in southwestern France. Its various provisions, when taken together and carefully analyzed, offer us an interesting picture of the nature of a Medieval manor and how it operated. The primary function of the manor was to grow crops with which to feed its serfs, who plowed the soil, planted the crops, and harvested them. They kept part for their own consumption and paid another part to their lord. In addition, rather than relying upon trade and manufacturing in towns for other non-agricultural necessities as had been the case in Roman times, the manor strove to be as self-sufficient as possible. It not only produced staple crops, a wide variety of fruits and vegetables, and all manner of farm animals, but it tried to produce everything else that its serfs needed. The serf population comprised craftsmen of all sorts: carpenters, metal-smiths, leather workers, etc.; and the women were employed in spinning thread, weaving it into cloth, dying the cloth, and making it into clothes, blankets, quilts, pillows, etc. In the last provision of this document (#70) there is a very long list of plants that should be grown on these estates. Such a garden would have served as the estate's rudimentary pharmacy, because many of these plants would have been used for making simple medicines to treat the serfs for various ailments. Other provisions imply that the serfs worshipped in a church on the estate and were punished for crimes not by some state official, but by the steward who managed the manor. These estates also raised horses and made barrels, wagons, and tools that were used by the Frankish army. Until the reemergence of town life during the High Middle Ages (1050-1350) self-sufficient manorialism defined how nearly everyone lived and worked throughout much of western Europe.

At the beginning of this lecture there is a short text, in which Charlemagne issued a summons to one of his vassals to be ready to go out on a military campaign. In this instance, however, the vassal was not the count of a county, but the abbot of a monastery. Here again we have an interesting illustration of the way in which politics and religion were entangled in Medieval society. The abbot was a religious functionary, a man who had been educated as a priest and was the head of a monastery. But as we will see when we survey monasticism in Lecture 23, Medieval monasteries were woven into the manorial system, in which the monastery owned (or was granted as a fief) a sizable piece of land to be worked in order to produce the food for the monks, but since land formed the basis of feudal obligations, the abbot, though a priest, was also a feudal vassal and was obligated to perform military service along with any knights who in turn happened to be his vassals. Thus, as we can see, the abbot had both religious and feudal obligations and duties, which at times might be in conflict with one another.

Although Charlemagne was primarily a war leader and could not read and write, he clearly understood the value of education. The vast geographical extent of his kingdom required a fair amount of record keeping, and the latter could only be accomplished by people who could read and write. In addition, as a devoutly Christian monarch, he knew that Christianity would flourish only if its clergy were well educated in the literature of *The Bible*. Moreover, realizing the very sorry state of learning throughout much of his realm, Charlemagne endeavored to bring about a major revival in Latin scholarship. He invited the most learned men of western Europe to his court at Aachen (located on the modern border between Belgium and Germany) and authorized them to promote education in the major churches and monasteries. As a result, schools for teaching monks and potential members of the clergy were created as a regular part of monasteries and cathedrals. Moreover, since book learning cannot succeed without books, Charlemagne's reign witnessed a substantial increase in book production. Of course, this was long before the time of the printing press and even before the use of paper in western Europe. In order to produce a book, a person had to copy out the entire text by hand; and since books at this time were almost entirely confined to churches and monasteries, one important duty carried out by monks was making copies of books, so that they could be handed on to the next generation. In fact, it was common for a monastery to have a room set aside for nothing but book production. This room was called the scriptorium, or writing room, where monks sat day after day, working at copying entire texts. In fact, Carolingian book production was so successful that many of the texts surviving from ancient times go back to manuscripts that were produced during this period. It has been estimated that perhaps as many as 10,000 books were produced by Carolingian copyists.

The principal writing material used in western Europe at this time was parchment or vellum, formed from the skins of sheep or calves respectively. Since it could not be produced as easily or as plentifully as paper, it was always in somewhat short supply. In order to make the most of their limited quantity of writing material, Carolingian copyists devised a new form of writing known as Carolingian minuscules, in which each letter of the alphabet was written in a smaller size so as not to take up as much space on the parchment as the letter forms in previous use. Before this time there had been only one type of letter forms used for the Roman alphabet, what today we call uppercase or capital letters. The Carolingian minuscules, however, are the ancestors to our lowercase letter forms. They not only looked nicer than the earlier letter forms, but they made reading easier; and the Carolingian scholars further enhanced the readability of their manuscripts by devising and employing a number of punctuation marks.

Perhaps the best example of Carolingian scholarship is Einhard's biography of Charlemagne, major portions of which form Text #27 in PSWC. Since Einhard regarded Charlemagne as one of the great figures of his day, he decided to write a biography of his life, so that people in later times would know of him. What is significant about this biography in the present context of this lecture is how Einhard composed this work. He wrote it in Latin in a style characteristic of the Roman Empire, not in the Medieval Latin of his own day, thus demonstrating his scholarly learning. In addition, he used as his basic model the Roman Imperial writer Suetonius, who was famous for having written a series of twelve biographies of the emperors of the Principate: Julius Caesar, and the emperors from Augustus to Domitian. In writing these imperial biographies Suetonius followed a basic model of organization: first treating the subject's family background, then the person's youth, followed by a chronological treatment of his actions as an adult, then listing the person's habits and describing his physical appearance and character, and finally ending with an account of the person's death. This was the way in which Einhard organized his material for his biography of Charlemagne. It is also noteworthy that the biographies of Suetonius had nothing at all to do with Christianity or Biblical studies. Although most of Medieval book production and study focused upon works that could aid in understanding *The Bible*, the Carolingian revival adopted a more expansive attitude toward the literature of the past, so that many scholars were interested in books in their own right, not because they could contribute to Christianity. Consequently, book production and learning during the Carolingian revival were not merely confined to Christian literature, but fortunately for us, they encompassed all areas of ancient learning and thereby took efforts to ensure the copying of numerous non-Christian texts. Thus, Einhard's biography of Charlemagne, based upon Suetonius' biographies of Roman emperors, is an excellent example of the educational program and success of the Carolingian revival.

As we will see in the next lecture, the Carolingian revival was disrupted by the great invasions of the ninth and tenth centuries carried out principally by the Vikings and Magyars, and to a lesser extent by the Arabs. As a result, western Europe's cultural advancement was cut short and was postponed for another two centuries until the intellectual reawakening of the High Middle Ages, beginning c.1050.

When Charlemagne died in 814, he was succeeded on the Frankish throne by his sole surviving son Louis, who was given the name "the Pious," because he continued the work of his father by trying to reform the monasteries in order to make them operate more in accord with their ideals of Christian devotion, piety, and asceticism. His reign, however, was troubled by unrest and rebellions, as his three sons and powerful nobles conspired and fought among and against themselves. For example, in 833 Louis' three sons (for once) banded together, stripped their father of his kingly power, and sent him off into retirement to a monastery; but in the very next year quarreling among the sons obliged them to restore their father to the throne. When Louis died in 840, the vast Frankish Kingdom created by Charlemagne devolved upon his three sons, who in 843 in the Treaty of Verdun agreed to divide it into three parts. Charles the Bald received the western portion, consisting of western and central France, and which ultimately developed into the modern nation of France. Louis was granted the area east of the Rhine, which was inhabited by German-speaking peoples; and this region became first the major portion of the Holy Roman Empire and then much later the modern nation of Germany. Lothair, the oldest of the three, ruled over the central area of the kingdom, the region now forming the nations of Belgium, the Netherlands, Switzerland, and even northern Italy. Much of this area was less unified than the other two in terms of language and its cultural identity. In a sense it formed a kind of no man's land or cultural gradient between the more culturally distinctive western and eastern regions, an intermediate status which is still reflected in the area's linguistic pattern today. In fact, one area, Lorrain, took its name from Lothair, as can be more easily seen from the German designation for this region: Lothringen. Indeed, modern historians sometimes refer to the Treaty of Verdun as the birth certificate of Europe, because it anticipated the modern-day national configuration of these three regions.

The Viking Age

IMPORTANT DATES AND TERMS

- **800-1050:** The Viking Age of Western European history.
- **895-955:** Period of Magyar destructive raiding throughout Europe.
- **911:** Creation of the duchy of Normandy.
- **955:** Decisive defeat of the Magyars at the Lech River by the German monarch Otto I.
- **1000:** Leif Erikson sails west and lands in "Vinland the Good" in North America.
- **Danelaw:** area of northern and eastern England colonized by the Danes.
- **Normandy:** area of northern France colonized by Norsemen.
- **Iceland:** large volcanically produced island of the North Atlantic, colonized by Vikings.
- **Greenland:** very large, glacier-covered island of the north Atlantic, whose southern edge was colonized by Vikings.
- **Vinland:** name given by Viking explorers to an area of North America.

As described in the previous lecture, Charlemagne attempted to carry out a revival in learning in the Frankish Kingdom of western Europe, and he was in fact rather successful. Unfortunately, before this revival could move forward significantly to repair all the damage caused by the Germanic invasions of the Roman Empire during the fifth century, this Carolingian revival was cut short by even more invasions that lasted about two and a half centuries, during the period 800-1050, and since the Vikings took the leading role in these invasions, this period of the Central Middle Ages is often termed the Viking Age, which will be the subject of this lecture.

But before we turn our attention to the Vikings, we will first treat more briefly two other peoples who also attacked parts of western Europe during this period. As we have seen, by the beginning of the eighth century the Arabs had overrun the lands bordering upon the southern coast of the Mediterranean, including all of northern Africa from Egypt to the Atlantic; and they had even crossed the Strait of Gibraltar and had added the Iberian Peninsula (modern Spain and Portugal) to their empire. During much of the ninth century the Arabs renewed their attempt to add more to their Islamic Empire by launching naval attacks upon the islands and coastal areas of the central Mediterranean. They succeeded in overrunning the island of Sicily and establishing their rule over it for the next two centuries. As a result, both Spain and Sicily became important multi-cultural areas in which there dwelled Jews, Christians, and Muslims, and from which Arab cultural influence, such as the use of Arabic numbers, eventually filtered into western Europe and played a role in creating the intellectual revival of the High Middle Ages (1050-1350).

These Arab attacks culminated in the capture of Rome in 846. The city was sacked, and Christian churches were desecrated. As the result of this humiliation, the pope began to construct a massive fortification to surround the small area of the Vatican (situated on the northwestern fringe of Rome), into which he could take refuge in the event of future attacks. These walls can still be seen today and served the popes well over the course of the next one thousand years, as Rome was occasionally attacked and captured by different enemies.

A second major cause of disruption was the Magyars. They arrived on the European scene in the year 895 and carried out destructive raids for the next sixty years until their crushing defeat at the Lech River in 955. They resembled the Huns in terms of their origin, lifestyle, and mode of fighting. They were a nomadic people of central or northeastern Asia, who moved about to find suitable pasturage for their herds of cattle. The women and children traveled in wagons that carried their rather sparse possessions, while the adult males rode on horseback. Like the Huns and Seljuk Turks, the latter of whom we have touched upon in connection with Byzantine history, the Magyars were fierce warriors. Boys were taught to ride from a very early age; and as the result of their nomadic lifestyle, the males virtually lived on horseback, became excellent horsemen, and were highly skilled in the use of the bow and arrow that they used for hunting and warfare. When they migrated westward into eastern Europe, they settled down in the plain of what is now Hungary, because the area provided their horses and cattle with ample pastures. In fact, the modern population of Hungary claim descent both from the Huns and the Magyars.

For sixty years large numbers of Magyar horsemen carried out raids into central Europe: primarily into what are now Austria, southern Germany, Switzerland, eastern France, and even across the Alps into northern Italy. They traveled light, and each horseman was served by more than one horse, so that the rider could switch from horse to horse as each one tired. In this way the Magyar raiders could travel rather quickly, appearing suddenly upon their victims and then riding off again before effective counter-measures could be taken. Since the goal of their raids was quick and easy plunder, they focused their attacks upon monasteries and churches that had valuable silver and gold objects and vessels for performing religious rites or to adorn the relics of saints. They killed people who attempted to stand in their way, and they carried off others as slaves. The predictable recurrence of their raids into the eastern part of the Frankish Kingdom prompted the inhabitants to build walled castle-like forts into which the people could take refuge. In addition, the Frankish kings slowly organized cavalry and infantry forces with which to oppose the Magyars.

These defensive measures culminated in the battle of the Lech River in 955 at Augsburg in southern Germany, where the Lech River flows into the Danube. Otto I, the Frankish king and later known as Otto the Great, led a large Frankish army against the Magyar raiders and succeeded in delivering a crushing defeat upon them. The Magyars who were not killed in battle were taken prisoner; and following the battle all but a few captives were slain. The few survivors were then allowed to return home in order to bear the news of this annihilating defeat to their people. The battle of the Lech River thus broke the back of the Magyars and persuaded them to turn their raiding attacks eastward and southward against the Byzantines, but by the year 1000 they began to abandon their raiding lifestyle, as many of them became farmers, and as they also were converted to Christianity and became part of the larger Christian culture of Western Europe.

The most prolonged series of attacks upon western Europe during this period was carried out by the Vikings or Norsemen. The latter is a term that simply means "the North Men," because they came from what are now the three Scandinavian countries of Denmark, Norway, and Sweden. The Swedes expanded eastward across the Baltic Sea into what are now the Baltic states and Russia, whereas the Danish and Norwegian Vikings expanded westward. The Viking expansion was carried out by sea and along rivers, and the vehicle employed was the Viking long ship, many examples of which have been recovered by archaeologists. They varied in length from forty to eighty feet. A few were as long as 100 feet. They were no more than about fifteen or twenty feet in breadth and were rather shallow, usually no more than about six feet. They were undecked and could be powered by sail or oars, the number of the latter depending upon the length of the ship. Given its relative small size and shallow draft, it could sail on both the open sea and along rivers and streams into fairly shallow water, thus making it ideal for travel by water.

One of the more interesting aspects of the Viking expansion has been revealed by the relatively new science of climatology. Despite hysterical claims made in the media in recent years about man-made global warming, climatologists have established beyond doubt that the Earth's climate is not a steady-state system, but for as far back as it can be traced, it has gone through cycles of warming and cooling, none of which has resulted from human activity. During the period 800-1300 the Earth's climate was warmer than it currently is, and climatologists term these centuries the Medieval Warm Period. Beginning around 1300 the Earth's climate began to cool down again and remained relatively cool until about 1850, after which the Earth's climate has been warming up again. Climatologists term the period 1300-1850 as the Little Ice Age. The arrival of the Medieval Warm Period played a crucial role

Vikings → seafarers, violent little people who appeared small.

in the Viking expansion across the North Atlantic. The warmer year-round temperatures created a much longer sailing season and thus enabled the Vikings to carry out much longer voyages than previously possible, because the northern latitudes of the Atlantic became free of ice at an earlier time in the spring and did not freeze over until a later time in the fall.

Our earliest reference to a Viking raid upon western Europe comes from an early English document known as The Anglo-Saxon Chronicle. It records an attack upon southeastern England in the year 789 and two more in 793 and 794 respectively upon the monasteries of Lindisfarne and Jarrow on the eastern coast of England. Once the Vikings discovered that the lands to the west of Scandinavia offered easy pickings, the news spread throughout Scandinavia, and Viking raids upon the British Isles and France became frequent. As in the case of the Magyars, Viking raiders concentrated their attacks upon undefended or poorly defended churches and monasteries, where they could carry off silver and gold objects. Like the Magyars, the Vikings killed those who offered resistance and seized others to be their slaves. Viking seamanship and the versatility of the long ship allowed them to appear with little advance warning, to carry out their attack, and then beat a hasty retreat. Viking attacks on England fell upon the coastal areas, but after establishing settlements there, they penetrated the interior on horseback by traveling along the roads that the ancient Romans had built. On the other hand, the rivers of Ireland and especially of France (Seine, Loire, and Garonne) gave the Vikings easy access to the interior, so that, for example, in 885 a large flotilla of Viking ships under the command of Sigfred the Dane sailed up the Seine and attacked Paris. The latter at this time was simply a small settlement on an island in the river. There the Vikings stayed for eleven months, and they did not withdraw until they had extorted the payment of 700 pounds of silver from the western Frankish king, Charles the Fat.

In addition to the frightful picture of the fierce Viking raider that we have from Western European sources, we have two other important sources of information about these people: archaeology and the Icelandic Sagas. Unlike the Magyars, the Norsemen were a literate people, and they have left behind tombstones and various artifacts inscribed with their Runic writing.

Excavations have shown that Norse craftsmen produced many daily objects of use with artistic refinement. But our best source of information about the Norsemen was written down in their own words in Iceland during the twelfth and thirteenth centuries. Before that time the Vikings had a rich oral tradition of story-telling in which myths, legends, and historical events were passed on from one generation to the next by word of mouth. These stories, or sagas, as they are usually termed, were not set down in writing until long after the end of the Viking Age when the Vikings had become Christian and no longer worshipped their pagan gods. During the twelfth century two important works were produced: The Book of the Icelanders, and The Book of the Settlements. Both were collections of stories concerning the families who settled Iceland, their genealogies, and their histories. Two works composed during the thirteenth century were the Elder Edda and the Younger Edda. The former was written in archaic poetry, whereas the latter was written in a more recent prose style. They contain the Norse myths of Creation and of their gods, such as Odin, Thor, and Balder, heroic stories about their kings and warriors, and other more ordinary tales. In addition to the Eddas, there were compiled at this time other collections of stories. All this written material gives us fascinating glimpses into Viking society. For example, despite their reputation among Western Europeans as savage and maniacal warriors (a reputation that they richly earned and deserved), most Norsemen were ordinary hard-working people, who had little tolerance for unsocial and destructive behavior within their own midst, such as homicide, which they regularly punished by banishing the murderer from their community. Moreover, given the hard living conditions of Norse society and the need for everyone to do their part, the sagas reveal that women enjoyed considerable freedom and independence.

The common pattern of the Viking expansion was initial raids, followed up by the more peaceful establishment of trading posts and colonization involving entire Norse families. The Vikings were truly intrepid seafarers and bold colonizers. In fact, given what they accomplished during the Viking Age, they could be accurately termed the pioneers or frontiersmen of Western Europe during the Central Middle Ages.

During the last third of the 800s Danish invaders had carved out their own territory around York in northeastern England. They received immigrants from Denmark and fought with the native Anglo-Saxons to take over more land until their expansion was halted during the first part of the 900s. Alfred the Great (871-899), the king of Wessics (the western Saxon kingdom), began the Anglo-Saxon resistance by establishing a series of forts. The Danes, however, renewed the fighting during the closing years of the 900s and the opening years of the 1000s. In fact, they became such a presence in northern and eastern England that the whole area became known as the Danelaw. The modern expression, "paying Danegeld," goes back to this period and refers to the Anglo-Saxons being forced to pay the Danes in order to keep them from launching attacks. During the period 994-1014 the Danes succeeded in extorting more than 100,000 pounds of silver from the Anglo-Saxons, who institutionalized these payments by establishing a Dane tax. Indeed, the Danes formed such a presence in England that although they were ultimately absorbed into the Anglo-Saxon population as they were in other areas where they settled, they affected the regional dialect of the area, and many common English words are of Danish origin: e.g., anger, awe, awkward, call, crooked, die, egg, fellow, flat, happy, hill, husband, law, leg, rugged, skin, skull, take, them, tight, till, ugly, and wrong.

A similar pattern of Norse colonization and attendant impact upon the local language occurred in northern France. By 911 the Norse had so heavily settled the area around the mouth of the Seine River that the French king recognized the Norse ruler of the district as duke of Normandy (land of the Norsemen), and the king received oaths of fealty and homage from him as his feudal vassal. The Norse population affected the way in which the language of this area developed by changing the pronunciation of vowels and consonants and thus creating what is known as Norman French. In addition, the Viking attacks all along the rivers of France during the ninth century contributed to the political fragmentation of this region and the emergence of strong local rulers who could provide the surrounding population with more effective protection than the king in Paris. The very predatory nature of Viking raids is evident from the fact that based upon our very incomplete records, the king of the Western Franks (i.e., France) paid out no less than 39,700 pounds of silver as Danegeld in seven payments during the years 845-886. The money for these payments was raised by the king imposing taxes upon his subjects. Normandy soon emerged as an important and powerful region, whose martial spirit owed much to the Vikings. In 1016 Normans in fact launched an attack upon the Mediterranean island of Sicily and eventually succeeded in making themselves masters of the island, which for the past several generations had been ruled over by Muslims. From Sicily the Normans overran both southern Italy and the western part of the Balkan Peninsula, which were still controlled by the Byzantines; and this Norman intrusion into the Mediterranean foreshadowed the crusading expeditions of the Franks (including many Normans) into the eastern Mediterranean during the following century.

The Vikings established trading posts in Ireland that eventually grew and became important modern cities (Dublin, Wexford, Limerick, etc.). They also settled the small North Atlantic islands of the Orkneys, Shetlands, and Faroes. Then around 870 they discovered the uninhabited island of Iceland, which they proceeded to colonize. Since the island was quite rugged from having been produced by volcanism and was covered in part by glacial ice and snow, they called this land Iceland; and despite its rather forbidding geography and northerly latitude, it was still quite suitable for human habitation, farming, and stock breeding. Rather than establishing a form of kingship, the settlers of this new land created a representative form of government. Beginning around 930 they agreed in designating one spot as their place of assembly, where representatives from the different districts of the island met for several days every year to have important issues and cases decided, as well as to hear a man orally recite the law. This person was known as the law speaker. He had to have a prodigious memory, held his position for three years, and recited one-third of the law at each of the three annual meetings at which he performed his duties.

Following the Norse settlement of Iceland, the westward expansion of the Vikings across the North Atlantic made its two biggest jumps around 985 and 1000 under the leadership of Erik the Red and his son Leif Erikson. When the Icelanders banished Erik the Red from their land for three years for having committed homicide, Erik sailed off to the west in search of a land that a few other Vikings had sighted when they had been driven off course. A few days sail to the west brought him to the enormous and glacier-covered island of Greenland; and after finding two areas on the southwestern and western coasts lush with green vegetation and perfectly suitable for human habitation during the height of the Medieval Warm Period, he returned to Iceland and persuaded others to join him in settling these two areas. According to the Icelandic saga, his expedition consisted of 25 ships laden with settlers and livestock, but only 14 of the ships reached their destination. The Vikings did in fact establish two settlements on Greenland; and they were able to eke out an existence for more than 400 years, but with the onset of the Little Ice Age and colder conditions, survival became increasingly difficult until the inhabitants dwindled in numbers and finally completely died out from cold and starvation during the fifteenth century, not long before Christopher Columbus sailed west from Spain in 1492 and landed in the New World. The fascinating history of these two settlements in Greenland and their ultimate extinction have been graphically reconstructed in recent years by archaeologists.

Around the year 1000 Leif Erikson and a small group of people from the Greenland colonies set sail and traveled even farther westward in search of a land more suitable for settlement than Greenland. They discovered an area that they called Vinland the Good, because it had a much milder climate than Greenland, so much so that it had wild grape vines, hence the name Vinland. For many years modern researchers used the topographical information in the so-called Vinland Sagas to try to locate the place in North America discovered by Leif Erikson, but it was not until the 1960s that archaeological excavations at a site called L'Anse aux Meadows in Newfoundland settled the question. Archaeologists were initially led to the site by the shoreline's resemblance to what is mentioned in the Vinland Sagas. Then they discovered the remains of eight sod houses and a garbage dump that contained a few metal artifacts of obvious Viking type. The houses were constructed of wooden beams and sod and were used for both living quarters and work. One building was the place where the Viking settlers repaired their ships, and another one was where the women did their weaving. They even had a small furnace for smelting iron that they made into nails. The remains of butternuts were found at the site; and since they did not grow in the immediate vicinity but had to come from warmer places farther to the south, it appears that this site was a base from which the Vikings set sail to explore areas to the south.

Possible confirmation of Viking settlement in North America has recently emerged from DNA analysis. A very small number of Icelanders today have DNA that seems to have originated centuries ago from someone or someones native to North America. This has led to speculation that at least one Native American woman sailed with Vikings to Iceland, where she (or they) contributed to the Icelandic gene pool.

The Vinland Sagas make it clear that these settlers were interested in peaceful colonization, but they soon had nasty and violent encounters with the natives, whom the Vinland Sagas call Skraelings. The latter certainly would have outnumbered the Viking settlers and could have therefore made it difficult for the newcomers. Thus, despite the great desirability of the area, which, unlike Greenland, possessed fine timber for ship construction, the Norse abandoned their settlement, but over the next few centuries they continued to make periodic voyages thither in order to obtain wood. The Viking movement across the North Atlantic from Iceland to Vinland was a truly remarkable phenomenon.

We will now trace the eastward expansion of the Vikings. When the Norse of Sweden sailed across the Baltic Sea, they found the mouth of the Dvina River in the Bay of Riga that led them inland to the Valdai Hills, out of which flowed two other important rivers of eastern Europe: the Dnieper and the Volga. By sailing along these two rivers they were able to explore a vast area. The Dnieper led them southward to the Black Sea, and sailing across it brought them to Constantinople. The Volga bore them eastward for a long distance before turning south and bringing them to the Caspian Sea and into contact with the Islamic Empire. In fact, Text #29 in PSWC is an Arab eye-witness account of a Viking funeral that occurred at a Norse settlement somewhere on the Volga. Given the Vikings' reputation as ferocious warriors, many were recruited into the Byzantine army as mercenaries, and by the eleventh century they formed their own military unit that served as the

Byzantine emperor's bodyguard. But as they did in other parts of Europe, these eastern Vikings established trading posts along the rivers, and two of them eventually arose to become important cities: Novgorod (New Town in Slavic) in northern Russia, and Kiev in Ukraine. The land at this time was relatively thinly populated and heavily forested and inhabited by wild animals. Thus, one of the main attractions of this region was its animal furs; and like the mountain men of our own western United States during the early nineteenth century, many of these Vikings were fur trappers, who brought their cargoes of furs by ship down the Dnieper, across the Black Sea, and to Constantinople to sell. One name by which these eastern Vikings was called was Rus, and from this name derives Russia. Kiev began as a Viking trading post and soon grew into the largest and most important town of this region. It served as the capital of a Slavic kingdom, whose monarch, King Vladimir, in 987 took the historic step of converting to Orthodox Christianity and therefore introduced Byzantine Christian culture among the Slavs of this area.

By 1050 Viking raids and major military expeditions were largely a thing of the past, although, as we shall see when we survey England during the High Middle Ages in Lecture 25, the battle of Hastings in 1066 was preceded by the last Viking invasion of northern England. By the close of the period covered in this lecture the Vikings had converted to Christianity and were becoming part of the larger Christian community of Europe, but their previous activity as intrepid seafarers, traders, and colonizers had done much to establish long distance trade routes and settlements that became very important during the High Middle Ages in the revival of town life, the economic growth of Europe, and the development of free-market capitalism.

Monasticism

IMPORTANT DATES AND TERMS

- **535:** St. Benedict founds the Monastery of Monte Cassino in west central Italy.
- **910:** Foundation of the Monastery at Cluny.
- **1182-1226:** Life of Saint Francis.
- asceticism < Greek *askesis* = 'training', involving physical hardship or denial, mortification of the flesh.
- *Rule of St. Benedict:* guidelines for the monastery.
- **abbot** - monastery - monks
- **abbess** - convent - nuns
- **Cluny:** under papal authority, ruled over many daughter houses, important in advocating Church reform.
- **Citeaux** - Cistertian order: return to the Benedictine model of both spiritual devotion and physical labor.
- **Franciscan Friars:** mendicant monks, living very simply, working among the people.

THE VOW OF A MONK

(Taken from *A Source Book for Medieval History: Selected Documents Illustrating the History of Europe in the Middle Age*, by Oliver J. Thatcher and Edgar Holmes McNeal, Charles Scribner's Sons [New York 1905])

Monasticism → life way in which one fully devotes oneself to religious ideals.

I hereby renounce my parents, my brothers and relatives, my friends, my possessions and my property, and the vain and empty glory and pleasure of this world. I also renounce my own will for the will of God. I accept all the hardships of the monastic life and take the vows of purity, chastity, and poverty in the hope of heaven; and I promise to remain a monk in this monastery all the days of my life.

In this and the following lecture we will complete our survey of the Early and Central Middle Ages by examining Christianity from two different perspectives: the phenomenon of monasticism, the subject of this lecture; and the papacy and the institution of the Roman Catholic Church in the next lecture. In an Anglo-Saxon document dating to the reign of Alfred the Great (871-899) contemporary society was described as consisting of three groups: those who work, those who fight, and those who pray. Those who worked were the serfs on the Medieval estates; those who fight were the various individuals immeshed in the feudal system for performing military service. Those who pray were the ordained members of the Church, especially the monks and nuns of the monasteries and convents.

Monasticism is a very interesting topic, but since, as usual, we have only a limited amount of time to cover roughly seven hundred years of a very complex subject (c.500-1200), we will have to be selective in covering four examples of monasticism that give us a representative picture of the whole phenomenon. We shall begin with some of the important philosophical and religious ideas and practices that led to the development of monasticism. It all goes back to Greek philosophy and the culture of the Greek eastern half of the Roman Empire. One important idea that ran through much of Greek philosophy was the dualistic contrast between the human body and the soul and between things material and things spiritual. Greek philosophers, of course, regarded things spiritual as superior to material things; and in some philosophical quarters this led to what we call asceticism, individuals leading very austere lives in order to avoid material things as much as possible and living a life of the mind in an attempt to develop their spiritual being to the maximum. Asceticism derives from a Greek word, *askesis*, which means "training" or "exercise." Just as an athlete needs to engage in hard and regular training in order to build up strength, so it was believed that humans should engage in activities that were thought to develop their spiritual being as much as possible partly in anticipation of death, at which time the human body and soul would be separated, and the soul would then embark upon its spiritual journey for the rest of eternity.

As Christianity became part of the larger religious environment of the Greek eastern half of the Roman Empire, these ideas of dualism (matter vs. spirit) and the notion of an ascetic lifestyle were absorbed into Christianity and gave rise to the phenomenon of hermits. These people were the ultimate loners. They were persons who wanted to live an ascetic life by shunning, as much as possible, the normal human interactions of this material world and to engage in religious or mystical contemplation of the divine in isolation from the distractions of everyday life. They divorced themselves from ordinary things and went off into a desert or heavily forested environment where they would not come into contact with other human beings. There they existed with little clothing and food, while they contemplated the divine and attempted to commune with it. Some of these hermits developed reputations as great holy men and attracted a following. Sometimes people simply wanted to consult them for advice, but others were impressed by their example and wished to follow in their footsteps. Thus, although he had intended not to do so, a hermit sometimes found himself leading a small band of like-minded individuals in a remote area, as they tried to live out in practical terms an ascetic and spiritual life. It was this sort of organized group activity that formed the basis of monasticism.

Now one common feature of the history of monasticism was this. First, a charismatic leader attracted followers and developed them into an organized group of monks. Secondly, since the charismatic founder would eventually die and not be around to personally supervise his followers, he attempted to institutionalize their ascetic lifestyle by drawing up a charter or constitution of regulations. Thirdly, the monastic following succeeded for a time in living out the ideals of the charismatic founder, but inevitably, being human and thus imperfect creatures, they slowly began to deviate more and more from the original goals, so that their lifestyle became increasingly mechanical in going through the motions; and at the same time the monks were involving themselves more and more in ordinary human activities. Finally, once this decline set in, some monks eventually noticed that they were really not doing what they were supposed to; and someone or someones then decided that it was time to reform things, and the whole cycle of charismatic founding, institutionalization, and decline played itself out all over again. This pattern resulted from two unchangeable things: the very high moral and ascetic ideals of the charismatic founder, and the basic imperfection of human beings.

We may now begin our historical overview of monasticism in the Middle Ages. By the fourth century monasticism was becoming an important phenomenon in the Greek eastern half of the Roman Empire, and from there it spread to the Latin western half of the empire. It received additional impetus with the invasions of the Germanic tribes from the late fourth century onwards, because many inhabitants of the Roman Empire, thinking that civilization was rapidly coming to an end, decided that it made good sense to withdraw from the ordinary world and to live out a simple, but spiritual existence that was detached from the hurley-burley of the material world.

Our first of four examples of Medieval monasticism is Saint Benedict. In 535 he established a monastery at Monte Cassino in Italy just north of the beautiful Bay of Naples and south of Rome. Out of this monastery grew the Benedictine order of monks. In order to provide a clear guide for his followers, Saint Benedict wrote a governing charter or constitution, known as The Rule of Saint Benedict, portions of which form Text #30 in PSWC. This became one of the most important and influential documents for all of Medieval monasticism, because it was copied and rewritten in various ways to serve as the operational guide for different orders of monks throughout western Europe for several centuries. As stated in The Rule, Saint Benedict regarded idleness as the enemy of the soul, because when people are idle, that is usually when they wind up doing things that they should not be doing. Thus, he designed a highly regimented life for all his monks, in which they were kept busy at all times of the day. Moreover, since the monastery was established in a remote area and needed to develop self sufficiency just like a Medieval manor, the monks had to spend some of their time in ordinary labor on the land and with other associated chores. Consequently, he devised a lifestyle that was roughly equally divided between physical labor and spiritual devotion. The monks' activities were performed together as a group. They arose from bed at the same time, had their meals together at the same time in a dining hall (termed a refectory), performed all their religious services together every three hours, eight times a day, in their chapel or church; and they went to bed at night at the same time in a barracks-like room with each person on his own small bed. The monastery was governed by the abbot, whose name derives from the Hebrew word for father (abba); and he was supposed to rule like a benevolent monarch. Although his authority was not to be questioned, he was expected to consult regularly and frequently with the monks in order to receive their advice and suggestions on how things should be run, and what decisions needed to be taken on various matters. He often had a second in command, a person called the prior, who assisted the abbot and could take over if the abbot needed to be absent to attend to other matters.

At the very beginning of this lecture there is a short text, "The Vow of a Monk," which gives you an example of the oath that monks had to take when they left lay society and became a member of a monastery. It was a decision for life. Once they became a monk, they remained one for the rest of their life. They formally renounced all connections with their relatives and friends, gave up all their property and possessions, and submitted themselves to the will of God and the monastery. They took a vow of poverty, humility, and chastity, the last ensuring that they would never engage in sexual activity. As The Rule of Saint Benedict spells out, monks were to cultivate the three virtues of humility, obedience, and silence. Humility was in keeping with the Christian notion that we are all rather insignificant in the whole scheme of things and in comparison to the majesty of God and of all eternity. Thus, what we as individuals do or think cannot be all that important. Monks were to be obedient to their abbot, who was to serve as God's deputy in regulating their lives. Monks were also expected to speak as little as possible. For example, their meals were eaten in silence while one of them was given the task of reading aloud from *The Bible* or some other religious work, so that their minds would be occupied with wholesome thoughts as they ate.

abbot → gaems the Monastery
abbess → gaems a convent

There was, of course, a female parallel to male monasticism. Just as a monastery was composed of monks under the rule of an abbot, there were also female monasteries called convents, composed of nuns, who were governed by an abbess. Since it was not often easy for the women to carry out all the hard physical labor on the land to provide them with food, it was not uncommon for a convent to be situated next to a monastery, so that the monks could donate part of their labor in working the land of the convent, or the nuns would reciprocate by providing the monks with woven textiles. Alternatively, convents were often established upon land with its own serf population for working the land for the nuns.

Charlemagne's son and successor to the Frankish Kingdom, Louis the Pious (814-840) received his name, the Pious, because he interested himself in reforming the monasteries throughout his kingdom. There was considerable variation from monastery to monastery in how things were done, and how rigorously they lived in accord with their regulations. For one thing, monasteries and convents often served as convenient dumping grounds for families eager or needing to rid themselves of a family member. I have already mentioned in Lecture 21 how the Venerable Bede at the age of seven was given by his parents to a local monastery, because his family simply had too many mouths to feed. Thus, there were always many instances in which a person became a monk or nun by necessity and not through his or her deliberate decision to live the rest of their life in a strict spiritual manner. Another important factor that contributed to monasteries not living up to their intended goals resulted from how they were embedded into the whole Medieval system of feudalism and manorialism. A monastery or convent was in large measure operated like any other Medieval manor in that it possessed a large tract of land that had to be farmed in order to provide the monks or nuns with their necessary food; but since land was the ultimate basis for feudalism and military service, the land attached to monasteries and convents usually had feudal military obligations to go along with them, thus forcing the monks to be part of the larger feudal structure and not simply being ascetic persons divorced from the rest of Medieval life and society. So, if you turn back to the beginning of Lecture 21 on the age of Charlemagne, you will find a short text entitled "A Military Summons." It was issued by Charlemagne to his vassals in preparation for one of his many military campaigns. In this particular case, however, the vassal being thus summoned was not a count or duke, as we might expect, but an abbot, who not only was the governor of a monastery, but also had feudal military duties to Charlemagne and was thus obliged to mount up on his horse with other subordinate knights to rendezvous with Charlemagne to go off and fight. As a result, there were always many abbots ready and willing to run a loose ship, because they were not entirely devoted to the ascetic life, but were more wrapped up with worldly concerns.

This brings us to our second case of Medieval monasticism: namely, Cluny, established in 910 by William the Duke of Aquitaine, and located in Burgundy in southeastern France. Duke William intended to found a monastery that would live up to the highest standards of monasticism; and in order to keep it from being contaminated by local church politics, he specified in the founding charter that rather than it being under the jurisdiction of the local bishop as was the general practice, his monastery would answer to none other than the pope himself. As we have already seen, a monastery could suffer from lax management by its abbot because of the latter's worldly concerns and preoccupations. The same was true, perhaps even more so, with regard to the local bishops under whom the abbot served, because many of these bishops were people who had not received their appointments due to their great piety and devotion to the Church, but because they came from a prominent family that wanted to have one of their members highly placed in the Church hierarchy, and in a position that brought in a nice regular income. Thus, if the local bishop did not exercise sufficient scrutiny over the monasteries in his district, monasticism could easily degenerate into a lifestyle more akin to ordinary Medieval life.

Cluny succeeded in revitalizing Medieval monasticism. It was fortunate to be governed by a series of very able and devoted abbots throughout the tenth and eleventh centuries. In fact, the hunger for a better form of monasticism was so strong throughout western Europe at this time that many monasteries willingly placed themselves under Cluny's rule to be reformed and to operate like Cluny. It therefore became the head of a large network of daughter institutions. In addition, since Cluny answered to the pope, not to the local bishop, its monks became very vocal advocates of the papacy and also urged that the Church undergo a much needed major reform of its ways. Indeed, Cluniac monasticism was responsible for the Catholic reform movement of the eleventh century that we will survey in the following lecture. Unfortunately, Cluniac monasticism experienced the pattern that we have outlined above: charismatic founding, institutionalization, and decline, leading to another round of reform. As Cluny took western Europe by storm in leading monasticism, there were numerous lay people who wanted to become part of the movement, and they were willing to give land and other things to Cluny to support its mission. This pattern resulted in part from people's desire to have monks pray for their own salvation or for that of deceased loved ones, because doing so could assist in the person progressing from purgatory to heaven. Consequently, by the later eleventh century Cluny had become a very wealthy institution, supporting monks in a rather lavish lifestyle, inconsistent with their vows of poverty and humility. We therefore come to the third case of monasticism in our survey, the Cistertian order, which takes its name from Citeaux, the place from which this new form of monasticism spread. It was founded in 1098 not too far from Cluny. It was located in a very remote place in the middle of a wilderness, because the founders wanted to make sure that their monks would have to work hard in clearing the land and would be far removed from other settled areas. They wanted to reinvigorate Saint Benedict's ideal of monks devoting about half their time to physical labor and the other half to spiritual matters. Like Cluny before it, Cistertian monasticism proved to be highly popular and successful, because it seemed to live out the high goals expected of monastic life. Its monks lived austere lives and worked hard in clearing land and bringing it under cultivation. In fact, Cistertian monasticism fell victim to its own great success, because due to its monks' austerity in living simple lives and their success in clearing land, by 1200 the Cistertian order had founded 525 houses and had become quite wealthy from its substantial land holdings. It therefore found itself more envied and resented than admired.

We now come to the fourth case of Medieval monasticism in our survey, and it is quite different from what we have thus far encountered. The three other examples of monasticism were typically Medieval in that they were very much a part of the Medieval pattern of manorialism that determined the overall social and economic structure of the Early and Central Middle Ages. As we shall see in Lecture 27, one of the most important phenomena of the High Middle Ages (1050-1350) was the emergence of town life as an important force in Western European society and its economy. During the High Middle Ages towns began to become much more numerous, and they emerged as the engines of economic growth and the beginnings of capitalism with their manufacturing of and commerce in many goods. This fourth case of monasticism was divorced from the earlier manorial model and was geared toward this newly emerging town life.

Around 1200 there came into being two types of this new monasticism: the Dominican and Franciscan orders. We will touch upon the former in Lecture 25 in connection with the early history of France. Therefore, in this lecture we will focus upon the latter. Both the Dominican and Franciscan orders are often termed the mendicant friars, or begging brethren, because rather than living upon a Medieval manor, these monks initially were itinerant priests, who moved from place to place to carry out their mission among ordinary people; and in order to have enough to get by, they took what day-job that they could find (e.g., working in a farmer's fields in return for their daily food), or if no such work were available, they obtained their minimal daily needs by begging from people.

I will end this lecture by briefly telling, as best I can, the amazing story of Saint Francis. If we had to choose one person as the most outstanding individual of the Middle Ages, there would probably be no contest. Saint Francis would win. In fact, he was a person of such extraordinary spirituality and charisma that many of his followers believed that he was the second coming of Jesus Christ, and that his mission on Earth signaled that The End of Days was at hand. He was born in 1182 in the town of Assisi, located in the mountains of northern Italy. His father was a well-to-do merchant of cloth, and Saint Francis grew up in a very comfortable family environment, in which he was the oldest child and was indulged by his parents. He had many friends and was widely regarded as the life of any party. But as he reached his later teen years, he had to decide what to do with the rest of his life. Like many young men of that time, he decided that he would become a knight and go off crusading. After all, this was the period of the great crusading movement. But after two very unsuccessful and unhappy experiences, one involving a war with the neighboring town of Perugia and resulting in Francis being imprisoned for almost a year, he gave up the idea of becoming a knight. He then had an important religious experience in which he believed that God spoke to him and ordered him to restore his church. Saint Francis took these words quite literally and thus began to devote considerable effort in rounding up bricks and mortar to fix up one of the dilapidated churches in Assisi. But after working on it for some time, Saint Francis came to the realization that God's admonition had meant something quite different. He was wanting him to somehow rejuvenate the entire Roman Catholic Church. At that point Saint Francis began to develop his own incredibly charismatic style of serving his fellow man and trying to convince others to awaken spiritually and to live truly Christian lives.

One of the most controversial issues involving the Catholic Church at that time was that of wealth and poverty, because the Catholic Church was by far the richest institution in all of Europe, and many of its clergy lived high on the hog, eating fine meals and wearing elegant clothes, which many regarded as inconsistent with the simplicity and poverty of Jesus and his disciples. In fact, many at this time criticized the Catholic Church for its wealth and for what they regarded as its relative indifference to the plight of the poor. Thus, one of the chief characteristics of Saint Francis' mission was his insistence that his followers assiduously cultivate poverty and avoid money and possessions. They had only the clothes that they wore (often little more than rags) and sometimes even went bare foot, and they provided themselves with only the minimal amount of food and shelter from day to day, regularly relying upon the charity of strangers. Saint Francis regarded this austere lifestyle as simply living and practicing what Jesus had instructed his disciples to do: "Heal the sick, cleanse the lepers, raise the dead, cast out devils. Freely ye have received, freely give. Provide neither gold, nor silver, nor brass in your purses, nor scrip for your journey, neither two coats, neither shoes, nor yet staves: for the workman is worthy of his meat" (*Matthew* 10.8-10). Saint Francis was himself the most inspiring example of simplicity and apostolic poverty. He and his followers were constantly on the move, coming into towns and preaching the need for people to practice charity and love of their fellow man. Although most people at this time regarded themselves as good Christians, many, as today, were living rather complacent lives, going through the basic motions of being a Christian, but not always attempting to live up to the highest spiritual standards spelled out in *The New Testament*. In addition, Saint Francis devoted much of his activity to aiding the sick and those suffering from incurable diseases by tending to their basic needs and trying to make them as comfortable as possible. This was a time in Europe when hospitals as we know them today did not exist, and many persons suffering from chronic diseases were often neglected or even cast out by their families. Saint Francis' service to the sick is perhaps best summed up by the words of one of his followers, who once remarked that he did what Francis did, but he could not find in it the joy that Francis did.

In 1219 Francis left Italy and traveled to the eastern Mediterranean in order to carry the word of Christianity to the Muslims. This was the time of the Fifth Crusade. He thought that the crusades should be a peaceful, not a warlike, enterprise. He was even prepared to be seized and executed for his activities and would therefore be martyred for the Christian cause. One day Francis and a single companion left the crusader army besieging Damietta in the eastern delta of the Nile and walked until they encountered Muslim soldiers. Rather than killing the two Christian strangers on the spot as they normally might have done, the soldiers instead conducted this odd unarmed pair into camp and right up to the magnificent tent of the caliph. Francis was hoping to persuade the caliph to convert to Christianity and was in fact allowed to engage him and his own Muslim religious leaders in an open discussion of their two religions. At the conclusion of this interchange, which lasted several days, the caliph (predictably) still adhered to his Muslim faith, but he was so impressed by Francis' simplicity and earnest piety that the caliph sent him away unharmed and attempted to shower him with rich gifts, which Francis refused to accept as being inconsistent with his avowed poverty.

Saint Francis' type of monasticism was designed to serve the new town life that was emerging in western Europe. He did not want Christian spirituality locked up and practiced inside an isolated monastery, but to be encouraged to develop among everyone in their daily lives. His personal example was so compelling that even during his own brief lifetime he attracted followers from all over Europe, who were eager to live more spiritually enriched lives. But as the number of his followers grew, it became increasingly difficult to maintain his high ideal of strict poverty, mendicancy, and itinerant service. Consequently, Francis and church authorities encountered major differences when they attempted to work out a rule to govern this new monastic order. Here we see a clash between Francis' charismatic example and the difficulty in trying to institutionalize it. Eventually, Francis had to make concessions with which he was not fully comfortable. The rule of the Franciscan order that was finally authorized by the pope allowed the friars to use money, to possess buildings, and to own books for educating themselves. After voluntarily stepping away from leading his followers and appointing someone else to take over this position, Francis spent the last few years of his life in accordance with his high ideals of poverty, asceticism, and spirituality. His example was so inspiring that it not only resulted in the creation of the new order of Franciscans, but it also spawned two other important religious organizations: the Poor Clares, an order of nuns founded by Clare, a dear friend of Francis, who was also from Assisi; and the order of the Penitents. The latter were members of lay society (not ordained members of the clergy) who wanted to incorporate Saint Francis' ideals, as much as possible, into their daily lives.

LECTURE 24
The Medieval Papacy

IMPORTANT DATES AND TERMS

- **1059:** Decree regulating papal elections.
- **1075:** Composition of the Dictate of the Pope (*Dictatus Papae*).
- **1075-1122:** Conflict over lay investiture between the pope and the ruler of the Holy Roman Empire, ending in the conference at Worms.
- **Petrine doctrine:** assertion of the bishop of Rome (pope) to speak and act authoritatively for the entire Church.
- *Donation of Constantine:* forged document of the Carolingian Age, offering a historical justification for the pope's intervention into the secular affairs of western Europe.
- **Papal States:** area of central and northern Italy given by Charlemagne to the pope to rule, thereby involving the papacy in secular matters.
- **penance:** atonement officially prescribed by a priest for one's confessed sinful acts.
- **simony:** the granting of priestly offices in exchange for money.
- **priestly celibacy:** restriction that priests abstain from sex and not marry.

In this lecture we will survey the history of the Roman Catholic Church and the papacy during the Early and Central Middle Ages, aspects of which are illustrated by three important writings forming Text #31 in PSWC.

As we have seen, Constantine was the first Roman emperor to embrace Christianity in 312, after which the religion spread rapidly throughout the Roman Empire, so that by 391 the Emperor Theodosius issued a decree that banned all forms of paganism, henceforth making Christianity the only religion tolerated by the Roman state. But with Theodosius' death in 395 the eastern and western halves of the Roman Empire began to drift apart; and during the fifth century the invasions of the Germanic tribes slowly destroyed the Roman Imperial government in the Latin west. Into the power vacuum in Italy created by these invasions stepped the pope, who soon emerged not only as the religious monarch of Christianity, but also as the actual secular ruler or king of Rome and central Italy. As western Europe dissolved into a motley collection of Germanic kingdoms, the only universal institution was the Roman Catholic Church, but as we will see later in this lecture, it initially did not possess the necessary strong organization to have the pope's will and decisions carried out and implemented swiftly and efficiently. Nevertheless, the Church did provide the one unifying factor in western Europe during the chaotic times of the Early Middle Ages. The whole region was divided into districts called dioceses that were placed under the rule of a bishop appointed by the pope. In fact, the pope himself was technically the bishop of Rome. Each diocese was in turn subdivided into parishes that were under the supervision of a priest, who, of course, answered to the bishop of the diocese. Moreover, each parish paid a tax to the Church, so that the latter quickly emerged as the wealthiest institution of Medieval Europe.

Perhaps the single biggest problem facing the early Medieval Church was simply trying to Christianize the inhabitants of western Europe. We speak very glibly of an emperor, such as Constantine, or a Germanic king, such as Clovis, or his people becoming Christian, but what did this actually mean? Did their conversion suddenly endow them with a full and clear understanding of what Christianity actually was, and how it should transform their lives? Probably not. We need to keep in mind that literacy was virtually non-existent in western Europe during the Middle Ages, so that almost no one except the priests of the Church could read *The Bible*, whose text existed only in Latin. Thus, what the ordinary person knew about Christianity probably consisted of nothing or little more than Jesus' death on the cross, his resurrection, and the promise of eternal salvation if the person was sure to do a few basic things as instructed by his local priest. Moreover, Medieval sources record numerous instances in which a Christian king defeated a non-Christian people and then forced them to be baptized. In such cases we are justified in doubting how fully Christian these people became. In fact, we have evidence that non-Christian beliefs and practices flourished for centuries among rural inhabitants who seem to have been largely untouched by Christianity. We therefore need to keep in mind that when we talk about someone or some people becoming Christian during these centuries, it is likely to have been a very complex phenomenon, in which a small number did succeed in becoming fairly Christian, but many simply continued on in their previous ways with a bit of Christianity added into the mix.

This point brings us to the first of the three passages (Text #31A in PSWC). It is a letter written by Pope Gregory in 594 to give advice to a missionary being sent to England to convert the Angles and Saxons to Christianity. The pope urges that the missionary not destroy the pagan temples of these people, because if they are well built structures, they can simply be recycled as churches, as long as they are desanctified as pagan shrines and then reconsecrated as Christian churches. In addition, Pope Gregory advises that popular pagan festivals not simply be abolished, but they can be recycled as Christian feast days associated with important saints in the Catholic calendar. You can therefore easily see that if a missionary did such things, it would have been quite natural for the newly converted to largely remain in their pagan ways while the priests in the Roman Catholic Church were of the opinion that their flock had become Christian.

During the course of the Middle Ages the Roman Catholic Church developed seven holy sacraments for regulating people's religious life and behavior: baptism, confirmation, holy matrimony, holy orders, extreme unction, the Eucharist, and penance. Baptism, of course, even preceded Christianity with John the Baptist in *The New Testament*. When Constantine converted to Christianity during the early fourth century, baptism was delayed in a person's life until the person was approaching death, because the person wanted the rite to cleanse him of all his sins, and he wished to have very little remaining time in which he might commit additional sins that could jeopardize his entry into heaven. During the Middle Ages, however, baptism was a rite performed on the newborn infants, because given the very high rate of infant mortality, people wanted to make sure that their baby would be cleansed of the original sin that they had inherited at birth from the disobedience of Adam and Eve in the Garden of Eden, so that they would be able to go to heaven. Confirmation was performed at the time of puberty and was designed to reaffirm that the person was a Christian. Then, of course, when people decided to marry, they did so with the sacrament of holy matrimony performed by a priest. On the other hand, if a person decided to enter the service of the Church as a priest, monk, or nun, he or she did so with the sacrament of holy orders. The Eucharist (or communion) was the taking of the bread sanctified by a priest, who, like a magician, transformed it from ordinary bread into the body of Christ through what the Church termed transubstantiation, i.e., changing the substance of the bread. In fact, our modern expression, "hocus pocus," associated with magic tricks, derives from the Latin spoken by the priest, "Hoc est meum corpus (this is my body)." Penance involved a person formally confessing his or her sins to a priest and having the latter prescribe the appropriate penance, so that the person could atone for those confessed sins. Penances consisted of so many days of fasting, abstaining from eating meat, abstaining from sexual intercourse with one's spouse, doing charitable works, or going on a pilgrimage to a holy site and seeking forgiveness. We can therefore see that in theory people's lives should have been affected by the religious environment provided by the Roman Catholic Church, but there was doubtless considerable variation from person to person, depending upon the individual's own circumstances of life, and how often they came into contact with the local priest.

We will now devote the remainder of this lecture to examining several of the important concepts and historical trends that shaped the papacy during the Early and Central Middle Ages, and we will begin with what is called the Petrine doctrine. It takes its name from Peter, the most important of Jesus' twelve disciples, and it is based upon the Roman Catholic Church's interpretation of a particular passage in *The New Testament, The Gospel According to Matthew* 16.18-9. It involves a verbal pun: namely, that the word for Peter in Greek (*Petros*) means "rock." In this passage Jesus is addressing Peter, and it reads as follows: "Thou art Peter, and upon this rock I will build my church; and the gates of hell shall not prevail against it. I will give to you the keys of the kingdom of heaven; and whatsoever you shall bind on earth, shall also be bound in heaven; and whatsoever you shall loose upon earth, also shall be loosed in heaven." It is from this passage that the popes derived their claim to be the supreme authority among all Christians, and this is how their argument ran. According to accepted tradition, Peter traveled to Rome, where he founded the city's first community of Christians, over which he served as its leader. Since Rome was the recognized capital of the Roman Empire, and since according to *Matthew* 16.18-9 Jesus, the son of God, had charged Peter as the founder of his Church, the church established by Peter in Rome was in fact established by God himself and was intended to head the entire community of Christians; and since the popes were the successors to Peter in Rome, the popes were God's chosen rulers over all Christians.

We now come to a second important concept that figured very prominently in the popes' self image and claim to authority: namely, the doctrine of the two swords. This idea formed a cornerstone of papal ideology during the Middle Ages and is attested as far back as c.500 when it was enunciated by Pope Gelasias. According to this doctrine, there exists two kinds of authority in the world, which can be thought of as swords. One is the temporal (or secular) sword, and the other is the spiritual (or religious) sword. Of these two, the spiritual sword is the mightier, because, after all, it is not simply concerned with the temporary and transient matters of this world, but with eternity. Moreover, since it is the spiritual sword that is wielded by the popes, it is superior to the temporal sword exercised by kings. Consequently, all kings are duty-bound to submit themselves to the popes. In this way the popes laid claim to supremacy in the secular sphere, as well as the religious; and by doing so they often came into conflict with Medieval kings, who sometimes obeyed or were forced to obey the pope, and on other occasions they succeeded in defying him.

Charlamagne → brought the Roman Catholic Church into western Europe.

Armed with these important papal concepts, let us now trace the history of the papacy for the period c.750-1150. As you may remember, Charlemagne and his father Pepin were the Frankish kings who first forged an alliance with the popes. This resulted in large measure from the popes' need to have a strong military ally to oppose the Lombards in northern Italy, who were hostile neighbors to the popes and threatened their control over central Italy. Both Pepin and Charlemagne invaded Italy, defeated the Lombards, added their realm to their Frankish Kingdom, and secured the popes' rule over central Italy, which was henceforth known as the Papal States. By doing so the popes were established as fully secular rulers, not simply the religious head of the Roman Catholic Church; and this ensured that they would play an important role on the stage of power politics in Europe for the next several centuries. In fact, the popes did not relinquish their rule over the Papal States until 1871 when Italy ceased being a collection of different states and small kingdoms and was unified into a modern nation. At that time the pope was stripped of his secular power, as represented by the Papal States, and was reduced to ruling over his tiny kingdom of the Vatican, measuring only a few square miles in the northwestern area of Rome.

PSWC #31
This brings us to the second of the three documents in PSWC (Text #31B), The Donation of Constantine. It purports to be a text written by Constantine, the first Christian emperor; and it bestows upon the popes not only their insignia of office and the Lateran Palace in Rome, but also their right to rule over all the western districts of the Roman Empire, because Constantine in acknowledgment of the pope's supreme authority has decided to move to the eastern half of the Roman Empire and to rule those areas from his newly founded capital of Constantinople. This document, however, was never composed by Constantine, but it was fabricated by some unknown person contemporary with Pepin or Charlemagne during the middle or late eighth century, more than 400 years after Constantine's death; and it was clearly designed to give the popes' claim to supremacy in the secular realm a solid historical foundation. In fact, the document was generally accepted as authentic until finally during the fifteenth century the Renaissance scholar Lorenzo Valla demonstrated that its Latin revealed it to be a Medieval forgery.

Nevertheless, before Valla's debunking of the document, it had served the papacy well in justifying the popes' high-profile involvement in the secular affairs and power politics of the Middle Ages.

The alliance between the papacy and the Frankish Kingdom nearly disappeared with the death of Charlemagne. This was in large measure due to the gradual breakdown and fragmentation of the Frankish Kingdom caused by the attacks and invasions of the Vikings and Magyars, as well as by the deliberate division of the Frankish Kingdom into three parts among the three grandsons of Charlemagne. The middle portion of the kingdom given to the oldest grandson soon fell apart, because there was little or nothing in common shared by its different districts to hold it together. The western and eastern portions, on the other hand, each shared a common language and culture that gave them internal cohesion and enabled them eventually to emerge as the modern nations of France and Germany. But given the very rudimentary and simple political organization of the Western and Eastern Frankish Kingdoms, they easily crumbled into their constituent feudal districts (counties and duchies) under the onslaught of the Vikings and Magyars: for since the two Frankish kings were unable to provide the local areas under attack with an adequate defense, the regional counts or dukes or local castellans who did provide some defense emerged as the acknowledged rulers of their areas, although they still theoretically owed homage and fealty to their Frankish kings.

This fragmented state of affairs finally began to change in the Eastern Frankish Kingdom during the middle of the tenth century. Since this region bore the brunt of the Magyar attacks, the people slowly mobilized themselves militarily against it by building fortresses into which the surrounding population could flee in times of attack, as well as organizing themselves into a fighting force. The latter was carried out by the Frankish kings and culminated under the reign of Otto I, the Great (936-973). As we have already seen in Lecture 22, he was responsible for delivering a crushing defeat upon the Magyars at the Lech River in 955, which ended the Magyar invasions. As part of his program of restoring the glory of Charlemagne to his realm, Otto reestablished an alliance with the papacy, invaded Italy, added Lombardy to his Eastern Frankish Kingdom, secured the pope's control over the Papal

States, and had himself crowned as emperor by the pope in Rome, just as had happened to Charlemagne on Christmas day in 800. Otto's coronation in Rome on February 2, 962 marks the beginning of the Holy Roman Empire, which according to Voltaire, was neither holy, nor Roman, nor much of an empire. Nevertheless, it took its name from the idea that Otto and his successors were reviving the grandeur of the ancient Roman Empire, and it was termed "Holy," because it was Christian. It did in fact unify the German-speaking peoples along with others into a kingdom that eventually evolved into the modern nation of Germany; and for its first 100 years or so it was the strongest kingdom in western Europe, but as we will soon see, its unsuccessful struggle with the papacy over the issue of lay investiture (1075-1122) resulted in it becoming the weakest region of western Europe for many centuries.

We now come to the papal reform movement of the eleventh century, which was crucial in the papacy emerging by 1100 as a well organized and powerful institution in western Europe. Despite being the one and only universal institution of Medieval Europe, the Roman Catholic Church in 1000 was not very effectively organized, nor was it well led or administered by the popes. This situation slowly changed over the course of the eleventh century as a series of strong-minded and devoted popes did much to eliminate long standing abuses and corruption in the Church and shaped it into a much more centralized institution. One common abuse that had long plagued the Church was termed simony. This was the practice of people buying their way into coveted positions, such as that of bishop, because it conferred considerable wealth upon its holder. Simony takes its name from Simon Magus (Simon the Magician), encountered in *The Acts of the Apostles* in *The New Testament*, and who attempted to purchase from Peter his powers to work miracles. Simony existed in the Medieval Church, because many prominent families wanted to have one of their members highly placed in the priestly hierarchy in order to exercise influence within the Church and also to benefit from the wealth that went along with the position. Obviously, this resulted in many people becoming bishops, abbots, or priests for reasons other than their sincere desire to serve the Church and to minister to the religious needs of their flock. Another major abuse was absenteeism. This consisted of a person obtaining a lucrative position in the Church and not bothering to come into the district to carry out its functions. Instead, the holder of the office stayed where he was, occupied in other matters, while raking in the monetary proceeds of the position and appointing another priest of much lower standing to carry out the actual duties of the office. Once again, of course, this resulted in ordinary people not being served by their religious leaders as they should have been. A third concern of the Church reformers at this time was the issue of celibacy for the priests. Although celibacy had long been required, it had never been effectively enforced. Many priests had actual legal wives; others took female companions as extra-legal concubines; and others simply satisfied their sexual needs through promiscuity or by visiting prostitutes, while some actually did live up to the requirement of celibacy.

By the beginning of the eleventh century there were many inside and outside the Church's priestly hierarchy calling for reform. As explained in Lecture 23, one of the leading voices in this movement came from Cluny; and it was also promoted by the Holy Roman Emperor. Pope Leo IX (1049-1054) made major advances in reforming the Church by traveling about, holding meetings among Church officials, and taking a direct hand in cleaning things up by deposing unsuitable priests and replacing them with new ones. In 1059 the papacy established a fixed procedure by which popes would be appointed, a procedure that is still in effect today. Henceforth, when a pope died, all the cardinals in the Church, who formed the highest ranking level of bishops, would be summoned to Rome, where they would meet and elect by majority vote the next pope. This procedure was intended to take the papal succession out of the hands of the powerful families in Rome, who for generations had largely determined who would be the next pope. The papal succession had previously been little more than a test of strength among the aristocratic families in Rome, each of whom wanted one of their own family members to become the next pope. The papal succession had often resulted in these families mobilizing popular support among the ordinary population in Rome, which led to the outbreak of violence until one party overpowered its adversaries and had its candidate installed on the papal throne. There had been one instance in which a teenager (i.e., Pope John XII, 955-964), clearly unfit for the office, was made pope.

In 1075 Pope Gregory VII issued a document known as The Dictate of the Pope, *Dictatus Papae*, which is Text #31C in PSWC. It is a list of 27 propositions that sum up the powers and privileges of the pope. They therefore constitute a charter or constitution by which the popes henceforth governed the Church. It was part of the on-going process of the papacy to set its house in order and to develop a clear and well defined organization. As we might suspect from what we have already encountered concerning the doctrine of the two swords and The Donation of Constantine, this list contains a number of extraordinary and breath-taking claims, such as the infallibility of the pope on matters of doctrine and Church policy, as well as his power to make and unmake emperors.

In the same year in which The Dictate of the Pope was issued (1075), Pope Gregory VII's attempt to reform the Church even further brought him into a direct clash with the Holy Roman Emperor. This clash stretched out for nearly fifty years, finally ending in 1122, and is known by modern scholars as the conflict over lay investiture. The conflict began when the bishop of Milan, the largest and most important city in northern Italy, died; and Pope Gregory and Emperor Henry IV could not agree on who should become the next bishop of Milan. This so-called conflict over lay investiture stemmed from the very messy and disorganized nature of Medieval feudalism. As we have already seen, political power and military service in the Middle Ages were mediated through the system of feudalism, in which a feudal lord created obligations by handing out fiefs in the form of counties, castle districts, or manors to his vassals, who were charged with keeping peace and order within their fiefs and serving their lord in wartime. The problem was that the whole structure of the Church was embedded in this feudal system, because all significant positions within the priestly hierarchy had land holdings that bore with them feudal obligations to a lord. As a result, the holders of these religious offices were not simply priestly members of the Church, but they also had to fulfill the ordinary political and military obligations of feudal vassals. Consequently, it had become very common practice for feudal lords to exercise an important role in deciding who became the next holder of a priestly office, because the feudal lord wanted to make sure that the priest would be a loyal and competent feudal vassal. Vacant positions in the Church were supposed to be filled by having the members of the clergy in the pertinent region elect the new occupant of the office, but in practice feudal lords of the area routinely played an important, if not dominant, role in this process; and such involvement was termed lay investiture.

Since Pope Gregory VII was determined to establish the Church's authority in making all ecclesiastical appointments and eliminating all influence from the laity, this brought him into a direct power struggle with the Holy Roman Emperor, who had long exercised a leading role in filling the more important priestly offices within his realm. When Henry IV, the Holy Roman Emperor, refused to accept Pope Gregory's insistence on this matter, the pope responded by excommunicating him from the Church and therefore endangering Henry's personal salvation. In addition, Gregory declared that Henry was deposed from his position as emperor, and that his vassals and subjects owed him no allegiance. Henry responded by crossing the Alps into northern Italy and came to the pope's castle at Canosa, where Henry humbled himself by standing outside, dressed in rags and bare-foot in the snow, until Gregory finally took pity on him, relented, and revoked the excommunication. But that was simply the first round in a very long power struggle between the emperor and the pope. Years later Henry IV invaded Italy, marched upon Rome, deposed Gregory from the papacy, and had his own candidate voted in to replace him. The power struggle polarized all the leading figures of Italy and the German states into one of the two camps, and it did so in a rather unexpected way. Henry's feudal vassals, his counts and dukes, wound up supporting the pope; whereas the leading Church officials in Henry's kingdom largely supported him. This odd alignment resulted from the feudal vassals not wanting Henry to emerge from the struggle too powerful, because then he would be able to lord it over them much more easily. They therefore preferred having a weaker, rather than a stronger emperor. Similarly, the leading Church officials in Henry's kingdom did not wish to come under the authority of a strengthened pope, but they wanted the somewhat ill-defined situation to remain as it was, because it allowed them to play one party off against the other. After decades of unresolved conflict, the struggle came to an end in favor of the papacy, which, after all, had always been technically in the right. When representatives from the pope and emperor met at Worms in Germany in 1122, they worked out an agreement, which was an obvious solution to the whole problem, but it had taken them nearly fifty years to arrive at it. Henceforth the clergy had the sole authority to make appointments to vacant Church offices; and priests were to receive from the pope or from his authorized representative the ring and staff symbolizing the priest's marriage to the Church and his duty to be a good shepherd to his flock. The emperor, on the other hand, had the right to accept or deny the priest's oaths of homage and fealty associated with the feudal fief that went along with the priestly office. Thus, the emperor in effect had a kind of veto power. The clergy and pope had the authority to make the appointment, but it could not be implemented until or unless the emperor consented. This arrangement, of course, obliged the two parties to come to an agreement on who should fill the vacant office.

There were two very important long term consequences of the conflict over lay investiture. One was that the power of the Holy Roman Emperor had been broken. During the nearly fifty-year struggle the German states had experienced both long term anarchy and civil war. The emperor's vassals had succeeded in turning this situation to their advantage. They emerged from the struggle with their positions having been greatly strengthened and with the acknowledged right to elect the emperor. Henceforth the Holy Roman Emperor was largely a figure-head, presiding over a collection of relatively sovereign and autonomous counties and duchies. Consequently, while England and France emerged as centralized and powerful monarchies during the twelfth and thirteenth centuries as we will see in the following lecture, the German states of the Holy Roman Empire existed for centuries as a relatively weak union of independent feudal districts. On the other hand, the pope emerged from this struggle as the victor and consolidated his power over the Church hierarchy. Indeed, the 200-year period of 1100-1300 witnessed the pinnacle of papal power in European history, and it did not begin to decline until it was overshadowed by the powerful monarchies of England and France.

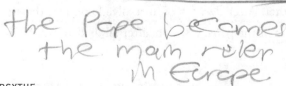
the Pope becomes the main ruler in Europe

LECTURE 25
The Rise of England and France

IMPORTANT DATES AND TERMS

- **871-899:** Reign of Alfred the Great of England.
- **1050-1350:** Period of the High Middle Ages, characterized by major political, social, economic, and cultural change.
- **1066:** Battle of Hastings.
- **1215:** Signing of Magna Charta by King John.
- **Danelaw:** northern and eastern England, settled by Danes.
- **William the Conqueror:** duke of Normandy and king of England.
- **Norman French:** language of the Norman conquerors of England.
- **English Common Law:** originating from the king's judges, common to the entire realm.
- **Angevin Empire:** England and much of France, resulting from Henry II's familial connections.
- **Cathars:** heretical sect of southwestern and southern France, object of a crusade.
- **parliament:** meeting periodically convoked by the English King on important matters, gradually evolved into a representative governmental assembly.

We are now embarking upon the fourth and final quarter of the course, in which we shall cover three major periods of Western European history: the

High Middle Ages (c.1050-1350), the Italian Renaissance (c.1350-1520), and the Early Modern Period (c.1520-1650). In doing so we will treat a number of different major topics, and the only overarching theme that ties them all together is the general advancement of Western European society along all fronts of human endeavor: important economic growth in the form of incipient free-market capitalism, political organization, religious diversity, developments in the fine arts and all areas of intellectual study, the discovery of the New World, and the beginnings of modern science. It was during these centuries that Western Europeans finally succeeded in surpassing the more sophisticated civilizations of Byzantium and Islam to create the world's most dynamic civilization that has continued to advance right up to our own day.

The subject of today's lecture is the rise of England and France during the High Middle Ages. We focus our attention upon England and France, because they now emerged as well organized and centralized feudal monarchies, but before we take up this subject, let us first devote some attention to see what was happening during this same period in Italy and the Holy Roman Empire. As we saw at the close of the previous lecture, the papacy emerged from the conflict over lay investiture as a very strong and well organized political institution. In fact, it was during the two centuries, 1100-1300, that the papacy enjoyed the pinnacle of its prestige and power in European secular affairs. Because of its political control over a significant part of Italy the papacy's emergence during this period can therefore be viewed as part of the larger phenomenon of the rise of states.

It is rather ironic that the rise in the papacy contributed significantly to increased political disunity within the Holy Roman Empire. Since the papacy and the Holy Roman Empire controlled lands in Italy that bordered on one another, the controversy over lay investiture during the late eleventh and early twelfth centuries had most immediate consequences for the Holy Roman Empire. This issue gave noble magnates especially in the German states a valid pretext for opposing the power of the emperor by siding with the pope. Thus, unlike France and England which experienced considerable political centralization during the High Middle Ages, the Holy Roman Empire's continued close involvement in the affairs of the papacy contributed to the opposite trend of political disunity. Even after the issue of lay investiture had been settled, conflict between the papacy and the Holy Roman Empire did not subside. In fact, their conflict actually escalated to periodic warfare in northern Italy during the reign of Frederick Barbarossa (1152-1190). He led six military campaigns across the Alps into northern Italy, but he was finally defeated decisively at Legnano in 1176. While he was occupied south of the Alps in trying to bring northern Italy under his control, his feudal vassals of Germany used his absence to strengthen their own positions. This process of decentralization accelerated further during the first half of the thirteenth century when Barbarossa's grandson, Frederick II, was emperor (1215-1250). Born of a Sicilian mother, he spent his youth in the island and was always far more interested in building up a powerful kingdom in Sicily and southern Italy than in Germany. This preoccupation led him to make major concessions to his German vassals, as well as to bishops and abbots, so that by the time of his death in 1250 the position of emperor had been greatly weakened, whereas the counts, dukes, and bishops had become largely sovereign. Germany therefore continued to be divided into several independent states until the late nineteenth century. On the other hand, Frederick's ambitions in Sicily and Italy posed a serious threat to and were resisted by the papacy, thus resulting in further destructive warfare and political conflict throughout Italy. In fact, the strife resulted in the creation of two opposing political groups in Italy during this period: the Guelphs who favored the cause of the papacy, and the Ghibellines who supported that of the emperor. So much for Italy and the Holy Roman Empire.

The single best example of political centralization during the High Middle Ages is England following the Norman conquest. During the years 600-800 England consisted of seven small independent kingdoms, the so-called heptarchy: Northumbria, East Anglia, Mursia, Essex, Kent, Wessex, and Sussex. These kingdoms warred with one another, which gradually led to groupings of smaller kingdoms into three larger ones of southern, central, and northern England. As we saw in Lecture 22, during the Viking Age England suffered considerably from the raids of Norsemen, many of whom even settled permanently in northern and eastern England to form a district known as the

Danelaw, because the culture and law of the Danish Norsemen prevailed in this area. By this means many words of Scandinavian origin entered the English language: e.g., anger, awe, awkward, call, crooked, die, egg, fellow, flat, happy, hill, husband, law, leg, rugged, skin, skull, take, them, tight, till, ugly, and wrong. Yet, by the end of the ninth century much of southern and central England outside the Danelaw had been unified into a single kingdom by Alfred the Great, the king of Wessex (871-899). This area remained unified and was ruled by native Anglo-Saxon kings until the early eleventh century.

Then, following a Viking victory over Anglo-Saxons at Maldon on the eastern coast of England in 991, Danish attacks intensified over the next generation along with large payments of Danegeld until finally in 1016 Cnut, the king of Denmark, became king of England, which he ruled with Denmark for nearly twenty years (1016-1035). After conquering Norway in 1028, he controlled three major areas of the North Sea. His rule marked the final flowering of Scandinavian power at the end of the Viking Age. His three-part kingdom, which had been forged by his own personal leadership, fell to pieces shortly after his death. For the next seven years England was ruled by Cnut's two sons, but in 1042 England again came under the rule of a descendant of Alfred the Great, Edward the Confessor. When he died childless in 1066, the kingly succession was disputed. An English nobleman named Harrold, who had been powerful during Edward's reign, and whose sister Edith had been Edward's wife, first took over as king, but his claim to the English throne was contested by two other people. One was the king of Norway, also named Harrold, who invaded England in the north, where the two Harrolds engaged one another in the battle of Stanford Bridge near York, fought on September 25, in which the Norwegian was defeated and killed. But the English Harrold was given no respite, because at the same time the other claimant to the throne was invading England from the south. This was William, the duke of Normandy. His claim to the English throne was based on the fact that he was related to Emma, the mother of Edward the Confessor. William gathered a considerable following, crossed the channel in numerous ships, and landed at Hastings on the southern coast right after Harrold's victory at Stanford Bridge. The latter therefore hastened southward, covering a distance of 240 miles.

The ensuing battle of Hastings, fought on October 14 of 1066, lasted nearly all day, but when Harrold was killed by an arrow in the eye, English resistance collapsed, and the Normans emerged victorious.

The battle of Hastings proved to be a major turning point in English history. it marked the end of the Anglo-Saxon Period and ushered in the Norman Age of English history. William's conquest of England took about five years to be completed. As a result, William, the duke of Normandy, is known to history as William the Conqueror. We possess a very interesting artifact concerning these events. It is known as the Bayeux Tapestry. It is a piece of cloth, measuring 19 inches high and 231 feet in length. It was embroidered by nuns of northern France with more than 70 scenes illustrating and narrating William's crossing of the English Channel and the battle of Hastings.

Putting down resistance allowed William to establish his power firmly over England by depriving English lords of their holdings and giving them to his Norman knights and nobles as feudal fiefs. This established William in a strong position by having local barons bound directly to himself by oaths of homage and fealty. Crucial to the Norman conquest was the throwing-up of numerous forts scattered throughout the land. At first these were very crude affairs, consisting of wooden towers on a hillock or artificial mound defended by an encircling earthen rampart, wooden palisade, and ditch, but they were eventually replaced by structures of stone, called castles, a word introduced into English from Norman French. The degree to which William succeeded in forging England into a well organized unified kingdom is further seen in the census taken at the end of his reign. Royal agents conducted a detailed survey of all households and their property holdings for the purpose of assessing taxes and determining military service. All this detailed information was organized into the so-called Domesday Book, which still survives and constitutes an important source of social and economic information for modern historians. No other kingdom in western Europe at this time was as centralized as England.

English history during the period 1100-1300 witnessed important developments in language, law, and government. As we have already seen in Lecture 22, the Norman conquerors of England traced their ancestry back to

Viking adventurers who settled in Normandy around 900. In the course of time these Normans adopted French as their native language. Thus, one important result of the Norman conquest of England was the establishment of Norman French as the language of the royal court and of the ruling class as a whole. But English (i.e., Anglo-Saxon) continued to be spoken by the large majority of native Englishmen. Consequently, English society during the twelfth and thirteenth centuries was bilingual. People of education would have spoken both English and Norman French and would have also known Latin. It was not until about 1400 that English finally replaced French as the prestige language of government and the royal court in England. The coexistence of English and French had important consequences for how English evolved as a language. It is most evident in English vocabulary, because during this period English adopted thousands of words from French. This process, as well as the class difference often associated with the two languages during this period, is well illustrated by words for domesticated animals and the meat resulting from them. English-speaking farmers raised pigs, cows, calves, and sheep for their Norman lords; and they also hunted deer. All these animal words are English words, but when these various animals were butchered and served up as meat to Norman lords, the terms used to describe them were all French in origin: pork, beef, veal, mutton, and venison.

This same period (1100-1300) was extremely important for the development of English common law. Since the High Middle Ages there have been two different legal traditions which have shaped the entire course of modern European legal history: Roman law and English common law. As we saw when we surveyed the Byzantine civilization in Lecture 19, the long and complex tradition of Roman law was codified by the Emperor Justinian during the sixth century, but Roman law was largely forgotten in western Europe during the Early and Central Middle Ages due to the destructive effects of the Germanic invasions, but in 1061 a text of Justinian's codification of Roman law (*The Digest*) was discovered in northern Italy. From that time onward Justinian's corpus of Roman law began to be studied seriously as one of the three major disciplines (the other two being theology and medicine) in the newly founded Medieval universities, and it was slowly incorporated into the legal systems of continental Europe. But what concerns us in this lecture is the other major legal tradition, English common law, which is the ancestor of the law of the United States. The only exception is the state of Louisiana, whose law is derived from France's Napoleonic law code of 1804, which in turn is based upon Roman law.

By the time that Roman law began to be studied in the Medieval universities, England was politically united more than any other European country, and it was in the process of developing its own legal system that had its origins in the earlier Anglo-Saxon Period preceding the Norman conquest. Consequently, there was little need for English judges and lawyers to borrow and adapt things from the currently studied body of Roman law, because their own independent legal tradition was sufficiently advanced and capable of further development to satisfy the needs of English society. The term "common" in the phrase English common law derives from the fact that this law was not of local origin enforced by the local lord but stemmed from the king and his judges and was common to the entire realm of England. Thus the term itself is another indication of the degree to which England was evolving into a centralized nation state. English common law grew out of custom and legal decrees issued by the various kings. Under King Henry II (1154-1189) England was organized into distinct judicial regions, and royal judges were appointed and sent out to tour the shires within their district for hearing and settling cases. They were often assisted in their inquiries by a group of twelve local citizens sworn to give relevant testimony. This practice later developed into the jury system. By the way, English shires were governed by local officials called reeves, and it is from the shire reeve that we derive our modern term sheriff. But to resume, if lawsuits could not be framed within existing case law, these royal judges had the authority to make innovations by extending existing law and custom to fit these new situations.

The reign of Henry II is also notable for two other things: a major religious dispute involving the archbishop of Canterbury Thomas Beckett, and the so-called Angevin Empire. The former can be regarded as the clearest English manifestation of a common historical phenomenon of the Middle Ages, the conflict between the power of the state and the authority of the

Church. This particular clash arose in connection with Henry II's assertion of the legal authority of his courts to judge and sentence clergymen guilty of crimes after they had been tried by an ecclesiastical court. There were many English clergy guilty of serious crimes such as murder, and the ecclesiastical court was far more lenient in its sentences. Becket maintained the Church's right to try and punish its own and denied the state's judicial authority over the clergy. The conflict between king and Church finally came to a head when Becket excommunicated the clergy who had participated in the coronation of Henry's son. This act so exasperated the king that he exclaimed in the presence of many, "Will no one rid me of this turbulent priest?" Thinking that they were doing the king's bidding, four barons traveled to Canterbury and stabbed Becket to death in the cathedral. In order to do penance for this murder for which he was indirectly responsible, King Henry humbled himself by walking barefoot through the streets of Canterbury and then submitted himself to be whipped by the monks. Becket was canonized as a martyr, and his grave in Canterbury became the object of religious pilgrimages in England, as made famous by Chaucer's *Canterbury Tales*.

Henry's reign was also notable for the Angevin Empire. William the Conqueror continued to be duke of Normandy after his conquest of England, and his successors were also both kings of England and dukes of Normandy. They therefore ruled domains on both sides of the English Channel. But we need to realize that these dukes of Normandy were also the feudal vassals of the kings of France, to whom they had to swear oaths of homage and fealty. This situation became even more complicated when Henry II became king. Not only was he descended from William the Conqueror and therefore the duke of Normandy through his mother Matilda, but through his father Geoffrey, the count of Anjou, he was the ruler of three districts in western and northwestern France: Anjou, Maine, and Touraine. In order to consolidate his control over these continental domains, Henry took to wife Eleanor, the duchess of Aquitaine, a large district of southwestern France, which also included the districts of Poitou and Gascony. Thus, through these familial ties Henry was not only king of England but also the ruler of several feudal districts that stretched across France from north to south. This feudal super-state has been termed the Angevin Empire by modern scholars. It endured only during the second half of the twelfth century, but while it lasted, it was the most dominant power of western Europe. Even after the Angevin Empire collapsed in the early thirteenth century, English kings continued to assert claims over these areas. The result was that for the next 300 years England and France fought numerous wars as invading English armies tried to win back areas of France.

The complicated and messy nature of Medieval feudalism is clearly revealed by the fact that although Henry II and his son Richard I the Lion Heart (1189-1199) were the vassals of the kings of France, they were more powerful than their feudal lords through their control of the Angevin Empire. Consequently, the kings of France were always trying to undermine Henry's and Richard's control of their feudal domains outside of England and thus obliged the two monarchs to spend much of their reigns in parts of France instead of England. In fact, Richard spent only six months of his ten-year reign in England. In addition, although they were kings of England, Norman French, not Anglo-Saxon, was the principal language spoken by these two monarchs.

Having traced English affairs up to this point, we now need to survey earlier French history. What is now France had formed the heart of Charlemagne's vast empire. After the death of his son Louis the Pious in 840 the Frankish Kingdomm was divided among his three sons, and France formed the western division ruled by Charles the Bald. But Viking raids and warfare between feudal districts contributed to political fragmentation and the weakening of centralized authority. The last Carolingian king of France died in 987 and was succeeded by the first of the new Capetian dynasty. Yet, this did not mark any significant change in French affairs. In fact, for the next 200 years the French king exercised direct control over a rather small area centering on Paris and Orleans, a district called the Ile de France, measuring about 50 miles wide and 100 miles long. The rest of France consisted of numerous feudal states that were technically bound by oaths of homage and fealty to the French king, but in reality the French king had little control over these areas. What prevailed in France was feudal anarchy.

As we have already seen, the Angevin Empire existed and flourished during the reigns of Henry II (1154-1189) and his son Richard the Lion Heart

(1189-1199), both of whom were very capable and energetic leaders. But the two English kings who succeeded Richard, his brother John (1199-1216) and John's son Henry III (1216-1272), were quite inept rulers. On the other hand, France was blessed by two very capable kings during much of the thirteenth century: Philip Augustus (1180-1223) and his grandson Louis IX (1226-1270). Consequently, this shift in the balance of royal leadership led to the destruction of the Angevin Empire and the rise of France as an important nation state. The twelfth century can therefore be regarded as the century of Medieval England, but the thirteenth century was the century of Medieval France.

The shift in the balance of power between England and France began in 1202 when King Philip Augustus, exercising his right as the feudal lord of King John of England, declared that since John had not performed the services required of a vassal, he was no longer entitled to the fief of Normandy. This formed the cause of war between France and England. France soon took back Normandy. Then after several years of inaction, the war finally ended with the battle of Bouvines in 1214 in which Philip Augustus led the French army in a decisive victory over the German allies of the English. The Angevin Empire of England was destroyed, and the French king was now able to establish firm control over the various districts of northern France.

At about the same time the papacy had declared a crusading war against the Cathars of southern France. For several generations this heretical form of Christianity had flourished in southwestern and southern France, where papal and French authority was very weak. The Cathars (also known as Albigensians) took their name from the Greek word *katharos*, meaning "clean" or "pure." They rejected the Catholic sacraments, the concept of the holy trinity, and the Catholic clergy in favor of their own rites and priests, whom they called the *perfecti*, the perfect ones. Catharism involved a strict division between matter and spirit. All things material were evil and the creation of the devil. Things of the spirit were good. Thus, catharist priests, who included many women and nobles, lived very austere lives. They were vegetarians and did not eat meat, milk, cheese, or eggs, because they came from animals. Although the *perfecti* did not marry and abstained from sex, lay believers could engage in sex as long as it did not result in conception and therefore the creation of new matter. This belief was directly opposed to Catholic doctrine, which maintained that the only legitimate purpose for sexual intercourse was procreation. The crusading war against the Cathars lasted twenty years (1209-1229) and was extremely brutal and destructive. Many towns were sacked, and their populations were driven off or slaughtered. The French king took up the cause of the papacy as the defender of orthodox faith and also used the war to destroy the power of feudal lords in this area and to assert the rule of the French monarchy. Both during and after the war the Dominican order, which had been established specifically to combat Catharism, worked to stamp out this heresy by conducting judicial proceedings authorized by another papal innovation, the inquisition. People suspected of unorthodoxy were arrested, imprisoned, questioned under torture, and often executed by being burned at the stake.

When Louis IX became king in 1226, France was on its way to becoming a nation state. Hereditary noble families continued to enjoy positions of considerable power in their feudal domains, but royal agents were also sent out into all districts to supervise the collection of taxes paid to the king. The judicial authority of local lords was also curtailed by the king establishing the right for people to appeal important cases to a royal court, so that France began to enjoy political, fiscal, and judicial centralization similar to England. The governmental system established at this time endured largely unchanged until the French Revolution in 1789. Louis IX was the first French king who issued decrees that applied to all of France. He was very devout and took his responsibilities as king very seriously. He was deeply concerned for the welfare of his subjects and carefully watched over his officials to curb abuses of power. Consequently, when he died in 1270 after a long reign of 44 years, his death was mourned by all classes in France, except for the Jews, whom his extreme Christian piety had led him to persecute. We will encounter him again in the following lecture when we survey the history of the crusades. He was eventually canonized as a saint by the Catholic Church and is the Saint Louis after whom the city in Missouri is named.

His grandson, King Philip the Fair (1285-1314), clashed with the papacy over the issue of taxes. When Philip disregarded the long standing tax exempt status of Church properties in order to increase his revenues, Pope Boniface VIII responded by issuing the decree known as *Unam Sanctam*, in which the pope reiterated the traditional papal notion of the two swords, the spiritual wielded by the popes and the temporal exercised by monarchs, and the former being superior to the latter. Philip, however, was not the least bit persuaded by the decree and responded by sending a French army into Italy. The pope was arrested and soon died after being released. The result was that the cardinals were intimidated to elect as the next pope a Frenchman who was far more compliant toward Philip the Fair than Boniface had been. So, unlike the earlier conflict over lay investiture between the papacy and the Holy Roman Empire, this later clash between spiritual and temporal authority ended in the victory of the latter. It also marked the end of papal supremacy in secular affairs and demonstrated the emergence of France as a powerful monarchy.

Let us now return to English affairs after the battle of Bouvines in 1214. This decisive defeat destroyed what little good will King John still enjoyed with his noble vassals. Even before that defeat King John had already become quite unpopular among his subjects due to his struggle with the papacy over who should be the archbishop of Canterbury. It was a struggle that King John lost. Consequently, in 1214 the English barons broke out into rebellion, and in the next year (1215) they forced the king to meet them at a place called Runnymede west of London to acknowledge their grievances and rights by signing *Magna Charta*, which is Latin for "great document." The text (being Text #32 in PSWC) contained 63 provisions that spelled out the barons' feudal rights and privileges in order to guarantee them against the king. John immediately repudiated his pledge by claiming that it had been obtained under duress, and he died in the next year. But his son and successor, King Henry III (1216-1272), quickly and wisely made it clear that he would abide by the provisions contained in *Magna Charta*. Like our Declaration of Independence, the document continued to play an important ideological role in the political and constitutional history of England. It was periodically reissued by later English kings at the beginning of their reigns to symbolize their acceptance of the notion that a true king does not place himself above the law, but he must recognize certain basic rights of his subjects. Among the many specific provisions of this document there are two which planted the seeds of two important constitutional principles. One was that the king could not levy taxes without the consent of his vassals; and the other was that no free man could be arrested, imprisoned, and punished except by legal judgment of his peers or by the law of the land. Our modern versions of these ideas in the United States are "no taxation without representation" and "every citizen accused is entitled to due process."

Another important English constitutional principle which had its origin during this period was parliament. This word derives from the French *parler*, meaning "to speak" or "to discuss." We therefore have here another example of French being the language of government in England during this period. Originally, a parliament was a conference of people called together by the king in order to discuss important matters of state, such as taxation and decisions about war. The king used these meetings to communicate his wishes to the most important people in the realm and to enlist their support. The people summoned to such meetings were originally Church officials and barons with hereditary landed estates. But by the end of the thirteenth century towns and cities in England had become so economically important that representatives of merchants and artisans also began to be included in these meetings summoned by the king. During the reign of King Henry III there was another major rebellion of nobles against the king, resulting in the promulgation of another important set of governmental rules known as the Provisions of Oxford (1258), according to which the king was supposed to summon a parliament three times every year. Parliament was still a rather shadowy institution by the end of the period covered in this lecture, but in the course of time the institution eventually took on the shape of a new branch of government, consisting of two houses: the House of Lords harkening back to the hereditary feudal barons, and the House of Commons that had its origin in the new economic forces of Medieval towns and cities. Consequently, when the framers of our own constitution considered how best to organize the legislative branch of the federal government, they adopted a similar two-chamber model, the U.S. Senate and the House of Representatives, the latter, like the English House of Commons, possessing the sole power to propose bills imposing taxes upon its citizenry. The basic political ideology of parliament can perhaps be glimpsed as early as 1295 in the official summons issued by King Edward I, "what affects all, by all should be approved." Thus, as the result of *Magna Charta* and the development of parliament, by 1300 the basic foundations were laid for the emergence of a constitutional monarchy in England.

LECTURE 26
The Crusades

IMPORTANT DATES AND TERMS

- **1096-1102:** First Crusade, which unfolded in three distinct phases with the second phase ending in the capture of Jerusalem.
- **1189-1192:** Third Crusade, involving King Richard I the Lion Heart of England and the Arab leader Saladin.
- **1204:** Fourth Crusade, ending with the crusaders seizing control of Constantinople.
- **1289-1292:** Mamluk warriors of Egypt recapture the last remaining crusader states in the Levant.
- **1492:** Spanish capture of Granada, ending the *Reconquista* of Arab Spain.
- **crusader:** warrior fighting under the cross, waging a holy war sanctioned by the papacy.
- **Venice, Pisa, Genoa:** important commercial states of northern Italy that benefited from the crusades.
- **Reconquista:** centuries-long Christian campaign of conquering Arab Spain.

In this lecture we will survey the nearly two hundred years of the crusades, 1096-1292, which formed a significant feature of the history of the High Middle Ages. It illustrated the harmonious synthesis between two important components that went into the making of Medieval culture: Christianity and the warlike traditions of the Germanic tribes that had invaded and destroyed the Roman Empire, as well as the warlike nature of the Vikings, who had more recently been absorbed into parts of western Europe. The crusades were in effect holy wars declared by the pope to recapture lands occupied by non-Christians. The papal declarations authorized the use of lethal violence in the name of religion. Moreover, it was during this period that knightly combat on horseback and Medieval chivalry reached its full glory.

Although the idea of the crusades immediately brings to mind knights in shining armor setting out from western Europe to do battle with Muslims for control of the Holy Land in the eastern Mediterranean, we need to realize that these were not the only military campaigns of this nature at this time. Indeed, both western and eastern parts of Europe experienced their own crusading movements during and even long after the period covered in this lecture; and they had at least an equal, if not a greater, impact upon European history. I will therefore devote a small amount of our time and space here to these other two major crusading phenomena before turning to the crusades involving the Holy Land.

As we have seen when surveying the Islamic world, the Arabs, after conquering all of North Africa, crossed the Strait of Gibraltar and added the Iberian Peninsula to their vast empire. This region, known as Andalusia, with its large and flourishing capital at Cordoba, formed an important part of the Islamic Empire bordering upon Christian Europe, and it was one of the main avenues along which Arabic cultural influence entered Christian Europe during the High Middle Ages. As Muslim power began to weaken during the eleventh century, small Christian kingdoms located in the far north of the Iberian Peninsula began to encroach upon Islamic areas to begin a 400-year process known as the *Reconquista*, or the reconquest of Spain. It ultimately resulted in the whole area becoming re-Christianized along with the formation of the two modern nations of Portugal and Spain. The latter was in turn formed from the union of Castile and Aragon, kingdoms of central and eastern Iberia respectively that had spear-headed the *Reconquista*. This long crusading movement ended in January of 1492 with the capture of Granada, the last remaining Muslim city. By this point Queen Isabella of Castile and King Ferdinand of Aragon had united their two kingdoms by their marriage. The year 1492 was rendered yet more famous by two other events: the Spanish monarchs sponsoring Christopher Columbus' first voyage to the New World, and their decree concerning the Jews living in their kingdom. Not only were the Spanish monarchs determined to stamp out Islam, but they wanted to fully re-Christianize their land by giving the non-Christian Jews the choice of converting to Christianity or leaving the country. Many did in fact convert and were known as the *Conversos*, but many others emigrated to different parts of Europe, North Africa, and western Asia that would receive them. This illustrates one of the other, often overlooked, aspects of the crusades, the hardening of Christian attitudes toward Jews and the development of religiously intolerant government policies.

During these same centuries the Germans of central Europe pushed eastward into the Slavic and Baltic areas of Poland and Lithuania. In German history this phenomenon is termed *der Drang nach Osten*, "The Push to the East." It resulted in an eastern Europe populated with pockets of Germans, who established numerous towns and cities that served as important nuclei of Western European Christianity and culture. Adolf Hitler later exploited this situation to justify his conquest of eastern Europe under the guise of uniting all German-speaking peoples.

The crusading movement involving the Holy Land began with the speech of Pope Urban II delivered before a large gathering of his fellow Frenchmen at Clermont in November of 1095, a version of which is set out as Text #33A in PSWC. In 1071 the Seljuk Turks, who had stormed across Asia from the east, inflicted a crushing defeat upon the Byzantines at a place called Manzikert in Anatolia. The battle resulted in the Turks becoming masters of the whole region and a severe reduction in the size and prosperity of the Byzantine Empire. The Turks had also disrupted the Abbasid dynasty's control over the Holy Land. Pope Urban's speech addressed these major crises by calling upon the knights of western Europe to cease fighting among themselves and to direct their energies much more constructively in the service of Christianity by bringing much needed military assistance to the hard-pressed Byzantine

PSWC
#33A

Empire and to recapture control of the Holy Land from the Turks and Muslims. The speech was met with an immediate enthusiastic response and led to the First Crusade, which unfolded in three different phases during the six-year period 1096-1102.

But before taking up the narration of the First Crusade, a few general points need to be made. We should remember that the Byzantine Empire was Christian, so that one goal behind the crusades was to unite all Christians in the common purpose of winning back the Holy Land that had long been part of the Islamic Empire. As we have seen in Lecture 24, by the time that Pope Urban II delivered his famous and pivotal speech, the papacy had emerged as one of the most powerful institutions in western Europe. In fact, these crusades, stretching over the period 1096-1292, coincided exactly with the pinnacle of papal power in secular affairs and represented a clear expression of that papal power. The term crusade derives from the Latin word for cross, because it was under the Christian cross that these holy wars were waged with the blessing and sanction of the popes. Crusaders routinely advertised their involvement in a crusade by sewing a cloth cross on their outer garments. The papal decrees that proclaimed these campaigns offered significant incentives for people to join up. People who died during a crusade was granted a full indulgence or pardoning of their sins, so that they would go immediately to heaven. Serfs who volunteered were freed of all their obligations that bound them to perpetual service on their Medieval manor. Anyone sentenced to death could have his impending execution commuted to a life sentence as a crusader in the Holy Land.

As already pointed out, there was an immediate enthusiastic response to Pope Urban's speech. The first phase of the First Crusade, often termed the People's Crusade, was characterized by more enthusiasm than clear headed organization. As they traveled overland across central and eastern Europe to Constantinople, they were often compelled to raid the surrounding countryside for provisions, so that their advance struck many as more akin to a swarm of ravaging locusts than a pious army. Moreover, fueled by religious zeal, they often attacked communities of Jews along their march, because they regarded them as killers of Christ who deserved punishment if they did not convert to the one true religion (see Text #33B in PSWC). When this poorly organized rabble finally arrived in Constantinople, Emperor Alexius was so appalled by their unruly nature that he wanted to have them out of his midst as soon as possible. He therefore ferried them across the Bosporus and disembarked them on the shores of Anatolia, where they were soon encountered by the Turks and largely destroyed. So ended the People's Crusade.

When news of this disaster reached western Europe, a second phase was organized with considerable care by many of the leading knights of France and the German states. Thus, this second phase is often termed the Barons Crusade. They too traveled overland to Constantinople, where the Emperor Alexius forced their leaders to swear oaths of homage and fealty to him and to promise to hand over any lands that they conquered. This created even more ill-feeling between the Byzantines and the crusaders and was to become even worse as time passed, so that the close cooperation between Eastern and Western Christians was a goal and dream never realized.

After landing in Anatolia, these well organized and determined crusaders, assisted by Emperor Alexius, recaptured from the Turks the important city of Nicaea in northwestern Anatolia. The crusaders then fought their way all across Anatolia and entered northern Mesopotamia, where they captured the important city of Edessa, which they established as the first of four feudal states. It was organized as a county and placed under the rule of one of their leaders, who thus received the title of count. They next turned their attention to Antioch in northern Syria, a large, flourishing, and strongly fortified city, which they also captured after a long siege. It became the capital of their second feudal state, a principality ruled over by another one of their leaders with the title of prince. They then eventually moved southward as they closed in on their ultimate goal, Jerusalem. When they first arrived there and failed to capture the strongly fortified city by assault, the priests in the army persuaded them to obtain God's favor by marching bare-footed around the city and blowing their trumpets in imitation of Joshua and the Hebrews in *The Old Testament* when the walls of Jericho came tumbling down before them. But when God failed to deliver such a miracle for the crusaders at Jerusalem, they resorted to their usual military siegecraft and captured the city, whose population they proceeded to systematically massacre. According to one eye-witness Christian (Text #33C in PSWC), the blood of the slain would have covered your feet up to the ankles. Jerusalem now became the jewel of the crusader states, designated as a kingdom ruled over by a king, who was chosen from among the leading crusaders.

Of all the crusading expeditions to the Holy Land, this second phase of the First Crusade was by far the most successful. It had benefited much from the organizational skills and considerable martial prowess of its participants. It also benefited from the fact that Anatolia, Syria, and the Holy Land were not the least bit united, but suffered from political fragmentation. Although this whole region belonged to the Abbasid dynasty of Baghdad, the caliph of Baghdad exercised rather little direct control over it. The area was divided among a large number of local rulers, who were constantly fighting with one another. In addition, the intrusion of the Seljuk Turks had created even more confusion, because they too were divided into different groups, each led by a war lord intent upon carving out his own area to rule, so that they were not united either. To complicate things even more, the Islamic sect of the Assassins (see Text #26 in PSWC) had been established just a few years earlier in 1092 in a mountain stronghold south of the Caspian Sea in northern Iran, but they soon spread westward into Syria, where they plagued Islamic leaders with their suicide terrorist attacks and hampered the creation of a united front against the invading Europeans.

When news of these successes filtered back to western Europe, there was great rejoicing, and a third phase of crusaders was hastily thrown together in order to become part of the victory. But since this expedition suffered from the same disorganization as the first wave, it suffered the same fate. After arriving in Constantinople and being ferried across the Bosporus to Anatolia, they were largely wiped out by the Seljuk Turks. Thus ended the First Crusade.

The crusaders of the second wave ignored their oaths of homage and fealty to Emperor Alexius and proceeded to rule over their newly conquered areas. As fighting continued, they soon captured Tripoli, designated it as their fourth feudal state, organized it as a county, and placed it under the control of a count. They then set about building large numbers of stone forts to defend themselves from Arab attack. Many of these forts still remain standing today and have been recycled to serve other purposes. These fortresses were often built on high ground to provide them with greater defense, and their elevated positions allowed them to communicate with one another by smoke signals. The crusaders heavily fortified Acre on the coast and had it serve henceforth as their main seaport. It lay on a peninsula on the northern side of a bay, on whose southern side now stands the modern city of Haifa, eight miles away. Acre was well defended with a wall that ran all across the neck of the peninsula that joined it to the mainland. Now that they had achieved their goal of taking back Jerusalem, many returned home, and others stayed behind. In fact, one of the main problems of the crusades was that the area that they controlled was almost always undermanned. Western Europe failed to provide adequate support and only responded in times of crisis with a new wave of crusaders, who were often not sufficiently strong to maintain the status quo or to roll back Arab gains.

Another indication of the harmonious synthesis between Christianity and the Germanic warlike spirit is the establishment of two knightly orders at this time. They were patterned after the orders of monks, but their members were knights, who took vows of humility, chastity, and poverty. They did not live in monasteries, but they performed their knightly duty of fighting and service to Christianity. One such order was known as the Knights Templar, or the Templars. They took their name from the fact that they established their headquarters in Jerusalem near the Temple Mount, the place where Solomon and King Herod the Great had built their famous temples to Yahweh. Herod's magnificent temple had been destroyed by the Romans in 70 A.D., and the site was now (as it is today) occupied by the Dome of the Rock, a massive and splendid Islamic mosque. The Knights Templar were pledged to defend the Holy Land and to make sure that it remained under Christian control, so that it could be safely visited by pious Christian pilgrims. They wore white clothing to symbolize their purity and devotion to Christianity, but they were well trained soldiers who often formed the hard core around which a crusading military force was formed. The knights Templar became quite numerous and wealthy and had their European headquarters in France. Not long after the

Muslims recaptured Acre and the entire Levantine coast by 1292, the French king, Philip the Fair, began to fear their numbers, power, and wealth. He therefore ruthlessly suppressed the order in 1307-8 by arresting many of the knights, by having them executed on countless charges, and by confiscating their properties.

The other principal knightly order was that of the Hospitalers. They took their name from the fact that they established and maintained hospitals for wounded crusaders or for pilgrims who happened to fall ill during the course of their travels, but they also provided military escorts for pilgrims, so that they could travel in safety. They wore black garments marked with a white cross; and like the Templars, they were well trained soldiers who comprised the crusading elite.

We will now run through the various crusading expeditions. When the Arabs succeeded in recapturing Edessa in 1144, western Europe responded with the Second Crusade (1147-1149) led by King Louis VII of France and Conrad of the Holy Roman Empire. But when they finally arrived at Antioch, their forces had been so depleted by disease and fighting that they were unable to launch a successful expedition to recapture Edessa. Then during the course of the next generation there arose among the Arabs their most able leader against the crusaders. This was Saladin. After bringing the disunited and quarrelsome Muslim leaders of the region under his command, he scored a decisive victory over the crusaders near Tiberias in the summer of 1187 and followed up this success by capturing Acre and other coastal strongholds. His ultimate victory was forcing Jerusalem to surrender; and unlike the crusaders who had captured the city in 1098, he did not carry out a gruesome bloodbath, but allowed most of the Christian inhabitants to ransom themselves.

When news of this reversal reached western Europe, there was much consternation and shock. The pope is said to have died of grief, and his successor immediately proclaimed the Third Crusade (1189-1192) to take back Jerusalem. Frederick Barbarossa (Red Beard), ruler of the Holy Roman Empire, was first to respond. But after traversing Anatolia, the aged emperor drowned in a river in 1190 when he fell off his horse and was borne down by his heavy armor. His expeditionary force then largely disbanded and came to naught. The crusade was then revitalized by the other two major monarchs of western Europe: Philip Augustus of France and Richard I the Lion Heart of England. The former, however, wound up accomplishing nothing, whereas the latter, along with Saladin, rendered this Third Crusade the most well known and picturesque. Rather than traveling overland to Constantinople, both monarchs of western Europe went by sea and arrived at the seaport of Acre, which the crusaders had under siege. Richard, however, first landed on the island of Cyprus, defeated the Byzantine prince who ruled it, and secured the island for the crusaders. Cyprus henceforth served as an important jumping-off point for subsequent crusading expeditions.

After landing at Acre, Richard took command of the siege and carried it to a successful conclusion. Then as he mobilized his forces and proceeded southward toward Jerusalem from Acre, he and his army were constantly harrassed by Saladin until the crusaders carried out a powerful counter-attack and inflicted a devastating defeat upon a much larger Muslim army. Over the course of two years of fighting (1190-1192) Richard succeeded in winning back the coastal strongholds that had recently been lost to Saladin; and although he came within sight of Jerusalem twice, he failed to recapture the city. His last battle in the Holy Land was fought against Saladin at Joppa on the coast. When Saladin was in the process of capturing the city, Richard unexpectedly showed up by sea; and although he was not prepared, he went immediately into battle and kept the city from falling into Muslim hands. Throughout these two years of campaigning Richard's exploits on the battlefield impressed everyone (including Saladin) and demonstrated that he was one of the greatest knightly warriors of the age and richly deserved his sobriquet, the Lion Heart. Yet, during this same time troublesome affairs back in the Angevin Empire and England were a constant source of worry and caused him to cut short his crusading enterprise. After engaging in lengthy negotiations with his worthy Muslim opponent, Richard and Saladin reached a settlement, according to which the crusaders would be allowed to retain control of the coast, while the Arabs maintained control of Jerusalem, but allowed Christian pilgrims safe access to the city. By March of 1193 Saladin had died of a lingering illness in Damascus, just a few months after Richard had departed from the Holy Land.

On his way back to his Angevin Empire, Richard was taken prisoner by the new ruler of the Holy Roman Empire, Henry VI, the son of Frederick Barbarossa; and he was kept in comfortable custody befitting a king for several months until the people of England secured the release of their monarch by paying an enormous ransom.

Since Jerusalem still lay in Muslim hands, the Fourth Crusade was soon organized (1202-1204), but it proved to be a real disaster and ended what little friendship there still existed between the Christians of the East and West. This crusade was composed of knights from France, who commissioned the Venetians of northeastern Italy to build ships to carry them and their horses to Acre. But when the Venetians presented the crusaders with their bill for having built the ships, it was too big for them to pay. They then worked out a deal. The Venetians at this time were the most important maritime traders of Medieval Europe, and they were eager to expand their commercial activity into the eastern Mediterranean at the expense of the Byzantines and Arabs. They therefore required the crusaders to first attack Zara, a place on the Balkan shore of the Adriatic Sea, so that the Venetians could add it to their growing overseas empire. Then instead of taking them to Acre, the Venetians sailed to Constantinople. An exiled prince of the Byzantine Imperial family had sought aid from the Venetians, and they were eager to have him installed in Constantinople as their puppet. The Fourth Crusade came to an end in 1204 when the crusaders treated Constantinople as an enemy city, captured it by force, plundered it for several days, drove out the Imperial family, and established their rule in their place. Crusader control lasted for 57 years (1204-1261) and succeeded in gravely weakening the Byzantine Empire. The crusaders alienated the Byzantines by establishing the Roman Catholic Church in place of their own Greek Orthodox faith, and they plundered the churches of saintly relics and other prized objects and shipped them back to western Europe. Venice, along with Genoa and Pisa, the other two commercially important states of northern Italy, benefited tremendously from the crusaders' capture of Constantinople, because they were now able to establish trading posts throughout the eastern Mediterranean and Black Sea. This was a striking testimony to the growing economic power of Western Europe.

The obvious greed and ambition exhibited by the Fourth Crusade seem to have prompted the so-called Children's Crusade of 1212. It was one of the most curious episodes of popular piety during the High Middle Ages and is described in Text #33E in PSWC. It was a mass movement among the teenagers of western Europe, primarily in France and the German states. These young people apparently believed that their youthful innocence and Christian piety would succeed where the greed and ambition of their elders had failed. As this movement gained support, large numbers of teenagers traveled in groups along the roads, descending upon the two seaports of Genoa in northwestern Italy and Marseille in southern France. When they arrived at their final destinations, the children were expecting a miracle: the Mediterranean Sea would open up before them, as God had laid open the Red Sea for the Hebrews during their exodus from Egypt. But when no such miracle was forthcoming, many pious crusaders became disillusioned and returned home. Some of those at Marseille were persuaded by two unscrupulous sea captains to go aboard seven ships that they provided for them. Unfortunately, two ships were wrecked with the loss of all aboard; and the other five ships conveyed their human cargo to Alexandria in Egypt, where the ship captains sold the children into slavery. Such was the tragic end of the Children's Crusade.

Since the Holy Land was under the jurisdiction of the caliph of Cairo in Egypt, the Fifth Crusade (1218-1219) set its sights on Egypt, but after moving inland from the coast of the Nile delta, the crusaders were thwarted by the inundation of the Nile, which blocked their advance. The Sixth Crusade (1228-1229) was led by Frederick II, the ruler of the Holy Roman Empire. He was perhaps the most intriguing monarch of his day. He was extremely well educated and spoke several different languages, including Arabic, because he had many Arab-speaking subjects in his island of Sicily. Through his unique combination of threatening military force and his knowledge of the Arabic language and culture, he was able to persuade the caliph of Egypt to hand over Jerusalem to the Christians without having to fight a single battle. But when the Muslims recaptured Jerusalem in 1244, this prompted the Seventh Crusade (1248-1254) led by King Louis IX of France. After setting sail from Marseille, he made first landfall on the island of Cyprus, where he organized his forces and supplies. From Cyprus the expedition sailed south to Damietta in the Nile delta; and after capturing it, the crusaders moved inland, but they were eventually defeated; and in order to keep his whole force from being annihilated, King Louis had to offer himself up in surrender to the Arabs, who kept him a prisoner until the people of France coughed up an enormous sum to ransom their king. Since Louis had set out with the highest of hopes based upon his piety, the utter failure of his crusade was very devastating to him, because he regarded his failure as God's judgment upon him and his shortcomings.

In 1258 the Abbasid dynasty of Baghdad came to an end when the capital of the Islamic world was captured and systematically sacked by the Mongols under the leadership of one of the three grandsons of Genghis khan. At about the same time the Arab rulers in Cairo in Egypt were overthrown and replaced by a class of warriors known as the Mamluks, who succeeded in checking the advance of the Mongols by defeating them near Damascus in Syria. Then in 1268 the Mamluks attacked the biggest city held by the crusaders, Antioch. After capturing it and either killing or selling its people into slavery, the city was destroyed and never reoccupied, after having enjoyed an illustrious history of nearly 1600 years since its foundation at the beginning of the Hellenistic Period. The much smaller crusader coastal sites, including Acre, were left undisturbed by the Mamluks for twenty years while they were busy establishing their control over the interior. When they finally mounted their attack upon these places by first attacking and capturing Tripoli in 1289, western Europe responded by sending out reinforcements, but it was too little too late. In 1291 the Mamluks began their assault on the last crusader stronghold, Acre, whose capture is described in Text #33F of PSWC. With its fall in 1292 the crusaders no longer controlled any land in Syria or the Holy Land. Nevertheless, many crusaders withdrew to the islands of Cyprus and Rhodes, where they lived for several generations as the eastern-most outpost of Western Europe.

Although this closed out this chapter of the crusading movement, it did not end the Western European phenomenon of crusading. Over the next three centuries there were popes and kings who called upon their fellow Europeans to mount another crusade to win back these lost areas, but they never succeeded in regaining a continental foothold in the region. This crusading movement, however, despite its ultimate failure, represented the great vitality, military power, and growing economic strength that was now enabling Western Europe to forge ahead as the world's powerhouse. The crusading movement had also brought about more peaceful interaction between western European Christians and Muslims, with the former adopting many habits and aspects of culture from the latter, such as the game of chess, sugar, and fabrics manufactured in the eastern Mediterranean. Despite the Islamic prohibition against drinking alcoholic beverages, the practice was widespread among Muslims, in fact, to such an extent that our word alcohol is of Arabic origin and entered European culture at this time. Moreover, despite religious intolerance displayed by both sides, Western European receptivity to the Arab world was symptomatic of the former's intellectual growth, which was a chief characteristic of the High Middle Ages, as embodied in the rise of the Medieval universities. On the other hand, as you can see from Text #33D in PSWC, Muslims looked down upon the crusaders as uncouth barbarians and so lacking in culture and civilization that they possessed nothing worth learning. Muslim writers displayed their contempt and prurient interests by their obvious enjoyment in recording scandalous jokes, rumors, and hearsay that portrayed European women as immodest harlots. Thus, while the crusaders were willing to learn from their Arab enemies, the reverse was generally not true, and this pattern of Western relative openness vs. Islamic isolationism has prevailed right up to our own day. Finally, whereas the crusades have largely been forgotten in the West, the converse has held sway among Muslims: for the wars of the crusades still figure prominently in the Arab world, where events from the twelfth and thirteenth centuries are routinely mentioned by Arab leaders as if they were part of the Arab world's recent hostile history with Western civilization.

LECTURE 27
Social and Economic Change in the High Middle Ages

IMPORTANT DATES AND TERMS

- **1050-1350:** Period of the High Middle Ages.
- **1348-1350:** First outbreak of bubonic plague in western Europe.
- **Burg** = town, burger = citizen (member of a town).
- **guild:** local town organization of craftsmen to control all major aspects of their trade, including wages, competition, and quality of their work (apprentice, journeyman, master, master piece).
- **gothic cathedral:** product of Medieval economic growth, embodying local pride and Christian piety, depicting Biblical scenes in its art and architecture.
- **Venice, Genoa, Pisa:** cities of northern Italy important for long distance maritime trade throughout the Mediterranean.
- **Hanseatic League:** league of northern European cities formed to promote long distance maritime trade in the North Atlantic and Baltic Sea.
- **Flanders:** area of northern Europe, comprising what is now both Belgium and the Netherlands, important for its textile industry and commercial centers.
- **Black Death** - bubonic plague: epidemic disease caused by micro-organisms in fleas carried by the black rat, periodic

outbreaks beginning in 1348 and lasting until 1721, responsible for curbing population growth in Western Europe.

In this lecture we will explore yet another major aspect of the dynamic High Middle Ages: significant changes in society and the economy.

You may recall that when we surveyed the Viking Age in Lecture 22, I pointed out that one of the primary factors contributing to the Viking expansion was climate change. During the period c.800-1300 the Earth's climate was warmer than it presently is; and this period is termed the Medieval Warm Period by modern climatologists. It enabled the Vikings to sail on longer voyages, because the sailing season in the North Atlantic was longer than it had been previously. These same warm climatic conditions played an important role in the social and economic changes of the High Middle Ages. Warmer weather meant that more land could be placed under cultivation, especially in higher latitudes or higher up on mountain sides. Thus, the High Middle Ages witnessed greater agricultural productivity. This in turn led to a better fed population, and a healthier population resulted in steady population growth. Moreover, as the population increased, there was a greater demand for all sorts of basic goods, such as food, clothing, shoes, furniture, etc.; and this increase in the demand for goods brought about one of the most important economic developments of this period, the increase in the number of towns.

As we have already seen, the major social and economic pattern of the Early and Central Middle Ages was determined by manorialism, with a large portion of the entire population living on large agricultural and relatively self-sufficient estates. Towns and cities were scarce and far between. This situation now began to change. You can think of this changing pattern in the following terms. Imagine a landscape that is almost entirely flat and uniform, like the surface of a lake, but with occasional tips of islands barely emerging from the surface. This is an accurate model of the earlier Middle Ages with the nearly uniform pattern of manorialism only occasionally interrupted by towns and cities scattered across the landscape. Now imagine what would happen if we were to slowly lower the lake's water level. Not only would these tips of islands grow larger and larger, but they would be joined by many other small islands emerging from the surface, whose uniformity would now be seriously disrupted.

As the population grew, there were more people available to become part of this growing town life. The primary purpose of these towns was to produce goods and to sell them. These new towns arose on lands already owned by feudal lords, who issued charters allowing people to associate at these sites to form towns. The reason why feudal lords allowed this to happen was that they could simply make more money, because a Medieval manor consumed almost all that it produced, whereas the economic activity inside a town produced a much larger surplus or greater wealth, and the feudal lord could make sure that he received his cut.

This brings us to an important document: Text #34 in PSWC, the Charter of the Liberties of Lorris. This charter was issued by King Louis VII of France in 1155 to allow people to form the town of Lorris. The document consists of 35 specific regulations that the townsfolk had to obey. Although some provisions spell out the rights and privileges granted to the townsfolk, notice that several of them involve issues of money: the people must pay so much for this and that, because the king, who was the feudal lord of this land, was making sure that it would be a profitable operation for him. In addition, he specified that a provost would serve as his overseer in the town to make sure that these regulations were followed, and the king received his money. You can therefore easily see how the creation of a town could have been quite desirable for a feudal lord.

Provision 18 in this document is of particular interest, because it specifies that if a person comes to Lorris and lives there an entire year without anyone laying claims upon him (i.e., as his serf), he will become a member of the town. This was a standard provision in these Medieval town charters and thus offered ordinary people, both men and women, a great opportunity to improve their lot in life. They could free themselves from their manorial serfdom and become a free person of a town. This concept is neatly summed up in an old German expression: "Stadtluft macht frei = town air makes [one] free." In 1190 there was established in southwestern Germany a town called Freiburg, whose name translates literally as Free Town.

People came to and lived in these towns for basic economic reasons, i.e. manufacturing and selling things. Towns therefore were often well placed to serve this goal. They were located on rivers, lakes, or the sea coast, so that they could import and export goods by ship, because transporting them overland in wagons was far more expensive and difficult. Towns might also be located where there was some natural resource to be exploited, such as stone, timber, clay, coal, or salt. Freiburg, which I have just mentioned, was established in order to mine silver.

Since local warfare was still a very common occurrence at this time, towns were also usually located on high ground in order to make them more defensible. Since the Germanic word for hill or mountain was *burg* or *berg*, many cities of modern Europe have that element in their names that derive from Medieval times: e.g., Augsburg, Bergen, Bergamo, Bettembourg, Bourges, Brandenburg, Canterbury, Cherbourg, Duisburg, Edinburgh, Esbjerg, Freiburg, Fribourgh, Goteborg, Hamburg, Heidelberg, Helsingborg, Kapfenberg, Koenigsberg, Luxembourg, Magdeburg, Mecklenburg, Nurnberg, Regensburg, Salisbury, Salzburg, Scarborough, Silkeborg, Strasbourg, Svendborg, Tilburg, Viborg, Wolfsberg, etc. Since many of these towns were named —-burg, the people living in the towns were often termed burgers, and in later times the whole class of townsfolk was called the *bourgeoisie* in French. This term came to mean the middle class, because earlier Medieval society had consisted of the two classes of the very small class of the rich and the very large class of the poor with virtually nothing in between. Medieval town life began to create a middle class of burgers positioned between the rich and the poor; and the emergence of this new middle class had very important consequences for the development of Western European society.

If we could travel back in time to visit a Medieval town, it would look very different from a modern-day small town in the United States. For one thing, the towns were usually enclosed by a stone wall for two different reasons. It obviously offered protection from enemy attack, but it also served an important economic purpose. It allowed the flow of goods in and out of the town to be strictly regulated, observed, and taxed. The gates in the town wall were closed at night, and during the day inspectors were stationed at the gates to see what people were bringing in or out, so that taxes could be assessed on them. They had very few paved streets, which, instead, were usually dirt paths or roads that became muddy messes when it rained. Most private dwellings would have been simple thatched cottages that one would have also encountered in the countryside. Many people kept farm animals to supplement their diet, such as chickens for eggs and pigs for pork. Thus, animals would have been seen roaming about in the yards and streets. In fact, during the twelfth century one prince of the French royal family died in Paris when his horse stumbled over a pig. Sanitation was virtually non-existent. Houses did not have plumbing systems for running water, and people dumped their waste material and garbage where they pleased or could. Some sources indicate that the smell and filth in these towns were quite hideous.

As already stated, the sole purpose for these towns was economic activity. Indeed, once towns began to multiply, they became the engine that drove the economy, led to the accumulation of wealth, and fostered the growth of free-market capitalism. Their growing economic importance is reflected in the changing composition of the English parliament. At first, when the kings of the twelfth century wished to consult representatives from their subjects on matters of taxes, they summoned the feudal lords and high ranking members in the Church. But as the towns emerged as the creators of wealth during the thirteenth and fourteenth centuries, kings overlooked members of the Church and summoned merchants from the towns.

All townsfolk, both men and women, had to belong to the guild of their particular craft or trade, such as metal working, glass working, pottery, woolen textiles, linen textiles, silk textiles, carpentry, masonry, leather working, etc. Guild members were of three different grades: apprentices, journeymen, or masters. Apprentices were at the bottom of the hierarchy and were required to work for several years in their trade in order to demonstrate that they possessed the necessary skills and application to deserve promotion to the next level of journeyman or day laborer. Both apprentices and journeymen were employed by masters, who owned and operated their own business. If a journeyman were sufficiently talented and lucky, he might eventually be authorized by his guild to become a master and could therefore go into business for himself. If his trade involved manufacturing specific items, such as shoes or furniture, his promotion to master consisted in part of him producing items of footwear or furniture that met the highest quality standards required by his guild. These objects, which served to display the journeyman's expertise, and which were carefully inspected by guild members, were known as masterpieces. In order to make sure that the workers did not overproduce their product and thus cause prices to fall, these guilds regulated all aspects of their particular trade: how many people were allowed to work, what were their wages, how many masters were allowed to operate businesses, etc. As towns grew and needed some form of government and administration, these needs were met through the guild system as well. The various officials of the towns were elected by their guilds to serve the town and to represent their interests. Consequently, in the course of time membership in a guild had both political and economic significance. A burger was not only a member of the economic class of townsfolk, but he was also a citizen of his town.

The economic prosperity produced by these Medieval towns resulted in a major building craze, the building of Gothic cathedrals. We can tell quite a bit about a society by seeing what kinds of monumental architecture it creates. For example, the Sumerians built ziggurats for worshipping their gods, the Egyptians built pyramids as tombs for their god-kings, the Greeks built beautiful marble temples, and the Romans built all sorts of massive structures: temples, public baths, and stadia. We moderns build sky-scrapers for business and gigantic sporting facilities to serve our mania for sports. Medieval burgers spent a sizable portion of their accumulated wealth to build cathedrals as testimonials to their Christian faith and as expressions of community pride. A cathedral advertised to the outside world the town's prosperity, faith, and sophistication. The large number of cathedrals built during the High Middle Ages is graphic proof of the towns' extraordinary economic power. Each structure required an enormous investment in labor, both skilled and unskilled: technical experts to oversee the construction, stone masons, brick layers, metal workers, glass makers, etc. The guilds were very civic minded and competed with one another in paying for the costs of construction, which were very large.

When completed, a cathedral was not only the community's most important church used for worship, but it also served as a community center. Guilds held meetings of their members there, and various forms of popular entertainment, such as simple morality plays, were performed in the open area outside the cathedral. Its floor plan was always in the shape of a cross with the top part of the cross pointing eastward toward Jerusalem. The cathedral was entered at the base of the cross at its western end. During church services the congregation sat in the long upright part of the cross, called the nave, while the priest stood at the far curved eastern end (called the apse) to conduct the services. The soaring height of the structure with its numerous windows for admitting light symbolized heaven and the illumination of the one true faith. The interior was richly adorned with works of art illustrating stories from *The Bible*. Besides being aesthetically pleasing, these scenes served an important didactic purpose. Because virtually no one could read the Latin text of *The Bible*, religious instruction was carried out by oral story telling assisted by these artistic renderings.

All this economic activity obviously resulted in the circulation of goods through trade. In earlier Medieval times there were relatively few commodities that were traded over long distances. They were usually various luxury goods not easily obtained and only purchased by the rich. As the Medieval towns produced more and more goods of all sorts, larger quantities began to be circulated to more and more people through a growing network of trade routes. Maritime trade in the Mediterranean was largely dominated by the three northern Italian cities of Venice, Genoa, and Pisa. As we saw in the previous lecture, the Venetians subverted the Fourth Crusade and used it to advance their commercial interests. Once the crusaders seized control of Constantinople, the Venetians, along with the Genoese and Pisans, established trading posts throughout the eastern Mediterranean and around the Black Sea. Their trade with the Islamic world introduced Western Europe to sugar, pepper, cinnamon, ginger, nutmeg, and cotton. Consequently, when in the fifteenth century the Ottoman Turks interrupted this flow of goods by disrupting the Asiatic trade routes, navigators, such as the Genoese Christopher Columbus, set about trying to reestablish the eastern trade by developing alternative trade routes, which resulted in the fortuitous discovery of the New World.

One important commercial alliance that arose during this period in northern Europe was that between England and Flanders. The latter was the area that eventually developed into the two modern nations of Belgium and the Netherlands. Since Flanders was now becoming a major manufacturer of woolen textiles, it needed a steady supply of wool, which was met by the large flocks of sheep kept in England. This trading connection endured for several centuries and created friendship between the two countries.

By the 1300s the towns and cities situated on the coasts of the North and Baltic Seas carried on such a thriving trade with one another that they gradually developed the Hanseatic League. This was an international trading association, designed to facilitate trade among its members by allowing traders from one city to use warehouse space in another city, or to have banking rights throughout the league, so that merchants did not have to carry large quantities of gold and silver with them everywhere in order to buy and sell. The league members also cooperated in suppressing piracy, which was bad for everyone's business. This league eventually comprised about 200 cities from as far west as London and as far east as Novgorod in Russia; and representativs from member cities met on occasion at the centrally located city of Lubeck on the southern shore of the Baltic in order to agree upon matters of common interest.

The economic growth of the High Middle Ages came to a screeching halt during the early 1300s. At that time the Medieval Warm Period came to an end, and the so-called Little Ice Age began. It ushered in much cooler climatic conditions and lasted up to about 1850, after which the Earth's climate has been experiencing another warm period. The years 1315-1322 were devastating for western Europe. Cool and wet summers caused crops either not to grow or to rot in the fields. Crop failure in turn created widespread famine and large numbers of people dying by starvation or by various diseases to which their weakened state made them more susceptible. It not only ended western Europe's population growth, but it reversed it. It has been estimated that during these years about six million people died, which would have been about one-eighth of the entire population of Europe at the time. Then in the next generation an even greater disaster struck western Europe. This was the bubonic plague or the Black Death. It arrived in the central Mediterranean in October of 1347 when a Genoese ship landed in Sicily. While conducting trade in the Crimea in the Black Sea, black rats that carried the disease in the microorganisms in their fleas came aboard the ship. By the time that the vessel landed in Sicily, the crew members were dead or dying, and both they and the rats spread the disease among the Sicilians. Thence it quickly spread through the islands of Sardinia and Corsica, and from there it struck the coastal areas and then spread inland. The disease raged for about two years (1348-1350). Modern historians estimate that during this time the epidemic wiped out 30- *PSWC #35* 40 percent of the entire population of western Europe. Some areas suffered much higher losses. Text #35 in PSWC is a famous passage from the prologue of Boccaccio's *Decameron*, which gives us a graphic portrait of how this plague affected Florence at this time. It was not uncommon for entire families to die out and to leave their farm or home unoccupied, and their farm animals abandoned and unattended. The death rate was so high that there were simply not enough coffins to give the dead proper burial, so that bodies were thrown into mass graves. It is hard for us to imagine the consequences produced by such massive and sudden human death.

Unfortunately, the epidemic of 1348-1350 was not the end of the story. Given the very unsanitary conditions of Medieval towns, there were major outbreaks of the bubonic plague in western Europe periodically up to 1721 when it afflicted the southern French seaport of Marseille. The disease returned in 1369, 1374-1375, 1379, 1390, 1407, and in every decade throughout the fifteenth century and less frequently during the sixteenth and seventeenth centuries.

One consequence of this phenomenon was that western Europe did not become overpopulated like India or China. Modern historians have therefore speculated that the Black Death in the long run turned out to be beneficial. It weakened manorialism and encouraged the development of alternative ways of employing human labor on the land. In fact, in many areas manorialism slowly withered away. Similarly, by keeping the European population at much lower levels for the next two centuries, the resulting chronic labor shortage served to stimulate Europeans to come up with-labor-saving ways of doing things and thus fostered a culture of technical innovations and experimentation, which played a role in the development of the Western scientific tradition.

Finally, I will end this lecture by mentioning just a few of the ways in which the people responded to this horrible disaster. Since this occurred long before the establishment of the germ theory of diseases, the Europeans had no clue as to what caused the Black Death. They at least understood that when it broke out, it always affected the towns worse than the countryside, so that those who could do so left the towns and lived elsewhere until the epidemic subsided. In any case, one explanation was that the disease emanated from one of the stars or planets, which agreed with the popular belief in astrology. Another view, common especially in the German states where Nazism centuries later exploited deeply entrenched anti-Semitism, was that the Jews had poisoned the water supply. Whenever this notion obtained currency within a community, it often resulted in the Christians attacking and killing many of the Jews living in their midst. A third view was that the epidemic was simply God's way of punishing humans for their sinful behavior. As a result, there were groups of flagellants (whippers) who traveled about from town to town, engaged in solemn religious processions. In addition to calling upon people to mend their ways, they set an example by standing together in public and beating each other with whips until they bled in order to do public penance. As they reasoned, if God was angry with humans, these flagellants were attempting to atone for everyone's collective burden of sin; and if they beat themselves enough, they just might persuade God to relinquish his wrath and to end the epidemic.

LECTURE 28
Religious Turmoil and the Hundred-Years War

IMPORTANT DATES AND TERMS

- **1309-1376:** Avignon papacy.
- **1337-1453:** Hundred-Years War between England and France.
- **1378-1417:** The Great Schism in the Church.
- **Joan of Arc:** uneducated French peasant girl, experienced visions and heard voices, rallied French to victory over the English, captured by the English and burned at the stake for witchcraft.
- **John Wycliffe:** English theologian, first translator of *The Bible* into English, advocating radical religious reform, basing everything upon the scriptures themselves rather than Church authority, allowing women to conduct church services.
- **Jan Hus:** Czech religious reformer, advocated clerical poverty, burned at the stake as a heretic at the Council of Constance.

In this lecture we will resume and advance the two themes treated in Lectures 24 and 25: the papacy and the history of England and France.

After enjoying the pinnacle of its power in secular affairs during the twelfth and thirteenth centuries, the papacy suffered a major loss in its power and prestige during the fourteenth and early fifteenth centuries, as the High

Middle Ages came to an end, and as the Renaissance began. The turning point for the papacy came in 1302 when King Philip the Fair of France, in order to increase his tax revenues, ignored the long standing tax-exempt status of Church properties and levied taxes upon them. When Pope Boniface VIII responded by issuing his decree, *Unam Sanctam*, in which he reasserted the papacy's claim to overrule secular monarchs, Philip brushed these arguments aside and resorted to force to decide the matter. He sent an army into Italy and had the Pope arrested for defying him. Pope Boniface was eventually released from custody and died shortly thereafter. But when the cardinals assembled to elect the new pope, Philip's military intervention had so intimidated them that they elected a Frenchman, who promptly moved the papal court from Rome to Avignon on the Rhone River in southern France, where the papacy remained for the next 67 years (1309-1376). Never before had the popes exercised their authority except from Rome. Although the move to Avignon pleased the French, it came as a great shock and disappointment to other Europeans, many of whom regarded it as simply another sign of the papacy being corrupted by politics and ignoring its one true purpose in the realm of religion. Indeed, the behavior and concerns of the seven popes at Avignon reinforced this perception, because they increased the size of the papal bureaucracy and seemed to be most interested in maximizing the sums of money that it took in by imposing fees on all transactions. Consequently, during the fourteenth century the papacy was the object of very severe criticism. There was certainly no shortage of things in the Church to be criticized, but the religious dissent of this period resulted in part from the general intellectual advancement of Western Europe and was led in large measure by professors in the Medieval universities.

One of the most important religious dissenters at this time was an Englishman, named John Wycliffe (1330-1384), a professor of theology at Oxford. Like many people at this time, he regarded the Church's vast wealth and land holdings as being inconsistent with both scripture and with its mission. Jesus and the apostles had all been poor; and, Wycliffe thought, the Church could not carry out its religious duties if it had to spend most of its time and energy in managing its property holdings. Wycliffe therefore believed that the Church should give up its wealth and cultivate apostolic poverty, because then and only then would it be able to devote its full attention to religious matters. He also had a low regard for many of the priests in the Catholic Church, because they were not men of piety. He believed that people should take an active role in their religious life and education. Rather than depending upon one's priest to interpret *The Bible*, people should read it and use their own intelligence to find meaning in it. He therefore began to make the first English translation of *The Bible*, so that its contents would be accessible to a larger number of people. In addition, he had no objection to women performing religious services, and they did so in the dissident religious movement (called Lollardism) that his ideas spawned in England. Also in keeping with the growing rationalism in the Medieval universities, Wycliffe rejected the canonical notion of transubstantiation, by which the bread consecrated by priests for the Eucharist was believed to actually become the body of Christ. He regarded the cult of the saints' relics and pilgrimages as superstitious folly. Like the Protestants of the sixteenth century, whom in many ways he anticipated, he based his convictions solely on sacred scripture, not Church tradition. Consequently, he rejected the notion of purgatory, because it had no scriptural authority. He likewise opposed monasticism for the same reason. Although Wycliffe's views and practices ran counter to Catholic doctrine and teaching, he was never molested by Church authorities, because he enjoyed unusually strong patronage and protection in the form of John of Gaunt, the Duke of Lancaster and the younger son of King Edward III. Thus, rather than being declared a heretic and being burned at the stake, Wycliffe was able to live out his life and die a natural death. Eventually, however, the Council of Constance in 1415 declared portions of his writings to be heretical, and in 1428 his body was exhumed, burned, and the ashes cast into a river so as to prevent his remains from being worshipped as saintly relics.

As the result of intermarriage between the royal families of England and Bohemia (now the Czech Republic), John Wycliffe's radical ideas found their way to Bohemia, where Jan Hus (1373-1415), a professor of Theology at Charles University in Prague, incorporated them into his own teaching, sermons, and writing against various Church abuses. For example, like Martin

Luther one century later, he denounced the Church's selling of indulgences in order to raise money for its various projects; and he argued that if a papal decree did not conform to written scripture, it was not valid and should not be obeyed. He further argued that if a pope was not a moral man (as many were not), they could not be infallible in their pronouncements. Like Wycliffe and many others at this time, he spoke out against the Church's wealth. While the large majority of Bohemians were poor, the Church owned half the country's land and many of its clergy lived in luxury. Hus became the leader of a major dissident movement against the Catholic Church, but unlike Wycliffe, he wound up being burned at the stake as a heretic in 1415 at the Council of Constance (treated below). When he was asked to attend the council to discuss abuses in the Church with a view to reform, he was given a guarantee for his personal safety. But after arriving there, he was seized, thrown into a sewer-filled dungeon, and kept there in chains for several weeks. When he was finally brought out and led before Church officials, he was shouted down when he attempted to defend his ideas. After being condemned as a heretic, he was burned at the stake, and his writings were burned as well. His martyrdom, however, caused an uprising in Bohemia. The people, led by their king and nobles, organized a Hussite Church to replace the Catholic Church. These people came to be known as Utraquists from the Latin word *utraque*, meaning 'both' or 'each', because the Hussites demanded that when they partook of communion, they be allowed, like members of the clergy, to receive both the bread and the wine instead of only the bread. But when these reforms did not go far enough to please the more extreme Hussites, the latter withdrew into the rural areas and formed their own sect, known as the Taborites. They took their name from an eminence that they called Mt. Tabor, a mountain in Galilee, whence Jesus was thought to have ascended to heaven. The Taborites believed that The End of Days was at hand. They abolished private property and established a form of communism in imitation of the supposed golden age at the time of Adam and Eve in the Garden of Eden.

Like the later Protestant Reformation, the Bohemian religious rebellion eventually resulted in warfare. The pope proclaimed a holy crusade against the Hussites, and a Catholic army from the surrounding regions was organized. But when the Catholics were repeatedly defeated, they succeeded in making common cause with the Utraquists against the Taborites, and the latter were defeated and wiped out, but the Catholic Church acquiesced in allowing the other Hussites to observe Utraquism. Nevertheless, these events in Bohemia clearly testify to the existence of widespread discontent with the Catholic Church that would explode a century later with the Protestant Reformation. John Wycliffe and Jan Hus, who have been profiled here, were only two of many out-spoken critics of the Catholic Church; and religious dissidence exhibited itself in many ways throughout Western Europe.

But let us return to the papacy itself. In 1376 Pope Gregory XI moved the papal court back to Rome and died during the following year. His successor, Pope Urban VI, was determined to end the many abuses in the Church and even threatened to excommunicate some of the cardinals who had just elected him. In 1378 the cardinals reconvened secretly at the small town of Anagni not far from Rome and deposed Urban VI on the grounds that they (the cardinals) had chosen him, because they had been intimidated by the people in Rome, who were demanding to have an Italian pope. The cardinals then chose the cousin of King Charles V of France to be the next pope, and he took up his official residence once again at Avignon. Since Pope Urban VI refused to step down, there were now two popes, each claiming to be the head of the Catholic Church. This confused situation, known as the Great Schism, lasted for nearly forty years (1378-1417). Some countries acknowledged one pope, and others recognized the other. France, of course, followed the pope in Avignon, whereas England and the Holy Roman Empire backed the one in Rome. The various states in Italy chose up sides as their interests dictated.

The schism led to the so-called conciliar movement, which takes its name from the Latin word *concilium* (plural, *concilia*), meaning "meeting." This movement was based upon the idea that the Church was a kind of Christian democracy of its clergy, rather than a papal monarchy. According to this doctrine, meetings of the clergy had the power to make fully binding and authoritative decisions for the Church. As the schism continued, this movement gained more and more support. In 1409 both colleges of cardinals, the one at Avignon and the other at Rome, met at Pisa, voted to depose both popes, and elected a new one in their place. Unfortunately, since neither pope refused to leave office, the problem was further compounded by there being three popes. Finally, a large Church council was convened at Constance in Switzerland (1414-1418), during which the participants voted to depose all three popes and elected a new one in their place. The three existing popes were forced out of office, and the new pope (Martin V, 1417-1431) returned the papacy to Rome. Although this marked a great triumph for the conciliar movement, Martin V and his successors made sure that the whole idea of conciliarism became a thing of the past, and they reestablished the traditional notion of the pope as absolute monarch of the Church. As we will see when we survey the Italian Renaissance, subsequent popes further damaged their religious leadership in the eyes of many Europeans by ignoring their religious duties in favor of pursuing military enterprises and-cut-throat political struggles in Italy.

Having traced the history of the papacy up to the beginning of the Renaissance, let us now do the same for England and France by surveying the Hundred-Years War. Despite its name, the war actually lasted 116 years (1337-1453), but that too is misleading, because it was more like a series of wars separated from one another by periods of truce or peace. Moreover, the war was simply a continuation of the conflicts between England and France that stretched back to the days of the Angevin Empire of Henry II and Richard I the Lion Heart and even earlier. There were three important causes for the war. One involved the two monarchs contesting their rights to the Duchy of Aquitaine. Although King Edward III of England had sworn oaths of homage and fealty to the King of France to be his feudal vassal for this region, the French king was eager to establish his direct control over it and therefore decided to revoke these oaths. Secondly, Edward III responded to the French king's revocation by laying claim to the French throne on the grounds that he was more closely related to the French royal family. Edward was in fact the grandson of Philip the Fair (1285-1314) and the nephew of Charles IV (1322-1328), whereas the current French king (Philip V, 1328-1350) was only the cousin of the latter. Indeed, one primary goal of English kings throughout the conflict was not only to restore the glory of the Angevin Empire, but to go even farther in making themselves kings of France. The third cause for the war involved Flanders. It was a county owing allegiance to the king of France, and its feudal nobility were in fact loyal to the French crown. But given the importance of Flanders' wool trade with England, the townsfolk were strongly sympathetic to the English.

Hostilities began in 1337 when the English invaded northern France. In fact, all the fighting during the war occurred on French soil, and it was the last major war involving large numbers of knights, who fought according to Medieval chivalry. At the very beginning of the war the English controlled only two small areas of France, one in the west around Bordeaux and another in northern France, which the English used as a beach-head. The first major battle occurred in 1346 at Crecy in northern France, where the English defeated the French. There were two factors crucial to the English victory. One was the English peasant infantry armed with long bows that could shoot three arrows to every one shot by a French cross bow. The other was the use of cannon, probably for the first time on a battle field in western Europe. Both succeeded in throwing the French into confusion and enabling the English knights to rout the French. In the next year the English captured Calais on the English Channel and held it for the next two centuries. In 1356 at Poitiers the English scored an even greater victory than at Crecy. In this battle a smaller force defeated a larger one. The French king was taken prisoner and held in England until he was ransomed for a sum that was five times more than what the English had paid to ransom Richard I the Lion Heart. In order to pay such a colossal sum, taxes upon the French people had to be increased; and since the peasants were already being pressed hard enough, the extra burden led to a peasant uprising in 1358, known as the Jacquerie. They attacked their manorial lords, their families, and property, killing, raping, and burning. The upper class responded by banding together and ruthlessly suppressing the uprising.

By 1360 the first major phase of the war came to an end. The French peasants were once again subservient to their lords. The French king had been ransomed, and the English had succeeded in enlarging their territorial holdings in France. At this point the fortunes of war shifted with the varying quality of leadership exhibited by both sides. Having achieved fame and fortune in the war, King Edward III (who did not die until 1377) slid into a life of ease and failed to give the war the attention that it required. The French, on the other hand, with their backs to the wall, pursued a cautious strategy under able leadership. By avoiding major engagements, but winning many small skirmishes, they slowly rolled back much of what the English had gained.

When King Edward III died in 1377, he was succeeded by his ten-year old grandson, Richard II (1377-1399). In order to come up with more money to fund the war, King Richard's regents decided to impose a head tax upon all English subjects. This resulted in an uprising of English peasants in 1381. Like the French peasants, their English counterparts rebelled, simply because they found their burdens to be more than what they could bear. The uprising began in southeastern England and involved both rural peasants and townsfolk. After plundering nearby areas, the rebels set their sights on London itself. They rampaged through the city for two days as they killed many people and engaged in more plundering. King Richard met with their representatives to hear their grievances. At this point the rebels desisted and began to celebrate, thinking that the worst of their troubles were now over. But as soon as they disbanded and left London, Richard and his advisors forgot all about the peasants' grievances and proceeded to stamp out the rebellion, although they did have enough good sense to repeal the head tax that had caused the uprising in the first place.

At this point the English war effort became bogged down in domestic politics with historically significant consequences. By now parliament had emerged as an important political institution in the English government and had even developed into its two chambers: the House of Lords and the House of Commons. The former comprised the feudal lords of the realm, whereas the latter drew its members from the lower nobility (termed the gentry) and rich townsfolk (called burgesses). Since the kings in recent decades had needed more and more money to fund the war, the House of Commons was now the body that controlled the purse strings. Its permission was needed in order for the king to levy taxes. Following the peasant revolt of 1381, King Richard II and parliament became locked in a power struggle that lasted for the rest of the reign (1399). Probably as a result of his youth and inexperience, Richard adopted an overly exalted view of kingship, according to which he did not think it at all necessary to render an accounting to parliament for the way in which he or his courtiers spent tax money. Parliament retaliated by using a procedure developed during the course of that century. It was termed impeachment and involved parliament accusing and putting on trial members of the king's entourage suspected of misconduct. It is from this procedure that we in the United States derive our own process of impeachment to remove elected officials from office. In these instances, however, the persons directly involved in the power struggle were playing for keeps. Those convicted were not simply removed from office. They were executed; and when Richard was able to turn the tables on the parliamentary accusers of his courtiers, they too suffered execution. Parliament reached its pinnacle of power in this struggle in 1388 when it succeeded in eliminating several of the king's favorites. Over the next few years Richard staged a comeback and shifted the balance of power in his favor, but then in 1399, while Richard was in Ireland conducting a military campaign, many of the most powerful feudal lords banded together and rebelled. When Richard returned and met with the leaders of the revolt to settle their differences, he was arrested and forced to abdicate in favor of his cousin, the son of John of Gaunt and grandson of Edward III, who now became King Henry IV. For Western Europe, which was ruled at this time by divine-right monarchs, Richard's forced abdication was a truly stunning event and demonstrated that within the English system of government not even the king himself could safely get away with ignoring the established procedures of government.

During the years of this power struggle the war in France dragged on with the English making no gains, but actually losing territory to the French. Eventually fighting ceased altogether as Richard negotiated a peace settlement that lasted for several years. Serious fighting did not resume until the English war effort came under the personal leadership of King Henry V (1413-1422), a very talented and charismatic monarch who nearly realized the dream of making himself king of France. King Henry won his most famous and brilliant victory in 1415 at Agincourt. William Shakespeare has summed up the military ethos so beautifully in the following lines that he attributed to King Henry on the eve of this battle:

> Whoever does not have the stomach for this fight, let him depart. Give him money to speed his departure, since we wish not to die in that man's company. Whoever lives past today and comes home safely, will rouse himself every year on this day, show his neighbor his scars, and tell embellished stories of all their great feats of battle. These stories he will teach his son, and from this day until the end of the world we shall be remembered, we few, we happy few, we band of brothers, for whoever has shed his blood with me shall be my brother. And those men afraid to go will think themselves lesser men as they hear of how we fought and died together.

The victory at Agincourt was largely achieved by the English footsoldier armed with the long bow, by which charge after charge of French knights ended in heaps of dead men and horses. The English lost only 112, whereas the French lost several thousands, many of them being prominent knights. Henry V had renewed the war at a time when France was suffering from a civil war. Since the English now formed an alliance with the Burgundians, their combined forces racked up one success after the next and became masters of much of France, including Paris. The king of France, Charles VI, who had long suffered from scizophrenia and had exhibited erratic behavior for many years, was persuaded by his Bavarian wife to disown his son as his successor to the throne and to marry his daughter Katherine to Henry, so that their son would be the next king of France. Meanwhile, the king's disowned son, Charles VII, continued to oppose the English and the Burgundians, but with little success. On June 2, 1420 Henry V and Katherine were married, and on December 6, 1422 Katherine gave birth to a son, Henry VI, who, according to the agreement, would be the next king of France. But these plans were soon undone when Henry V died of dysentery on August 31, 1422, and Charles VI died less than two months later on October 21. The latter's disowned son immediately assumed the title of King of France, but his war against the English and Burgundians continued to go nowhere. At this point something totally unexpected happened to alter the entire nature and ultimate outcome of the war. While the English were pressing the siege of Orleans, Joan of Arc arrived on the scene and rescued the French nation.

Joan's brief, but remarkable life began about 1412 in the village of Donremy in eastern France on the western bank of the Meuse River. She was the child of ordinary peasants. When she was twelve (1424), Joan began hearing the voices of angels and saints, who, as she reported it, told her that the English had no right to be in France, and that she must help to drive them out. Five years later (1429) at the age of seventeen, she persuaded the captain of a nearby garrison to give her a small military escort to the castle of Chinon, where Charles VII feebly presided over a government in exile. The journey took eleven days, and during it Joan dressed in male clothes for the first time in order to conceal her female identity and thereby to protect herself from physical molestation. Joan's arrival at court occurred at a time when a mystic, who was thought to have the power of prophecy, had predicted that France would be restored by a virgin. Joan now urged Charles to believe that her voices were genuine, and that she was sent by God to save the French. After spending three weeks in having Joan's religious orthodoxy and virginity investigated, Charles armed her, placed her in command of a large military force, and sent her off to relieve Orleans from its English besiegers. After all, what did he have to lose? Everything else had thus far failed.

Arriving at Orleans, Joan ordered the English to lift their siege, but of course, they simply scoffed at this peasant girl wearing soldier's armor. First, she slipped through their lines with a sizable force that relieved the French troops trapped inside the castle. Then exhibiting extraordinary courage, she personally led a series of successful counterattacks on the English camp. Rattled and forced to lift their siege after only nine days of Joan being on the scene, the English retreated, leaving Joan to be forever after revered as the Maid of Orleans. One month later, she won a second major victory at the battle of Patay. By then, all French and English troops knew that a peasant girl had reversed the momentum of the war. Joan continued to campaign until she fought a path to Reims, in whose cathedral Charles VII was finally properly crowned as king of France. Yet, having revived her king's cause, Joan's own luck ran out, in part because after his coronation Charles distanced himself from her. While attacking Pans, she was wounded and taken prisoner by the Burgundians. Since King Charles was short of money, he decided not to ransom her. The Burgundians therefore sold her to the English. Whereupon she was put on trial in the city of Rouen for heresy and sorcery.

Since the English authorities were determined to discredit and destroy her, she was mistreated both physically and mentally. When in her cell, she was kept tightly bound with chains; and before her actual trial, she was subjected to 34 consecutive days of gruling interrogation, during which she was denied counsel and had to defend herself. Of course, the English ignored other legal procedures that would have been to her benefit. Her interrogators focused especially on her dressing as a male soldier, her voices, and her military successes. Her responses in the surviving transcript suggest that she, a young and illiterate peasant woman, answered the educated men who judged her in steadfast, articulate, and clever ways. For example, when asked if God hated the English, she replied, "Of the love or hate which God has for the English and of what He does to their souls, I know nothing, but well I know that God will send victory to the French over the English." When worried that the clerk might be keeping an inaccurate record, she demanded that his notes be read aloud and then revised to reflect more truly her actual words. She was eventually found guilty of heresy, witchcraft, and other things and condemned to death, being not yet twenty-years old. She was publicly burned at the stake in Rouen, and it took about a half an hour for her to die. One of the on-lookers was Jean Froissart, who wrote a history of the Hundred-Years War, and who was serving as an official to the court of Henry VI. he was deeply shaken by Joan's execution and thought that it spelled the ruin of the English cause. The English burned her body twice in order to reduce it completely to ashes, which they then cast into the Seine River, so that no one could possess any part of her as a holy relic.

By 1435 the war began to tilt in favor of the French. The ruler of the Holy Roman Empire began making noises as if he would intervene on the

the way English interrogate, makes Joan look bad

French side. The English-Burgundian coalition eventually fell apart, and Charles VII and the duke of Burgundy reconciled their differences. Nevertheless, it took several more years of fighting for the French to achieve ultimate victory. When they finally did in 1453, the English held only the port of Calais on the English Channel, which served as a beach-head for the English in future wars with the French.

On November 7, 1455 Joan's aged mother appeared in Paris and petitioned that her daughter's case be re-examined. This request was the culmination of several years of various theologians and lawyers studying the transcript of the earlier interrogation of Joan and her trial, which were found to be deficient in justifying the English verdict and her execution. Over the next several months a panel of judges, including representatives of the pope, took testimony from people who had known Joan. Then following their scrutiny of all the available evidence, the judges on July 7, 1456 delivered their verdict, which nullified the English judgment against Joan and found her innocent of the charges. Then in 1920 Joan was finally canonized as a saint by the Roman Catholic Church.

LECTURE 29
Medieval Universities and Vernacular Literature

IMPORTANT TERMS AND PERSONS

- Medieval university: institutions of higher learning for the teaching of theology, law, and medicine, important in fostering intellectual and literary activity.

- Vernacular Languages: native languages spoken by the various peoples of Western Europe as opposed to Latin learned as a second language by the educated members of society.

- Dante: Italian author of *The Divine Comedy* (Inferno, Purgatorio, and Paradiso).

- Boccaccio: Italian author of *The Decameron*, collection of 100 tales.

- Chaucer: English author of *The Canterbury Tales*, a collection of 24 stories somewhat similar to *The Decameron*.

As we have seen from the preceding four lectures, the High Middle Ages (1050-1350) were characterized by considerable change and growth in many sectors of Western European society. This was certainly true for the overall intellectual climate, which we shall explore in this last lecture devoted to this period. During the Early and Central Middle Ages book learning and formal education virtually disappeared and was confined to a very small number of people, who learned how to read and write in Latin as part of their training to become priests in the Catholic Church. The only schools that existed were associated with monasteries and cathedrals. Formal education consisted of being taught the very basics in seven different fields, which were grouped into one set of three (the *trivium*) and another set of four (the *quadrivium*). The former comprised grammar, logic, and rhetoric, which were designed to teach the student how to read, write, speak, and think in Latin, because that was the language of *The Bible* and of the literary works surviving from earlier ancient Roman times. The *quadrivium* comprised arithmetic, geometry, music, and astronomy and gave the student a very rudimentary knowledge of these areas. During the High Middle Ages, however, Western Europeans began to absorb a large body of new scholarship from the Arabs of Spain and Sicily. As heirs to the scholarship of the ancient Greeks, the Arabs had translated works of Greek philosophy, medicine, mathematics, and astronomy into Arabic, and this knowledge was now being transmitted to Western Europe as these Arabic works were translated in turn into Latin. As a result, the very basic and simple curriculum of the *trivium* and *quadrivium* had to be updated and expanded in order to assimilate all the new learning borrowed from Islamic Spain and Sicily. This required an entirely new system of education to be developed, the Medieval university, which is the ancestor of our own modern-day system of higher education.

During the High Middle Ages about eighty universities were founded throughout western Europe, some of which still exist today as venerable and leading institutions of higher learning. One of the earliest Medieval universities came into being around the middle of the eleventh century (c.1050) at Salerno on the western coast of southern Italy, just north of Sicily. At about the same time (1088) the University of Bologna was founded in northern Italy. Universities at Oxford and Paris came into being during the late twelfth century (1100s). The University of Padua in northeastern Italy was founded in 1220, and the University of Naples was established in 1224.

There were three major fields of specialized study taught in these Medieval universities: medicine, law, and theology. The ancient writings of Hippocrates and Galen now became the standard texts for Medieval medicine and were not significantly improved upon until the sixteenth and seventeenth centuries with the beginning of the scientific tradition during the Early

Modern Period of Europe. Justinian's *Digest* on Roman Law was rediscovered in Italy in 1061 and led to Roman law becoming the central focus of legal studies, because *The Digest* embodied a system of law that was much more sophisticated than what currently existed in western Europe. As Medieval university students mastered Roman law and found employment as lawyers in their countries' governments, they incorporated ancient Roman law into their legal work. Consequently, the legal systems of modern-day continental Europe derive from Roman law; and even today students in European law schools are usually required to take at least one semester on Roman law.

Perhaps the single most influential figure of Medieval education was Aristotle. Since he had written treatises on virtually every important area of human knowledge and had employed such rigorous and convincing logic in analyzing things, Aristotle's numerous works, translated into Latin from Arabic texts, became the unchallenged authority, so that Aristotle reigned supreme in Western European thought for five centuries (c.1100-1600). Aristotle's views on nature and biology were accepted as true as Biblical scripture. Indeed, his method of logic was adopted by Medieval theologians, who used it to construct a coherent and logical system of Christian theology, culminating in the comprehensive *Summa Theologica* of Thomas Aquinas (1225-1274).

The one area of scholarship most dramatically affected by the new learning was mathematics. Earlier Medieval arithmetic and geometry, which formed part of the *quadrivium*, had been very simple and still employed the cumbersome system of Roman numerals, which made it very difficult to carry out complex calculations. This situation changed with the Western European adoption during the twelfth century of the system of Arabic numbers. Euclid's geometry now became available in Latin, as did the new field of algebra developed by Arab scholars. The earlier simple Medieval study of astronomy was also now updated. The comprehensive astronomical work of Ptolemy (dating to the second century) with its geocentric view of the universe became the unquestioned authority in its field until challenged in the sixteenth and seventeenth centuries by Copernicus, Kepler, and Galileo.

Having outlined the basic ways in which Medieval learning was revolutionized by ancient Greco-Roman and Arabic scholarship, we will now survey the nature of Medieval universities themselves. To begin with, the term "university" comes from a Latin word, *universitas*, meaning "union" or "guild." It was used to refer to the guild of students and teachers who carried on their activities within a Medieval town, just as other craftsmen and workers were organized into their respective guilds. Just as the guilds of the various crafts specified the conditions of work, wages, and quality of manufacture, so the "university" of students and teachers regulated their activities, both among themselves and with other members of the town. Since during this period the Medieval universities did not possess their own land (campus) or buildings, space had to be rented, and the "university" helped to establish the conditions by which teachers and students could find appropriate accommodations in their town or city. The "university" also specified how much the students paid their teachers, and exactly what subjects and texts had to be taught.

All instruction was delivered by the teachers in Latin, and students were required to speak to each other in the same language, thus making Latin the one universal language of scholarship throughout Western Europe. Books were expensive and hard to come by, so that many students could not afford having their own. Instead, they had to rely upon copious notes that they took on their professors' lectures. Conditions within the classroom were often quite primitive. While the professor usually had a chair in which to sit at a table on which he read from an open book, the students sometimes did not have tables and chairs. For example, the famous Italian poet Dante (1265-1321) complained of having to take notes while sitting on a cold stone floor. Students decided when they were prepared to graduate. In order to do so, they had to pass a very rigorous oral exam, in which they were asked numerous questions by their professors, who then decided whether or not the student demonstrated sufficient learning to justify his receipt of his license for teaching (*licentia docendi*). By the way, our modern-day custom of wearing caps and gowns at graduation ceremonies is Medieval in origin. As we have seen, "master" was the highest of three levels within a Medieval guild. Thus, the graduating student became a master of arts (our M.A.) and was certified to teach the seven liberal arts of the *trivium* and *quadrivium*. Students who only mastered the lower level of the *trivium* received a degree known as the bachelor of the arts (B.A.). Those who were judged as having achieved complete command of medicine, law, or theology were awarded the higher degree that designated them a doctor (i.e., professor) of philosophy (love of wisdom), *philosophiae doctor* (Ph.D.).

The culture surrounding Medieval education was very similar to what we have today with our own universities and colleges. Just like today, when many parents want their children to obtain a good education in order to provide them with a secure livelihood, so peasant farmers or craftsmen of sufficient means wanted their sons (there were no females admitted to Medieval universities) to become educated, so that they could obtain a secure niche in life and earn a living with their minds instead of having to labor with their hands and backs. The few letters of students that survive most frequently request money from their parents for buying books, clothing, and other things. What a big surprise! Since these students were young men living on their own and out of reach of parental control, their extra-curricular activities were predictable: gambling, drinking in taverns, and gallivanting around with the young lasses. Of course, the ordinary townsfolk often complained of their rowdy behavior.

The intended consequence of Medieval university education was to produce a steady crop of persons well trained in the areas of the seven liberal arts, medicine, law, and theology in order to serve society. But as young people obtained education in these areas, they developed skills and habits of thought that enabled them to give expression in writing to their own feelings, thoughts, and experiences, which lay outside the structured curriculum of the university. We see this very clearly, for example, in "Flora" and "The Confession of Golias" forming Texts #36A-B in PSWC. By the fourteenth century (1300s) the Medieval universities had produced an intellectual climate that was spawning "vernacular" literature, i.e. works of literature written not in Latin, but in the actual languages spoken by ordinary people (in early forms of Italian, German, French, English, etc.). We shall therefore conclude this survey of the Medieval universities by looking at three examples of this vernacular literature, two in Italian and one in English: Dante's *Divine Comedy*, Boccaccio's *Decameron*, and Chaucer's *Canterbury Tales*.

Dante Alighieri (1265-1321) was a native of Florence in Italy, but as the result of political turmoil in his city, he spent much of his adult life living in exile. By the end of his life he had succeeded in producing one of the world's greatest works of literature, written in Italian verse, an epic poem called *The Divine Comedy*. As we have seen in the cases of the Epic of Gilgamesh, Homer's *Iliad*, and *Beowulf*, epics embody the basic values and world views of their societies. Dante's poem was written at the end of the Medieval period and neatly sums up its God-centered Christian world view. It is a fictional account of how Dante was taken on a personal tour of hell, purgatory, and heaven, during which he encountered the ghosts of many famous, infamous, and ordinary people, who were either punished or rewarded for their respective sins or virtues. The poem is structured to symbolize the unity or oneness of God, as well as the holy trinity. Thus, the whole poem (being a unity) is divided into three parts: *Inferno* (hell), *Purgatorio* (purgatory), and *Paradiso* (heaven). In addition, the whole poem is structured into blocks of verses called cantos, so that the entire poem consists of 100 cantos with each third comprising 33 cantos (3x11) along with the single introductory canto. At the very beginning of the poem Dante encounters the ghost of Vergil, the greatest poet of ancient Rome, the author of the epic poem, *The Aeneid*, written during the early years of Augustus' reign as Rome's first emperor. Just as Vergil described in the sixth book of *The Aeneid* how his hero, the Trojan Aeneas, ancestor of the Roman people, was taken on a tour of the pagan underworld, so Vergil conducts Dante on a tour of hell. This forms the first third of the entire poem and is the most famous part of the work.

Over the entrance into hell is written "Abandon all hope, ye who enter here." But before Dante and Vergil descend into the places where the souls of sinful people are punished, they first travel through the top most level that is devoid of actual torments. It is the place where dwell people of virtue who lived before the advent of Christianity. These souls of good non-Christians therefore spend eternity in a kind of imperfect heaven. Here Dante encounters many great figures of ancient Greece and Rome: Homer, Socrates, Plato, Aristotle, Euclid, Ptolemy, several noble Roman women, and even the great Islamic warrior Saladin. From here they enter hell proper, and they first meet

Minos, the judge of the dead. He has the form of a human but with a very long tail. After newly arrived souls tell him of what crime(s) or sin(s) they are guilty, he condemns them to one of the nine levels of hell by wrapping his tail around his body as many times as the number of the level to which they have been condemned. You may recall from Lecture 4 that the Bronze Age civilization on the island of Crete is termed Minoan from the ancient Greek myth that made King Minos ruler of the island in early times, and because of his reputation for justice he was one of the three judges of the ancient Greek underworld. Having Minos serve as the judge of the souls entering hell is only one of countless instances in which Dante ingeniously incorporates figures of ancient Greece and Rome into his graphic description of Christian hell.

Each of the nine levels of hell are circular, and they become larger as they descend from top to bottom, so that, taken together, they form something like a cone embedded beneath the surface of the Earth, with the bottom level positioned at the center of the Earth. Souls guilty of less serious offenses wind up in the upper levels, whereas the worst offenders are consigned to the lower ones; and each offense is punished in its own particular and appropriate way. The offenses include lust, gluttony, avarice, bribery and graft, hatred and wrath, fraudulent and deceptive behavior of all sorts, murder and bloodshed, and treason. For example, those guilty of murder or bloodshed are forced to stand in a river of boiling blood. The less serious offenders stand in the boiling blood only up to their ankles, whereas the mass murderers, such as Alexander the Great and Attila the Hun, are almost entirely immersed. Those guilty of bribery or graft are fully immersed in a gigantic pool of hot pitch; and if they raise themselves above the surface, demons immediately attack them and tear them to pieces. People guilty of theft are constantly tormented by snakes. The lowest level of hell is a lake of ice, and people guilty of treason are embedded in the ice up to their necks. The most grievous perpetrator of this crime is, of course, Satan, who is frozen in the ice around his waist, which marks the very center of the Earth; and his constantly flapping wings stirs up a steady cold wind that afflicts people's heads above the surface of the ice.

As Dante and Vergil make their way from one level and area to the next, Vergil explains the sins committed and the rationale for their punishment.

They encounter the souls of famous persons of the past and more ordinary folk as well. Dante frequently engages many of these unfortunate souls in conversation to learn about them and their misdeeds; and he sometimes encounters someone whom he knows from his native Florence, and whom he either reviles for their misconduct, or whose condemnation to hell he laments. In short, the whole work is imaginative, striking, and powerful.

Our other two examples of vernacular literature resemble one another in being large collections of short stories shaped into a single literary work. We have already encountered *The Decameron* of Giovanni Boccaccio (1313-1375) in connection with the outbreak of the bubonic plague in 1348-1350. Although this work is fictional, it is placed in an actual historical setting, the arrival of the Black Death in Florence in 1348. After describing the actual horrors of the disease in the work's preface, which forms Text #35 in PSWC, Boccaccio sets up the remainder of the work by having ten young people (seven males and three females) band together and flee the disease-ridden city. When they come upon a very nice, but abandoned house, they stay there for ten days, whence the work derives its name: from Greek *deka* (meaning "ten") and *hemera* (meaning "day"). Since in those days there was no TV or internet to while away the time, the ten people are described as having passed these ten days by each of them telling one story each day for a grand total of one-hundred stories. They range from the serious to the very funny and sometimes obscene. They present us with a full cast of characters representing all walks of contemporary life and situations.

The same applies to *The Canterbury Tales* of Geoffrey Chaucer (1343?-1400). The work was written in Middle English, the vernacular language of England at that time. In this fictional work Chaucer brings together a group of English men and women traveling along the roads as they make a religious pilgrimage to the tomb of St. Thomas Becket at the cathedral of Canterbury in southeastern England. Chaucer's characterization of his cast of thirty travelers and the 24 stories that they tell give us a broad and lively cross-section of contemporary English society. As in *The Decameron*, Chaucer's characters while away the time, as they slowly make their way to Canterbury, by exchanging stories that reflect the full range of human behavior, both good and bad, serious and humorous.

Finally, I will close this lecture with several examples of technological innovations testifying to the creativity of Western Europeans during this period. During the Middle Ages there was an increasing use of water mills for grinding grain and fulling cloth. During the High Middle Ages wind power began to be harnessed as well by wind mills that were used for both grinding grain and pumping water out of swampy areas. Mechanical clocks were developed and became a common feature of town life, because they were made to chime and adorned many churches and monasteries to announce the times for the various daily services. The magnetic compass began to be used on ships during the 1200s and helped to take some of the guess-work out of sailing on the open sea. By 1280 we encounter our earliest evidence for glass being shaped into lenses and formed into eye glasses in Italy. The spinning wheel was invented during the 1300s, thus allowing wool, silk, or linen fibers to be spun into thread much more easily and quickly than by hand with a spindle whorl, as had been done since Neolithic times.

LECTURE 30
The Italian Renaissance

- **1350-1520:** The period of the Italian Renaissance.
- **1434-1494:** Political dominance of the Medici family in Florence.
- **1450:** Approximate date for the beginning of printing by movable type.
- **Note:** You do not need to know the dates given with the following famous persons
- **renaissance:** period of rebirth, rediscovery of Greek and Roman Classical culture, literature, and the arts.
- **Humanism:** world view in which man, not God, is at the center of things.
- **commune:** free self-governing state of Italy, such as Florence or Venice.
- **Papal States:** area of central and northern Italy controlled by the pope.
- **Machiavelli:** 1469-1527, author of *The Prince*, offering practical and realistic advice for rulers regarding their acquisition and use of political power.
- **perspective** - foreshortening: artistic technique used to produce a realistic representation of three-dimensional scenes in two dimensions.

- **Vasari:** author of *Lives of the Artists*.
- **Filippo Brunelleschi:** 1377-1446, great Renaissance architect, responsible for designing the great dome for the Cathedral in Florence.
- **Leonardo da Vinci:** 1452-1519, painter of The Last Supper and The Mona Lisa, military architect, famous for his notebooks of drawings.
- **Michelangelo:** 1475-1564, painter of the ceiling of the Sistine Chapel, sculptor of the Pieta and a colossal statue of David.

In these last five lectures we will survey major aspects of the Early Modern Period for western Europe that were extremely important in shaping Western Civilization in our own day. This lecture will focus upon the Italian Renaissance (1350-1520). It was a period of extraordinary creativity, especially in the visual arts (painting, sculpture, and architecture). As a result of the advances accomplished during this period, western Europe surged ahead of both the Byzantine and Islamic civilizations to become the leading civilization on the planet, a position which it has still not surrendered to any other.

The term "renaissance" comes from French and simply means "rebirth." It refers to the rebirth in western Europe of the learning of the ancient Greeks and Romans. To be sure, the Renaissance was in many ways simply the continuation of the intellectual progress that had been taking place in western Europe during the High Middle Ages, but it occurred at an accelerated pace and thus produced a qualitative difference from the Medieval culture that had gone before. Indeed, from c.1350 onwards many learned persons throughout western Europe began to think that they were living in a new and exciting age very different from earlier times, which they began to call the Dark Ages or the Middle Ages. To them, the latter had been a period of nearly one thousand years that separated them from the glories of ancient Greece and Rome, which the Germanic tribal invasions of western Europe had destroyed. These men now saw themselves as reviving the learning and intellectual brilliance of the Greeks and Romans. Eventually, the term "humanism" began to be used to characterize the overall cultural and educational goals of the Renaissance. It marked a real change from the world view of the preceding Middle Ages. The latter had stressed the relative unimportance of human affairs in this world and had placed God, personal salvation, and eternity at the center of things. Renaissance humanism, on the other hand, like the cultures of ancient Greece and Rome, placed human beings and their actions in this world at the center of things. When we surveyed Medieval monasticism in Lecture 23, we noticed how the Medieval God-centered world view emphasized that monks must be humble, obedient, and silent. The man-centered world view of the Renaissance placed great value upon the individual and individual achievement, so that it was acceptable for people to take pride in their abilities and what they could accomplish. Along with this new sense of individualism was the notion of "the Renaissance man," a concept that we still have today. "A Renaissance man" was someone who was well educated in all fields of knowledge, and at the same time he was physically fit, possessing considerable athletic abilities, and also having the social skills and polish of a gentleman. All these interrelated concepts (humanism, individualism, and "the Renaissance man") can be seen very clearly in the following passage taken from the autobiography of Leon Baptista Alberti (1404-1474):

(Taken from *The Portable Renaissance Reader*, ed. by J. B. Ross and M. M. McLaughlin, Penguin Books 1968)

Finally, he embraced with zeal and forethought everything which pertained to fame. To omit the rest, he strove so hard to attain a name in modeling and painting that he wished to neglect nothing by which he might gain the approbation of good men. His genius was so versatile that you might almost judge all the fine arts to be his.... He played ball, hurled the javelin, ran, leaped, wrestled, and above all delighted in the steep ascent of mountains; he applied himself to all these things for the sake of health rather than sport or pleasure. As a youth he excelled in warlike games. With his feet together, he could leap over the shoulders of men standing by; he had almost no equal among those hurling the lance. An arrow shot by his hand from his chest could pierce the strongest iron breastplate.... On horseback, holding in his hand one end of a long wand, while the other was firmly fixed to his foot, he could ride his horse violently in all directions for hours at a time as he wished, and the wand would remain completely immobile. Strange and marvelous! That the most spirited horses and those most impatient of riders, when he first mounted them, would tremble violently and shudder as if in great fear. He learned music without teachers, and his compositions were approved by learned musicians. He sang throughout his whole life, but in private, or alone.... He delighted in the organ and was considered an expert among the leading musicians. When he had begun to mature in years, neglecting everything else, he devoted himself entirely to the study of letters, and he spent some years of labor on canon and civil law.... Since his relatives were neither kind nor humane to him in his illness, by way of consoling himself between his convalescence and cure he wrote the play Philodoxeos.... But in truth, because he could not live without letters, at the age of twenty-four he turned to physics and the mathematical arts.... From craftsmen, architects, shipbuilders, and even from cobblers he sought information to see if by chance they preserved anything rare or unusual or special in their arts; and he would then communicate such things to those citizens who wished to know them. He pretended to be ignorant in many things, so that he might observe the talents and habits and skill of others. And so he was a zealous observer of whatsoever pertained to inborn talent of the arts.... He wrote some books entitled On Painting, and in this very art of painting he created works unheard of and unbelievable to those who saw them.... By some defect in his nature he loathed garlic and also honey, and the mere sight of them, if by chance they were offered to him, brought on vomiting. But he conquered himself by force of looking at and handling the disagreeable objects, so that they came to offend him less, thus showing by example that **men can do anything with themselves if they will.**

Notice those last few words. They agree exactly with the tenor of Text #38 in PSWC, the beginning of an essay entitled "Oration on the Dignity of Man," written by an Italian named Picio della Mirandola. In this passage Pico glorifies the human being as God's most noble creation. According to Pico, we humans are situated between the other animals and the angels. What we make of ourselves is left up to us as individuals. We can fail to develop our abilities and simply live ordinary lives not all that different from the other creatures, or we can reach for the stars, become the very best that we can be, and thus be akin to the angels themselves in our knowledge and intellectual abilities. Furthermore, in this brief passage Pico cites several authorities in support of his opinions. He does not confine himself to *The Bible* or to ancient Greek and Roman writers, but he even cites Arab sources. This agrees with the idea that Renaissance learning did not confine itself to study of *The Bible*, but its field of study was the entire world and all of human experience.

Another excellent example of Renaissance individualism is encountered in Text #40 in PSWC, a series of excerpts taken from the autobiography of Benvenuto Cellini (1500-1574). He was a native of Florence and became a highly skilled artist in working silver and gold. Luckily for us, he thought that his life was so worthy of record that he wrote an autobiography, which gives us a detailed picture of what it was like to live and work as a Renaissance artist. For example, as a young man visiting Rome, he went one night with other people to the ruins of the ancient Roman Colosseum, where a magician conducted rites to summon up the ghosts of dead gladiators; and it became so hair-raisingly spooky that everyone fled away in terror. He traveled about from place to place (Pisa, Siena, Rome, Mantua, and Paris), being employed by different wealthy patrons for various works of art. His employers and patrons included the pope and the king of France. He was once imprisoned in a dungeon and describes (quite unashamedly) how he murdered a man for disrespecting him. What clearly emerges from all his escapades is his great sense of personal worth and as a great artist.

Having sketched the basic Renaissance values of humanism, individualism, and the ideal of "the Renaissance man," let us turn to the realm of politics. Italy at this time was largely dominated by the big five. The kingdom of Naples controlled southern Italy and Sicily. Rome and the popes ruled over central Italy as the Papal States, and northern Italy was dominated by Milan, Venice, and Florence. Venice, as we have already seen, was a thriving commercial maritime state that dominated trade throughout the whole Mediterranean, and it possessed a republican form of government that was primarily controlled by aristocratic families who had grown rich through trade. Milan was ruled by a series of strong men from the Visconti and Sforza families. Although they possessed the title of duke, they actually ruled Milan with an iron hand and can be regarded as tyrants. Florence, the real heart and soul of the Renaissance, possessed a republican form of government in which various boards of officials were elected to represent the 21 guilds and four quarters of the city. But besides these big five, there were numerous smaller communities in Italy at this time, such as Verona, Brescia, Bologna, Rimini, and Siena. In fact, Italy possessed the most vigorous town life of any region in all of western Europe.

This situation, when we compare it to the Classical Period of ancient Greece, can help explain why Renaissance Italy was so creative during this period. Indeed, Classical Greece and Renaissance Italy were two of the most creative eras of human history. Why was this? It clearly resulted from the fact that during these times the people living in these two societies enjoyed a considerable degree of personal, political, and economic freedom; and their cultures both expected and encouraged them to take full advantage of them in pursuing their dreams and becoming the best that they could be. Both cultures fostered a very strong sense of competition in all areas of human endeavor; and given the great value placed upon the individual, competition urged people to realize their full potential as they strove to outdo others. We can see this very clearly in the lives of the Renaissance artists, who, as the result of their great talents, possessed big egos that often clashed as artists tried to surpass one another.

This keen spirit of competition pervaded all aspects of Italian life and spilled out into the international arena. As we have seen, the ancient Greeks were never united as a nation, but they organized themselves into numerous self-governing city-states, which were often competing with one another in various ways in both peace and war. Renaissance Italy resembled this same pattern. The large number of self-governing towns (termed *communi*, [*commune* in the singular]) along with the big five created fierce competition and nearly incessant warfare. Indeed, the cut-throat nature of Italian politics and international affairs during the Renaissance produced what is generally regarded as the first Early Modern work of political science, *The Prince*

Niccolo Machiavelli
→ The Prince (first early political modern work)

authored by Niccolo Machiavelli. This man was a native of Florence and was an avid student of history, especially of ancient Greece and Rome. He possessed an excellent Renaissance education, served the Florentine Republic as a diplomat, and firmly believed that states should be ruled through the consent of their inhabitants. Nevertheless, when the Florentine Republic went down to defeat in 1512 and had to submit to the monarchical rule of the Medici family once again (after an earlier period of Medici supremacy, 1434-1494), Machiavelli retired from public life, but he set down his political thoughts and experiences in the form of this treatise, which he addressed to the new Medici ruler of Florence in order to give him concrete advice on how he could maintain himself in power. The treatise approaches the subject of power politics, both internal and external, from a completely rational perspective. It views human behavior in very practical terms by acknowledging that we humans are not angels, but we are flawed creatures; and although it would be nice if rulers could always operate from the moral high ground, the reality is that they must be hard-headed and practical if they wish to remain in power. In order to illustrate his general conclusions, Machiavelli, like a true Renaissance man, draws upon human history from ancient Greece onwards and gives his reader specific examples of how some leaders of the past or in contemporary times either succeeded or failed, because they understood or failed to understand the principles that Machiavelli set forth. The following two passages from *The Prince* should give you a good sense of the nature of this work.

(Taken from the translation of W. K. Marriott, 1908)

Coming now to the other qualities mentioned above, I say that every prince ought to desire to be considered clement and not cruel. Nevertheless, he ought to take care not to misuse this clemency. Cesare Borgia [the bastard son of Pope Alexander VI] was considered cruel; notwithstanding, his cruelty reconciled the Romagna [part of the Papal States], unified it, and restored it to peace and loyalty. And if this be rightly considered, he will be seen to have been much more merciful than the Florentine people, who, to avoid a reputation for cruelty, permitted Pistoia to be destroyed. Therefore, a prince, so long as he keeps his subjects united and loyal, ought not to mind the reproach of cruelty; because with a few examples he will be more merciful than those who, through too much mercy, allow disorders to arise, from which follow murders or robberies; for these are wont to injure the whole people, whilst those executions which originate with a prince offend the individual only. And of all princes, it is impossible for the new prince to avoid the imputation of cruelty, owing to new states being full of dangers.... Nevertheless, he ought to be slow to believe and to act, nor should he himself show fear, but proceed in a temperate manner with prudence and humanity, so that too much confidence may not make him incautious and too much distrust render him intolerable. Upon this a question arises: whether it be better to be loved than feared or feared than loved? It may be answered that one should wish to be both, but, because it is difficult to unite them in one person, it is much safer to be feared than loved, when, of the two, either must be dispensed with. Because this is to be asserted in general of men, that they are ungrateful, fickle, false, cowardly, covetous, and as long as you succeed, they are yours entirely; they will offer you their blood, property, life, and children, as is said above, when the need is far distant; but when it approaches they turn against you. And that prince who, relying entirely on their promises, has neglected other precautions, is ruined; because friendships that are obtained by payments, and not by greatness or nobility of mind, may indeed be earned, but they are not secured, and in time of need cannot be relied upon; and men have less scruple in offending one who is beloved than one who is feared: for love is preserved by the link of obligation which, owing to the baseness of men, is broken at every opportunity for their advantage; but fear preserves you by a dread of punishment which never fails. Nevertheless, a prince ought to inspire fear in such a way that, if he does not win love, he avoids hatred; because he can endure very well being feared whilst he is not hated, which will always be as long as he abstains from the property of his citizens and subjects and from their women. But when it is necessary for him to proceed against the life of someone, he must do it on proper justification and for manifest cause, but above all things he must keep his hands off the property of others, because men more quickly forget the death of their father than the loss of their patrimony. Besides, pretexts for taking away the property are never wanting; for he who has once begun to live by robbery will always find pretexts for seizing what belongs to others; but reasons for taking life, on the contrary, are more difficult to find and sooner lapse. But when a prince is with his army, and has under control a multitude of soldiers, then it is quite necessary for him to disregard the reputation of cruelty: for without it he would never hold his army united or disposed to its duties. Among the wonderful deeds of Hannibal this one is enumerated: that having led an enormous army, composed of many various races of men, to fight in foreign lands, no dissensions arose either among them or against the prince, whether in his bad or in his good fortune. This arose from nothing else than his inhuman cruelty, which, with his boundless valour, made him revered and terrible in the sight of his soldiers, but without that cruelty, his other virtues were not sufficient to produce this effect. And short-sighted writers admire his deeds from one point of view and from another condemn the principal cause of them.... Returning to the question of being feared or loved, I come to the conclusion that, men loving according to their own will and fearing according to that of the prince, a wise prince should establish himself on that which is in his own control and not in that of others; he must endeavour only to avoid hatred, as is noted.

Everyone admits how praiseworthy it is in a prince to keep faith, and to live with integrity and not with craft. Nevertheless, our experience has been that those princes who have done great things have held good faith of little account, and have known how to circumvent the intellect of men by craft, and in the end have overcome those who have relied on their word. You must know that there are two ways of contesting, the one by the law, the other by force; the first method is proper to men, the second to beasts; but because the first is frequently not sufficient, it is necessary to have recourse to the second. Therefore, it is necessary for a prince to understand how to avail himself of the beast and the man. This has been figuratively taught to princes by ancient writers, who describe how Achilles and many other princes of old were given to the Centaur Chiron to nurse, who brought them up in his discipline; which means solely that, as they had for a teacher one who was half beast and half man, so it is necessary for a prince to know how to make use of both natures, and that one without the other is not durable. A prince, therefore, being compelled knowingly to adopt the beast, ought to choose the fox and the lion; because the lion cannot defend himself against snares and the fox cannot defend himself against wolves. Therefore, it is necessary to be a fox to discover the snares and a lion to terrify the wolves. Those who rely simply on the lion do not understand what they are about. Therefore, a wise lord cannot, nor ought he to, keep faith when such observance may be turned against him, and when the reasons that caused him to pledge it exist no longer. If men were entirely good, this precept would not hold; but because they are bad and will not keep faith with you, you too are not bound to observe it with them. Nor will there ever be wanting to a prince legitimate reasons to excuse this non-observance. Of this, endless modern examples could be given, showing how many treaties and engagements have been made void and of no effect through the faithlessness of princes; and he who has known best how to employ the fox has succeeded best. But it is necessary to know well how to disguise this characteristic and to be a great pretender and dissembler; and men are so simple and so subject to present necessities that he who seeks to deceive will always find someone who will allow himself to be deceived. One recent example I cannot pass over in silence. Alexander the Sixth [pope 1492-1503] did nothing else but deceive men, nor ever thought of doing otherwise, and he always found victims; for there never was a man who had greater power in asserting, or who with greater oaths would affirm a thing, yet would observe it less; nevertheless, his deceits always succeeded according to his wishes, because he well understood this side of mankind. Therefore, it is unnecessary for a prince to have all the good qualities that I have enumerated, but it is very necessary to appear to have them. And I shall dare to say this also, that to have them and always to observe them is injurious, and that to appear to have them is useful; to appear merciful, faithful, humane, religious, upright, and to be so, but with a mind so framed that should you require not to be so, you may be able and know how to change to the opposite. And you have to understand this, that a prince, especially a new one, cannot observe all those things for which men are esteemed, being often forced, in order to maintain the state, to act contrary to fidelity, friendship, humanity, and religion. Therefore, it is necessary for him to have a mind ready to turn itself accordingly as the winds and variations of fortune force it, yet, as I have said above, not to diverge from the good if he can avoid doing so, but, if compelled, then to know how to set about it. For this reason a prince ought to take care that he never lets anything slip from his lips that is not replete with the above-named five qualities, that he may appear to him who sees and hears him altogether merciful, faithful, humane, upright, and religious. There is nothing more necessary to appear to have than this last quality, inasmuch as men judge generally more by the eye than by the hand, because it belongs to everybody to see you, to few to come in touch with you. Everyone sees what you appear to be, few really know what you are, and those few dare not oppose themselves to the opinion of the many, who have the majesty of the state to defend them; and in the actions of all men, and especially of princes, which it is not prudent to challenge, one judges by the result. For that reason, let a prince have the credit of conquering and holding his state, the means will always be considered honest, and he will be praised by everybody; because the vulgar are always taken by what a thing seems to be and by what comes of it; and in the world there are only the vulgar, for the few find a place there only when the many have no ground to rest on.

Italian internal and inter-state politics during the Renaissance did in fact often resemble the rule of the jungle. The Republic of Florence, for example, was frequently rocked by violent clashes and power struggles between noble families or nobles with the middle or working classes, which often led to mass armed violence in the streets, assassinations, grisly public torture and executions, and people being sent into exile for years at a time. In 1342/3 a prominent figure succeeded in establishing himself as tyrant for eight months, but his cruelty ultimately led to his downfall when he was torn to pieces by a furious mob of Florentine citizens eager to regain their liberty. In 1378 the working class rose up against the nobles and the middle class, seized control of the government, and remained in power for three years. Moreover, as had been the case in ancient Greece, where there had been dozens of separate city-states to form ever-shifting alliances, the large number of self-governing *communi* created competing interests and chronic warfare. The dukes of Milan were always succeeding or failing in extending their power over smaller neighboring states; and Venice and Florence did the same. Some of the popes of the later 1400s and 1500s were among the most warlike and brutal leaders of their day. Although they had taken an oath of chastity and celibacy, popes routinely fathered children through mistresses or casual affairs and used their offspring as important elements in their power politics. Daughters were married off to form alliances with prominent families, and sons were set up as lords to rule over states and districts. In fact, our modern term "nepotism," meaning a person abusing his or her power to advance a relative into a coveted position, originates with the popes and how they abused their power to place family members in high positions.

Having looked at the politics of Renaissance Italy in general terms, let us focus more closely upon Florence, the one city that above all others was most responsible for the cultural revolution of the Renaissance. In 1300 Florence had a population that has been estimated at 90,000, which was quite large for a Medieval city. Of course, this number was reduced (probably by about one-third) as the result of the Black Death of 1348-1350. By the late 1200s Florence had developed a republican form of government based upon the 21 guilds into which its population was organized according to their trades. During the fourteenth and fifteenth centuries Florence enjoyed considerable economic prosperity based largely upon two things: its textile industry and banking. Probably about one-third of all workers in Florence were part of the textile industry, both wool and silk. Most of these people would have been ordinary laborers hired to spin fibers into thread and to weave the thread into cloth, or to thicken or soften the cloth in various ways or to dye it in different colors. Florence during the Renaissance manufactured some of the highest quality cloth in western Europe, and it was traded widely. As a result of the prosperity from its textile industry, Florence became one of the more important economic centers; and its coinage, the gold Florin, was greatly respected throughout the rest of Europe.

Two families, the Bardi and the Medici, became very rich and powerful through their banking activities. When the Medici succeeded in becoming the bankers for the popes in Rome, they emerged as Florence's wealthiest and most prominent family. By October of 1433 Cosimo di Medici had made such excellent political use of his vast wealth by loaning money to numerous people and gaining their favor that many Florentines regarded his prominence as endangering the Republic's freedom. But after he had been arrested and sent into exile, his friends in Florence orchestrated his triumphal return in August of the following year; and for the remaining thirty years of his life (1434-1464) he ruled Florence as a quasi-tyrant and was able to pass this power on to his son Piero (1464-1469) and to his grandson Lorenzo (known as The Magnificent, *Il Magnifico*) until his death in 1492. At that point Medici power devolved upon Lorenzo's twenty-year old son, Piero, who was totally unsuited for public affairs. He was a young man of mediocre character, spoiled by his family's wealth, and absorbed with horses, fine clothes, and his handsome appearance. Consequently, by November of 1494 long standing, but quiet resentment with Medici rule finally came to a full boil and led to Piero di Medici being driven out of Florence and the reestablishment of the Republic. But the restored Republic enjoyed a second life of only 18 years, itself being overthrown and replaced in 1512 by a Medici monarchy.

Cosimo and Lorenzo di Medici had been great patrons of artists and had used a large portion of their wealth to support talented men and to give them commissions that beautified the churches, monasteries, convents, public buildings, and homes of the wealthy throughout northern Italy. By the time that the restored Florentine Republic came to an end, patronage of the arts began to shift away from Florence, as the Renaissance spread throughout the rest of Italy and even across the Alps into other European countries. Initially, the popes in Rome emerged as figures who dominated both the politics of the Italian Peninsula and the patronage of the arts. Pope Alexander VI (1492-1503) and Pope Julius II (1503-1513) were not pious monarchs of the Catholic Church, but instead, they typified all too well the hard-headed and ruthless nature of warfare and politics as embodied in Machiavelli's *Prince*. Julius II had no qualms in putting off his papal robes and donning armor to lead armies to secure his hold over the Papal States. Even by the lowest standards of the papal court, which was quite corrupt at this time, Alexander VI was scandalously immoral with respect to women, and he employed his bastard son Cesare Borgia as his papal commander of military forces to maintain and enlarge his territorial possessions. In addition, the popes of the sixteenth century used their vast wealth to patronize the best artists and architects of the day to beautify Rome and to surround the popes with artistic splendor, whose extravagance played an important role in provoking the violent religious reaction known as the Protestant Reformation treated in the next lecture. It was during these years that the Basilica of St. Peter, built more than 1100 years earlier by the Emperor Constantine, was pulled down; and the popes employed the greatest artists and architects of the sixteenth and early seventeenth centuries to rebuild a much more magnificent structure, the modern-day Basilica of St. peter that still stands in the Vatican.

We will now survey the great artistic achievements of the Italian Renaissance, which we will explore more fully with the slide show in the next class meeting. But first, I need to say a few things more about Renaissance humanism, because the Renaissance movement began in the literary, not the artistic, sphere with the careful study of Greek and Latin texts. Petrarch (1304-1374) is generally regarded as the first Renaissance scholar. He saw himself as living in a new age, and he viewed the time interval between himself and Greco-Roman antiquity as a dark age. He loved the Latin language of the ancient Romans, which, of course, was very different from Medieval Latin. His two favorite authors were Cicero and Livy, whose ancient style of Latin he imitated in his own writings and letters to other scholars of the day. During the Middle Ages knowledge of ancient Greek and Roman literature had not entirely disappeared, but it had become very limited and restricted to serve the greater goal of Christianity. If an ancient text could aid in understanding sacred scripture, then it was prized by the very small number of priests and monks able to read and write, but if it had nothing to offer in this regard, then it was usually neglected and deemed unimportant. The rebirth of Classical learning that characterized the Renaissance came about in large measure, because the town life that had grown up during the High Middle Ages closely resembled the town life of ancient Greece and Rome. Consequently, the literature produced by the latter now seemed fully relevant to Western

Europeans of Petrarch's day. Thus, many ancient works, which had long been neglected by Medieval priests and monks, were now avidly sought out by Renaissance scholars, who appreciated these writings in their own terms, not simply in terms of Medieval Christianity. This resulted in what we could term a treasure hunt, in which Renaissance scholars traveled to long existing monasteries and churches to see if they could find manuscripts of ancient Roman writers that had lain neglected and uncopied for centuries. They did in fact make numerous discoveries and succeeded in preserving many works that otherwise would have disappeared.

During the fourteenth century, as the Ottoman Turks gradually conquered one part of the Byzantine Empire after another, there was an exodus of Greek-speaking Byzantines from their homeland to western Europe; and the scholars who fled westward from the Turks brought with them ancient Greek texts that had long been forgotten in western Europe. As a result, the Renaissance humanists were reacquainted with the great literary works of the ancient Greeks, so that humanist education consisted in large measure of the learning of ancient Greek and Latin and the reading of their texts. Since both Greek and Latin are very complex languages, this training made humanists very self-conscious about language generally and how words should be used, used properly, and to best effect. The learning of Greek and Latin therefore was very important in developing Early Modern literature in Italian and in the other so-called vernacular languages. The careful study of ancient languages and texts required the humanists to develop mental discipline and contributed significantly to the overall rational approach that these scholars adopted toward everything around them. By the early 1400s this rational outlook, coupled with the desire to revive the artistic traditions of the ancient Greeks and Romans, produced the extraordinary artistic revolution of the Renaissance. This period witnessed so many artists of great genius that one of them, Giorgio Vasari, compiled a multi-volume collection of their biographies, which provide us with invaluable evidence about the lives of these talented people. Text #39 in PSWC comprises excerpts from two biographies (Filippo Brunelleschi and Leonardo da Vinci) out of this large body of fascinating writing.

Filippo Brunelleschi (1377-1446) was one of the most outstanding Renaissance artists and was a pioneer in many ways. Although he is most famous as an architect for having constructed the world's largest masonry dome over the cathedral in Florence, he was a highly talented painter and played an important role in developing and establishing foreshortening (also termed perspective) as the standard technique among Renaissance painters. Foreshortening or perspective requires the painter to represent figures in a graduated scale according to strict mathematical proportions, so that the end-result is to create the visual illusion of three dimensions on a two-dimensional surface. In 1401 he was one of seven artists who competed for the commission to make bronze castings to decorate the northern and eastern doors of the baptistery of San Giovanni in Florence. Each of the artists had to make a bronze sample of their work to be viewed by a panel of judges. His sample and that of Lorenzo Ghiberti were considered the best, but in the end the commission was granted to Ghiberti. Brunelleschi was so disappointed and angry that he left Florence and went to Rome, where he and his friend Donatello spent years in studying the ruins of the ancient Romans. As a sculptor, Donatello was primarily interested in finding and studying ancient Greek and Roman statues, whose realism he reproduced in his own works. Brunelleschi, however, was fascinated with the Pantheon, which had been built during the reign of the Emperor Hadrian (117-138), because it was surmounted by an enormous free-standing masonry dome, the largest in the world at the time. By carefully studying this dome Brunelleschi was able to recreate in his own mind the complex building techniques used by the ancient Romans to construct such a marvel. He eventually returned to Florence, obtained the commission to build a similar dome over the cathedral, and constructed one slightly larger than the Pantheon's by reinventing ancient Roman architecture. It is still one of the great architectural marvels of the world. Brunelleschi's extraordinary career demonstrates the tremendous power of rational observation and artistic execution that characterized Renaissance art. We should also notice that such powers and skills led to significant technological advances and played a very important role in the development of the tradition of experimentation in Early Modern science. For example, in order to construct the dome, Brunelleschi had to build a gigantic crane (driven by oxen) for lifting tons of building material from the ground, hoisting it hundreds of feet into the air, and then maneuvering it horizontally to exactly where the workers needed it.

The career of Leonardo da Vinci is perhaps the most famous and well known case of the close interaction between artistic representation and scientific observation. For example, when he was commissioned by the duke of Milan to cast a bronze statue of the duke mounted on a horse, Leonardo undertook an exhaustive study of the anatomy of the horse, so that he could reproduce a horse's statue with complete realism. He even wrote a treatise on the subject in order to place his findings on record for others to use. Similarly, since he wished to represent the human form in painting with as much accuracy as possible, he dissected the bodies of executed criminals, so that he could see exactly how the human body was constructed. Once again, we can see how artists' great powers of perception and observation were an important forerunner to the development of observation and experimentation that were fundamental to the emergence of the modern Western scientific tradition.

One of the greatest sculptors of all time was Michelangelo (1475-1564). He spent his childhood as a foster-child, living with a family whose father worked in a stone quarry as a mason. This environment was doubtless an important formative experience for his later life: for Michelangelo seemed to possess an uncanny ability to examine the grain and texture of a block of stone and to know exactly how it could best be sculpted. At the age of twenty-two he produced one of his great masterpieces: The Pieta, portraying the Virgin Mary holding the dead body of Jesus in her lap after he had been taken down from the cross. When commissioned by Pope Julius II to design his tomb, Michelangelo produced a series of sculptures to adorn a chapel that stands inside the church of San Pietro in Vincoli in Rome, whose most famous statue is one of Moses, seated and portrayed with a delicately rendered, long flowing beard. The same pope also commissioned Michelangelo to paint the ceiling of the Sistine Chapel, covering an area of 6300 square feet. The latter structure had been built during the papacy of Sixtus IV (1471-1484) for musical performances. After years of difficult work Michelangelo and his team of artists succeeded in filling this enormous space with representations from *The Bible*, thereby making this ceiling one of the most visited attractions in Rome today. Later in his life Michelangelo was commissioned by another pope to adorn the eastern wall of the Sistine Chapel with a scene depicting The Last Judgment. He did so by portraying Jesus as signaling with his hands the elevation of some persons to heaven and the condemnation of others to hell. As was the custom of Renaissance artists, he portrayed all these human forms as nude, as ancient Greek and Roman artists had done. But many people were disturbed by this nudity, so that a modicum of clothing was added to some of these figures by later artists. Out of an enormous block of marble Michelangelo sculpted a gigantic statue of David, showing him at the moment when he has released his sling to kill Goliath. The statue is eighteen feet high and portrays the nude male form with anatomical accuracy. It also portrays David in a very heroic pose. It now stands on display as the centerpiece of Michelangelo's work in a small museum in Florence; and the Florentines have adopted this statue as their city's mascot.

I will now close this lecture by touching upon one of the most important inventions that occurred at this time, the invention of the printing press with movable type. It occurred around 1450 not in Italy, but in Germany in the Rhine Valley. Although it seems to have been the product of several people working on the same problem, Johann Gutenberg has traditionally been given credit for this invention. The printing press is an excellent example of Western European technological innovation at this time. One of the basic ideas behind the printing press was first devised by the Chinese, passed on to the Arabs, and then came to Europe.

The Chinese developed the idea of block printing. This involved taking a block of wood and carving on one of its flat surfaces the relief of the image (actually a mirror image) that the craftsman wanted to be reproduced. The relief image could then be smeared with dye or ink and then stamped onto cloth or paper in order to impress the image on it. When the Arabs learned this technique from the Chinese, they used it to produce playing cards. Eventually, Gutenberg and others incorporated it into their design of the printing press. This apparatus consisted of a metal rack into which there could be placed small metal stamps bearing the reverse images of the various letters of the alphabet. A worker could set up an entire page by placing the proper sequence of letters into this rack one line at a time. Then when the type had been set, ink was smeared on the metal stamps, and the rack, which was fixed into its own proper mechanism, could be pressed against a blank piece of parchment or paper to produce a printed page. Once a page of type had been set, it was easy to stamp out as many copies of the page as were needed. If the printed text was more than one page, then other pages of type had to be set and then printed or stamped out as well.

Once Gutenberg perfected this machine, news of its invention spread like wild fire throughout western Europe, and printing presses were being built and put to work in all the major cities. It had a tremendous impact upon Western European society, because it made written material far easier to reproduce than ever before, more inexpensively, and in much greater volume. It therefore led to a virtual explosion in the quantity of material and information circulated by the written word. As a result, it helped to foster the rise in literacy throughout Western Europe (especially among the growing middle class of the towns and cities), and it greatly facilitated the exchange of information in written form. The geometric progression at which printed material was henceforth produced can be seen from the following estimate that has been made. During the first fifty years of the printing press' existence (1450-1500) there was printed as much material as had been produced by hand-copying from Greek and Roman antiquity up until then. The same volume was printed during the first decade of the 1500s, and twice as much was printed during the following decade. As we will see in the following lecture, the printing press played a pivotal role in the career of Martin Luther and the Protestant Reformation.

LECTURE 31
The Protestant Reformation

IMPORTANT DATES AND TERMS

- **1517:** Luther posts his 95 Theses against indulgences.
- **1521:** Luther refuses to recant before Church and governmental authorities at Worms.
- **Erasmus:** great Christian humanist from Dutch Rotterdam in northern Europe, great Classical and Biblical scholar, critic of papal corruption and advocate for Church reform.
- **Protestantism:** Lutheranism, Anabaptists, Anglican Church, Calvinism (including Puritanism).
- **Martin Luther:** reliance upon biblical scripture not papal tradition, priesthood of believers, salvation attained through justification by faith rather than through penance and good works.
- **John Calvin:** predestination, the elect vs. the damned.
- **Geneva:** Protestant puritanical model-society.
- **Anglican Church:** formed out of King Henry VIII's marital desires.

In these last four lectures we will encounter three major developments that revolutionized Western European civilization. One was the Protestant Reformation that shattered the religious unity of the Middle Ages. A second important phenomenon was the European discovery of the New World that shattered the long prevailing European concept of the globe and its continents and peoples. The third development was the rise of modern science, which we shall explore by examining the amazing discoveries of Copernicus, Tycho Brahe, Johannes Kepler, and Galileo, which, taken together, shattered the long prevailing Medieval notion of the Earth's position in the overall cosmic order of the universe.

The Protestant Reformation involved large numbers of people, who rejected various practices and doctrines of the Catholic Church, breaking away from that Church and organizing themselves into new forms of Christianity. The term "reformation," however, based upon its current meaning in English, is misleading. If we were to classify this movement today, we would instead call it a revolution, because the latter refers to a really major break with tradition, which is what the Protestant Reformation did. It involved people breaking away from the Roman Catholic Church and forming their own entirely new Christian organization. It was therefore a true revolution. The term "reformation," on the other hand, implies a process of reform taking place inside an institution with that institution remaining basically intact, but since the term "reformation" began to be used by people of the sixteenth century to refer to this major development, and since it has therefore become part of the standard historical vocabulary, we will follow others in using this term, despite its somewhat misleading nature.

Before turning directly to the Protestant Reformation, we first need to consider the career and work of Erasmus (1466-1536). He is generally regarded as the greatest humanist scholar of that age, and his life and writings form the perfect bridge from the Renaissance to the Protestant Reformation. He was born in Rotterdam in Flanders (now the Netherlands) and was the member of a devoutly Christian organization in his early adulthood. In addition to his deep Christian piety, he was an extremely well educated man in the literature of ancient Greece and Rome, so that he combined in himself both the Greco-Roman and Christian traditions that have been so very important in shaping Western civilization. Many Europeans during the Middle Ages and on into the Early Modern Period often viewed the Greco-Roman tradition as either irrelevant to or incompatible with Christianity, but Erasmus thought that the two had much to offer one another, and that Greco-Roman learning could and should be put to good use in furthering the goals of Christianity. In fact, his career involved this very program. He thought that the logic and ethical teachings of ancient philosophy should be used to reinforce and further sensitize us to the ethical and moral teachings contained in Christianity. In addition, he thought that the sophisticated training in ancient languages, which was such a large part of humanist education at the time, was not only desirable, but actually essential for conducting scholarly inquiry into *The Bible*. We see this latter idea illustrated in one of Erasmus' most important works, the publication of a Greek text of *The New Testament* with his own Latin translation. Although *The New Testament* had originally been written in Greek, the only text used by Western Europeans during the previous one thousand years had been the Latin Vulgate translation made by St. Jerome c.400. Erasmus deemed it essential to read and study *The New Testament* in its original form, not to rely upon a Latin translation. He therefore spent years in studying Greek texts of the work and produced his own edition. This work was published in 1516, the year before Martin Luther posted his 95 Theses and sparked off the beginning of the Protestant Reformation. Erasmus also believed that *The Bible* should be translated into all the so-called vernacular languages, so that rather than relying upon priests to tell them what the Latin text said and meant, ordinary people could read it for themselves, arrive at their own understanding, and have it touch their lives directly. This latter notion, as we will see, was a common feature of the Protestant Reformation.

Throughout his life Erasmus wrote numerous essays, of which Text #41 in PSWC is an example. He had a great sense of humor and often used it to get his points across to his readers, as we see very clearly in this reading. It is cast in the form of a Platonic philosophical dialogue, but rather than considering some high-minded theme such as the nature of justice or piety, this dialogue is very funny and uses humor to criticize aspects of the Roman Catholic Church, such as people going on pilgrimages to famous churches, their belief in the magical properties of saintly relics, and the Church's exploitation of this widespread belief by seeking donations from the devout. Like many well educated people of this time, Erasmus regarded these traditional aspects of the Catholic Church as nothing more than superstition that should be eliminated from people's lives, so that they could focus their attention upon much more meaningful things, such as living a truly Christian life by being charitable to the poor and loving one's neighbors. Here again we see Erasmus espousing views that were typical of the Protestant Reformation, so that in many ways his career anticipated the Protestant Reformation. Yet, when the latter finally came, and while many people were breaking away from the Roman Catholic Church to form their own Christian organizations, Erasmus did not join them, because although he shared many of their same deeply held convictions that were critical of the Catholic tradition, he felt very strongly that rather than there being a revolutionary break from Catholicism, the religious unity of Western Europe needed to be maintained, and the Roman Catholic Church should be reformed from top to bottom.

Having thus surveyed the work of Erasmus as a forerunner to the Protestant Reformation, let us now turn to the latter phenomenon, which we will examine by looking at four different movements: Martin Luther and the Lutheran Church, King Henry VIII and the Church of England, John Calvin and Calvinism, and the Anabaptists. Martin Luther (1483-1546) was the son of a German miner and mine owner, who wanted his son to obtain his law degree from a university and become a successful and prosperous lawyer. Although he did in fact receive a university education, Martin Luther had a profound personal religious experience that convinced him to study theology instead of the law. Consequently, after receiving his Ph.D. in theology, he became a professor of theology at a college in the small German town of Wittenberg. While teaching there, he became involved in a major theological dispute that set off a fire storm, which created the Protestant Reformation.

During the late 1400s the popes tore down the Basilica of St. Peter in the Vatican that had been erected more than 1100 years earlier by the Roman Emperor Constantine. By this time the structure had become dilapidated and in serious need of repair. The popes therefore demolished it and decided to erect in its place a much larger and grander structure. It took about a century and a half to complete and was extremely expensive. The final result is what now stands in the Vatican, a truly marvelous and beautiful cathedral. During the 1510s the pope was in need of money to keep the construction going. He therefore launched a fund-raising campaign in which indulgences figured prominently. The basic idea was that instead of going through the tedious process of confessing one's sins and having to perform good works to atone for them, a person could receive a papal indulgence in return for making a contribution to the Church. As we saw in Lecture 28 in looking at the careers of John Wycliffe and Jan Hus, there had long been objections to papal indulgences. When the Catholic representative came into Martin Luther's region of Germany to raise money in this way, Luther was greatly disgusted by what he viewed as the pope's unscrupulous selling of salvation. He therefore composed a lengthy document in which he stated all his objections, after which on Halloween of 1517 he posted it on the door of the cathedral in Wittenberg in the hope of stirring up a serious debate on this issue. The document has come to be known as the 95 Theses, because Luther listed 95 separate objections to Church policy in this and related matters. He composed the document in Latin; and as often happened during these and earlier times, he was expecting to be able to participate in a public debate over these issues with some leading local priest. But what actually happened was something very different. Somehow or other, the document was translated into German and found its way to a printing press, where copies were made and sent out. Since it summed up many other people's objections to various abuses in the Catholic Church, the document was passed around, traveled to other communities, printed again and again with other printing presses, and kept being circulated. It therefore soon created a major stir throughout the Holy Roman Empire, because there was widespread discontent with the Catholic Church. It was as if this discontent were the dried out vegetation and wood in a large forest, and the 95 Theses was a spark that resulted in a massive forest fire.

In this connection it is interesting to notice that the printing press, invented around 1450, played a pivotal role in the Protestant Reformation. This relatively new printing technology enabled public opinion to be mobilized in a way that would have been thought impossible in earlier times. In fact, if we look back at the career of Jan Hus, we can easily see the difference between that time and the later one of Martin Luther. As you may recall, Jan

Hus had many objections to the Catholic Church. When he was summoned to the council at Constance in Switzerland, he was examined by a panel of Church officials, who condemned him as a heretic and had him burned at the stake. Although this did spark off a religious uprising in Hus' native Bohemia that lasted for several years, it did not result in the massive fire storm that the 95 Theses created. Moreover, when Martin Luther was eventually summoned before Church and governmental authorities at Worms in 1521 to answer questions about his views on things, he was not arrested and burned at the stake, because by then he had stirred up such massive popular support that he had powerful backers, who guaranteed his safety.

When questioned at Worms in 1521, Martin Luther did not back down from his deeply held convictions; and since he did have the support of the local feudal ruler, he was able to walk away from his interrogators with his skin intact. He then went into hiding under the protection of Frederic the Wise, Elector of Saxony, one of the great barons of the Holy Roman Empire. From May of 1521 to March of 1522 Luther resided in Wartburg Castle (Eisenach, Germany), during which time he carried out by himself his German translation of *The New Testament*, because, like Erasmus, he firmly believed that ordinary people should be able to read *The Bible* for themselves. Luther later worked together with other scholars to produce a German translation of *The Old Testament* from the original Hebrew. Like the King James version of almost a century later (1611), this translation of *The Bible* forms one of the earliest and most important works in modern German literature. As time passed, and as Luther gained more supporters, he found himself at the head of a popular religious movement that eventually evolved into the Lutheran Church.

Before examining some of the more important views of Luther and his new Church, I wish to make two important points about the Protestant Reformation in general. As already noted, one was the idea that *The Bible* should be translated into the people's own language, so that they could read it themselves and not have to depend upon a priest to interpret the text for them. This notion was clearly the outgrowth of town life and the growth of a middle class. Before the revival of town life in the High Middle Ages, the overwhelming majority of people in western Europe were simple uneducated peasants. In those conditions the Catholic Church more or less satisfied the basic religious needs of the people by priests telling them in simple terms what they needed to do in order to be assured of salvation. But as towns came into being with a growing middle class, many of whom could read and write, a big gap developed between traditional Catholic ways and the spiritual needs and aspirations of this growing middle class. Many people were not content with being spoon-fed their religion by a priest. They felt the need and desire to take personal charge of their spiritual life and salvation, hence the idea that they should be able to read *The Bible* themselves. You can therefore see how and why the printing press played such an important role in creating and defining the Protestant Reformation. One interesting outgrowth of the notion that people should read *The Bible* themselves was the idea of universal education in the form of a public school system. Since Protestantism assumed one's ability to read, Protestants organized elementary schools in their communities, so that their children would learn to read and write and thereby be able to become proper Protestants.

A second factor that characterized the Protestant Reformation was the doctrine of *Sola Scriptura*, Scripture Alone. Luther and others thought that in order to be good Christians, they had to follow, as best they could, what they actually found written in *The New Testament*, because scripture alone was the authoritative source in defining Christianity. Over the centuries, however, there had grown up many Catholic traditions for which there was no scriptural authority, such as penance, indulgences, and purgatory. As a result, the different Protestant denominations defined their beliefs and practices by relying upon what they found in the text of *The Bible*; and they also rejected long established Catholic practices and ideas, because they had no scriptural authority.

We will now turn our attention to Luther and his new Church. To begin with, you can obtain a first-hand perspective by reading the sample of Martin Luther's writing that is Text #42 in PSWC. Throughout his life Luther was a prolific writer. He expressed his opinions forcefully, persuasively, and in no uncertain terms. You can see this very clearly in this reading. One doctrine that was central to Lutheranism was "justification by faith." This involved the way in which we obtain salvation. The long established Catholic tradition had

PSWC
#42

been that one obtained salvation for one's soul in eternity by regularly confessing one's sins to a priest and then atoning for these sins by performing good works as instructed by the priest. Thus, the Church in the form of its priests was essential in this process. According to Martin Luther's reading of Paul's letters in *The New Testament*, this was not at all how it worked. In fact, Martin Luther could not find any scripture in *The Bible* that specified the need for confession and good works, and certainly not the pope's power to secure one's salvation through the granting of an indulgence. Indeed, Martin Luther discovered in the writings of Paul that salvation was a very simple matter of faith, placing one's trust in having Jesus as one's personal savior and believing that he had been the son of God and by his death on the cross had taken upon himself the entire burden of mankind's sin. This idea was termed "justification by faith," because if one simply had this faith in Jesus, then he was rendered proper or just in the eyes of God in terms of his burden of sin.

Another crucial belief that separated Luther from the Catholic Church was the notion of a priesthood of believers. It had long been the established Catholic doctrine that the pope alone could appoint priests, and they alone could carry out the various rites of the Church, upon which people's good standing in the Church depended. Consequently, in a sense the popes and priests had long claimed a monopoly on religious authority. Luther did not accept this idea. As he explains in Text #42 in PSWC, if a group of Christians happen to become isolated in a forest and need to observe religious services but have no priest in their midst, there is no reason why they cannot elect one of themselves to serve as their priest. They do not need to have the pope appoint someone to do this. The Christian believers are fully capable and justified in creating their own priest. Obviously, such a notion had the effect of rendering much of the Catholic Church apparatus unnecessary.

There were other important ideas that came to define Lutheranism and to separate it from Catholicism. Given the emphasis upon the need to ground one's faith and religious practices upon actual scripture, Luther's new Church rejected five of the seven canonical Catholic sacraments, retaining only baptism and communion. Moreover, since Luther could find no scriptural evidence for priestly celibacy, he decided that there was no reason why priests could not be married. He set the example in this regard by marrying a nun, and the two of them enjoyed a very happy life together. Indeed, Luther saw nothing the least bit shameful or sinful about sexual intercourse inside the institution of marriage. To him, they were perfectly natural and normal bodily functions, like eating and drinking. Along these same lines Luther made religious music an important part of Lutheran services. He was himself an accomplished musician and believed that music was a very powerful and moving way in which people could express their religious devotion. He therefore authored many hymns that are still performed and sung in churches today.

Another important feature of Lutheranism and of the Protestant Reformation in general involved monasticism, which, as we have seen, had formed a major part of the Medieval Catholic Church. One big source of popular resentment toward the Catholic Church had long been its extraordinary wealth. It was not only the largest landowner in all of Europe, but it also enjoyed tax-exempt status on its properties, while other people were required to pay property taxes. Moreover, since Protestants saw no need for monastic celibacy, they favored the abolition of monasticism altogether. As a result, in regions where Protestantism became the established state religion, monasticism was ended, and the various properties owned by monasteries and convents were confiscated or sold off by the state, and the monks and nuns were turned out and had to adopt a new way of life. In the course of time northern Germany embraced Lutheranism, as did the Scandinavian countries of Denmark, Norway, and Sweden, as well as Finland. Southern Germany and Austria, on the other hand, remained Catholic.

We will now examine the creation of the Church of England, or the Anglican Church. As we have seen, Lutheranism was the product of a massive grass-roots religious movement. This was not the case with the Anglican Church, at least not in its earliest days. It came into being out of the personal desires of King Henry VIII, a very domineering man, who almost always succeeded in getting his way in things. When the break between Luther and the pope occurred, King Henry was in full support of the papacy and opposed Luther, but a few years later, when Henry was in need of the pope nullifying his marriage to Katherine of Aragon, so that he could marry Anne Boleyn, he changed his tune when the pope refused to go along with his desires. After years of marriage, Henry and Katherine succeeded in producing only one offspring, a daughter named Mary, the later Queen Mary of England (1553-1558). Henry, however, wanted a son; and when it looked as if he was not going to get one from Katherine, he decided that it was time to divorce her and take a new wife, who could give him his son. But when Henry approached the papal court for an annulment of the marriage, he was rebuffed. Years earlier a previous pope had actually issued a special decree that authorized the marriage between Henry and Katherine and found no fault in it. The current pope was most unwilling to reverse his predecessor's ruling, in part because by doing so he would provide the Lutherans with a clear example in showing that the popes were not in fact infallible, but they made mistakes and changed their minds on things. Consequently, when Henry ran into a wall on this issue, he came up with a new plan. By the early 1530s he badgered parliament into passing a series of laws that divorced England from the papacy and made King Henry the head of a new religion, the Anglican Church, also termed the Church of England. Having accomplished this separation by passing laws, Henry could then quash his marriage to Katherine and take Anne Boleyn as his new wife. As things turned out, she was no more successful in producing a male heir than Katherine. Anne and Henry wound up having another daughter, Elizabeth, the later Queen Elizabeth (1558-1603). Henry eventually tired of Anne and ridded himself of her by having her accused of witchcraft that she had allegedly used to cause him to fall in love with her; and after she was beheaded, Henry went through four more wives before passing on to meet his Maker. His third wife, Jane Seymour, did produce his desired son, Edward VI. Jane died in child birth; and Edward did succeed Henry on the English throne (1547-1553), but died at an early age and was followed by his older two half sisters as English monarchs.

Let us now turn to John Calvin and Calvinism, which wound up being the most widespread and most influential of the Protestant movements. Born in 1509 in northern France of a well-to-do family, John Calvin received a very good Catholic Christian education. But as he entered early adulthood and witnessed the unfolding of the Reformation, he found himself agreeing with many of its ideas and proceeded to develop his own distinctive Protestant theology, which he set forth in his most famous work, a massive work entitled *Institutes of the Christian Religion*, parts of which form Text #43 in PSWC. Contrary to what we have encountered in the previous lecture concerning the Renaissance, which viewed humans as God's most glorious creation and capable of achieving virtually anything, Calvin adhered to the earlier Medieval view of God and humans in regarding the former as all-powerful and the latter as insignificant and hopelessly sinful. But the two most important ideas of Calvin's theology were predestination and the elect vs. the damned. In brief, here is how Calvin arrived at these ideas. Since God is all knowing and all powerful, everything that has or will ever happen has been known and determined by him from the very beginning of Creation. This is the doctrine of predestination. Although it appears that we all do things according to our free will, we are actually only doing what God has predestined us to do. Moreover, since God's wisdom is so vastly superior to the feebleness of human reason, there is no way that we can ever understand why God has planned things to happen in the way that they do. Since God has rigged everything from the very beginning, this includes our salvation or damnation. For reasons that we cannot ever hope to understand, God has chosen (elected) some of us to receive eternal salvation, while the rest of us will be damned to hell. Accordingly, the Catholic idea of earning one's salvation through confession and the performance of good works, as well as Luther's justification by faith, are utterly ridiculous. Yet, despite everything being predestined in this Calvinist scheme, Calvin did not advocate that people therefore simply do as they pleased, because they had no control over whether or not they would be saved. Instead, he believed that Christians should strive with all their might to live upright, God-fearing, Christian lives; and as they did, they could live in the hope that God would send them a sign indicating that they were among God's elect.

John Calvin was a very serious thinker and probably would have been most content if allowed to live in his study, surrounded by books and having the leisure to think and write. But in 1540 he was invited to come to Geneva in Switzerland to become part of a new and exciting phenomenon, the creation of a devout Christian community. The invitation was a welcome one, because by now France was being torn apart by conflict between Catholics and Protestants, and it was not a very wholesome environment in which to live. Calvin therefore came to Geneva and served as the spiritual engine, as it were, for the community. The people had decided to carry out a Protestant reform of their whole community and to try to create a society in which they could all live good Christian lives. In order to guard against conflict between religious leaders and public officials, they created a board called the consistory, which was composed of both religious figures and public magistrates. Since both were committed to realizing the same goal of forming a community that functioned well and embodied Christian values, the members of the consistory were generally inclined to cooperate with one another instead of working against each other. They met every Thursday to confer on what needed to be done to maintain good public order. One of their functions was to decide what to do about people's reported misbehavior, such as gambling, drinking, dancing, spousal abuse, adultery, etc. People's private lives were constantly under scrutiny. Mild forms of misconduct resulted in the person being admonished to reform. More serious misconduct could result in judicial action, such as being whipped or imprisoned. The most serious offenses were punished by banishment from the community or even by execution. In this way a very strict code of conduct was enforced, and from this Calvinist tradition came the Puritans of England, some of whom first settled New England in North America. As we have seen, Luther was very fond of music and had it serve a vital role in his new Church. To the Calvinists, however, music was the handiwork of the Devil, because it inevitably led to men and women dancing together, and that in turn opened the door to hanky-panky between the sexes.

We will now conclude our survey of the Protestant Reformation by touching upon the Anabaptists. Unlike the three previous cases, Anabaptism did not enjoy coherence. Although it stemmed from a common origin, the notion of re-baptizing (Greek *ana-* means "again"), there were different Anabaptist groups that sprung up in many areas, each having their own distinctive views and lifestyles. Anabaptists were so called, because they opposed the long established tradition of baptizing newborn babies. This practice, of course, had developed in order to try to make sure that infants would have a chance to go to heaven if they died at a very young age, which happened all too often in those days of very poor medical care. Anabaptists, however, pointed out that the only instances of baptism in *The New Testament* involved adults. From this they argued that people should be baptized only when they reached the age of reason, when they could make a conscious decision to embrace Christianity. Moreover, since Anabaptists had been baptized as infants, they had themselves baptized again as adults to signify their well informed decision to be Christians. Most of them were ordinary people who worked as craftsmen or shop keepers in the towns, and many of them had little concern for established religious rituals. Instead, they emphasized the need to lead upright lives and to treat their fellow man with charity and honesty. They also had a general distrust or indifference toward government, because they did not want governmental officials telling them how they should live and worship. Modern-day descendants of the Anabaptists include the Mennonites, Amish, Quakers, and Baptists.

The early years of Anabaptism contains one of the most extraordinary events of this period. Around 1530 some Anabaptists began to espouse the idea that The End of Days was at hand, because it had now been nearly 1500 years since the crucifixion. Many Anabaptists were therefore caught up in a messianic fervor. This eventually resulted in them taking over the small town of Munster in northwestern Germany. As more Anabaptists poured into the town to await the second coming and the arrival of the millennium, they were able to take control of the local government by voting their own people into office. On February 27, 1534 the Anabaptists drove the Catholics and Lutherans out of the city. The bishop of the region then mobilized military forces that began to blockade the city. The ensuing siege dragged on for sixteenth months. It finally ended on June 25, 1535 when the besiegers captured the town. But in the interval the townsfolk had undergone quite a remarkable series of events, which other fanatical religious movements since then have replicated. Early on during the siege a man named John Bockelson (also known as Jan van Leyden = John of Leyden) emerged as the leader and established a cult-like devotion to himself, which was reinforced by the threat of violence at the hands of his bodyguard. He soon decreed that all private property had to be abolished, so that everyone was forced to turn in their clothing and other things to go into common stores, from which items were distributed to people according to their needs. Then Bockelson decreed the ending of all money, so that people had to turn in all their gold and silver, but of course, Bockelson went about in the finest of clothes decked out in jewelry. Then he decreed the establishment of polygamy, so that men could have more than one wife, but no woman could have more than one husband. Bockelson wound up having fifteen wives under the age of twenty. Surprise! Surprise! By this point the Anabaptists had renamed the town New Jerusalem, and Bockelson was known as King David. The true believers thought that they would soon miraculously overcome their enemies and become rulers of the world with the arrival of the new millennium. The townsfolk eventually ran out of food and began dying of starvation until a few deserters, driven by utter desperation, betrayed the defense works to the besiegers, who then captured the city and carried out a massacre of the survivors. Bockelson was captured and led about the country in chains as if he were an exotic beast on exhibit, and to show people what happened if they followed such a raving religious fanatic. He was then brought back to Munster, where he was tortured to death along with two other leaders. Their bodies were placed in iron cages and hung from a tower of the cathedral in Munster, where they are still today. Their bodies were allowed to rot away where they were out of people's reach, because authorities did not want parts of their bodies becoming treasured relics to inspire future fanaticism.

LECTURE 32
Counter Reformation and Wars of Religion

IMPORTANT DATES AND TERMS

- **1545-1563:** Council of Trent.
- **1555:** Peace of Augsburg, allowing the rulers of the feudal districts of Germany to determine the Christian faith of their realm.
- **1558-1603:** Reign of Queen Elizabeth of England, younger daughter of Henry VIII and his second wife Anne Boleyn.
- **1581:** Formation of the nation of the Netherlands.
- **1588:** English defeat of the Spanish Armada.
- **1618-1648:** The Thirty-Years War in Germany, resulting from religious intolerance among Catholics, Lutherans, and Calvinists.
- **1648:** Peace of Westphalia, ending the Thirty-Years War on the earlier conditions of the Peace of Augsburg.
- **Counter Reformation:** reform movement within the Catholic church to counter the advance of Protestantism.
- **Ignatius Loyola:** Basque soldier turned Catholic leader.
- **Jesuits** = Society of Jesus: new religious order, unquestioning loyalty to the pope, concept of the mission to educate the young, to reconvert Protestants, and to convert the heathens of the newly discovered lands of Africa, Asia, and the Americas.

- **Index:** list of books officially banned by the Catholic church.
- **Inquisition:** judicial apparatus of the Catholic church, used to expose heretics and to force them to recant or be burned at the stake.

In this lecture we will finish our treatment of the Protestant Reformation by examining two other aspects of this important historical development: namely, the Catholic response to Protestantism and the various wars that arose from this deep division caused in Western European society. The Catholic response to the Protestant Reformation is termed the Catholic Reformation or the Counter Reformation. We will treat it by looking at four different things: the Council of Trent (1545-1563), the index of forbidden books, the inquisition, and the creation of a new monastic order called the Society of Jesus (also more commonly known as the Jesuits).

Text #44 in PSWC is a series of decrees resulting from the Council of Trent. During the early years of the Protestant Reformation (i.e., the 1520s and 1530s) there were numerous meetings between Protestant and Catholic clergy in an attempt to work out their differences and thereby to maintain the religious unity of Western Europe, but all these meetings failed to realize this goal, because the differences between the two sides were too large to be closed. In response to the storm of protest and critical publications from Protestants against Catholicism that poured out during these years, the Catholic Church decided to hold a major council in order to examine all aspects of Catholicism with a view to reform. Protestants were invited to attend, but they chose not to, because by then it had become all too apparent that the differences between Protestants and Catholics were unbridgeable. The council therefore wound up being a totally Catholic affair. The northern Italian city of Trent (Latin Tridentum) was chosen for the meetings, which began in 1545 and lasted until 1563. This northern Italian city was chosen, because it could be reached by travel fairly easily by Catholic priests and bishops from areas north of the Alps. As its participants discussed matters of theology and practice and reached agreements on things, they formalized their agreement by issuing decrees, of which you have samples in Text #44 of PSWC. Let me run through them briefly.

The validity of indulgences was reasserted. Thus, the issue that had caused Martin Luther to compose the 95 Theses was not changed in any way from previous Catholic tradition. The use of the Latin Vulgate text of *The Bible* was reaffirmed. This too was fully in keeping with previous Catholic tradition and was opposed by the Protestants, who insisted on translating the Hebrew and Greek texts of *The Bible* into the various vernacular languages, so that the text could be read and understood by ordinary people. The Council of Trent reasserted the Catholic belief in the doctrine of original sin, according to which we humans are all born as imperfect creatures, because we have inherited a sinful nature going back to the original disobedience of God by Adam and Eve in the Garden of Eden. The council, however, rejected the notion of predestination, which was so crucial in defining Calvinist theology. Instead, the Catholic Church maintained its traditional belief in free will, according to which we all have and exercise free will in making our individual decisions and in doing what we do. The council reaffirmed the validity of the traditional Catholic seven sacraments, many of which the Protestants abolished in their own redefined Christianity, because there were no scriptures authorizing them. In addition, the Council of Trent asserted that not just anyone, but only priests duly appointed by the pope, could perform these rites. This too was aimed against the Protestant idea of "the priesthood of believers," by which a group of Christians could decide among themselves whom they wished to have as their priest or minister. The council also reaffirmed the traditional Catholic idea of transubstantiation, according to which the bread and wine of the Eucharist or communion actually did become the body and blood of Christ through the proper performance of the rite by a Catholic priest. This matter had been widely debated among theologians in earlier times, and Protestants generally viewed communion in symbolic terms, rather than regarding it as a kind of religious magic. The council reaffirmed the need for priests to be celibate, which Protestants rejected, because there was no scriptural authority for it. The council also reasserted the propriety of using paintings, mosaics, and statues in churches to represent figures from *The Bible*, and it also affirmed the belief in the holiness of sacred relics. Protestants, of course, rejected the latter as superstition and regarded the former as being in violation with one of the

Ten Commandments, which specified that "thou shalt not make any graven images." Finally, the Council of Trent addressed the long standing criticism against priests living luxuriously and using their position to enrich their relatives. The council urged priests to lead sober lives characterized by an avoidance of extravagance. In sum, despite the intention to carry out sweeping reforms, the Council of Trent left unchanged all major aspects of Catholicism.

One important innovation resulting from this council was the institution of seminaries or schools for training Catholic priests. Before this time there was no real systematic training given to people who came forward to be priests in the Church, and this had obviously led to a widely criticized phenomenon: namely, that many Catholic priests were unfit to carry out their duties, and many were simply not interested in doing so, because they had become priests, not because of some compelling inner spiritual desire to do so, but because their family wanted to have a member in the Catholic hierarchy, or the person wanted to have a nice comfortable and secure job for the rest of his life. Seminaries were designed to screen applicants for the priesthood in order to make sure that they did in fact have a strong personal commitment to being priests for the rest of their lives; and the seminaries provided these candidates with a systematic education and training to equip them for their duties. By destroying the Catholic Church's monopoly in the area of religion, the Protestant Reformation forced Catholicism to try to do a much better job in serving the spiritual needs of its members.

Once the Protestant Reformation was underway, the printing presses in Europe were kept busy in churning out a huge volume of religious pamphlets and books, as both Protestants and Catholics set forth their ideas and arguments in favor of their views and in attacking the positions and practices of the other side. This on-going war of ideas fought out in print was responsible for one aspect of the Catholic Reformation: the index of forbidden books. This was an official list maintained by the papacy. It contained all those published works that the Catholic Church deemed dangerous for its members to read, because by doing so they might be led astray and into theological error. According to the Catholic Church, it was unlawful for anyone to print, sell, circulate in any way, or read books listed on the index.

Related to the index was a third component of the Counter Reformation: the inquisition. This, if you will remember from Lecture 25, was a judicial institution established by the papacy during the early 1200s to deal with the Cathar heresy that flourished in southern and southwestern France. It had been placed under the administration of the Dominican friars, who had the power of arresting, imprisoning, and interrogating under torture anyone suspected of unorthodox religious beliefs; and if the person undergoing investigation refused to renounce such beliefs, he or she was burned at the stake. The inquisition was now brought back into action by the papacy to combat Protestantism. Since Spain and Italy remained staunchly Catholic, the inquisition became a dreaded institution in these areas, where people suspected of non-Catholic beliefs could be subject to its powers; and the fear of what it could do played an important role in keeping the populations of these areas obedient to the Catholic Church.

Perhaps the single best illustration of both the index and the inquisition is the case of Galileo, whom we shall treat in Lecture 34. Toward the end of his life he published a scientific work written in the form of a dialogue, in which the discussants debated evidence for two competing theories of the universe: the geocentric (Earth at the center) vs. heliocentric (sun at the center). Of course, the Catholic position on this matter followed Aristotle and Ptolemy in placing the Earth at the center of the universe, which was thought to show how God had positioned mankind at the center of his entire Creation. Galileo, however, in this dialogue made it rather clear that he supported the notion that the Earth revolved around the sun. Not only was this book placed on the index and became banned in Catholic areas, but Galileo was summoned before the inquisition and questioned concerning his views. He was so intimidated that he submitted himself to the authority of the Church; and as punishment, he was confined to house arrest for the remainder of his life and was forbidden to discuss these matters with anyone.

The fourth aspect of the Counter Reformation that we shall consider is the Society of Jesus, a new monastic order founded by Ignatius of Loyola (1491-1556). This man came from the Basque area of the Pyrenees Mountains between France and Spain. As a young man, he had the desire to become a chivalrous knight and actually was involved in a minor local uprising in Pamplona, during which he received serious wounds in his legs from cannon fire. He then had to spend months in bed, recovering from these injuries. In order to pass the time, he read his way through most of the books available to him in the place where he was convalescing. Since most of these works concerned the Catholic religion, by the time that he was back on his feet, he had decided to give up knighting and go into the priesthood. He therefore enrolled himself into the University of Paris, which had long been the leading European university for teaching theology. While studying there, he quickly emerged head and shoulders above his fellow classmates, largely due to his charismatic and powerful personality. He succeeded in collecting around himself other like-minded students, including Francis Xavier. When this small group had finished their education and had received their degrees, they decided to devote themselves to preaching Christianity among the Muslims and thereby to carry out a religious crusade. But when they arrived in Rome to receive the stamp of approval for their activities from the pope himself, they were dissuaded from this goal. Since the Protestant Reformation was now posing a very serious challenge to the Catholic Church, these men were persuaded to turn their efforts into this direction. They were now formed into a new monastic order that combined monastic celibacy with missionary fervor and a kind of military mentality, in which the pope served as their commander in chief to give them their marching orders that they would proceed to carry out with single-minded dedication. Their primary goal was to go into hostile territory, as it were, and to win people back to Catholicism and away from Protestantism. In order to increase their effectiveness, these Jesuits were highly educated men capable of debating all points of theology in order to convince their listeners of the rightfulness of Catholicism.

In many ways the religious climate throughout much of western Europe at this time resembled the cold war atmosphere following World War II, in which much of the world was divided into the two opposing camps of the free world vs. the communist world, which conducted warfare upon one another through spies and the battle of ideas (termed propaganda by the opposing side). In this sense the Jesuits represented the secret agents of the Catholic Church, because they often infiltrated Protestant areas under the cover of false names and identities and moved quietly among the population as they tried to locate Catholic sympathizers and to spread Catholicism while avoiding detection. If caught doing so in an area in which Protestantism was the state religion, like spies caught in the act during the cold war, they were often executed.

There are two other important aspects of Jesuit activity that we should touch upon. One is their emphasis upon the need to educate the young. Like Protestants, who promoted the founding of public schools to teach ordinary people how to read and write, so that they could understand *The Bible*, so the Jesuits regarded education as fundamental for the success of Catholicism. They took the lead in establishing Catholic schools, so that many young people would be exposed to Catholic teachings at a very early age and would be more prone to remain faithful to the Catholic Church for the rest of their lives. Secondly, since the foundation of the Society of Jesus coincided not only with the Protestant Reformation, but also the European discovery of the New World, which we will cover in the next lecture, Jesuits began to be sent out as members of the voyages of discovery and colonization in order to bring knowledge of Christianity to the non-Christian peoples of Africa, Asia, and the Americas. In fact, Francis Xavier, Loyola's closest associate, was one of the very first Christian missionaries to India, Japan, and China.

Having covered these four important aspects of the Counter Reformation, we will now turn to the wars of religion that characterized this period of European history, ending with the Thirty-Years War of 1618-1648. These wars played an important role in the affairs of France, England, Flanders, and the German states of the Holy Roman Empire. Much of this fighting strikes us modern-day inhabitants of the United States as bizarre, because we are so accustomed to the notion of the state not imposing one form of religion upon us, but allowing us to engage in religious belief and practice as we each see fit. We should realize that what we take for granted in this regard was a very hard-won liberty paid for by the lives of thousands of people who died during the Early Modern Period in these wars of religious intolerance. The latter largely stemmed from the commonly accepted idea that a society could not function harmoniously if its people did not share the same religious beliefs. It was generally assumed that if some people believed one thing, and others another, the society would be torn apart by constant religious quarreling. Consequently, in order to maintain peace and order, the state had to make sure that everyone belonged to the same religion. It took decades and decades of terrible warfare and the loss of human life for Western Europeans to slowly realize that a policy of religious toleration actually made good practical sense.

The first major fighting over religion erupted during the late 1540s in the Holy Roman Empire, which consisted of about 300 small counties, each under their own ruler. By this time these counties had become either Lutheran or remained Catholic, and they had grouped themselves into two opposing leagues, a Lutheran League and a Catholic League. After several years of fighting the two sides negotiated a peace settlement, the Treaty of Augsburg of 1555. It established the earliest form of religious toleration, but in a very limited fashion. It allowed the different counties to be either Lutheran or Catholic; and which it was, was to be determined by the county's ruler. If he was Lutheran, he could require all his subjects to be Lutheran; but if he were Catholic, he could force all the inhabitants of his district to be Catholic. Thus, the only persons actually granted freedom of religion under this arrangement were the rulers themselves. If they were lucky, ordinary people would just happen to share their ruler's religion. If not, then they had to make some hard choices. They could convert to the other religion, or they could vote with their feet and move into an area where their religion was the one of the district. In fact, during this period of the religious wars there were large numbers of people who did vote with their feet. Catholics left their homes and moved into Catholic areas, and many Protestants left their native lands and lived in exile in places where their religion was that of the state. Another choice that people had was to keep to their religious beliefs in secret and hope that they avoided detection and punishment for it. There was another problem created by the deaths of the local rulers, because they would sometimes be succeeded by a relative who belonged to the other faith. As a result, when he became the ruler, everyone in the district had to convert, move, or pretend to comply with their new ruler's religious preference.

We will now turn our attention to England. As we saw last time, the Anglican Church came into being not through a grass-roots Protestant movement, as did Lutheranism, but through the desires and needs of King Henry VIII. Consequently, while Henry was king (he died in 1547), the Anglican Church did not differ all that much from the Catholic Church, because Henry was primarily interested in breaking ties with the papacy in order to be the head of a new Church of England. There were, however, two aspects of Henry's new Anglican Church that did correspond to the wider Protestant movement. One was his abolition of monasticism, but this was not done out of any doctrinal conviction on Henry's part, but it was simply the product of the king's opportunism. He simply wanted to confiscate all the property and wealth of the monasteries and convents in England to have it for himself or to sell it to his closest associates at bargain-basement prices. He did, however, authorize the use of an English translation of *The Bible*, prepared by a man named Miles Coverdale. A few years earlier, before the Anglican Reform, another man, William Tyndale, had undertaken to translate *The Bible* into English, but his efforts were condemned, and Tyndale was eventually arrested and executed. The famous and very influential King James version of *The Bible* was not published until 1611 during the reign of King James I (1603-1625), who followed Queen Elizabeth on the English thrown.

It was not until the brief reign of Henry's son, Edward VI (1547-1553), that the Anglican Church was reformed significantly along Protestant lines under the leadership of Thomas Cramner, the archbishop of Canterbury. He had Catholic altars removed from churches and had priests dress in much less elaborate clothing. He also presided over the composition of "The Book of Common Prayer," written in English and used as the basic guide for church services. The worship of saints was abolished; and religious paintings, reliefs, mosaics, and statues were removed from churches. But when King Edward died, he was succeeded on the English throne by his older half sister, Mary, the daughter of Henry and his first wife Katherine of Aragon, who had raised her daughter Mary as a Catholic. Thus, during her brief five-year reign (1553-1558) Queen Mary attempted to roll back the Anglican Reform and to reestablish Catholicism in England. Protestants rash enough to oppose these efforts were arrested and burned at the stake as heretics. 288 people suffered such a fate under her rule and were responsible for bestowing upon her the name "Bloody Mary." When she died in 1558, the English throne was occupied by her younger half sister, Elizabeth, the daughter of Henry and his second wife Anne Boleyn. Since Elizabeth had been raised as an Anglican, she reversed Mary's policy and reinstated Anglicanism.

Unlike her half brother and half sister, Queen Elizabeth enjoyed a very long reign of 45 years (1558-1603), during which she succeeded in outliving many of her subjects and was able to make sure that her religious policy took hold throughout the realm. She was one of that era's ablest monarchs, who would have doubtless received Machiavelli's approval, because she was very politically astute and pragmatic. Knowing that religion was a very volatile issue and wanting to keep the peace inside her kingdom, Elizabeth set herself against religious extremism from both the Catholics and the Puritans. The latter were ardent Calvinists, who regarded the Anglican Church as not going nearly far enough in reforming things. Elizabeth's middle course in matters of religion was practical and proved to be fairly successful. Although both Catholics and Puritans continued to exist as religious minorities, she was wise enough to look the other way, as long as they did not do something to bring attention to themselves, at which point she would bring the full fury of the law down upon them. This usually meant arrest and public execution.

Let us now look at religious conflict in Flanders. This land, also known as the Low Countries because of its low elevation (often being below sea-level and thus requiring the famous Dutch dikes), was in essence two different areas, which eventually developed into the two modern nations of Belgium to the south and the Netherlands to the north. The southern districts were largely rural and were dominated by their old feudal nobility. Given this social and economic reality, these areas largely remained Catholic as the Protestant Reformation unfolded. Just the opposite was the case in the north, whose economy was dominated by the towns with their important textile industry, which we mentioned in Lecture 27. By the mid 1500s Calvinism had become widely accepted among the middle-class population of these northern districts. Through a very complex chain of monarchical inheritance Flanders at this time came under the rule of Spain, whose king, Philip II (1556-1598), prided himself on being the most Catholic monarch of all Europe. He was therefore determined to wipe out Protestantism in this part of his realm.

In 1566 high taxes combined with resentment over the introduction of the inquisition into their land caused the Protestants of Flanders to rise up in revolt. During the autumn of that year mobs assaulted Catholic churches and smashed their paintings, mosaics, statues, altars, and other physical manifestations of Catholic worship. In response, King Philip of Spain dispatched a huge army into Flanders to carry out an all-out conquest of the region. The fighting dragged on for years. The Spanish army was eventually successful in taking control of the ten southern counties, largely because they were already well disposed toward Catholicism, but this was not at all the case with the other seven counties in the north, which, under the leadership of William of Orange, resisted the Spanish. Like Queen Elizabeth, in order to mobilize the maximum amount of support against the Spanish, William tried to play down people's religious differences and instead appealed to their basic patriotism as inhabitants of Flanders. Since he was often so closed-mouthed about religion, he received the name William the Silent. Atrocities committed by Spanish troops played into his hands, because many people were horrified and angered by the ruthlessness with which the Spanish army carried out its activities. Finally, in 1581 the seven northern counties of Flanders formally declared their independence from the Spanish crown and organized themselves into a federation of states, thus creating the modern nation of the Netherlands. Despite its small geographical size, the Netherlands was the most economically advanced region in western Europe at this time and enjoyed considerable prosperity as the result of its free-market capitalism. In fact, once they became an independent people, the Dutch rapidly emerged as Western Europe's economic powerhouse throughout the seventeenth and early eighteenth centuries, establishing a far-flung commercial empire into the newly discovered regions of Africa, Asia, and North America (including New York, which was originally called New Amsterdam).

There is one final aspect of this war that deserves our attention. As the Spanish army conquered the southern counties and threatened to do the same to the north, Queen Elizabeth began sending financial and military support to the Netherlands. In order to cut off this important line of support, King Philip of Spain in 1588 sent a fleet of 130 ships against England. This was the famous Spanish Armada, which the English encountered in a fierce naval battle in the English Channel and succeeded in defeating and driving back. If the Spanish had been successful, they had intended to land in England, depose and kill Queen Elizabeth, and bring England back into the Catholic community of other European states. The English continued to give valuable support to the Netherlands, which eventually forced Spain to recognize their independence. Moreover, the English victory over the Spanish Armada consolidated Elizabeth's position in England and unleashed patriotic energies that found expression in the flowering of English literature at this time (e.g., William Shakespeare, Christopher Marlowe, Ben Jonson, Edmund Spenser, and Sir Walter Raleigh).

Let us now take a look at France. After Calvinism had won over large numbers of converts in all areas of France during the ten-year period 1552-1562, a Catholic massacre of Calvinists in 1562 sparked off a religious war in France that raged for nearly thirty years, 1562-1589. The conflict divided the French population into three groups, each headed by one of the three most powerful noble families in France. The Calvinists (known as Huguenots) were led by the Bourbon family, whose most prominent member was Henry of Navarre. The Catholics were led by the Guise family, while the Valois royal family, though Catholic, attempted to steer a moderate course that was conciliatory toward Calvinism. One aspect of this religious war, which was also true of the one in Flanders, was mob violence. Priests often worked their church members up into such frenzy over the supposed faults and misguided beliefs and practices of the other side that they went rampaging along the streets of their community, attacking members of the opposite faith. Protestants often attacked Catholic churches and destroyed paintings, mosaics, and statues, which they regarded as idolatrous. In the late summer of 1572 it looked as if the religious war would end, because Henry of Navarre had agreed to marry the sister of the king, thus uniting the heads of two of the three warring factions. But as Paris was filled with celebrants for the wedding on Saint Bartholomew's Day (August 24), the leaders of the third faction carried out a massacre of Calvinists in the city in order to make sure that no settlement would be reached with the Huguenots. This was the notorious Saint Bartholomew's Day massacre, whose violence soon spread to other cities throughout France and resulted in the estimated deaths of about twelve thousand Calvinists. Consequently, the war resumed and raged on for another seventeen years, causing enormous losses of lives and the destruction of property. Finally, in 1589 after the king and the leading member of the Guise family had been assassinated, Henry of Navarre brought the war to an end when he agreed to convert to Catholicism and became King Henry IV of France (1589-1610).

In 1598 King Henry IV issued the famous Edict of Nantes, which established a very limited form of religious toleration throughout the land. Catholicism was acknowledged as the official state religion, but various areas throughout France were designated as Calvinist, but even within these Calvinist areas Catholics could live and worship as they pleased. No such right was given to Calvinists outside their designated areas. During the subsequent seventeenth century the French monarchy gradually withdrew the limited privileges granted Huguenots, thereby ending even this limited form of religious toleration. In 1685 King Louis XIV rescinded the Edict of Nantes altogether and declared France to be a Catholic nation.

We will end this survey of the religious wars by returning to the Holy Roman Empire, where we began. The Treaty of Augsburg of 1555 gave this area relative peace for about sixty years until the outbreak of the Thirty-Years War in 1618. During this period of tranquility Calvinism, which was not accommodated in the Treaty of Augsburg, made major gains throughout the Holy Roman Empire. Some local rulers embraced Calvinism and thus expected their subjects to do likewise. This had the ultimate effect of upsetting the balance of power between Lutherans and Catholics and introducing a new destabilizing element into an already delicate situation. The cause for the Thirty-Years War was an event that occurred on May 23 in 1618, known as the Defenestration of Prague. Bohemia, whose capital was Prague, was staunchly Protestant, but when the area came under the rule of a Catholic, the stage was set for a major showdown. On that day representatives of the

Bohemian Protestants came to a castle to confer with the agents of the new Catholic ruler. When neither side expressed their willingness to budge from their deeply held positions, the Bohemians seized the three royal agents and threw them out a nearby window, hence the term defenestration, from the Latin meaning "down from the window." The three men fell fifty feet, landed in the castle's moat, and were not seriously injured, because it was full of manure that cushioned their fall. Nevertheless, the event marked the intransigence of both sides, which soon broke out into all-out war.

Although the ensuing conflict is known as the Thirty-Years War (1618-1648), it was actually a series of four wars joined together by a common theme: Protestants vs. Catholics, but the warring parties varied somewhat from one phase to the next. It was the most destructive war ever fought in Europe up to the time of World War I (1914-1918). It is estimated that as many as seven million died during this period, most from diseases or starvation. The war was conducted with enormous armies, the largest that Europe had ever seen, often numbering more than 100,000. They devastated the land like locusts, often leaving the inhabitants without food. During the first phase of the war (the Bohemian phase of 1618-1625) the emperor of the Holy Roman Empire, based in Vienna in Austria and leading the Catholic cause, defeated the Protestants in the battle of the White Mountain just west of Prague (November 1620), took over Bohemia, and reinstituted Catholicism. This ultimately brought about the Danish or second phase of the war, in which Lutheran Denmark felt obliged to come to the support of their beleaguered fellow Protestants. The Danes, however, did not fare any better during this four-year interval in the war (1625-1629). They suffered defeat and withdrew from the war, leaving the Catholics preeminent and threatening to dominate northern Germany. The Catholics used their position to dispossess many Protestants of their property and to restore it to Catholics. At this point Sweden, another Scandinavian Lutheran state, intervened under the leadership of its very capable king, Gustavus Adolphus. This third Swedish phase of the war lasted five years, 1630-1635. After winning a smashing victory in 1631, over the Catholics at Breitenfeld near Leipzig, the Swedish king was killed in battle in the following year, but his success enabled the Swedes to remain dominant over the next few years and to roll back Catholic gains. But as the Catholics rallied and began to stage a comeback under the emperor of the Holy Roman Empire, the French intervened on the side of the Swedes and Protestants, thus bringing about the fourth and final French phase of the war (1635-1648). Although the French were also Catholic, they did not want Austria to emerge from the war victorious and strong, because this would pose a threat to France. Eventually the war came to a negotiated end in 1648 with the Treaty of Westphalia, which was a variation on the Treaty of Augsburg. It allowed Lutheranism, Calvinism, and Catholicism to be worshipped according to the will of the rulers of the various counties. Thus, once again, the religion of the local ruler became the official religion of that area. France emerged from the war with major gains by taking over lands west of the Rhine that had previously belonged to the Holy Roman Empire. This helped to pave the way for French dominance in European affairs during the seventeenth century.

In conclusion, by 1648, the year that marks the terminal date for this course, these wars of religious intolerance had succeeded in developing the idea of religious toleration in only a very limited sense. The first espousal of full religious toleration came with the American Revolution and the U.S. Constitution.

LECTURE 33
European Discovery of the New World

IMPORTANT DATES AND TERMS

- **1492:** Columbus sails across the Atlantic and lands in the Caribbean.
- **1516:** Sir Thomas More publishes his *Utopia*.
- **1519-1522:** Circumnavigation of the earth by the Spanish expedition led by the Portuguese Ferdinand Magellan.
- **Portugal:** western-most country of Europe, fifteenth-century exploration of the Atlantic and African coast, its colonial and commercial empire of Brazil and southern Asia.
- **New-World crops:** corn, tomato, potato, tobacco, peanuts, and cocoa.
- **Syphilis:** venereal disease introduced into Europe from the New World by Columbus' first voyage.
- **African slave trade:** resulting from tribal warfare, established long before by the Arabs, used by Europeans to supply the labor needs of plantations in the New World, accompanied by an ideology of racial inferiority.

We now come to the second of these last three transformative developments of the sixteenth century: the European discovery of the New World. It shattered the long accepted European notion of how the Earth's land masses were configured, because since ancient Greek and Roman times, it was believed that there existed only three continents: Europe, Africa, and Asia, all of which were joined together around the Mediterranean Sea, and the rest of the Earth's globe was occupied by a gigantic ocean that encircled these three continents. The European discovery of the New World and the voyages of exploration were a truly phenomenal development in the world's history. It resulted from the continuous growth of Western European society, which from the High Middle Ages onward had been responsible for the foundation of the Medieval universities, the crusades, various technological advances (including navigation and ship construction), and the extraordinary cultural revolution of the Renaissance. It therefore played an important role in the Europeans of this time realizing that they were living in a new age of discoveries and inventions; and this in turn fostered the development of the modern idea of progress that we now take for granted, but which was a new idea at the time. Of course, the European discovery of the New World also led to the economic growth of Western Europe through the emergence of an Atlantic system that brought Europe and the Americas together. In that sense it represents the first giant step in the globalism that has become such an important element in the economy of our own day.

The European discovery of the New World was accidental and stemmed from the need for the Europeans to reestablish the spice trade that had been disrupted by the Ottoman Turks and their conquest of the Byzantine Empire. During the High Middle Ages maritime trade throughout the Mediterranean grew, and through it there flowed into western Europe from the eastern Mediterranean large quantities of spices that were grown in southern Asia, principally in India: pepper, cinnamon, ginger, nutmeg, and cloves. The volume of this trade had grown during the period of the crusades, as the Venetians, Genoese, and Pisans of northern Italy penetrated this lucrative trade in the eastern Mediterranean. Moreover, the establishment of the Mongol Empire during the thirteenth century, which stretched all across Asia, further facilitated trade between Europe and Asia. The best example of this trading system is revealed by the career of the Venetian Marco Polo. Born in 1254, as a young man in 1271 he accompanied his father and uncle on a trading journey. After sailing from Venice to the Crimea in the Black Sea, they traveled overland across Asia to China, where they lived for twenty years, not returning until 1292. But when the Ottoman Turks conquered the Byzantine civilization and established themselves as the new imperial power of the eastern Mediterranean, they adopted a hostile attitude toward western Europe, which they wished to add to their empire. Consequently, this trading system that had long linked Europe and Asia was now disrupted, and with its disruption the flow of spices to western Europe was cut off. Thus, one European goal during the fifteenth century was to figure out how trade with Asia could be reestablished.

Portugal pioneered one avenue to develop direct European contact with Asia by sailing around Africa. It was well positioned geographically for this undertaking, because it lay on the extreme southwestern edge of the European continent, facing out onto the Atlantic and just north of northwestern Africa. By this time Europeans had developed the caravel, a decked ship driven by a series of sails and armed with cannons. It was an extremely sea-worthy vessel that could cope with the Atlantic open sea and could also defend itself from attackers. During the fifteenth century the Portuguese began carrying out voyages of exploration along the western coast of Africa, from which they obtained salt, ivory, gold, and slaves, but their ultimate goal was to discover if they could sail around Africa and reach Asia. In fact, shortly after Columbus accomplished his epoch-making voyage to the New World, the Portuguese explorer, Vasco da Gama, in 1496-1497 finally succeeded in reaching the southern tip of Africa, sailed across the Indian Ocean, and landed in northwestern India. He returned with a large cargo of spices and thus opened up southern Asia to the economic penetration by the Portuguese. They did battle with the Arabs, who were in control of the sea lanes; and after deposing them as the lords of the Indian Ocean, the Portuguese were able to found trading posts throughout southern Asia to form a very lucrative global empire. They did the same along the African coast and joined the Arabs as being important middle-men in the African slave trade.

The other strategy for reestablishing European trade with Asia was pursued by Christopher Columbus. He was a native of Genoa in northwestern Italy, and by the time of his first voyage to the New World he was a highly experienced navigator and sea captain. His idea was to sail due west across the Atlantic until he came to the eastern coast of Asia, because according to the European prevailing view of the Earth's geography, the only thing that lay between western Europe and eastern Asia was a vast open sea. He eventually succeeded in persuading the monarchs of Spain, Ferdinand and Isabella, to finance his venture. If it were successful, it would enable Spain to equal or surpass its neighbor, Portugal, in trying to corner the market on the Asian spice trade. As a result, on August 3 in 1492 Columbus set sail with his fleet of three caravels (the Nina, Pinta, and Santa Maria). They sailed southwestward across the Atlantic, and in the early hours of October 12 they caught their first sight of land since having left the islands of the eastern Atlantic. They had sailed into the Caribbean and spent the next few months exploring the various islands to learn about their natural resources and their human populations. They sailed back to Europe in early 1493, convinced that they had stumbled upon the offshore islands of eastern Asia.

Text #45 in PSWC is a most fascinating document, a letter that Christopher Columbus wrote in early 1493 as he was sailing back to Europe across the Atlantic. In this letter he records for his patrons, Ferdinand and Isabella, what he had observed in these newly discovered lands. It is therefore our earliest account of the encounter between Western Europeans and the natives of this region. From the European perspective the inhabitants seemed to be living in a state of primitive innocence akin to that of Adam and Eve in the Garden of Eden, as described in the opening chapters of *Genesis* in *The Bible*. Since they were living in a hot humid environment, the people went about naked or nearly so. They had no knowledge of iron or steel and were thus living in a kind of stone age, although they did possess gold, but their weapons were bows, arrows, and spears fashioned out of wood. As far as Columbus could tell, they were monogamous, although their chiefs had more than one wife; and Columbus could not tell whether they acknowledged private property or lived in a state of primitive communism, because they seemed to be quite generous in sharing their food and other meager possessions with one another. These natives had never encountered men of this sort, who wore clothes, shoes, and hats, traveled aboard large sail-driven ships armed with cannons, and possessing objects made of glass and iron. They therefore thought that these explorers must be divine beings, whom they accordingly somewhat feared and treated with extreme deference.

Columbus carried out three more voyages, in which he further explored the Caribbean, probably going as far west as the coast of Central America. He never realized that he had stumbled upon a huge land mass, whose existence was hitherto unknown to Western Europeans. He remained convinced that this area was simply the offshore region of Asia, and he was determined to find exactly where the eastern coast of Asia was. It was left up to another Italian navigator, Amerigo Vespucci, a Florentine, to realize that this was an entirely new land. Vespucci served as navigator aboard other voyages to the New World at about the same time as Columbus' later three. He startled his fellow Europeans with his findings that he published after completing his final voyage. When he came upon the coast of northern South America and sailed along it for a long distance, he realized that this was a huge land mass that had nothing to do with Asia. Like Columbus, he describes his interesting (and sometimes hair raising) encounters with the natives, some of whom were cannibals. In 1507 a German map maker, using the knowledge about these newly discovered lands, drew and printed a map of the world, in which he first used the Latin phrase *Terra America* (Amerigo's Land) to label this region. Consequently, the North and South American continents received their names not from Columbus, but from Amerigo Vespucci, who was the first man to realize the true significance of what these early explorers had come upon.

These early discoveries created a real sensation in western Europe and prompted a flurry of other voyages. Portugal and Spain were now joined by France and England, who did not want to be left out in making discoveries and laying claim to these new lands. The Spanish, however, had the jump on everybody and soon hit the jackpot, as it were, with the expeditions of Cortes and Pizzaro. During the years 1519-1521 Cortes carried out his conquest of the Aztec Empire. In the spring of 1519 he landed on the eastern coast of Mexico and founded a settlement that grew into the city of Vera Cruz. He had with him only 600 soldiers, armed with steel swords, muskets, and horses, none of which the natives possessed. But besides his superior military technology,

Cortes mastered the Aztec Empire, largely because its subjects hated their rulers and greeted the Spanish invaders as liberators from Aztec oppression. As the Spanish made their way inland from the coast toward the Aztec capital, they entered towns in which the people regularly engaged in human sacrifice and even butchered the bodies of the victims to be eaten. This was an integral aspect of their religion. Since the Aztecs carried out human sacrifice on a very large scale and took their victims from conquered peoples, the latter were understandably very unhappy subjects of the Aztecs. Consequently, Cortes was able to persuade some of the Aztecs' disaffected subjects to join him as allies. The Aztec capital city, Tenochtitlan, was probably the largest city on the planet at the time and was well built and organized. It was situated in a large lake, and the city was entered along three long causeways. The emperor of the Aztec Empire, Montezuma, lived in a gigantic palace amid wondrous splendor. The city was dominated by a massive pyramid on whose top priests sacrificed human beings to the Aztec gods in order to ensure the daily rising of the sun, rainfall, and abundant harvests. Four priests held down the sacrificial victim by his or her legs and arms, while a fifth priest cut open the chest with an obsidian knife and then tore out the heart as the choicest offering to the Aztec sun god. One area in the city housed racks of thousands upon thousands of skulls of those sacrificed. After Cortes had succeeded in taking Montezuma prisoner, the latter's brother was acknowledged as the new Aztec ruler and led his people in an unsuccessful uprising against the Spanish.

In 1532 Pizzaro led an even smaller band of 150 soldiers against the Inca Empire in Peru and succeeded in conquering it, because they arrived at a time when the Inca throne was being fought over by two contenders, and the Spanish were able to play one side off against the other. Both these American empires were rich in gold and silver, which the Spanish then proceeded to haul off and ship back to Spain. As a result, the latter emerged during the sixteenth century as the richest nation in Europe. While the Portuguese were establishing a trading empire along the African and south-Asian coasts and also laying claim to Brazil in South America (where Portuguese remains as the national language), the Dutch were creating their own equally far-flung empire of trading posts that also took in the Americas, Africa, and Asia. The Spanish laid claim to a vast territory in the Americas: the islands of the Caribbean, Central America, the northern part of South America, and the southern area of what is now the United States, from Florida to California. Meanwhile, the English and French were conducting their own voyages of exploration in the more northerly areas of North America, where there were no easy pickings like the Aztec and Inca Empires, and where the colder climate offered much greater obstacles to settlement. Thus, while the Spanish succeeded in developing the economic potential of the tropics during the sixteenth century, French and English settlement farther to the north did not begin to produce results until the next century.

As these two very different worlds came into contact with one another, the two populations inadvertently exchanged germs and their attendant diseases with catastrophic consequences for both parties, but especially for the natives of the Americas. Since these two peoples had been living in biological isolation from one another for thousands of years, their immune systems were quite different. Measles, for example, which did not bother Europeans, was a deadly disease for the natives. What devastated the native population more than anything else were these various diseases to which they were vulnerable. We have seen how the Black Death wiped out about one-third of the population of western Europe during the years 1348-1350. This never could have been achieved through warfare. Likewise, despite the military and technological superiority of the Europeans, what devastated the indigenous American population was the spread of these diseases. Just as entire villages in Europe had been wiped out by the bubonic plague, the same happened in the Americas. Desoto and other explorers occasionally came upon villages that had few or no inhabitants because of epidemics. On the other hand, the natives transmitted to the Europeans a deadly form of syphilis. This occurred during Columbus' very first voyage. When his crew returned to Europe along with some natives, this deadly form of syphilis rapidly spread throughout western Europe and resulted in thousands of deaths. It continued to plague the European population until the middle of the sixteenth century when the germ either mutated into a less virulent and deadly form, or the European population developed a limited immunity against it.

One positive result of contact between Europe and America was Europeans becoming acquainted with several crops native to the Americas: corn, the potato, the tomato, tobacco, peanuts, and cocoa. These food items eventually made their way back to Europe, where they began to be grown and became staples of the Western diet. Can you just imagine what your diet would be like without corn, popcorn, potatoes, tomatoes, peanuts, and chocolate? God, Glory, Gold.

European leaders and their explorers were seeking two things in the New World: wealth and human souls to be converted to Christianity. With regard to the latter, these expeditions were usually accompanied by Dominicans, Franciscans, Jesuits, or other priests who were to introduce the natives to Christianity. The other goal, however, the extraction of wealth, was realized in different ways. Following the quick and easy smash-and-grab conquests of the Aztecs and Incas, the Spanish continued to extract precious metals from the existing mines by using native labor, but in the long term wealth was more effectively created in this newly emerging Spanish empire by the production of cash crops grown on large plantations throughout the Caribbean islands. The hot and wet conditions of this region was perfectly suited for the growing of sugar and coffee, which had been borrowed from the Arabs and were being grown in limited quantities in the Mediterranean. These crops were now brought to the New World, and along with tobacco they soon became important cash crops consumed by Europeans in increasing amounts. At first the Spanish enslaved natives and forced them to provide the necessary human labor for these plantations, but as their numbers diminished through disease, they began to import slaves from Africa. As a result, there evolved a triangular Atlantic trading system, involving Europe, Africa, and the New World. In fact, the people heading the European governments developed a theory of state economy, called mercantilism, that guided their policies. According to this theory of mercantilism, a nation could best foster economic growth by promoting manufacturing in the home country and shipping the surplus abroad to holdings in the New World, where these goods were exchanged for various raw materials, such as gold, silver, sugar, coffee, or tobacco. In addition, ships stopped off along the western African coast, where they purchased slaves, who were transported to the holdings in the New World to keep the plantations in full operation.

During the period 1519-1522 one of the most extraordinary voyages of this era was carried out by the Portuguese Ferdinand Magellan. It was the first successful circumnavigation of the entire planet. At that time it was as phenomenal as my generation's witnessing the first landing on the moon by the astronauts of Apollo XI on July 20, 1969. Magellan's expedition set out with five ships manned by 270 men. They sailed southwestward across the Atlantic, made landfall on the eastern coast of South America, sailed southward along the coast, worked their way through the bewildering archipelago of islands at the southern tip of South America (the Strait of Magellan), and finally emerged into the vast Pacific. After landing in the Philippine Islands, where Magellan met his death and was buried, the expedition sailed westward across the Indian Ocean, rounded Africa, and sailed along its western coast to return to Europe. When the expedition finally came to an end, there was only one ship left with a crew of only seventeen men. The four other ships had been lost during the long journey, as well as 94% of the original crew. Besides being a tremendous feat of human skill, daring, and perseverance, the voyage added valuable evidence to Europe's growing body of geographical data concerning the oceans and land masses of the planet, as well as offering a clear demonstration of European nautical supremacy.

I will close this lecture by examining a literary work of this period that neatly incorporates the many different strands that were now coming together to form a distinctive Western European culture, which included the earliest European perceptions of the New World. This is Utopia, written by Sir Thomas More and published in 1516, shortly after the voyages of Columbus and Vespucci. Portions of this little work form Text #46 in PSWC. Thomas More was an Englishman and one of the leading humanist scholars in England during his lifetime. He was a very close friend of Erasmus and was well educated in both Greek and Latin and the literature of the ancient Greeks and Romans. After being trained as a lawyer, he went into government service and became a leading figure during the reign of King Henry VIII, but when in 1535 Thomas More refused to take an oath acknowledging Henry as head of the newly created Anglican Church, he was imprisoned in the Tower of London and beheaded. But in 1516 when More published *Utopia*, he was still fairly young and enjoying great success and prominence as one of King Henry's trusted advisors. This small work embodies and encapsulates much of Western European culture at this time. It reflects the important role of Renaissance humanism and thus represents the ancient Greco-Roman tradition. At the same time it is fully grounded in the events and attitudes of its day; and it combines the European excitement over the discovery of the New World with these other two strands to create a very complex literary work that uses an imaginary and idealized portrait of the New World to offer a scathing criticism of contemporary Western European society and politics.

The work is clearly patterned after the famous philosophical dialogues of Plato and especially his most famous work, *The Republic*, in which a discussion of the nature of justice leads to a long and detailed description of how one would organize the perfect state. Moreover, throughout the work More, who seems to have had a great sense of humor, uses his knowledge of Greek to make up words that turn out to be puns. For example, utopia, a word first invented by More and used in this work, simply means "nowhere" in Greek. Therefore, this Utopia, More is telling us from the very beginning, really exists nowhere. It is simply the creation of his own imagination, although he has set it in the New World. Similarly, the main river that flows through the land of Utopia is called the Anhydor, which translates from Greek to mean "waterless." It is therefore a river that does not really exist.

The work is divided into two books with Utopia discussed in Book II. The work begins with what appears to be a real setting, just like a dialogue of Plato. Thomas More has been dispatched by King Henry VIII to Flanders to represent England in some negotiations. While there, More is drawn into a learned discussion with other people concerning the general state of affairs in Europe. This is not a case of literary window-dressing with Book I simply serving as a preface to the real meat of the work. It is, to be sure, prefatory, but it is a lengthy and necessary long preface, because More is interested in contrasting the sad state of affairs in Europe with the perfection of Utopia in order to further emphasize his criticisms of European society and politics spelled out in Book I.

Here is the basic plot of the work. One of the discussants is a man named Raphael, who has just returned from a long stay in Utopia in the New World. He had been a member of one of Vespucci's voyages, but he stayed behind for several years. After traveling inland, he came upon Utopia, where he lived and learned how this people organized a perfect society. This should sound familiar, because it is More's own adaptation of Columbus' idealized portrait of the natives whom he first encountered, but rather than living in a perfect state of primitive innocence, More's Utopians are just as sophisticated as Europeans, but, of course, they have figured out how to do everything perfectly. When one of the group's discussants observes that Raphael would therefore be an ideal advisor for an European monarch, he denies this most vigorously, because, as he observes, these people are not interested in knowing how to rule their kingdoms justly. They are too preoccupied with conquests to make them bigger. Besides, what these monarchs like most is not someone who will tell them the truth, but people who will simply flatter them and tell them what they want to hear. There then follows a lengthy discussion of conditions in England. The rich have been taking over more and more land as pasturage for their herds of sheep. In doing so they have displaced many small farmers, who have turned to highway robbery as a means of survival, but to combat such criminality, the state has imposed the death penalty (by hanging) upon robbers. Despite the severity of the law, robbery has continued to flourish and has even become worse, because robbers try to avoid detection of their crime by killing their victims, instead of simply robbing them, so that there are no witnesses. Consequently, the death penalty has resulted in the deaths of the criminals' victims. More concludes this discussion with the famous maxim from Plato's *Republic*: "a truly good government will not be established until or unless a king becomes a philosopher, or a philosopher becomes king." This is followed by another assertion. There will never be justice or happiness in a society unless private property is abolished, as argued by Plato for his ideal state. Here we encounter a standard feature of all subsequent utopian literature: the idea that injustice stems from private property, so that in order to ensure justice, private property must be abolished in favor of communism. To the utopian dreamer, the grass does not just seem, but actually is greener on the other side of the fence. His own society is plagued with so many evils, but if a society could be created without private property, everyone would live happily ever after. The problem, of course, with this utopian view is that as the historical record of modern times has clearly demonstrated, whenever this has been tried by a society, it has failed miserably and has caused far more human misery than the flawed society that the utopian one has replaced.

At this point Book II begins, and Raphael proceeds to describe all the wonders of Utopia. In order to account for this people's sophistication, More has the Utopians learn much from some Romans and Egyptians, who were blown off course 1200 years ago and landed in the New World. Of course, the Utopians have no private property. Things are given out from common stores of goods as people need them, and no one goes without or in need. Gold and jewels are despised and held in contempt. There are no beggars. Everyone works at some job six hours a day. Everyone wears exactly the same kind of clothes, so that people do not waste their resources by trying to outdo each other with fashion statements. There is no gambling in Utopia, nor are there any taverns for drinking. Instead, people amuse themselves with a mentally demanding game similar to chess. There are no lawyers in Utopia, because they are not needed. Since the laws are so few, everyone knows them, so that whenever there is a lawsuit, people represent themselves. This is a very interesting point, because More was himself a lawyer. As such, he must have witnessed and understood all too well the countless injustices carried out by the so-called justice system.

These are only a few aspects of More's portrait of Utopia. Although this literary work owes much to Plato's *Republic*, More spawned a minor genre in early modern literature, in which other writers, such as Francis Bacon and Tommaso Campanella, not only devised their own Utopias, but like More, they situated them in a remote area of the New World, where conditions were believed to be much better than those in the old tired world of Europe. But in a much more practical and down-to-earth sense, of course, as Europeans began to establish in this New World permanent settlements, not just trading posts or plantations, many were fleeing grinding poverty or religious persecution brought about by the Protestant Reformation and Counter Reformation that we have treated in the previous two lectures. To many of these people, who were in search of a new and better life, the New World did in fact represent "a shining city on a hill," "a place where the streets were paved with gold," "the land of opportunity."

LECTURE 34
The Beginnings of Modern Science

IMPORTANT DATES, TERMS, AND PERSONS

- **European Witch Craze:** superstitious belief system concerning worshippers of the Devil who cause harm within their communities; accused, convicted, and executed in substantial numbers during the sixteenth and seventeenth centuries.
- **1543:** Death of the Polish mathematician Copernicus and publication of his *On the Revolutions of the Heavenly Spheres*.
- **1609:** By using the newly invented telescope Galileo discovers the moons of Jupiter.

(You need not know the dates given in connection with the following important persons)

- **Copernicus:** (1473-1543) Polish mathematician, revived the heliocentric theory of the solar system to explain planetary motion.
- **Tycho Brahe:** (1546-1601) Danish noble, great observational astronomer.
- **Galileo:** (1564-1642) great Italian scientist, discovered that all objects fall and accelerate due to gravity at the same rate, condemned by the Catholic church for advocating a heliocentric universe and placed under house arrest.

- **Johannes Kepler:** (1571-1630) German mathematician and astronomer, discovered three important laws of planetary motion.

In the preceding three lectures we have examined two transformative developments in early modern European history: the Protestant Reformation that shattered the religious unity of Western Europe, and the discovery of the New World that shattered the ancient and Medieval notion of the Earth's continents and peoples. In this last lecture we will survey a third transformative development, the beginnings of modern science, which in the area of astronomy shattered the ancient and Medieval notion of the Earth's position in the universe and paved the way for a rational (i.e., mathematical) way in which celestial phenomena could be understood and explained. We will survey this development through the careers of four early modern scientists: the Polish Nicolaus Copernicus (1473-1543), the Danish Tycho Brahe (1546-1601), the German Johannes Kepler (1571-1630), and the Italian Galileo Galilei (1564-1642).

Before taking up this subject, it is worth contrasting the sophisticated scientific work of these four men with the so-called European Witch Craze. Most of the European population during the sixteenth and seventeenth centuries (1500-1700) firmly believed in the existence of witches, who did all sorts of evil things: causing people to fall sick with a mysterious illness, blighting a person's crops, making a farmer's cow not give milk, cursing men and women with infertility, etc. The belief in witches was such an integral part of European culture at this time that it resulted in thousands of people being arrested, interrogated, and executed for witchcraft. In fact, it has been estimated that eighty to one-hundred thousand people lost their lives as victims of the European Witch Craze, at least 90% of them being women. The notion of witches and black magic had always existed during the Middle Ages, but it had never been a significant part of the culture. This changed in 1486 with the publication of a work entitled *The Hammer of Witches* (*Malleus Maleficarum*). It was written by two Dominican priests who had conducted investigations into charges of witchcraft in the German states. This book presented their findings and succeeded in creating the standard European mythology about witches and witchcraft that became widely accepted and formed the underlying belief system for the witch craze. The book was printed and widely circulated, so that it became part of the whole European culture, both Protestant and Catholic; and once the witch craze began, other people wrote their own treatises on the subject and thus created an entire literature on the topic. The witch craze finally died out, as a growing number of Europeans were influenced by the developing scientific tradition, which required rational inquiry to be used to investigate natural phenomena. Therefore, the juxtaposition of the European Witch Craze with Copernicus, Brahe, Kepler, and Galileo serves to remind us of the complexities and contradictions inherent in any society. While these four scientists were engaged in their remarkable work, most Europeans still harbored many superstitious notions. This renders the work of these scientists even more remarkable.

In 1500 Aristotle and Ptolemy still reigned supreme in the universities of Europe, and it was from them that Europeans derived their views about the configuration of the universe, according to which the Earth remained motionless at the center, while all other heavenly bodies revolved around it. The earliest Greek philosophers had thought that these orbits were precisely circular, and that the heavenly bodies traveled in uniform motion. But as Greek astronomers made more and more careful observations, they realized that the planets did not travel at a constant speed, but they seemed to speed up and slow down. In order to contrive a model that would account for these variations, Greek astronomers devised the notion of epicycles, a small circle positioned on the periphery of a planet's orbit, and around which the planet also moved. Consequently, the astronomical work of Claudius Ptolemy, *The Almagest*, employed a geocentric theory of the universe along with a very complicated mathematical system of circles inside of circles.

People of Medieval and early modern Europe accepted the idea of a geocentric universe, in part because it harmonized with their view that God had placed Earth and mankind at the very center of his Creation. In addition, there was a widespread belief that the various planets were attached to transparent crystalline spheres, one inside the other, and that as they rotated at different speeds, their motion produced sounds at different frequencies, but taken together, their sounds formed a celestial harmony. This Medieval concept of the spheres and their music was incorporated by Dante into his *Paradiso*, the part of *The Divine Comedy* in which he was taken on a tour of heaven.

The modern revolution in astronomy began in 1543 with the publication of Nicolaus Copernicus' *On the Revolutions of the Heavenly Spheres*. In this work the Polish mathematician used the most accurate observational data then available to provide his readers with tables that predicted the motions of the various heavenly bodies. Moreover, in explaining all this material Copernicus replaced Ptolemy's geocentric theory of the universe with a heliocentric one, in which the sun was positioned at the center of the solar system with the Earth and other planets revolving around it. In doing so Copernicus was reviving a theory propounded by some ancient Greek astronomers, whom Copernicus actually cited in order to have ancient authority for his ideas. One thing that attracted Copernicus to the heliocentric model was his observation that the two inner-most planets, Mercury and Venus, were never observed too far away from the sun. This suggested that they might actually be circling the sun instead of the Earth. Copernicus also noticed that the variation in speed of the other planets all seemed to have the same period of one year. This would be the case if the Earth completed one revolution about the sun in the course of one year. By placing the sun, rather than the Earth, at the center of things Copernicus was able to account for celestial motion without some of the more complicated devices needed to do so in the Ptolemaic geocentric system. Here we encounter one common aspect of modern scientific theory: namely, although natural phenomena may be difficult to explain, their explanations often turn out to be both elegant and simple. This notion conforms to a famous maxim stated by the fourteenth-century Medieval English scholar, William of Ockham, and this principle is known as Ockham's Razor: "entities must not be multiplied without necessity (*non sunt multiplicanda entia sine necessitate*)," which is often commonly rephrased as "the simplest explanation is the correct one." Copernicus' revolutionary treatise was published in the year of his death and was the culmination of many years of diligent work on his part. Since it put forth an idea that ran counter to the accepted contemporary view of the universe, a man named Osiander wrote a preface to the work, in which he discounted the heliocentric theory by explaining that it did not represent reality, but was simply adopted in this work as a more convenient way to calculate planetary motion.

The next major advance in modern astronomy was achieved by Tycho Brahe, a Danish nobleman who possessed the necessary leisure and resources (including his own island and castle) to indulge his interest in observational astronomy. Over his career Brahe made countless observations, which he recorded very accurately by using compasses with gigantically long arms for measuring very precisely the angular motion of the planets and stars. In fact, during his lifetime Brahe compiled the most accurate astronomical data in the world. Two of his findings provided key evidence that cast serious doubt upon the prevailing European concept of the universe. In 1572 a bright new star appeared in the sky near the constellation Cassiopeia. It was so bright that for a time it was visible during the day. This was a nova or supernova, a star exploding before collapsing to become either a dead neutron star or black hole. By carefully observing this new star with respect to the other planets, Brahe determined that it was located far beyond the orbits of the planets in the outer-most sphere where the other fixed stars were located. According to accepted Aristotelian doctrine, however, the universe above the moon was changeless and perfect since The Creation. If this were true, how could a new star suddenly appear and spoil this supposed changeless perfection of the universe? Then in 1577, when a comet appeared in the sky, Brahe charted its course and determined that it was traveling far beyond the moon. Comets had been a known astronomical phenomenon since ancient times, but the orthodox Aristotelian view was that since they were transient and not part of the regular motion of the other heavenly bodies, they must come into being and then disappear in the so-called sublunary sphere, where all material change in the universe was thought to occur. Not only did Brahe's observation of the comet's path disprove this idea, but it also cast doubt upon the whole notion of there being crystalline spheres, because if they existed, how could a comet travel erratically in the region above the moon without crashing through them?

The next major advances in modern astronomy were accomplished by Johannes Kepler. He was a highly gifted German mathematician, who early on in his teaching career stumbled upon what he regarded as a key to unlocking the organizational scheme of the universe. As it turned out, Kepler's initial insight proved to be wrong, and he was a good enough scientist to realize his error and to develop other, actually valid, ideas in their place. Yet, in order to try to prove and refine his early erroneous theory, Kepler succeeded in convincing Brahe to take him on as his assistant, because Kepler wanted to have access to Brahe's most accurate observational data with which to prove his theory. When Kepler became Brahe's assistant in January of 1600, the latter was living in Prague in Bohemia at the court of Emperor Rudolph II, ruler of the Holy Roman Empire, whom Brahe was serving as chief astronomer and astrologer of the imperial court. Brahe, however, was not terribly cooperative with Kepler. In order to keep his assistant busy and out of his hair, Brahe gave him a seemingly unsolvable problem: namely, to come up with a convincing model to explain the orbit of Mars, the most irregular of the planets. Kepler diligently worked at the problem for a very long time and tried various solutions, but none of them did the trick until he finally figured out that the planet's orbit could be explained as an ellipse. Once he came upon this realization and applied it to the other planets, he had succeeded in making a monumental discovery that had defied all earlier astronomers and became the first of Kepler's three laws of planetary motion.

Kepler's first law states that all the planets move about the sun in elliptical orbits with the sun located at one of the two focal points of these ellipses. Now in case you do not remember or never did learn analytic geometry, let me explain what an ellipse actually is. Here is how you can trace one out on paper or a piece of cardboard and see its basic properties. Take a piece of string, and thumbtack each end down onto the paper or cardboard, so that the two thumbtacks are slightly apart. Now by using a pen or pencil, stretch the string out to its fullest extent and trace out one half of the ellipse. Then after flipping the string to the other side of the paper, but keeping its ends thumbtacked down, trace out the other half of the ellipse. This geometric shape has both a major and minor axis. The two points where the string has been thumbtacked are the focal points (or foci) of the ellipse. If you have drawn the ellipse properly, the one constant is that the sum of the two line segments from any point on the ellipse to the two focal points is always the same. As the distance between the two focal points increases, the eccentricity or irregularity of the ellipse increases. On the other hand, as the two points are moved closer together, the ellipse becomes more circular. In fact, a circle is simply an ellipse with zero eccentricity, because the two focal points have been moved together to merge into one another, and there is no difference in length between the major and minor axes. They are the same and are the radius of the circle.

Kepler's first law of planetary motion assumed the validity of the heliocentric theory of the universe. Moreover, by using the ellipse Kepler was able to provide an elegant and simple solution to the long standing puzzle of how the planets moved in non-circular patterns. His elliptical model eliminated all the complicated circles inside of circles that had hitherto plagued all theories of planetary motion.

Having arrived at this beautiful solution, Kepler posed another follow-up question, whose solution became his second law of planetary motion. Empirical data indicated that the planets traveled more quickly as they drew nearer to the sun in their elliptical orbits and went slower as they were more distant from the sun. Kepler asked himself what was the relationship between these variations in speed and distance. He figured out that if you draw a line from the sun to a planet and then chart the angular motion of the planet along its elliptical orbit, what you find is that in equal periods of time the planet sweeps out equal areas in its elliptical orbit.

When Tycho Brahe died in October of 1601, Emperor Rudolph appointed Kepler to succeed him as imperial astronomer and astrologer, a position that Kepler held until 1612 when the emperor died. In 1609 Kepler published a work entitled *Astronomia Nova, The New Astronomy*, in which he set forth a new astronomical system that included his first two laws of planetary motion. Toward the end of his life he developed his third law. Kepler noticed that the inner planets of the solar system travel much more quickly around the sun, and the outer ones move at much slower speeds. In the process of working out other matters that interested him, he came upon another elegant mathematical expression for this phenomenon. If one cubes the mean radius of a planet's orbit and divides it by the square of its period (the time needed to complete one orbit around the sun), one always winds up with the same number. There therefore existed a mathematical constant for the entire solar system in this regard. Kepler arrived at this mathematical relationship by trial and error. Decades later, when Sir Isaac Newton developed his own three laws of motion, Kepler's third law could be easily derived by combining Newton's second and third laws. By establishing his three laws of planetary motion Kepler was removing astronomy from the realm of theology and bringing it into the field of exact science, where phenomena could be explained neatly through mathematics. It was a truly extraordinary intellectual accomplishment.

At the very time that Kepler was revolutionizing astronomy with the publication of his *Astronomia Nova*, Galileo was doing the same by using the newly invented telescope. In 1608 German craftsmen in the Rhine Valley, where the printing press had been invented, succeeded in making the first telescope when they discovered that they could magnify the image of a distant object by combining convex and concave lenses in the right way. When news of this astounding discovery spread through the academic world and reached Galileo in Italy, he proceeded to conduct his own experiments to replicate this discovery; and once having figured out the basic principle, he fashioned his own telescope. By January of 1609 Galileo was using his newly constructed instrument to observe the heaven at night, and he was soon making new astronomical discoveries. He was the first person to observe moons orbiting around the planet of Jupiter. He noticed that the surface of the moon appeared to be irregular, and he postulated that it was not a perfectly shaped sphere as was generally supposed, but it more likely resembled the Earth in being a globe with mountains and other imperfections on its surface. He also discovered that the planet Saturn was not perfectly spherical, but it seemed to have what he called ears. Galileo had discovered the famous rings around the planet, but his telescope was not strong enough to reveal their actual shape.

When Galileo published all these discoveries in his *Siderius Nuntius* (*Starry Messenger*) in 1610, they were not well received by the Catholic Church, because they cast serious doubt upon the theological interpretation of the universe. It was generally assumed that only the Earth had a moon revolving about it because of the Earth's special position in God's Creation. How could this be so if Jupiter had not just one, but several moons revolving about it? Galileo's findings concerning the surface of the moon also ran counter to the accepted theological astronomy of the day, because it assumed that all the heavenly bodies were perfectly smooth spheres. Only the Earth, placed at the center of things and below the sublunary sphere, was an imperfectly shaped object. Galileo's discoveries suggested that the heavenly bodies were not the perfectly made objects designed by God to adorn the heavens, but they were large natural objects akin to the Earth itself. In fact, this line of reasoning led Kepler at the end of his life to speculate that there might be intelligent life on the moon, and he explored this idea by writing one of the earliest works of science fiction.

Despite these extraordinary discoveries made by Kepler and Galileo, the Ptolemaic geocentric view of the universe continued to be the orthodox view taught in the universities, and many professors heaped scorn upon the silliness of the new astronomy in arguing that the Earth and other planets moved around the stationary sun. In 1616 the Catholic Church placed Copernicus' work on the index of forbidden books and ordered Galileo not to believe such nonsense, but he continued his astronomical work, which included his study of sun spots. Since he did so by looking at times directly at the sun, he slowly went blind, but the discovery of sun spots reinforced his earlier findings in suggesting that the heavenly bodies were not the perfect objects of God's Creation, but were flawed physical bodies. Then in 1629 Galileo finished writing a very lengthy work, *Dialogue on the Two Chief World Views*, in which the discussants argued the pros and cons of the two competing theories, but with the heliocentric view emerging victorious. When this work was published in 1630, it so angered the pope and other Catholic officials that the work was placed on the index of forbidden books, and in 1633 Galileo was brought before the inquisition, questioned, and forced to denounce his belief in a heliocentric universe. He was then punished by house arrest for the remainder of his life (until 1642), and he was forbidden to discuss these matters with anyone. Although his scientific dialogue was banned by the Catholic Church, it was widely circulated in Protestant areas and became an integral part of the newly emerging scientific tradition.

I will close this lecture by touching upon another important aspect of Galileo's work, which reveals his extraordinary ability as an experimental scientist, as well as the intellectual power that the Western European tradition was beginning to exhibit. One commonly accepted aspect of physics at this time was that when various objects were dropped to fall, they fell at different rates according to their weight. Since this notion had been stated as being so by the great Aristotle himself, it had been accepted as the gospel truth for nearly two thousand years until Galileo decided to try it out. Since it was difficult to time how long it took objects to fall vertically, Galileo instead used a pendulum as his timer to find out how long it took balls of varying weight to roll down an inclined plane. He discovered that if one ignored friction, all balls rolled down at exactly the same rate, thereby disproving Aristotle. Galileo's work on falling bodies exhibits his great skill in being able to device an experiment to test a hypothesis. But his work also shows that like any good modern scientist, he did not accept any claim or theory on faith. It required testing to see if it conformed to reality; and if it did not, it had to be abandoned in favor of other ideas, even if it had been propounded by the great Aristotle himself.

As we end this course, let us look back upon what we have covered during its last quarter. We have traced how Western Europe emerged from the intellectual darkness of the Early and Central Middle Ages to surpass both the Byzantine and Islamic civilizations. By 1648, the terminal date for this course, Western Europeans had also surpassed the achievements of the ancient Greeks and Romans, whom they so much admired. They had discovered the New World. They were making important technological advances, such as the printing press; and as we have seen in this lecture, their greatest minds were developing the modern scientific tradition. As we saw when surveying the ancient world, those people regarded the distant past as a golden age in which people lived in a kind of paradise or Garden of Eden, and that their own times were an iron age of decline. By 1600 Western Europeans were beginning to adopt a new idea, the idea of progress, which we take for granted today. The clearest statement of this notion at this time was expressed in the following words by the English intellectual Francis Bacon in his *Novum Organum* published in 1620:

(Taken from the Translation of James Spedding [1858])

Printing, gunpowder, and the compass: these three have changed the whole face and state of things throughout the world. The first in literature, the second in warfare, the third in navigation; whence have followed innumerable changes, insomuch that no empire, no sect, no star seems to have exerted greater power and influence in human affairs than these mechanical discoveries.

THE END

CPSIA information can be obtained
at www.ICGtesting.com
Printed in the USA
LVHW082157090821
694964LV00025B/747

9 781648 040634